# 60 HIKES *within* 60 MILES
## RICHMOND
### INCLUDING WILLIAMSBURG, FREDERICKSBURG, AND CHARLOTTESVILLE

# 60 Hikes *within* 60 MILES

## RICHMOND

### INCLUDING WILLIAMSBURG, FREDERICKSBURG, AND CHARLOTTESVILLE

## Nathan Lott

**MENASHA RIDGE PRESS**
Birmingham, Alabama

Library of Congress Cataloging-in-Publication Data

Lott, Nathan, 1977–
60 Hikes within 60 miles, Richmond : includes Williamsburg, Fredericksburg, and
Charlottesville/Nathan Lott.—1st ed.
p. cm.
ISBN 0-89732-594-X
   1.Hiking—Virginia—Richmond Region—Guidebooks. 2. Trails—Virginia—Richmond Region—Guidebooks. 3. Richmond Region (Va.)—Guidebooks I. Title: Sixty
hikes within 60 miles, II. Title


GV199.42.V8L68 2005
796.51'09755'451—dc22
                                                            2005049563

Cover design by Grant M. Tatum
Text design by Karen Ocker
Cover photo by Nathan Lott
Author photo by Elizabeth Lott
All other photos by Nathan Lott
Maps by Scott McGrew

Menasha Ridge Press
P.O. Box 43673
Birmingham, AL 35243
www.menasharidge.com

**Dedication**
This book is for Lucy, who hiked more miles with me than
anyone else and would have hiked them all had I let her.

# TABLE OF CONTENTS

# TABLE OF CONTENTS

# ACKNOWLEDGMENTS

Many thanks to my friends at Menasha Ridge Press for encouraging me to take on this project and patiently awaiting the manuscript. Sincere appreciation is due the land managers, volunteers, and preservationists who safeguard the parks profiled in this guide. Similar gratitude goes to the authors, ecologists, and amateur historians who rewarded my research with fascinating stories and insights.

I owe my father and grandfather for my first walks in the woods and my mother for nurturing my childhood love of books. Their ongoing support, and that of my brother, is reflected in this volume. This book would remain unwritten, however, were it not for the tireless support of my wife, Elizabeth, who brought me to Richmond and who makes it feel like home.

—*Nathan Lott*

# FOREWORD

Welcome to Menasha Ridge Press's *60 Hikes within 60 Miles,* a series designed to provide hikers with information needed to find and hike the very best trails surrounding cities usually underserved by such guidebooks.

Our strategy was simple: First, find a hiker who knows the area and loves to hike. Second, ask that person to spend a year researching the most popular and very best trails around. And third, have that person describe each trail in terms of difficulty, scenery, condition, elevation change, and all other categories of information that are important to hikers. "Pretend you've just completed a hike and met up with other hikers at the trailhead," we told each author. "Imagine their questions; be clear in your answers."

An experienced hiker and writer, author Nathan Lott has selected 60 of the best hikes in and around the Richmond metropolitan area. From casual strolls through manicured suburban parks to history-rich explorations of colonial and Civil War sites, from bird-watching excursions in Chesapeake Bay marsh to long backcountry treks through Piedmont forest, Lott provides hikers (and walkers and trail runners) with a great variety of routes—and all within roughly 60 miles of Virginia's capital.

You'll get more out of this book if you take a moment to read the Introduction, which explains how to read the trail listings and will prove of particular value to those of you who have hiked extensively. The Maps and GPS Data section will help you understand how useful topos will be on a hike and will also tell you where to get them. The section also explains the relationship between a topo map and the GPS trailhead coordinates given for each hike.

As much for the opportunity to free the spirit as to free the body, let these hikes elevate you above the urban hurry.

*All the best,*
*The Editors at Menasha Ridge Press*

# ABOUT THE AUTHOR

The child of an Air Force officer, Nathan Lott has lived and traveled widely in the United States, Europe, and the Near East. He credits his parents with fostering the appreciation for history, culture, and the natural world that serves him well as a writer. Turning his native curiosity to storied Virginia proved a rewarding, if time-consuming, task. In particular, the experience reinvigorated his environmentalism, and Nathan has since accepted a public-relations position with the Virginia Department of Conservation and Recreation. Nathan holds a journalism degree from Samford University in Birmingham, Alabama, but maintains that the most valuable thing he did in college was meet his wife Elizabeth, a minister. It was her seminary education that brought the couple to Richmond, where they reside with two cats and a dog.

# PREFACE

Hikers in Richmond and Central Virginia enjoy a surprising array of choices. They have their pick of urban parks, suburban greenways, and more bucolic settings; of tidal wetlands, rolling hills, and riparian forest; of colonial homes, Civil War battlefields, and state parks built by the Civilian Conservation Corps (CCC). All this exists despite a dearth of public land.

While national forest blankets the western mountains of Virginia, public land in the Tidewater and the Piedmont is at a premium (largely because the region was divvied up by royal land grants in the seventeenth and eighteenth centuries). There is no shortage of guidebooks devoted to the trails of Virginia's Blue Ridge Mountains. Likewise, there are volumes cataloguing hikes throughout the commonwealth, firstly Allen De Hart's copious tome, *The Trails of Virginia*.

But this book is different. I don't ask that you drive three hours west just to go for a Sunday afternoon stroll. I don't provide a multitude of curt trail descriptions and ask you to choose without maps. This is, above all, a *guide*book. My intent is not only to get you to the trail, but to keep you on the path and help you appreciate sights along the way. I have erred on the side of lengthier description to better equip novices, and I have peppered each profile with anecdotes and insights to enhance your experience.

Having moved to Richmond as an adult, I undertook writing this guide as something of a novice myself. I walked many of the profiled trails for the first time in the course of my research and found hiking a marvelous way to discover more about my adopted home. My goal in writing was to enable you to discover more as well. What better way to explore the storied Old Dominion than on foot, just as the first English speakers and the native Indians before them did? How else can one fully appreciate Virginia's ecological diversity and beauty?

In writing, I attempted to make this guide as serviceable as possible. A few notes on my approach: A hike's listed mileage is generally a minimum distance, with optional extensions provided. Many of these hikes can be significantly elongated. As a rule, these are circuit hikes; that is to say, you start and stop at the parking area. Only the longest non-loops are profiled as end-to-ends. Even parks and forests with extensive trail networks are not divided into multiple profiles. Thus, the guide provides 60 distinct destinations, However, though some are adjacent to others, they are administered by different agencies. Finally, in order to include a broad range of hiking experiences, the within-60-miles criterion was applied to metro Richmond and as the crow flies. A few hikes require a noticeably longer drive. This makes the guide more useful to residents of peripheral communities like Charlottesville and helpful to Richmonders planning weekend trips.

Inevitably, some noteworthy destinations remain just beyond the geographic scope of this guide. First Landing State Park and Natural Area in Virginia Beach pays homage not only to Jamestown-bound settlers who landed here on April 26, 1607, but also to the delicate estuarine environment at the mouth of the Chesapeake. It is home to the Virginia Marine Science Museum and 18 trail miles. Roughly equidistant from Fredericksburg and Alexandria, Prince William Forest Park, managed by the National Park Service, offers 30 rustic trail miles in the midst of the burgeoning Northern Virginia suburbs. There is also a 6-mile trail at Appomattox Court House National Battlefield, site of Lee's famed surrender. Also worth mentioning is one bike and pedestrian trail still in the works. When completed, the Virginia Department of Transportation's paved Capital Trail will stretch from Williamsburg to Richmond, closely following the VA 5 corridor.

So, while I don't purport to have included every worthwhile trail east of the Blue Ridge, I believe you'll be surprised to learn what great trails are in your proverbial backyard. I also think you'll find trails geared to your personal needs and interests. Whether you're out for an after-work jog or a trail-runner's half marathon, a romantic weekend getaway or a serious overnight backpack, my suggestions will help you choose. My suggestion now is that you take your pick. Find a trail near your home and make a brisk walk part of your routine. Take the kids; take the dog. Watch the changing seasons paint your favorite trail in new colors. Learn to identify the trees and birds. You'll find yourself healthier for it, mind and body.

# HIKING RECOMMENDATIONS

(*Note:* The number in parentheses next to each hike title corresponds to its number in the Table of Contents.)

▶ **HIKES BY MILEAGE (SHORTEST TO LONGEST)**

# HIKING RECOMMENDATIONS

## ▶ HIKES FEATURING COLONIAL OR EARLY AMERICAN SITES

Caledon State Park and Natural Area (8)
Chippokes Plantation State Park (11)
Freedom Park (21)
George Washington Birthplace National Monument (22)

Greensprings Greenway (23)
Henricus Historical Park (25)
Wahrani Nature Park (54)

## ▶ HIKES FEATURING CIVIL WAR SITES

Belle Isle and Brown's Island (5)
Cold Harbor Battlefield (13)
Crump Park (14)
Henricus Historical Park (25)
James River Park Main Section (30)

Newport News Park (35)
North Anna Battlefield Park (36)
Petersburg National Battlefield Park (38)
Spotsylvania Court House Battlefield (50)

## ▶ HIKES FEATURING HISTORIC HOMES OR HOME SITES

Belle Isle State Park (6)
Caledon State Park and Natural Area (8)
Chippokes Plantation State Park (11)
Crump Park (14)
Fluvanna Heritage Trail (20)
George Washington Birthplace National Monument (22)

Hardware River Wildlife Management Area (24)
Ivy Creek Natural Area (29)
Observatory Hill (37)
Powhatan Wildlife Management Area (42)
Saunders-Monticello Trail (48)
Zoar State Forest (60)

## ▶ HIKES FEATURING MUSEUMS OR NATURE CENTERS

Belle Isle and Brown's Island (5)
Chippokes Plantation State Park (11)
George Washington Birthplace National Monument (22)
Henricus Historical Park (25)

Mariners Museum Park (33)
Petersburg National Battlefield Park (38)
Pocahontas State Park (39)
Three Lakes Park (51)

## ▶ HIKES FEATURING LAKES OR PONDS

Amelia Wildlife Management Area (1)
Bear Creek Lake State Park (3)
Beaverdam Park (4)
Cumberland State Forest (16)
Deep Run Park (17)
Dorey Park (18)

Holliday Lake State Park (28)
Ivy Creek Natural Area (29)
Lake Anna State Park (32)
Mariner's Museum Park (33)
Motts Run Reservoir (34)
Newport News Park (35)

# HIKING RECOMMENDATIONS

## ▶ HIKES FEATURING LAKES OR PONDS *(continued)*

Pocahontas State Park (39)
Powhatan Wildlife Management Area (42)
R. Garland Dodd Park at Point of Rocks (44)
Ragged Mountain Natural Area (45)
Three Lakes Park (51)

Twin Lakes State Park (52)
Waller Mill Park (55)
Walnut Creek Park (56)
York River State Park (59)

## ▶ HIKES FEATURING MAJOR RIVERS

Belle Isle and Brown's Island (5)
Belle Isle State Park (6)
Caledon State Park and Natural Area (8)
Canal Park Trail (9)
Chickahominy Wildlife Management
  Area (10)
Chippokes Plantation State Park (11)
Chubb Sandhill State Natural Area
  Preserve (12)
Dutch Gap Conservation Area (19)
Fluvanna Heritage Trail (20)
George Washington Birthplace National Mon-
  ument (22)
Hardware River Wildlife Management
  Area (24)

Henricus Historical Park (25)
Hog Island Wildlife Management Area (27)
James River Park Main Section (30)
Mariners Museum Park (33)
North Anna Battlefield Park (36)
Pony Pasture Rapids (40)
R. Garland Dodd Park at Point of Rocks (44)
Rivanna Trail (46)
Rockwood Park (47)
Voorhees Nature Preserve (53)
Westmoreland State Park (57)
Willis River Trail (58)
York River State Park (59)
Zoar State Forest (60)

## ▶ HIKES FEATURING WETLANDS

Beaverdam Park (4)
Bush Mill Stream State Natural Area Preserve (7)
Cumberland Marsh Nature Preserve (15)
Dutch Gap Conservation Area (19)
Greensprings Greenway (23)
Henricus Historical Park (25)

Hog Island Wildlife Management Area (27)
Newport News Park (35)
R. Garland Dodd Park at Point of Rocks (44)
Voorhees Nature Preserve (53)
Westmoreland State Park (57)
York River State Park (59)

## ▶ HIKES FEATURING HILLY TERRAIN

Appomattox–Buckingham State Forest (2)
Holliday Lake State Park (28)
Ragged Mountain Natural Area (45)

Wahrani Nature Park (54)
Walnut Creek Park (56)

# HIKING RECOMMENDATIONS

## ▶ HIKES FOR WILDLIFE- OR BIRD-WATCHING

Amelia Wildlife Management Area (1)
Appomattox–Buckingham State Forest (2)
Belle Isle State Park (6)
Bush Mill Stream State Natural Area
  Preserve (7)
Caledon State Park and Natural Area (8)
Chickahominy Wildlife Management
  Area (10)
Chubb Sandhill State Natural Area
  Preserve (12)
Cumberland Marsh Nature Preserve (15)
Dutch Gap Conservation Area (19)

Hardware River Wildlife Management
  Area (24)
Hog Island Wildlife Management Area (27)
Ivy Creek Natural Area (29)
Pony Pasture Rapids (40)
Powhatan Wildlife Management Area (42)
Ragged Mountain Natural Area (45)
Scheier Natural Area (49)
Voorhees Nature Preserve (53)
Westmoreland State Park (57)
Willis River Trail (58)

## ▶ HIKES FOR FAMILIES WITH CHILDREN

Bear Creek Lake State Park (3)
Belle Isle and Brown's Island (5)
Bush Mill Stream State Natural Area
  Preserve (7)
Chippokes Plantation State Park (11)
Crump Park (14)
Deep Run Park (17)
Dorey Park (18)
George Washington Birthplace National
  Monument (22)
Greensprings Greenway (23)
Henricus Historical Park (25)

Hickory Hollow State Natural Area Preserve
  (26)
Ivy Creek Natural Area (29)
Joseph Bryan Park (31)
Mariners Museum Park (33)
Motts Run Reservoir (34)
Newport News Park (35)
Pony Pasture Rapids (40)
Rockwood Park (47)
Saunders-Monticello Trail (48)
Three Lakes Park (51)
Waller Mill Park (55)

## ▶ HIKES FOR JOGGING OR TRAIL RUNNING

Beaverdam Park (4)
Belle Isle and Brown's Island (5)
Belle Isle State Park (6)
Caledon State Park and Natural Area (8)
Canal Park Trail (9)
Deep Run Park (17)
Fluvanna Heritage Trail (20)
Freedom Park (21)

Greensprings Greenway (23)
Hickory Hollow State Natural Area
  Preserve (26)
James River Park Main Section (30)
Mariners Museum Park (33)
Observatory Hill (37)
Poor Farm Park (41)
Ragged Mountain Natural Area (45)

# HIKING RECOMMENDATIONS

## ▶ HIKES FOR JOGGING OR TRAIL RUNNING *(continued)*

Rockwood Park (47)

Twin Lakes State Park (52)

Wahrani Nature Park (54)

Walnut Creek Park (56)

## ▶ HIKES ON MULTIUSE TRAILS

Amelia Wildlife Management Area (1)

Appomattox–Buckingham State Forest (2)

Beaverdam Park (4)

Chickahominy Wildlife Management
 Area (10)

Cumberland State Forest Multiuse Trail(16)

Dutch Gap Conservation Area (19)

Freedom Park (21)

Hardware River Wildlife Management
 Area (24)

Hog Island Wildlife Management Area (27)

James River Park Main Section (30)

Lake Anna State Park (32)

Observatory Hill (37)

Petersburg National Battlefield Park (38)

Poor Farm Park (41)

Powhatan Wildlife Management Area (42)

Prince Edward–Gallion State Forest (43)

Walnut Creek Park (56)

Willis River Trail (58)

York River State Park (59)

## ▶ HIKES WITH WHEELCHAIR-ACCESSIBLE PORTIONS

Belle Isle and Brown's Island (5)

Canal Park Trail (9)

Deep Run Park (17)

George Washington Birthplace National Monument (22)

Ivy Creek Natural Area (29)

Petersburg National Battlefield Park (38)

Rockwood Park (47)

Saunders-Monticello Trail (48)

Waller Mill Park (55)

## ▶ HIKE LOCATIONS THAT OFFER CAMPING OR CABINS

Bear Creek Lake State Park (3)

Belle Isle State Park (6)

Chippokes Plantation State Park (11)

Holliday Lake State Park (28)

Newport News Park (35)

Pocahontas State Park (39)

Twin Lakes State Park (52)

Westmoreland State Park (57)

York River State Park (59)

# INTRODUCTION

Welcome to *60 Hikes within 60 Miles: Richmond*. Whether you're new to hiking or a seasoned trail veteran, take a few minutes to read the following introduction. We'll explain how this book is organized and how to make the best use of it.

## ▶ HIKE DESCRIPTIONS

Each hike profile contains seven key items: a brief description of the trail, an at-a-glance information box, a detailed description of the hike, directions to the trail, GPS coordinates for the trailhead, a trail map, and an elevation profile. Combined, the maps and information provide a clear means of assessing each trail from the comfort of your favorite chair.

### KEY AT-A-GLANCE INFORMATION

The At-a-Glance Information boxes give you a quick idea of the specifics of each hike. There are 13 basic elements covered.

**LENGTH**   Provides the length of the trail from start to finish. There may be options to shorten or extend the hikes. Consult the hike description to help you decide how to customize the hike to your ability or time constraints.

**CONFIGURATION**   Describes what the trail might look like from overhead. Trails can be loops, out-and-backs (that is, hikers use the same path to and from the trailhead), figure eights, or balloons.

**DIFFICULTY**   Notes the degree of effort an "average" hiker should expect on a given hike. For simplicity, difficulty is described as "easy," "moderate," or "difficult."

**SCENERY**   Describes the environs of the hike and what to expect in terms of plant life, wildlife, streams, and historic buildings.

**EXPOSURE**   Suggests how much sun you can expect on your shoulders during the hike. Descriptors used are self-explanatory and include terms such as "shady," "exposed," and "sunny."

**TRAFFIC**   Indicates how busy the trail might be on an average day and if you might be able to find solitude out there. Trail traffic, of course, varies from day to day and season to season.

**TRAIL SURFACE**   Indicates whether the trail is paved, rocky, smooth dirt, or a mixture of elements.

**HIKING TIME**   Notes how long it took the author to hike the trail. (He averaged 2 to 3 miles an hour, depending on the terrain.)

**SEASON**   Notes times during which the trail is open for use.

**ACCESS**   Notes fees or permits needed to access the trail, indicates accessibility to wheelchairs, and notes other types of trail uses.

**MAPS**   Notes where to find the best, or easiest-to-use (in the author's opinion), map for this hike.

# INTRODUCTION

**FACILITIES**  Describes what to expect in terms of restrooms, phones, water, and other niceties available at the trailhead or nearby.

**SPECIAL COMMENTS**  Provides you with those little extra details that don't fit into any of the above categories. Here you'll find information specific to the hike being described.

## IN BRIEF

This short passage offers a "taste of the trail," a snapshot focused on the historical landmarks, beautiful vistas, and other interesting sights you may encounter on the trail.

## DESCRIPTION

The trail description is the heart of each hike profile. Here, the author provides a summary of what you'll encounter along the trail and highlights any special features the hike offers. Ultimately, the hike description will help you choose which hikes are best for you.

## DIRECTIONS

Each hike includes a set of concise driving directions. In some instances, distance is sacrificed for simplicity. Do not rely solely on the driving directions in this guide. Instead, obtain a detailed, up-to-date road map to augment them.

## ▶ MAPS AND GPS DATA

The maps in this book have been produced with great care and, used with the hiking directions, will help you stay on course. But as any experienced hiker knows, things can get tricky off the beaten path.

## ELEVATION PROFILES

Each map is accompanied by an elevation profile, a graph with the elevation above sea level plotted on the vertical access and mileage along the hike plotted on the horizontal access. This graphic enables you to gauge the number of climbs and their steepness. Note, however, that differences in distance produce an "accordian" effect. What looks like a steep climb on a long hike might not be so bad. Keep each axis in mind.

## GPS TRAILHEAD COORDINATES

To collect accurate map data, each trail was hiked with a handheld GPS unit (Garmin Etrex Venture). Data collected was then downloaded and plotted onto a digital USGS topo map. In addition to rendering a highly specific trail outline, this book also includes the GPS coordinates for each trailhead. More accurately known as UTM coordinates, the numbers index a specific point using a grid method. The survey datum used to arrive at the coordinates is NAD27. For readers who own a GPS unit, whether handheld or onboard a vehicle, the UTM coordinates provided on the first page of each hike can be entered into the GPS unit and used to navigate directly to the trailhead. Just make sure your GPS unit is set to navigate using the UTM system in conjunction with NAD27 datum.

Most trailheads, which begin in parking areas, can be navigated to by car. However, some hikes still require a short walk to reach the trailhead from a parking area. In those cases, a handheld unit would be necessary to continue the GPS navigation process. That said, however, all trailheads in this book are easily accessed using the directions given, the overview map, and the trail map, which shows at least one major road leading into the area. But for those who enjoy using the latest GPS technology to navigate, the necessary data has been provided. A brief explanation of UTM coordinates follows.

## UTM COORDINATES: ZONE, EASTING, AND NORTHING

Within the UTM coordinates box on the first page of each hike, there are three numbers labeled zone, easting, and northing. Here is an example from the Ragged Mountain Natural Area hike on page 184.

| | |
|---|---|
| Zone: | 17S |
| Easting: | 0714511 |
| Northing: | 4211375 |

The zone number (17) refers to one of the 60 longitudinal zones of a map that uses the Universal Transverse Mercator (UTM) projection. Each zone is six degrees wide. The zone letter (S) refers to one of the 20 latitudinal zones (horizontal) that span from 80° South to 84° North.

The easting number (0714511) references in meters how far east the point is from the zero value for eastings, which runs north–south through Greenwich, England. Increasing easting coordinates on a topo map or on your GPS screen indicate you are moving east. Decreasing easting coordinates indicate you are moving west. Since lines of longitude converge at the poles, they are not parallel as lines of latitude are. This means that the distance between easting zones is 1,000 meters near the equator but becomes smaller as you travel north or south. The difference is small enough to be ignored but only until you reach the polar regions.

In the Northern Hemisphere, the northing number (4211375) references in meters how far you are from the Equator. Above the Equator, northing coordinates increase by 1,000 meters between each parallel line of latitude (east–west lines). On a topo map or GPS receiver, increasing northing numbers indicate you are traveling north.

In the Southern Hemisphere, the northing number references how far you are from the equator, which is given a value of 10 million meters. Below the equator, northing coordinates decrease by 1,000 meters between each line of latitude. On a topo map, or on your GPS unit, decreasing northing coordinates indicate you are traveling south.

# INTRODUCTION

## TOPOGRAPHIC MAPS

The maps in this book, when used with the route directions provided with each hike profile, are sufficient to get you to the trail and keep you on it. However, you will find superior detail and valuable information in the United States Geological Survey's 7.5 minute series topographic maps. Recognizing how indispensable these are to hikers and bikers alike, many outdoor shops and bike shops now carry topos of the local area.

If you're new to hiking, you might be wondering, "What's a topographic map?" In short, it indicates not only linear distance but elevation as well. One glance at a topo will show you the difference; contour lines spread across the map like dozens of intricate spiderwebs. Each contour line represents a particular elevation, and at the base of each topo, a contour's interval designation is given. It may sound confusing if you're new to the lingo, but it's truly a simple and helpful system. Assume that the 7.5 minute series topo reads "Contour Interval 40 feet," that the short trail you'll be hiking is two inches in length on the map, and that it crosses five contour lines from its beginning to its end. Because the linear scale of this series is 2,000 feet to the inch (roughly 2.75 inches equals one mile), the trail is approximately 0.8 miles long (2 inches equal 2,000 feet). You'll also be climbing or descending 200 vertical feet (5 contour lines are 40 feet each) over that distance. The elevation designations written on occasional contour lines will tell you if you're heading up or down.

In addition to outdoor shops and bike shops, you'll find topos at major universities and at some public libraries, where you might try photocopying the ones you need to save the cost of buying them. But if you want your own and can't find them locally, contact USGS Map Sales at Box 25286, Denver, Colorado, 80225; (888) ASK-USGS (275-8747); or www.mapping.usgs.gov. They accept Visa and MasterCard. Ask for an index while you're at it, plus a price list and a copy of the booklet "Topographic Maps." With a little practice you'll be reading them like a pro.

## ▶ WEATHER

Virginia's weather is often dynamic but rarely extreme. It is jokingly said that the state has four distinct seasons but that they do not occur in any particular order. Hence, a modicum of planning should precede a hike of any significant distance—or of any significant distance from home. Obtain a reliable weather forecast, dress appropriately and in layers, and bring a raincoat just in case.

In general, as the accompanying temperature chart shows, Central Virginia summers and winters are relatively mild. As a rule the eastern periphery of the area covered by this guide stays a few degrees warmer in the winter and a few degrees cooler in the summer than the rest of the state. The area to the west is typically a few degrees cooler during the winter than the rest of Virginia. Precipitation in Richmond peaks during the month of July, which averages five inches of rain, but it is a year-

# INTRODUCTION

round possibility. Other warm months average four inches, and cool months average three inches.

Blizzards and thunderstorms aside, a well-equipped, well-prepared hiker can enjoy these trails year-round. In fact, hiking in the wake of a snowfall rewards the intrepid with stunning scenery. Nevertheless, you'll find trail traffic spikes in the spring. To avoid the crowds, head east of Richmond, where you'll find blossoms, particularly mountain laurel, on Tidewater riverbanks, and migratory birds returning north along the Atlantic flyway. In the autumn, head west to the hardwood forests of the Piedmont and Appalachian foothills. You'll find stunning foliage and sweeping vistas near Charlottesville, without the throngs that flock to Skyline Drive.

### AVERAGE DAILY TEMPERATURES BY MONTH (°F)

|      | JAN | FEB | MAR | APR | MAY | JUN |
|------|-----|-----|-----|-----|-----|-----|
| MIN. | 26  | 28  | 36  | 45  | 54  | 63  |
| MAX. | 46  | 49  | 60  | 70  | 78  | 85  |

|      | JUL | AUG | SEP | OCT | NOV | DEC |
|------|-----|-----|-----|-----|-----|-----|
| MIN. | 67  | 66  | 59  | 47  | 38  | 30  |
| MAX. | 88  | 87  | 81  | 71  | 64  | 50  |

## ▶ REGULATIONS AND TRAIL ETIQUETTE

Though the hike profiles note some restrictions (generally in the Access category of the At-a-Glance Information box), it is your responsibility to learn and obey the rules of any park or preserve that you visit. Some commonplace regulations that apply to most of the sites listed in this guide include:

- ▶ Use or display of alcoholic beverages is not allowed.
- ▶ All state and local ordinances apply, including those governing fishing and hunting.
- ▶ Pets must be leashed. Pets are not allowed at most nature preserves.
- ▶ Though hours vary, parks generally close at dusk.
- ▶ Camping is not allowed without the permission of park management. Established campgrounds are often closed in the off-season.
- ▶ Fires are not allowed without the permission of park management. Even campfires are subject to seasonal bans.
- ▶ Swimming is not allowed unless otherwise specified. Many rivers, lakes, and ponds are closed to swimmers, and some lake beaches are open only in summer.

Whether you're on a city, county, state, or national park trail, always remember that great care and resources (from nature as well as from your tax dollars) have gone into creating these trails. Treat the trail, wildlife, and fellow hikers with respect.

# INTRODUCTION

Here are a few general ideas to keep in mind while on the trail:

1.  Hike on open trails only. Respect trail and road closures (ask if not sure), avoid possible trespass on private land, and obtain all permits and authorization as required. Also, leave gates as you found them or as marked.

2.  Leave no trace of your visit other than footprints. Be sensitive to the dirt beneath you. This also means staying on the trail and not creating any new ones. Be sure to pack out what you pack in. No one likes to see the trash someone else has left behind.

3.  Never spook animals. An unannounced approach, a sudden movement, or a loud noise startles most animals. A surprised snake or skunk can be dangerous to you, to others, and to themselves. Give animals extra room and time to adjust to your presence.

4.  Plan ahead. Know your equipment, your ability, and the area in which you are hiking—and prepare accordingly. Be self-sufficient at all times; carry necessary supplies for changes in weather or other conditions. A well-executed trip is a satisfaction to you and to others.

5.  Be courteous to other hikers and to bikers and horseback riders that you meet on the trails.

## ▶ WATER

"How much is enough? One bottle? Two? Three?! But think of all that extra weight!" Well, one simple physiological fact should convince you to err on the side of excess when it comes to deciding how much water to pack: a human working hard in 90° heat needs approximately ten quarts of fluid every day. That's two-and-a-half gallons—12 large water bottles or 16 small ones. In other words, pack along a bottle or two even for short hikes.

Serious backpackers hit the trail prepared to purify streamwater found along the route. This method, while less dangerous than drinking it untreated, comes with risks. Many hikers pack the slightly distasteful tetraglycine hydroperiodide tablets (sold under the names Potable Aqua, Coughlan's, and others). Some invest in portable, lightweight purifiers that filter out the crud. Unfortunately, both iodine and filtering are now required to be absolutely sure you've killed all the nasties you can't see. Giardia, for example, may hit one to four weeks after ingestion. It will have you bloated, vomiting, shivering with chills, and living in the bathroom. But there are other parasites to worry about, including E. coli and cryptosporidium (affectionately known as "Crypto," and even harder to kill than Giardia).

For most people, the pleasures of hiking make carrying water a relatively minor price to pay to remain healthy. If you're tempted to drink "found water," do so only once you thoroughly understand the risks involved.

# INTRODUCTION

## ▶ FIRST-AID KIT

A typical kit may contain more items than you might think necessary. Pack the items in a waterproof container such as a Ziploc bag. You may want to include more, such as a snack for hikes longer than a couple of miles. These are just the basics:

Ace bandages or Spenco joint wraps

Antibiotic ointment (Neosporin® or the generic equivalent)

Aspirin or acetaminophen

Band-Aids

Benadryl or the generic equivalent—diphenhydramine (an antihistamine, in case of allergic reactions)

Butterfly-closure bandages

Gauze (one roll)

Gauze compress pads (6 each, 4 in. by 4 in.)

Hydrogen peroxide or iodine

Matches or pocket lighter

Moleskin/Spenco "Second Skin"

Snakebite kit

Sunscreen

Prefilled syringe of epinephrine (for those known to have severe allergic reactions to such things as bee stings)

Water-purification tablets or water filter (see note under "Water")

Whistle (more effective in signaling rescuers than your voice)

## ▶ SNAKES

If you hike enough of these trails, you'll eventually spot a snake, usually sunning on the trail ahead, or perhaps slithering into the underbrush at the sound of your footfalls. The odds that you will happen upon a poisonous snake are significantly less. Still, it's recommended that you give all legless reptiles a wide berth—and other wildlife as well.

Among the snakes native to Central Virginia are the nonpoisonous garter, black rat, and king snakes, and the venomous water moccasins, copperheads, and Canebrake rattlesnakes. Snakes like warm—but not hot—weather and are active from midspring through midautumn. If you're worried about snakes, you may want to spend a few minutes studying the various species and their habits before heading into the woods. A field guide such as *Dangerous Wildlife of the Mid-Atlantic* (Menasha Ridge Press) may help you feel more informed and empowered. Basic precautions, such as wearing sturdy shoes and long pants and carrying a cell phone, should also assuage your fears, while minimizing more likely risks like twisted ankles and poison ivy.

## ▶ TICKS

Ticks tend to lurk in the brush, leaves, and grass that grow alongside trails. May through August is the peak period for ticks in the Mid-Atlantic, but arachnids can remain active all year. Scientifically, ticks are ectoparasites, living on the outside of a host for the majority of their life cycles in order to reproduce.

Of the two varieties that may hitch a ride on you while you're hiking—wood ticks and deer ticks—extensive research suggests that both need several hours of actual bloodsucking attachment before they can transmit any disease. Deer ticks, the primary vector for Lyme disease, are very small (often as tiny as poppy seeds), and you may not be aware of their presence until you feel the itchiness of their bites. The best avoidance strategy is to wear light-colored clothing (so that you can spot the ticks more easily); tuck the bottoms of your pant legs into your socks (it looks geeky but helps); lather your ankles, wrists, and neck with a DEET-rich insect repellant; and remain on the beaten path, avoiding trails overgrown with tall grass. At the end of the hike, check yourself thoroughly before getting in the car, and later, when you take a post-hike shower, do a more thorough check of your entire body.

Also, when hiking with your dog, take precautions to ensure your pet's safety. Regularly apply a topical anti-flea, anti-tick medication (such as Frontline Plus or KP Advantix), and brush your dog after hiking to look for ticks, which tend to crawl up to the head and chest. Ticks that haven't bitten are easily removed but not easily killed unless you burn or crush them. Tweezers work best for plucking off attached ticks.

## ▶ POISON IVY, OAK, AND SUMAC

Recognizing and avoiding contact with poison ivy, oak, and sumac are the most effective means of preventing the painful, itchy rash associated with these poisons. In the Mid-Atlantic, poison ivy occurs as a vine or ground cover with three leaflets to a leaf; poison oak appears as either a vine or shrub with three leaflets to a leaf; and poison sumac grows in swampland as a shrub with 7 to 13 leaflets per leaf. Consult a field guide to learn how to identify these species and distinguish them from benign counterparts like Virginia Creeper.

Urushiol, the oil from these plants, is responsible for the rash. Thus, you may contract a case of poison ivy either by direct contact with the plant or by touching something—your clothing, boots, or pets—that brushed against it. Within 12 to 24 hours of exposure, raised lines and/or blisters appear, accompanied by a terrible itch. As with insect bites, scratching makes the situation worse, and bacteria under your fingernails may cause an infection. Wash and dry the rash thoroughly, applying a calamine lotion or other desiccant to help dry out the rash. If the itching or blistering is severe, seek medical attention.

## ▶ HIKING WITH CHILDREN

No one is too young for a hike in the woods or through a city park. Be careful, though. Flat, short trails are probably best with an infant. Toddlers who have not

# INTRODUCTION

quite mastered walking can still tag along, riding on an adult's back in a child carrier. Use common sense to judge a child's capacity to hike a particular trail, and always expect that the child will tire quickly and need to be carried.

When packing for the hike, remember the child's needs as well as your own. Make sure children are adequately clothed for the weather, have proper shoes, and are protected from the sun with sunscreen. Kids dehydrate quickly, so make sure you have plenty of fluid for everyone.

A list of hike recommendations for children is provided on page xv. Finally, when hiking with children, remember the trip will be a compromise. A child's energy and enthusiasm alternate between bursts of speed and long stops to examine snails, sticks, dirt, and other attractions.

## ▶ THE BUSINESS HIKER

Whether you're in the Richmond area on busines or are a resident, these 60 hikes offer perfect quick getaways from the busy demands of commerce. The city of Richmond is home to some of the best urban parkland on the East Coast. Instead of eating inside, you can pack a lunch and head out to picnic on a boulder beside the James River at Belle Isle. Or plan ahead and take a small group of your business comrades on a nearby hike in Pocahontas State Park or at Dutch Gap Conservation Area. A brief outdoor getaway is the perfect complement to a business day in Richmond.

## ▶ THE TOURIST HIKER

A wealth of historic sites, homes, and battlefields are scattered across Virginia's Tidewater and Piedmont, with Richmond at the hub. Many of these destinations offer trails of their own; others lay en route to hikes profiled in this guide. Each year, thousands of visitors flock to Monticello, Petersburg Battlefield, Jamestown, and George Washington's birthplace. Sadly, many never leave their vehicles. America's history unfolded on Virginia's soil, and this guidebook invites you to tread in the footsteps of English settlers, American revolutionaries, rebellious slaves, Civil War soldiers, and Civilian Conservation Corps workmen. Don't forsake the opportunity to walk a mile in their shoes.

# AMELIA WILDLIFE MANAGEMENT AREA

## KEY AT-A-GLANCE INFORMATION

**LENGTH:** 6.1 miles (plus shorter and longer options)

**CONFIGURATION:** Loop

**DIFFICULTY:** Moderate

**SCENERY:** Mostly hardwood forest, fishing lakes, fields, and hedgerows

**EXPOSURE:** Moderate

**TRAFFIC:** Low

**TRAIL SURFACE:** Dirt and gravel double-track, mowed grass paths

**HIKING TIME:** 3 hours

**SEASON:** Open daily during daylight year-round, but avoid trails during autumn and winter hunting seasons

**ACCESS:** No fee; horseback riding and mountain biking allowed; no ATVs; wheelchair-accessible boat launch and fishing pier on Amelia Lake

**MAPS:** Available online at www.dgif. virginia.gov/hunting/wma/amelia.html.

**FACILITIES:** Pier, boat launch, shooting ranges (open daily except Wednesday), informational signboards, resident staff; primitive camping permitted, but do not leave campfires unattended

**SPECIAL COMMENTS:** All wildlife management areas are open to hunting. Check with VDGIF to determine annual hunting seasons (call (804) 370-1000 or visit www.dgif. virginia.gov/hunting). It is recommended that you not hike during deer and wild turkey seasons; if you do, wear blaze orange and hike only during peak daylight hours.

UTM Trailhead Coordinates for Amelia Wildlife Management Area

UTM Zone (NAD27)  18S

Easting   0241980

Northing  4148896

## IN BRIEF

The 2,217-acre Amelia Wildlife Management Area (WMA) encompasses forest, rolling fields, and wide hedgerows that offer great bird-watching. The 100-acre Amelia Lake and a smaller pond entice anglers with largemouth bass, channel catfish, walleye, redear sunfish, and other species.

## DESCRIPTION

The commonwealth's wildlife-management areas, operated by the Virginia Department of Game and Inland Fisheries (VDGIF), greatly expand outdoor recreation options in Central Virginia. With no national forests east of the Appalachian Mountains, avid hikers look to WMAs to effectively double the state-owned land at their disposal. And while these areas lack the conveniences associated with state parks, they are, as the name suggests, great for wildlife-watching.

If you have more than watching in mind, you can bring your fishing pole (and fishing license) anytime. Hunting is allowed in season, and the seasons vary with the game. It's advisable

## DIRECTIONS

Amelia is approximately 25 miles west of Richmond via US 60 (the Midlothian Turnpike). Continue through Midlothian and turn left onto VA 13 just east of Powhatan. The road leads through Powhatan, but take a left onto VA 603 after a quarter mile. Continue almost 6 miles on VA 603 to a T intersection with VA 604 in the hamlet of Genito. Turn right onto VA 604 and continue 2.8 miles to equally small Mason's Corner. Here VA 604 turns southward (left), but continue straight, now on VA 616, for another 1.4 miles. Next, turn right onto VA 652, which enters Amelia WMA after less than a mile. Park in the first lot, immediately on the right as you enter the WMA.

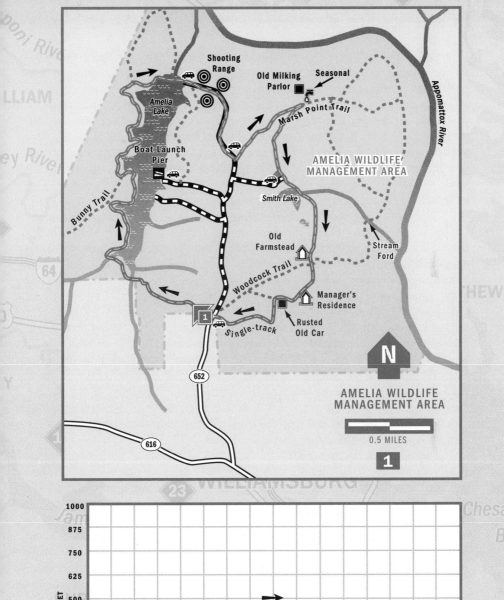

Shooting Range

Old Milking Parlor · Seasonal

Amelia Lake

Boat Launch Pier

Marsh Point Trail

AMELIA WILDLIFE MANAGEMENT AREA

Appomattox River

Bunny Trail

Smith Lake

Old Farmstead

Stream Ford

Woodcock Trail

Manager's Residence

Rusted Old Car

Single-track

N

652

616

AMELIA WILDLIFE MANAGEMENT AREA

0.5 MILES

1

| MILES | | | | |
|---|---|---|---|---|
| 1.5 | 3.0 | 4.5 | 6.1 | |

FEET
1000
875
750
625
500
375
250
125
0

to avoid hiking in Virginia's wildlife areas during the popular deer- and wild-turkey–hunting seasons. Hunting seasons typically begin with bird hunting in September and continue intermittently through February.

But don't let the preceding caveat dissuade you from visiting, particularly if you're one of the many Chesterfield County residents just half an hour away. In actuality, aquatic wildlife constitutes the main draw at Amelia, and you'll inevitably spot anglers casting from the shore or from small watercraft. If it's not hunting season and you hear gunshots, keep in mind the firing ranges northeast of the lake. This loop takes you past them along a gravel road—a short, necessary link between trails on either side of the main gravel road.

The north–south road bisects the area, with Amelia Lake and the firing ranges located in the western half and the much-smaller Smith Lake and former farm buildings in the east. Scenic Amelia Lake reflects the tall trees along its shore, while the cumulative effect of the fields and buildings—which include barns still used by the VDGIF, and a decrepit, abandoned manor—is not one of wilderness but of bucolic decay. Come in the winter and you may fancy seeing the old manor located on an abandoned Dust Bowl farmstead—there's even a Model-T rusting in the woods. In the summer the pastoral scene is positively shaggy with greenery. At any time of year this loop presents an intriguing and endearing dichotomy.

Unlike nearby Powhatan Wilderness Management Area, where equestrian use keeps overgrowth at bay, Amelia's trails are sometimes shrouded in waist-high grass. With that in mind, the loop described avoids the easternmost trails in favor of the westernmost path, which is easier to follow because it traces the shoreline of Amelia Lake. Of course, you may well find the grassy paths freshly shorn, especially in the early spring, when the fields are tilled and planted.

The VDGIF elected to maintain the fields and hedgerows of this former farm, as they constitute an ecosystem unto themselves. The hedges provide habitat to rabbits and other woodland mammals, which in turn draw the owls and raptors you may see circling overhead. Smaller birds, like doves and quail, forage in the fields and nest in the hedges. Rotund, long-billed woodcocks reportedly favor the banks of the Appomatox River, which forms the WMA's northern and eastern borders but is not along the trail network. You're more likely to spot wild turkeys feeding near the many stands of oak. I was surprised to flush a pair but was even more surprised to see them fly over nearby trees almost 100 feet tall. According to the VDGIF, Amelia's turkey population is on the rise, in keeping with a nationwide renaissance. Hunted nearly to extinction a century ago, the wild turkey is now a conservation success story.

Begin by crossing the park road to a yellow metal gate that signals the trail's departure westward toward Amelia Lake. After a half mile of mostly level walking through hardwood forest, the trail descends steeply to meet the lake at the end of the first mile. The trail then traces the lakeshore northward, looping occasionally into the woods, but it promptly returns to the waterside. Bear right when spur trails head left, and you'll soon reach the earthen dam at the lake's northern edge. The grassy slope with views across the lake is a pleasant spot at which to catch your breath.

Almost halfway through your hike, ascend westward through a parking lot and follow the gravel road past the firing ranges. Turn left at a signboard that signals the Milking Parlor Trail (erroneously labeled Marsh Point Trail on some maps). Shaggy cedars border the gravel double-track, which is closed to vehicles. Cedars commonly line the state's rural roads, indicating that the road predates the establishment of this wildlife-management area. Ahead on the left is the trail's namesake, an open-sided milking barn that now houses maintenance tractors. A newer cinderblock structure nearby serves as a seasonal hunting headquarters and has restrooms. Turn sharply right onto another double-track before passing the building.

Head south past a series of fields and hedgerows. The bands of brush between fields have been allowed to widen beyond those of a working farm in order to increase animal habitat. A hardwood forest of oak and hickory towers at the periphery of the field. You'll descend to reach a small pond abutting Smith Lake on the right. Its twin lies across peaceful Smith Lake to the south. Pass a spur path to a nearby parking area on your right and continue uphill past the water.

Soon the old grain silos and abandoned manor of the former farmstead rise into view on the horizon. The WMA now uses the barns, including a quaint red one, for storage and workspace, but vines are overtaking the brick manor house. Shaded by a mammoth oak, its shutters still hang despite missing windowpanes, and its roof, though rusted, appears to be intact. The house fronts the Woodcock Trail, a gravel road that leads past a quail-restoration demonstration back to the trailhead parking area. To follow the route as shown on the trail map, continue southward.

You'll soon reach the newer manager's residence, passing directly beside the domicile. A few hundred yards ahead, a dirt double-track veers to the left. Turn here and look for the rusted car that has collapsed in the leaves to the left of the trail. Proceed between two stands of hardwood to see a field opening on the left. Look for a narrow dirt path on the right. Though brief, this lone stretch of single-track is Amelia's best footpat, wending past some younger pine forest and through more mature trees back to the parking area.

# APPOMATTOX-BUCKINGHAM STATE FOREST: CARTER-TAYLOR MULTIUSE TRAIL

## KEY AT-A-GLANCE INFORMATION

**LENGTH:** 10.9 miles

**CONFIGURATION:** Loop

**DIFFICULTY:** Hard (due to length)

**SCENERY:** Mature-hardwood forested valleys, mixed and pine-forested hills, rocky Holliday Creek

**EXPOSURE:** Shaded except on forest roads

**TRAFFIC:** Low, but autos are permitted on forest roads

**TRAIL SURFACE:** Dirt single-track and gravel forest roads

**HIKING TIME:** 5 hours

**SEASON:** Trails are open daily during daylight year-round but should be avoided during hunting seasons.

**ACCESS:** No fee to enter the forest; mountain biking and horseback riding are allowed on multiuse trail; no ATVs

**MAPS:** Available at forest office and online at www.dof.virginia.gov/stforest/index-absf.shtml

**FACILITIES:** Grass and gravel parking areas, forest office, small horse stable; adjacent Holliday Lake State Park offers restrooms, a campground with showers, a lakeside beach, and a snack bar

**SPECIAL COMMENTS:** Portions of the state forest are open to hunting with the proper license. Call the forest office (434) 983-2175 for details; check with the VDGIF to determine annual hunting seasons (call (804) 370-1000 or visit www.dgif.virginia.gov/hunting).

UTM Trailhead Coordinates for
Appomattox-Buckingham State Forest

UTM Zone (NAD27)   17S

Easting   0706393

Northing   4145591

## IN BRIEF

Though it does rely on gravel forest roads to make a complete loop, the Carter-Taylor Trail features long stretches of single-track. Three stream crossings entail some ups and downs, but the generally level nature of the trail counterbalances its length.

## DESCRIPTION

You'll find echoes of Appalachia in Appomattox-Buckingham State Forest, the westernmost of Virginia's three major Piedmont forests. Instead of sandy streambeds, you'll cross creek beds dotted with stones. There are even black bears residing in these woods. However, you're more likely to spot their diminutive relative the racoon, as well as white-tailed deer and wild turkey.

Anglers may hope to find a rainbow dangling from their line. The rocky Holliday Creek is

## DIRECTIONS

From Richmond, travel west on US 60 (the Midlothian Turnpike). Continue through Midlothian, Powhatan, and Cumberland to the crossroads of Sprouses Corner (just east of Buckingham, 57 miles from Chippenham Parkway). Turn left here onto VA 640, which you will follow generally southwest for 10.7 twisting miles. Turn left after 2.1 miles to stay with VA 640 when it joins VA 633, then veer right after 0.1 mile to stay with VA 640. After passing through tiny Andersonville, make a right onto VA 636. In 1.7 miles, turn left onto Richmond Forest Road, a gravel double-track. The dirt parking lot, complete with a small stable, is located 0.2 miles downhill on the right side. Maps and a trail log are located across the road. You may also elect to park at the forest headquarters, located 0.2 miles farther along VA 636 on the right side of the road. There is also a trailhead, linked to the loop by a half-mile connector, in Holliday Lake State Park (see page 118.)

APPOMATTOX-BUCKINGHAM
STATE FOREST

To 60

640

636

Richmond Forest Rd.

2

North Holliday Creek

Rinehart Forest Rd.

640

Walker Forest Rd.

614

Holliday Creek

BUCKINGHAM CO.
APPOMATTOX CO.

640

692

N

614

Sanders Creek

692

Forbes Creek

APPOMATTOX-BUCKINGHAM
STATE FOREST:
CARTER-TAYLOR
MULTIUSE TRAIL

0.5 MILES

2

626

HOLLIDAY LAKE
STATE PARK

Holliday Lake

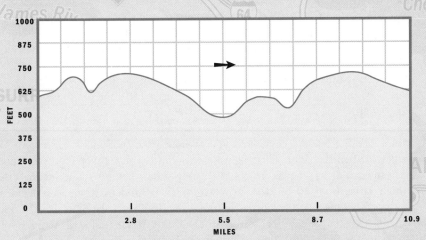

| FEET | | | | |
|---|---|---|---|---|
| 1000 | | | | |
| 875 | | | | |
| 750 | | | | |
| 625 | | | | |
| 500 | | | | |
| 375 | | | | |
| 250 | | | | |
| 125 | | | | |
| 0 | 2.8 | 5.5 | 8.7 | 10.9 |

MILES

a designated delayed-harvest trout stream. The Virginia Department of Game and Inland Fisheries stocks the creek October through May, and catch-and-release fishing is permitted with artificial lures and a trout license. From June through September general state regulations apply.

This hike begins westbound along Richmond Forest Road, which the loop follows west for almost half a mile. But take heart: if hiking the loop counterclockwise, you'll get most of the road walking out of the way first. Near the starting point, where the North Fork Holliday Creek funnels beneath the road, the blended forest includes yellow poplar, red maple, and white pine. Younger white and scarlet oaks and Virginia pines shade the gravel road on its gradual climb.

Cresting the hill, the Carter-Taylor turns left onto Rinehart Forest Road. A small red sign indicates the turn, and intermittent red blazes help keep you on track. A meadow stretches away on the left then again gives way to Virginia pines. The double-track, sometimes dotted with puddles, bypasses multiple gated roadbeds as it gradually descends toward Holliday Creek. Carefully fording the stream, you leave Buckingham County and enter Appomattox County.

The trail curves right to meet and then parallel a feeder branch. Shrouded in mountain laurel, the rivulet runs close by on trail left. A recently logged hilltop is scarcely discernable uphill on the right. A red sign soon directs you left, off the roadbed and across the feeder stream. Once across, you'll make your first appreciable climb through a forest of white, chestnut, and black oaks.

Shortly after the trail levels, a sign on the right indicates that your route makes a sharp left. If you reach an asphalt road, you've missed the turn. The Carter-Taylor makes its first single-track run through a tunnel of mixed evergreens. Reentering hardwood forest, the trail reaches a road crossing, with an intersection visible to the right. Bisect VA 640 and continue ahead on the single-track path that parallels VA 692 on the right. The Carter-Taylor keeps the road within sight for more than a mile as it heads east beneath chestnut oaks. Fortunately, the road is seldom busy. Don't be tempted off the path by several dirt roads. The trail turns left 90 degrees only after first crossing VA 614 and proceeding a quarter mile southeast.

A grassy stretch of trail passes through a parcel of younger forest before crossing a power-line clearing. Make a steep descent to reach the Holliday Creek Valley, where the connector from Holliday Lake State Park joins your path from the right. Appomattox-Buckingham State Forest envelops the park. With swimming, fishing, camping, and a hiking trail around the lake (page 118), the park makes an excellent base camp.

In the valley, dead pines, victims of disease or infestation, lay scattered beneath young beech trees and cedars. As you approach the creek, look for a sign directing pedestrians to the right. This slight detour affords you a bridged crossing not available to equestrians. Grass fringes the sandy shoals behind stones in the creekbed, which varies from 10 to 20 feet in width. The rudimentary wood-on-cement-pipe bridge also serves as the northern stretch of Holliday Lake State Park's loop trail, which enters and departs on trail right. The Carter-Taylor Trail turns left, rejoining the equestrian path to weave north through the bottomland forest.

A steep, rocky climb follows, then the trail reaches an oak-hickory ridge, cresting at an old home site distinguishable both by the remnants of a stone foundation and the glade of broad-crowned white oaks that once shaded the house. Then, upon intersecting an old logging road, the Carter-Taylor turns left with the double-track. Meadows on either side of the trail precede younger pines.

Just before reaching VA 614, the trail doubles back. It makes a sharp left to run through a wide clearing between dense pines then back down a steep hillside to Holliday Creek. Stay with the broader path as it curves to the right, rather than taking a signed fishing trail left. Just ahead, within the stocked trout-fishing stretch, the steep-sided, rocky creek has a mountainous character. Laurel crowds the trail, which runs upstream, pressed against the hillside. The fenced-off contraption on trail left is part of a depth-gauging station. A steel cable links it to a twin across the stream.

The trail bends right, away from the water, before cutting left. The creek flows beneath VA 614 on the left, while your path rises away to meet the road. Turn left briefly, but before spanning the creek, cross VA 614, and head uphill on gated Walker Forest Road. Bypass another fishing trail on the left and climb out of the valley.

Shortly after leveling out, the trail opens upon a sweeping meadow vista. Upon closer inspection, the remnants of a logging operation are discernable among the recovering brush. Continue through the open area, passing beneath a few spared white oaks. After more than a quarter mile, reenter the forest of young pines and spindly hardwoods. The level trail continues north; you'll pass a gravel road on the left before a small meadow, also on the left, signals your next turn.

Follow the Carter-Taylor Trail as it makes another sharp left here, keeping the meadow on your left before turning right. The trail promptly joins the just-mentioned gravel road, an extension of Walker Forest Road, and follows it a short distance to VA 636. Cross the blacktop then turn left immediately. The trail follows a power-line swath through deciduous forest.

Follow the path west, paralleling VA 636 for about a mile. Look for a brown sign directing you left through the woods and back across the road. The Carter-Taylor Trail now makes its final stretch along a wide, grassy path. Lichen spots the bark of young hardwoods along the trail, which makes a distinct right away from a small meadow. A short distance ahead, another brown sign signals a left turn. The trail makes a final descent through moist forest carpeted in clubmoss on the north bank of North Fork Holliday Creek. But, rather than crossing the stream, it emerges back at the Richmond Forest Road trailhead.

While in the area, consider visiting Appomattox Courthouse National Historic Park, site of Robert E. Lee's famed surrender (just a few miles west but beyond the radius of this guidebook). In the park you'll find a 6-mile trail weaving through the battlefield, leading from the visitor center across the Appomattox and past the site of the McLean House, where Generals Grant and Lee convened on Palm Sunday 1865. Three days earlier, on April 6, Lee's Army of Northern Virginia had suffered 7,700 casualties on what became known as the Black Thursday of the Confederacy. The site of that conflagration, Sailor's Creek Battlefield State Park, just east of Farmville via US 460 from Appomattox, is also open to visitors.

# BEAR CREEK LAKE STATE PARK

## KEY AT-A-GLANCE INFORMATION

**LENGTH:** 2.9 miles, plus 2.5 miles to be reopened

**CONFIGURATION:** Balloon

**DIFFICULTY:** Easy

**SCENERY:** Hardwood and mixed forests, small streams, Bear Creek Lake

**EXPOSURE:** Shaded except along lakeshore

**TRAFFIC:** Moderate

**TRAIL SURFACE:** Dirt single-track

**HIKING TIME:** 1.5 hours

**SEASON:** Trails open daily during daylight year-round, camping in season

**ACCESS:** Parking $2–$3 on weekends in season. Restrooms, snack bar, and some campsites are wheelchair accessible; trails not recommended for wheelchairs

**MAPS:** Available at park and online at www.dcr.virginia.gov/parks/bearcreek.htm

**FACILITIES:** Visitor center, campground, restrooms, showers, beach on lake, boat launch, playground, snack bar, RV dumping station, pay phones. Swimming, $2 for children ages 3–12, $3 for adults. In-season canoe, kayak, and rowboat rentals (prices vary with watercraft type and the time of day). Campsites cost $20 per night with hookups or $14 without hookups.

**SPECIAL COMMENTS:** As of publication, construction of new cabin facilities was underway, closing trails on the lake's southeastern shore. For more information, contact the park office at (804) 492-4410.

**UTM Trailhead Coordinates for Bear Creek Lake State Park**

**UTM Zone (NAD27)** 17S

**Easting** 0741440

**Northing** 4157156

## IN BRIEF

This compact jaunt showcases the natural beauty of the park's eastern woodlands. Birds linger on the marshy eastern periphery of Bear Creek Lake, and hardwoods tower over Little Bear Creek. Extend this hike along the creek using the Willis River Trail as an out-and-back if you like.

## DESCRIPTION

Just 326 acres, Bear Creek Lake State Park is engulfed by the 16,000-acre Cumberland State Forest. But the park has the larger lake (at 40 acres) and all the amenities to make it a popular weekend-camping destination. On crowded days, the surrounding forest makes it easy to escape the throng for either hiking or fishing. But you may find that with everyone lounging on the beach, this hike is surprisingly serene. It skirts the eastern shore of Bear Creek Lake, crossing Little Bear Creek then tracing a stretch of Bear Creek proper.

It's hard to believe, threading beneath tall oaks along the creek, that this land was farmed as early as the 1740s. Though most of that former cropland has reforested, evidence of its agrarian past remains. A monument on VA 663 marks the

## DIRECTIONS

From Richmond travel west on US 60 (the Midlothian Turnpike). Continue through Midlothian and Powhatan to Cumberland, seat of its eponymous county (approximately 40 miles west of Chippenham Parkway). East of town you will pass VA 622 on the right, which is signed for Bear Creek Lake State Park. Follow the road 3.4 miles north to turn left onto VA 629. Veer left again after 0.8 miles to pass the park office and entrance-fee station. The trailhead, marked for the Cumberland Multiuse Trail, or CMT, is on the left 0.4 miles ahead, beyond the campgrounds and before the beach.

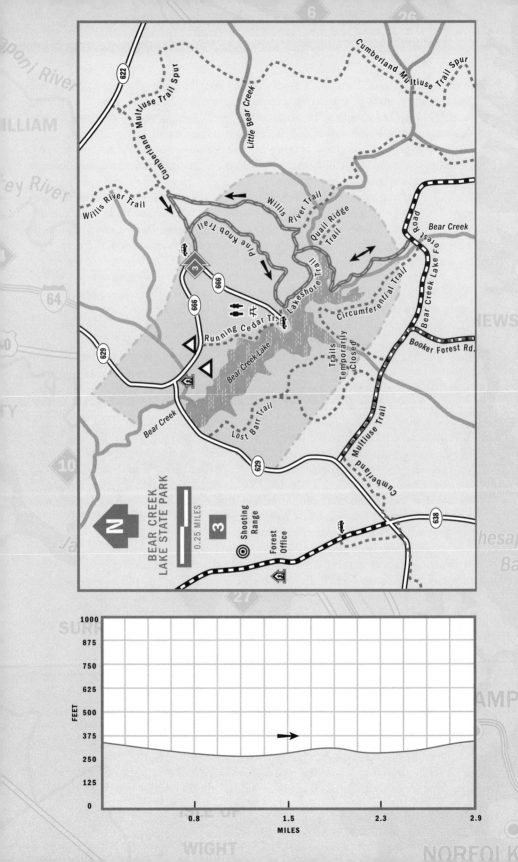

homestead of Jesse Thomas, a Revolutionary War colonel who famously warned Baron Von Streuben of Cornwallis's impending attack. On a rainy June 2, 1781, he road his horse Fearnaught as far north as the James then swam the river to the Continental camp. Also in Cumberland State Forest is the Charles Irving Thornton tombstone, a registered landmark bearing an inscription written by Charles Dickens. Found in the small Oak Hill Cemetery off VA 629, the tombstone marks the infant's grave with an original 31-line epitaph.

The federal government purchased most of the surrounding land from struggling farmers under Franklin Roosevelt's New Deal then leased it to the commonwealth. Some 100 farmers and laborers left jobless by the Depression found work with the Virginia Department of Agriculture, damming Bear Creek and erecting the park's first pavilions and grills. You can still identify their handiwork near the park's beach: shelters made with rough-hewn logs and freestanding stone hearths. In 1940 the park was deeded to the nascent state park system, one of six original parks. It was operated as a day-use recreation area until 1962, when campgrounds were added.

This hike begins at the trailhead parking area for the Cumberland Multiuse and Willis River Trails. (It's possible to augment this loop by using the Running Cedar Trail to access the Lakeside Trail, but the route mapped here offers the best parking for noncampers.) Set out on the double-track spur that leaves from the trailhead signboard. Ferns and clubmoss grow beneath trailside pines, and fallen needles carpet the path. After a short distance, fork right onto the wide, gray-blazed Pine Knob Trail.

Virginia pines grow thick on this hilltop, seemingly loathe to drop their lower, dead branches and brighten the forest. Examine the canopy, however, and you'll spot a few longleaf pines growing at the northern extend of their range. Boundary markers here and elsewhere along the path indicate the border between state park and forest. Veer right to cross a road that was recently cleared to facilitate the construction of cabins. The Pine Knob Trail continues, entering mixed forest as it extends onto a ridgeline. Southern red oak, white oak, beech, and shagbark hickory overtake pines before you turn right at an intersection, staying with the Pine Knob Trail.

Now a narrower single-track, the trail descends nearing the lake. Wooden beams form steps in the trail, taking you to a bridge over a rivulet on trail right. This provides access to the lake beach, with picnic areas, restrooms, and a snack bar. Your hike continues forward, now on the orange-blazed Lakeside Trail.

Look for yellow poplar, red maple, and hornbeam as you near the lake, then follow the shoreline southeast. The trail bends inland alongside slow-flowing Little Bear Creek, and birch trees shade a spit of land opposite. Rising just slightly, you reach a trail junction. Straight ahead is a spur trail to the Willis River Trail, but turn right to stay with the Lakeside Trail as it rounds the easternmost finger of the lake on a lengthy boardwalk. Beaver-gnawed stumps spike the flat where smaller streamlets convene and flow into the lake. Look for salamanders in the pools that dot the floodplain. On your right, the lake extends beside the aforementioned birch trees.

Across the boardwalk, step over a small streamlet to reach another junction. The Quail Ridge Trail leads here toward the Cumberland Multiuse Trail, but bypass it to continue on through Northern red and white oaks. Rounding a peninsula in the lake, look for waterfowl and songbirds amid the shrubs and sycamores on the small islands below. Trace a finger of the lake south as it narrows to the point where Bear Creek empties into its namesake. Birches arc from another spit of land here and shade the creek as the path turns to follow it.

Sandy banks flank the greenish water on your right, and a chorus of frogs is audible in all but the coolest months. Look for a beaver dam in the creek before the trail veers left to wind between younger mixed forest and riparian bottomland. White blazes indicate you're now on the Circumferential Trail, which takes you beyond the park boundary to Bear Creek Lake Forest Road. At the time of publication, construction had closed the trail ahead. Once the work is complete, however, you'll be able to follow the Circumferential Trail to the Lost Barr Trail. The two paths create a small loop south of the lake, then the latter continues northwest to VA 629. To make a complete circuit of the lake, you must walk VA 629 back into the park.

To follow the route mapped here, turn around and backtrack beyond the board-walk, then turn right onto the spur for the Willis River Trail. This short and pleasant path traces Little Bear Creek beneath lofty hardwoods. Signs warn you that the trail doesn't reenter the state park; however, you needn't worry. By making a left on the Willis River Trail, you'll return to the trail on which you set out. First pass over some quartzite rock in the trail bed atop a small rise. Descend into the valley of a branch that feeds Little Bear Creek; it's shaded by sycamore and birch trees. Just ahead, ford a rivulet then make a left onto the northbound stretch of the Willis River Trail. Note that it is only signed from the opposite direction.

If you've got the time and energy, consider hiking forward for an out-and-back stint on the southeast-bound Willis River Trail. The next half mile is representative of the best hiking the long trail has to offer. You'll make a slight rise to rocky bluff then descend to ford a tributary of Little Bear Creek. Tracing the rocky creek through open, mature hardwoods, you'll find calm pools created by industrious beavers. A parcel of pines just ahead makes a good turnaround.

Once on the northbound Willis River Trail headed back toward the trailhead, you'll steadily climb up a draw. Pass several downed trees, then bisect a pipeline clearing. A deep-channeled rivulet with mossy banks meanders along on trail left, shaded by beech, Southern red oak, and bear oak. The trail turns left to cross the dwindling streamlet then continues uphill with the streamlet on trail right. Step over a pair of narrow feeder rivulets as you reach the top of this drainage and enter a darker forest of Virginia pines.

Shortly, the trail intersects the double-track on which you set out. Turn left and follow the level path 0.2 miles back to the parking area.

Cumberland State Forest envelops the park. In it are the Willis River Trail (see page 235), a 16-mile end-to-end trail, and the Cumberland State Forest Multiuse Trail (page 70), an 8.4-mile loop with optional extensions. Both intersect the state park's trail network at multiple points and afford numerous route permutations (for a three-day backpacking option see the Willis River Trail profile). While camping is allowed only within the state park, there are four lakes, each smaller than Bear Creek Lake, where you can generally fish in solitude. Bonbrook, Arrowhead, Oak Hill, and Winston Lakes have boat launches and are stocked with largemouth bass, sunfish, and channel catfish. The forest also operates a wheelchair-accessible sporting-clay range.

# BEAVERDAM PARK

## KEY AT-A-GLANCE INFORMATION

**LENGTH:** 5.8 miles, plus almost 10 miles of multiuse trails

**CONFIGURATION:** Loop, plus seven multiuse loops and a connector

**DIFFICULTY:** Moderate

**SCENERY:** Beaverdam Reservoir, creek-fed marshes, hillside hardwood forest

**EXPOSURE:** Mostly shaded, open on Backbone Trail and along the river

**TRAFFIC:** Low; higher near boat launch

**TRAIL SURFACE:** Dirt and boardwalks

**HIKING TIME:** 3 hours

**SEASON:** Open daily during daylight year-round

**ACCESS:** No fee; jon boat, paddleboat, and canoe rentals (prices vary with craft, time); restrooms and picnic shelters accessible but wheelchairs not recommended on trails.

**MAPS:** Available at the park office and trailheads

**FACILITIES:** Park office, restrooms, fitness trail, vending machines, playground, boat launch, boat-rental pier, fishing pier, picnic tables and shelters, outdoor classroom, meeting lodge, and group camp; restrooms, boat launch, and multiuse trailhead at Fairy's Mill Road entrance

**SPECIAL COMMENTS:** The multiuse trail that traces the shoreline of Beaverdam Reservoir totals 12 miles one way. For details, contact the park office at (804) 693-2107 or visit www.gloucesterva.info/pr/parks/welbvd.htm

---

**UTM Trailhead Coordinates for Beaverdam Park**

**UTM Zone (NAD27)** 18S

**Easting** 0364316

**Northing** 4145520

## IN BRIEF

This route begins on Beaverdam Park's nature trail then joins its hiking path to trace the southeastern arm of Beaverdam Reservoir, bisecting numerous stream-fed marshes along the way. A return leg across forested hills on the park's multiuse trail completes the loop.

## DESCRIPTION

Were it solely the work of tree-felling, semi-aquatic mammals, Beaverdam Reservoir would be quite a feat. But in fact the 350-acre lake is the product of a manmade dam. Prior to its 1990 inundation, the submerged area was a tangle of creeks and wooded beaver ponds known as Beaverdam Swamp. Today, the beavers are relegated to the lake's many marshy inlets, and the reservoir is home to 20 fish species. Consequently, the lake is a popular destination with anglers, who vie for largemouth bass, bluegill, and several varieties of sunfish but could inadvertently land an American eel.

## DIRECTIONS

From Richmond, take I-64 east to Exit 220. Exit onto VA 33 heading northeast. Proceed through West Point and turn right onto VA 14 after 14 miles. Heading east, you will intersect US 17 after 6 more miles. Veer right and continue another 8 miles southeast on US 17 to Gloucester. Turn left onto US 17 Business (Main Street), then take the first left onto VA 616 (Roaring Springs Road). The park's main entrance is located at the road's terminus, 2.4 miles ahead. The park's secondary entrance—the multiuse trail's optional trailhead—is located off VA 606 (Fairy's Mill Road), which intersects US 17 2.4 miles northwest of Business US 17. To use this entrance, take 606 north 2.6 miles to the entrance on your right.

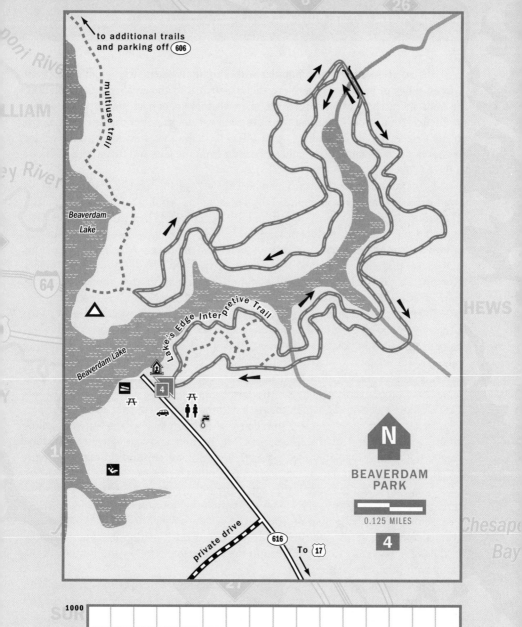

to additional trails
and parking off 606

multiuse trail

Beaverdam
Lake

Lake's Edge Interpretive Trail

Beaverdam Lake

4

private drive

616

To 17

**N**

**BEAVERDAM
PARK**

0.125 MILES

4

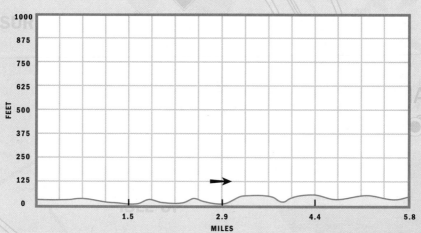

The adjacent park is also popular with mountain bikers, who enjoy more than a dozen miles of multiuse trail. Nevertheless, thanks to the area's relative isolation, the trails are rarely crowded. Moreover, many visitors linger near the playground, picnic shelters, and fitness trail just south of the boat docks rather than heading north on the nature, hiking, or multiuse trail. All three leave just downhill of the outdoor classroom, with the multiuse trailhead farthest from the lake and the hiking trailhead in the middle.

Begin your loop on the aptly named Lake's Edge Interpretive Trail, picking up a trail-guide brochure at the trailhead to deposit at the terminus. This booklet details 20 stations along the quarter-mile nature trail, each denoted by a numbered signpost. Outlining many familiar aspects of Virginia's ecology—common tree species, riparian reptiles and amphibians, and migratory waterfowl—the Lake's Edge Trail serves as an informative primer for your hike. Look closely and you'll easily find all the plants identified by the booklet, as well as some of the animals, as you traipse along the shore of Beaverdam Reservoir.

After crossing a small, algae-blanketed inlet on a sturdy wooden bridge, turn left to stay on Lake's Edge Trail; straight ahead is one of several connectors to the hiking path. You'll wind past a beaver-scarred tree trunk and, in late summer, flowering stalks of blue lobelia, which was once believed (erroneously) to cure syphilis. The path then curves slightly away from the water's edge to terminate at a T intersection opposite an attractive three-tiered wood. Sweetgum and yellow poplar trees shade a glade of shorter dogwoods, which themselves stretch above thickets of pawpaw.

Deposit your brochure and turn left on the footpath, which you will follow around a lengthy arm of the lake, as well as around and through many smaller, marshy inlets. The first of these swampy sloughs soon appears through a narrow screen of trees on your left. Fallen logs and truncated tree trunks project from the water amid reeds and grasses. Turtles are commonly found sunning on dry logs but slip noisily into the water at the sound of approaching footsteps.

Before crossing the inlet on the first of several earthen levees, the nature trail meets a connector to the multiuse trail. Remember this junction if, when returning via the latter, you wish to veer right onto the connector to follow the portion of the hiking path otherwise omitted.

This is the first of several inlet crossings, which vary in scale but are similar in design. The hiking path traverses an earthen levee, with the lake visible on the left and a small pond on the right. Above that pond is another earthen dam along which the multiuse trail passes. The modest streams that feed these marshy inlets are routed through the earthen dams in metal pipes. In summer, clusters of pinkish swamp milkweed and orange jewelweed grow alongside the trail, while pale lotus blossoms dot the still water. Approach the lake's sloughs with a watchful eye and you will likely spot a great blue heron or snowy egret stalking prey amid the marsh grass and cattails.

Once across, the hiking path turns left, then veers inland, bypassing a closed trail section, through a forest of beech, white oak, scarlet oak, and Virginia pine filled out by American holly and younger ironwoods. Stay with the green blazes, and the trail is easy to follow as it continues along the southern edge of Beaverdam Reservoir's southeastern arm. Following the second inlet crossing, ignore any arrows you find spray-painted on the trail, telling you to leave the main path and veer right. These directions, accompanied by the letters XC, are intended for local high-school cross-country runners. You should, of course, abide by any trail closures and may find one beyond Morgan Bridge, where the multiuse trail was temporarily routed onto the hiking path following storm damage.

At Morgan Bridge the two paths share treadway, specifically a long boardwalk, to cross the marshy farther reaches of the lake's southeastern arm. Once across, the hiking path begins tacking south and west, mirroring itself across the water. If you wish to cut this hike roughly in half, use the bridge as your turnaround point. The clearly marked multiuse trail climbs uphill on either end of the bridge, so it's possible to hike a smaller loop—or, for that matter, to convert this hike to a figure eight.

To continue the hike as mapped, stay on the trail as the sycamores and red maples growing at the lake's edge give way to beech, chestnut oak, and tulip poplar. Follow the green blazes as an older trail segment (now closed) runs nearer the lake and a connector takes the temporarily rerouted multiuse trail to the right. Continue over the undulating and winding root-studded path repeatedly approaching the water in marshy inlets then bearing inland. The boathouse comes into view across the lake, signaling the hiking path's impending terminus at the multiuse trail.

As it heads north from this well-marked junction, the multiuse trail crosses an old double-track near a spur trail leading west to the peninsular group camp. Eight miles and four bridges on, the multiuse trail reaches its trailhead at the park's Fairy Mill Road entrance. The prescribed route here, however, doubles back eastbound on the multiuse trail, which runs uphill from and roughly parallel to the hiking path. Blue iconic blazes, indicating hiker, cyclist, and equestrian use, dot the route, which is sometimes muddier that its pedestrian-only counterpart. There are also mileage markers, which are absent on the hiking path.

Though these are upland woods, which drain toward the lake, the soil remains damp enough to sprout numerous ferns along the path. That you are traversing hilltops and ridges is evidenced by the increased presence of trees downed by the wind; where blocked the trail circumvents the trees on improvised paths. You'll also notice more frequent elevation change, particularly when the trail dips to cross lake sloughs south of Morgan Bridge.

After recrossing the bridge, the trail rises steeply to enter a very fragrant pine-dominated wood, where needles carpet the trail. Ahead, the path dips to a break in the woods with three sturdy benches. A streamlet runs beneath the trail here. Rest a moment, knowing your hike is almost complete—a pair of piney knolls and one more lake inlet away.

While in Virginia's Middle Neck, consider visiting the Gloucester Museum of History located south of the county seat at the junction of VA 616 and VA 614. The museum is housed in a circa 1770 brick tavern on Main Street named for colonial governor Lord Botetourt and the birthplace of Walter Reed. The son of a Methodist minister, Reed was an army physician in the Spanish-American War who helped eradicate Yellow Fever after discovering its transmission by mosquitoes.

# BELLE ISLE AND BROWN'S ISLAND

## KEY AT-A-GLANCE INFORMATION

**LENGTH:** 2.7 miles, plus optional spur trails

**CONFIGURATION:** Two balloons with one trailhead

**DIFFICULTY:** Easy

**SCENERY:** James River, ruins of industrial buildings, an abandoned quarry, Tredeger Iron Works, a canal alongside the James, sculptures

**EXPOSURE:** Open, with limited shade

**TRAFFIC:** High, especially on warm weekends

**TRAIL SURFACE:** Paved and dirt

**HIKING TIME:** 1–2 hours

**SEASON:** Open daily during daylight year-round

**ACCESS:** No fee

**MAPS:** Belle Isle map available online at www.jamesriverpark.org

**FACILITIES:** Interpretive signage; the adjacent Tredeger Iron Works is managed by the National Park Service as Richmond National Battlefield Park Visitor Center

**SPECIAL COMMENTS:** Stop by the Richmond National Battlefield Park Visitor Center at Tredeger Iron Works as you complete your hike. For more on the center and the park's other offerings, visit www.nps.gov/rich.
  Alternate access to Belle Isle is available via a footbridge from the southern shore of the James, but the James River Park 22nd Street parking lot is not reliably open. Contact James River Park at (804) 646-8911.

UTM Trailhead Coordinates for
Belle Isle and Brown's Island

UTM Zone (NAD27)   18S

Easting   0283651

Northing   4156757

## IN BRIEF

In the James River near the heart of the city, Belle Isle is a de rigeur Richmond outing, augmented here by a short stroll around Brown's Island, itself a popular, park-like destination on the north shore of the James with an amphitheater that hosts summer concerts. For newcomers and lifelong Richmonders alike, these islands reveal much about the city's industrial and wartime past.

## DESCRIPTION

One of five waterside parcels jointly managed as the James River Park (see also James River Park Main Section and Pony Pasture Rapids, pages 126 and 166, respectively), Belle Isle is one of Richmond's most historic and most popular outdoor destinations. What hard-trammeled Belle Isle lacks in wilderness, it compensates for with views of the James River and the downtown skyline across the water. Its proximity to the National Park Service–run visitor center at Tredeger Iron Works, Brown's Island, and the Haxall Canal (as well as the city's 1.25-mile Canal Walk) make Belle Isle a natural addition to any tourist itinerary. However,

## DIRECTIONS

Belle Isle and Brown's Island are easily accessible from both I-95 and I-195. From I-95, exit onto 7th Street heading south (Exit 75). If entering the city from the west via the I-195 downtown expressway (toll required), exit eastward onto Byrd Street and make an immediate right onto 7th Street. Continue south to a roundabout intersection with 10th Street and Tredeger Street. Turn right onto Tredeger. You may park along the road at the Tredeger Iron Works, now the main visitor center for Richmond National Battlefield Park, or farther down the road in a gravel lot on the right. The lot is closest to the footbridge from Tredeger Street to Belle Isle.

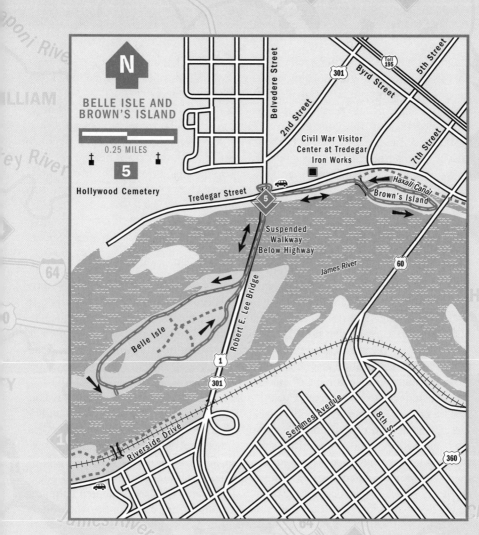

N

BELLE ISLE AND
BROWN'S ISLAND

0.25 MILES

**5**

Hollywood Cemetery

Civil War Visitor
Center at Tredegar
Iron Works

Tredegar Street

Haxall Canal

Brown's Island

James River

Suspended
Walkway
Below Highway

Robert E. Lee Bridge

Belle Isle

Riverside Drive

Semmes Avenue

8th St.

Belvedere Street

2nd Street

5th Street

7th Street

Byrd Street

Toll 195

301

60

1

301

360

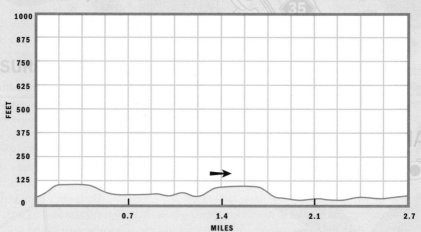

it's equally suited to lunchtime trail running or after-work mountain biking. Many visitors simply stretch out to sunbathe on the many boulders surrounding the island and watch kayaks darting about in the Class IV Hollywood Rapids.

The only safe and reliable way to reach Belle Isle is via the concrete footbridge suspended beneath the Robert E. Lee Bridge, with traffic rumbling along US 301 overhead. A parking lot adjacent to the James River Park Main Section provides theoretical access from the James's southern shore via a police-access bridge, but it is routinely closed. Intrepid souls even rock-hop to the island from the southern shore in low water (at their own risk, of course). If you elect to venture onto any of the numerous boulders and granite slabs that flank the island, exercise extreme caution and keep a close eye on any children in your party.

To follow the route mapped here, begin by strolling west on Tredeger Street, then ascend, by ramp, to the footbridge and traverse the James, which flows some 30 feet below. After descending to the dusty trails of Belle Isle, head west along the island's north shore. But first read the informative sign at the crux of the trails. It outlines the island's past and its role in the Civil War in particular. The flat expanse of land on Belle Isle's eastern shore (now directly beneath the Lee Bridge) was the site of a Confederate prison that housed upward of 8,000 Union prisoners of war. Two or three times that number passed through the mostly tent brig during the course of the war. Many perished of disease and were interred on the island, their remains later moved to Richmond National Cemetery.

There are no visible remains of the prison, but in the course of your hike, you will see numerous remnants of industrial operations that were housed on the island in the nineteenth and early twentieth centuries. For instance, the metal awning on the opposite, eastern, edge of the prison site was once part of a steel factory. First, however, you'll pass Hollywood Rapids on the right. These granite shoals were the site of the island's first industry, fishing. Native Americans who inhabited the island relied on the James for sustenance. Kayak and raft guides are the island's modern entrepreneurs. Keep your eyes peeled for their colorful crafts darting about in the whitewater.

Next you will pass a pond, complete with a fishing pier, on your left. Granite cliffs tower over the pond, the product of a bygone mining operation. After you round the island's western edge, you will pass a strainer gate that still gathers debris, although the hydroelectric plant downstream no longer functions. Across the gate, a ladder provides access to the rocks and pools below. The rounded rocks are a popular side trip for Belle Isle visitors, who explore the pools and lounge on the smooth stone. Perhaps more popular are the dirt trails that crisscross the island's interior. Popular with mountain bikers, these short spur trails are not particularly scenic but do offer far-reaching views to anyone willing to make the climb. Of course, the photogenic sweep of Richmond's skyline from the footbridge is hard to beat.

Continuing along the wide, sandy main path on the island's southern shore, you will soon pass the ruins of the hydroelectric plant once operated by Virginia Electric, a precursor of Dominion Power, and the ruins of an iron foundry, also on trail right. Born of a humble nail-producing factory in 1832, the Old Dominion Iron and Steel Company operated metal works on Belle Isle well into the twentieth century. For much of that time, the island, dubbed Broad Rock Island by city founder William Byrd, was known as Bell's Isle in homage to a resident Scotsman who operated a

Lounging on the rocky shore fronting Hollywood Rapids is a popular pastime.

horseracing track on the site. Upon his departure the island's nomenclature was recast in French for respectability's sake. Or so the legend has it.

As you round the bend heading northeast back to the footbridge, you will pass the roofless remains of a stone building on the left and then the Environmental Center maintained seasonally by James River Park. Return to the north shore via the footbridge and trace Tredeger Street east to make a quick loop of Brown's Island. You will pass the Tredeger Iron Works on your left and a small demonstration garden opposite it on your right. Pause to read the garden sign, which briefly describes the native ecosystem. Save the iron-works-turned-visitor-center for last. A self-guided tour highlights the role played by the 1861 gun foundry in the Civil War.

Ahead is Brown's Island, separated from the mainland by Haxall Canal. A pedestrian bridge crosses the canal at the western tip of Brown's Island. Ten History Medallions on the island commemorate the site's role in Richmond's past. The island's centerpiece is a bronze statue by Paul DiPasquale (who also sculpted the likeness of Arthur Ashe on Monument Avenue) depicting one of the black bateaumen who, well into the twentieth century, navigated barges through the canal using wooden poles. To complete the route as mapped, simply circle Brown's Island and return to Tredeger Street.

You may extend your outing by continuing east for the full length of Richmond's Canal Walk, a pleasant stroll along canals that once ferried tobacco and other goods through the city. The Haxall Canal ends at the Kanawha Canal Locks near 12th Street. However, the Canal Walk extends along the Kanawha Canal until reaching the Turning Basin, which is the end of Virginia Street. The Turning Basin was constructed so that mule-drawn barges could be turned around once loaded or unloaded at the city's tobacco market. The larger canal system was part of an unrealized effort, proffered by George Washington, to link the Ohio River and Atlantic Ocean.

# BELLE ISLE STATE PARK

## KEY AT-A-GLANCE INFORMATION

**LENGTH:** 5.3 miles

**CONFIGURATION:** Out-and-back with 3 arms

**DIFFICULTY:** Easy

**SCENERY:** Estuarine Mulberry and Deep Creeks, the tidal Rappahannock River, woodlands, marsh, crop fields

**EXPOSURE:** Shaded at outset but mostly open

**TRAFFIC:** Moderate

**TRAIL SURFACE:** Dirt, gravel double-track

**HIKING TIME:** 2.5 hours

**SEASON:** Open daily from 8 a.m. to dusk year-round; main season runs May–October

**ACCESS:** No camping allowed; parking $2–$3 on weekends in season; restrooms, picnic shelters, and a short trail are wheelchair accessible

**MAPS:** Available at park and online at www.dcr.virginia.gov/parks/bellisle.htm

**FACILITIES:** Picnic shelters, 2 boat launches, restrooms, vending machines, park office; in-season bike, canoe, and motor-boat rentals (prices vary with craft, time); the Bel Air Mansion and guest house are available for overnight stays

**SPECIAL COMMENTS:** The park's only lodging options, the 1942 Georgian-style Bel Air Mansion and guest house, are fully furnished, and either one makes an excellent base from which to explore the Northern Neck. Contact the park office at (804) 462-5030 for more information.

**UTM Trailhead Coordinates for Belle Isle State Park**

**UTM Zone (NAD27)** 18S

**Easting** 0358823

**Northing** 4182648

## IN BRIEF

Surrounded by water on three sides, Belle Isle State Park is a boon for anyone looking to cast off or cast a line into the Rappahannock River and its tributaries. However, at 733 acres, the park is also rich with agrarian history and ecological diversity, easily accessible via wide, level trails.

## DESCRIPTION

Belle Isle State Park, on the northern shore of the Rappahannock River, is not to be confused with the Belle Isle of downtown Richmond (see page 26), though, like the latter, it was home to a Powhatan Indian fishing village. Specifically, the Moraughtacunds tribe inhabited the area concurrent with the earliest English colonization. The name Belle Isle is telling because it nods to one of the peninsula's first European-born landholders, the Huguenot John Betrand, who acquired the property in 1692. Often persecuted at home, French Calvinists arrived in Virginia with a wave of mostly Protestant Europeans—Germans, Scotch-Irish, Dutch, Swiss, and Swedes—whom the

## DIRECTIONS

From Richmond, follow US 360 northeast across the Rappahannock to the small town of Warsaw (approximately 45 miles beyond I-295). Turn right onto VA 3, and proceed 14 miles southeast before turning right onto VA 354. Continue 3.1 miles, then make another right onto VA 683. A kiosk collecting vehicle-entry fees is less than a mile ahead, with a final right following within another half mile. At the road's terminus, you'll find the trailheads in the southwestern corner of the parking area. From Fredericksburg, take US 17 for 47 miles to Tappahannock, then US 360 for another 7 miles to Warsaw.

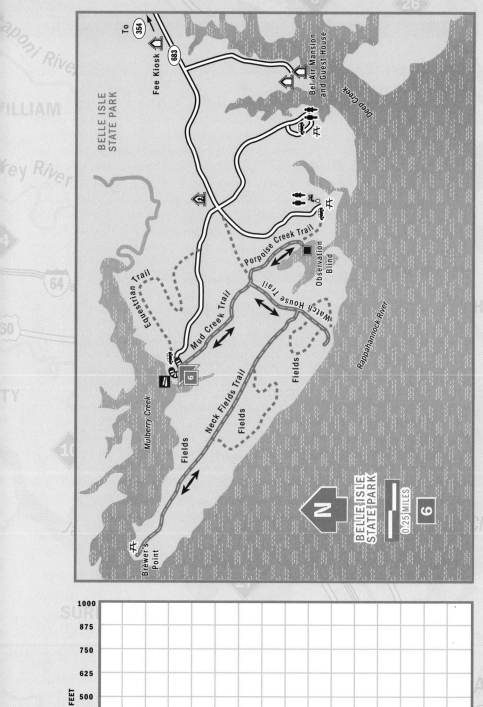

BELLE ISLE STATE PARK

BELLE ISLE
STATE PARK

Deep Creek

Bel Air Mansion
and Guest House

Fee Kiosk

To 354

683

Rappahannock River

Observation Blind

Porpoise Creek Trail

Watch House Trail

Equestrian Trail

Mud Creek Trail

Neck Fields Trail

Mulberry Creek

Fields

Fields

Fields

Fields

Brewer's Point

N

BELLE ISLE
STATE PARK

0.25 MILES

6

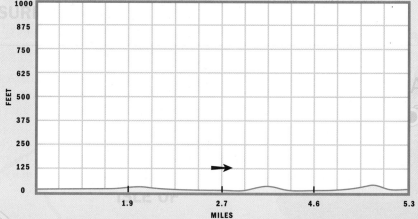

Anglican gentry admitted in order to settle vast tracts of land and provide a buffer against native tribes pushed westward by war.

Belle Isle is misleadingly named, however, in that, like Hog Island on the James (page 114), it is now contiguous with the mainland. Betrand likely found the peninsula's westernmost spit of land inaccessible, enveloped by Mulberry Creek to the north, the Rappahannock to the west, Deep Creek to the south, and swampland to the west. Yet at ten feet above sea level, the land was arable. Subsequent plantation owners built levees and roadways through the swamp to enlarge their cropland. The trail to the mouth of Mulberry Creek passes over a raised roadbed then threads between cultivated cornfields. Crops still blanket much of the park's interior, and you will pass an old barn opposite the office en route to the trailhead.

The fields now model sustainable agriculture practices intended to mitigate tainted runoff into the Chesapeake Bay. The health of the wetlands buffering the park is evidenced by the breadth and abundance of wildlife. Noisy migratory waterfowl favor the shallow, protected waters between the Mud Creek and Neck Fields Trails, while bald eagles, ospreys, and hawks hunt just offshore near Brewer's Point, which is this hike's northwestern turnaround.

Begin your hike with a brief out-and-back along the paved trail that leaves right from the trailhead. Passing a marsh-fringed inlet a few feet away on the left, this spur soon reaches a boardwalk and curves right to front Mulberry Creek. Here you may find anglers tempting rockfish, flounder, croaker, and other species tolerant of these brackish waters. Venture out onto the pier for far-reaching views of the estuary before backtracking to begin Mud Creek Trail in earnest. The path turns to dirt as it heads southwest through a sweetgum grove, the narrowing inlet still visible to the west.

The trail passes beneath pine and ash trees before curving right to emerge alongside the forest. There is a cultivated field on the left, the expanse of which may be obscured by tall cornstalks, depending on the season. The Mud Creek Trail soon dead-ends at the Watch House Trail. Belle Isle proper lies to the right, but turn left first to follow the Porpoise Creek Trail as a spur. You will walk a short segment of the Watch House Trail before turning right into the woods on the Porpoise Creek Trail, which weaves through the trees as an earthen path before emerging as a grassy corridor alongside a cornfield.

At the corner of the crop field, there is a short access trail to the observation blind to the right. Straight ahead, across a small meadow, are a playground and picnic area with restrooms and vending machines. This area overlooks Deep Creek's confluence with the Rappahannock and can readily serve as alternate trailhead—perhaps a more convenient one for families looking to spend a day at the park. The observation blind doesn't face the river but does offer a view of a wide, still inlet linked to the Rappahannock by a narrow channel. Almost landlocked and ringed with pines, the placid water recalls a pond rather than an estuary. Patient wintertime hikers enjoy good prospects for spotting tundra swans and snow geese through the short, wide windows of the observation blind.

Backtracking to the Watch House Trail, head southwest (left) toward the Rappahannock. On your left you will pass fingers of the calm inlet that you recently scanned from the observation blind. On your right a wall of cedars rises to a stand of pines before yielding to marsh grasses as the trail approaches the state park's name-sake former island. As you pass along this narrow stretch of trail, the croak and chirp of frogs give way to splashes as they retreat from your oncoming footsteps into the shallow waters.

Continue beyond an intersection with the Neck Fields Trail, departing on your right, to reach a small clearing on the shore of the Rappahannock River. Wild persimmons grow alongside the trail, and a picnic table nearby invites hikers to pause for a moment's respite. Deer also frequent this part of Belle Isle, and you may spot a few bounding away should you disturb their grazing.

Return to the Neck Fields Trail and head northwest (left) toward Brewer's Point. The park map shows several subloops in this area of Belle Isle; however, these are merely the grassy corridors that ring cornfields. Explore them if you like. The Neck Fields Trail itself is a gravel double-track that emerges from a stand of pines to squeeze between crop fields. Sycamores also abut the fields, thriving in the moist soil. On trail right a swampy pond shelters geese more often heard than seen through the screen of trees.

Ultimately the fields give way to reforesting meadows, edged by locust and mulberry trees. A smattering of wildflowers vies for sunlight amid the dense, vine-clad shrubs. Just ahead, beyond a portable toilet cloistered in a thicket of cedars, a pair of picnic tables overlooks the Rappahannock River, with Mulberry Creek entering on the right.

Approach quietly and you may find, as I did, a bald eagle perched on a dead-but-still-standing tree and scanning the glistening water. From Brewer's Point, you can watch the sun set beneath the Rappahannock, painting the entire sky flaming orange. Time your hike to enjoy the nightly vista, but be prepared to quickly back-track along the Watch House and Mud Creek Trails, as the park closes at dusk.

If you're looking to pair history and ecology on your visit to the Northern Neck, stop by the Kilmarnock Museum, which focuses on the maritime heritage of Northumberland and Lancaster Counties. Farther northeast the Reedville Fisherman's Museum is a beacon to avid anglers. It chronicles the evolution of Chesapeake Bay fishing and aquaculture, beginning with the region's Native American tribes.

# BUSH MILL STREAM STATE NATURAL AREA PRESERVE

## IN BRIEF

Though not long, the trail at Bush Mill Stream is a valued resource for denizens of Virginia's Northern Neck. Bring binoculars for bird-watching or a picnic lunch to enjoy on your leisurely descent through mixed forest to the marshy banks of the preserve's namesake Chesapeake Bay tributary.

## DESCRIPTION

After descending the mountain laurel–cloaked hillside to brackish Bush Mill Stream, you may think it unlikely that these quiet waterside woods were once a bustling port. Yet, as its name recalls, Deep Landing once harbored large sailing ships. The forestry industry began here in the colonial era and peaked in the early nineteenth century. Local foresters hauled timber and lumber products to the mouth of Bush Mill Stream, this trail's terminus. The goods were then transported downstream via the Great Wicomico River.

Over time, however, silt accumulated in the upper Wicomico and its tributaries, rendering them impassable for large vessels. When the lumbermen departed, the forest returned and with it a host of wildlife. Though the woods overlooking Bush Mill Stream evidence ongoing reforestation in the size and variety of trees, the entire preserve has a noticeable unspoiled air. You may well spot

## DIRECTIONS

From Richmond, follow US 360 northeast across the Rappahannock to the small town of Warsaw (approximately 45 miles beyond I-295). Continue east on 360 an additional 19 miles to VA 201. Turn right and proceed 3.5 miles south to VA 642. Turn left and look for the preserve entrance 0.4 miles ahead on the left. The small parking area is just down the gravel road. From Fredericksburg, take US 17 for 47 miles to Tappahannock, then US 360 for 7 miles to Warsaw.

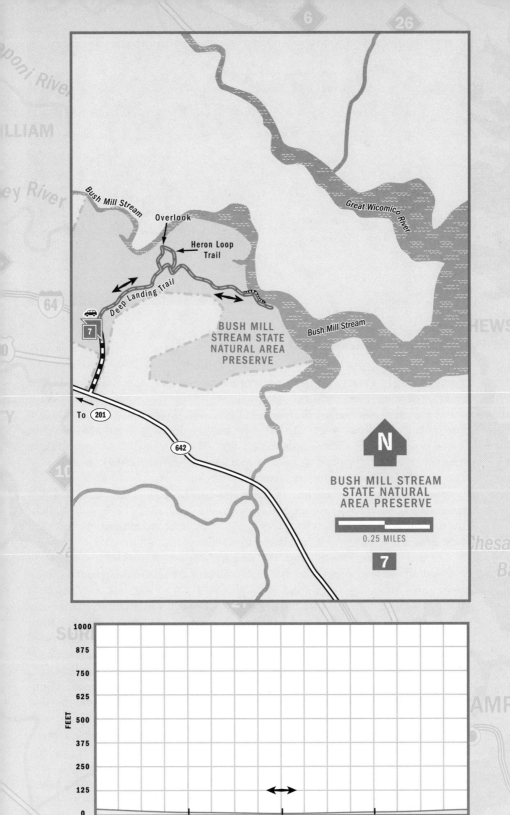

BUSH MILL STREAM
STATE NATURAL
AREA PRESERVE

0.25 MILES

7

herons nesting in a marsh upstream of Deep Landing or pale, diminutive Indian pipe flowering beneath laurel thickets.

A cluster of pale stalks about five inches tall with downward-drooping flowered tips, Indian pipe feeds not on chlorophyll but on decaying vegetation, hence it thrives in shade where there is little competition. Though named for its resemblance to a soapstone pipe, the plant's ghastly color and fragility have earned it other names, including ghost flower, corpse plant, and fairy smoke.

You probably won't see one of the major beneficiaries of the preserve's protected status: the tidewater amphipod *Stygobromus indentatus*. The rare shrimp-like creatures are only millimeters long and live in pockets of groundwater beneath the forest floor, though they occasionally surface at springs.

Setting out northbound from the parking area on an obvious trail (not the cordoned-off old road a short distance east), you find the first of the preserve's interpretive signs welcoming you with an aerial photo. Accompanying text describes Bush Mill Stream's estuarine character and lists a few of the birds you may spot on the water or in trees overhead. Besides herons, these include eagles, mallards, ducks, and teals.

Level at the outset, the path passes beneath tulip poplars and loblolly pines before weaving down the hillside where large gnarled mountain laurel replace holly in the understory. Common throughout the preserve's forests are Southern red, American white, and chestnut oaks. And while trailside sassafras saplings are plentiful, this path features a rarer mature specimen. Sassafras, of course, is the tree that put the root in root beer, and when colonists boycotted British tea in opposition to hefty import duties, the commonwealth's more politically active ladies took to brewing sassafras tea instead.

You'll soon come to a trail junction with the orange-blazed Heron Loop Trail to the left. This short spur leads to a wooden deck overlooking the heron rookery before rejoining the blue-blazed main trail. The latter continues on a switchback descent through a cluster of red maples.

A pair of benches is built into the heron-observation platform, and mounted on its rails is a pair of interpretive signs. One outlines the ecology visible around you, from the bluffland forest through which you've just passed to the marsh of cordgrass, rose marrow, and arrow arum visible below. Its twin describes the great blue heron's habit of nesting in colonies and depicts the sort of nests you may spot in the treetops surrounding the meandering river below.

Shortly after the Heron Loop rejoins the main trail downhill, the pathway begins to level. The edge of the woods is discernable on your left, with Bush Mill Stream just beyond it as you approach an interpretive sign devoted to the coastal plain. A map depicts the fall line that runs along the eastern seaboard separating the Piedmont and low-lying coastal plain. Waterfalls and rapids commonly delineate these geologic regions. Richmond is one of several cities strategically situated along the line for purposes of river navigation; others include Philadelphia, Raleigh, and Washington, D.C.

Ahead, a view of the river opens on your right, while a dense hedge of mountain laurel runs on your right. Laurel thrives here and on other Tidewater hillsides because it prefers well-drained, sandy soil. Likewise, the hardy Virginia pines found growing here are common to eastern Virginia riverbanks. Moss flanks the earthen bank running alongside the now steadily descending trail.

The trail emerges onto a well-built wooden boardwalk, which leads across a marshy inlet and offers views of a wide cordgrass-and-cattail marsh backed by a wall of deep-green pines. If the water level is low enough, inspect the sand below for scuttling blue crabs, which make their nursery in these brackish waters. If you're visiting in early autumn, scan the woods to your right for swamp tupelo trees, hydrophilic relatives of the dogwood that turn vibrant red after the first cold snap.

Before you, the trail continues a short way along the river to an interpretive sign marking the aforementioned Deep Landing. The trail fades into the brush just ahead, but a grassy clearing near the shore invites picnickers to enjoy a respite.

As I admired the view from this shoreline, a pair of bald eagles passed overhead, and I jerked my head upward at the audible flapping of their wings. The great blue herons, however, proved more elusive. Perhaps put off by the midday sun, the wading birds saved their stalking for dusk. Exercise patience, and you may have better luck.

If you're looking to combine history and ecology in your Northern Neck itinerary, begin at the Richmond County Museum in Warsaw. Housed in a hip-roofed brick jail (circa 1782) next to a Palladian courthouse (circa 1748), the museum traces the county's history from the pre-Columbian era through the present. Nearby is historic St. John's Church (circa 1836). In its courtyard stands a memorial to Congressman William Jones given by the Philippines in appreciation for his role in granting that nation independence.

If the neck's maritime heritage interests you, head east toward the Chesapeake. Not long after sailing ships ceased to dock at Deep Landing, the vessels were replaced by steamboats better suited to river travel. With photos, artifacts, and stories, the Steamboat Era Museum in Irvington recalls the nineteenth-century heyday of Chesapeake paddlewheel steamers. En route to Irvington from Bush Mill Stream is the Kilmarnock Museum, which highlights that town's centrality in the Northern Neck's commercial and cultural heritage.

# CALEDON STATE PARK AND NATURAL AREA

## KEY AT-A-GLANCE INFORMATION

**LENGTH:** 4 miles

**CONFIGURATION:** Loop with connectors for shorter options; the park has a network of fire roads subject to seasonal closures

**DIFFICULTY:** Moderate

**SCENERY:** Hardwood-forested hillsides and creek drainages south of the Potomac

**EXPOSURE:** Well-shaded

**TRAFFIC:** Low

**TRAIL SURFACE:** Dirt single-track

**HIKING TIME:** 2 hours

**SEASON:** Trail open daily 8 a.m.–dusk year-round; double-track Boyd's Hole Trail to the Potomac closed April–October; visitor center open in season Wednesday–Sunday 10 a.m.–6 p.m. and in April, May, September, and October on weekends noon–5 p.m.

**ACCESS:** Parking costs $2 or $3 on weekends; visitor center and some picnic tables are wheelchair accessible; trails are not recommended for wheelchairs

**MAPS:** Available at park office and on signboard at trailhead

**FACILITIES:** Park office, visitor center, restrooms, picnic shelter, grills, playground, small amphitheater; interpretive programs, including an eagle-viewing outing, are available by reservation; fees apply

**SPECIAL COMMENTS:** If bird-watching is your aim, inquire about guided eagle tours held June–September. Contact the park office at (540) 663-3861.

---

**UTM Trailhead Coordinates for Caledon State Park and Natural Area**

**UTM Zone (NAD27)**   **18S**

**Easting**   **0312650**

**Northing**   **4244771**

## IN BRIEF

A series of interconnected loops, the network of hiking trails at Caledon State Park and Natural Area is easily customized to a shorter loop or figure eight. This loop descends through oaks to wind along a riparian floodplain then makes an undulating return over beech-studded hillsides.

## DESCRIPTION

Provided it's open, start your visit to Caledon with a walk through the visitor center, where you'll find exhibits on the property's history and the bald eagles that roost along its stretch of Potomac shoreline. The exhibits are housed in the white-clapboard colonial that Lewis Smoot built in 1910, shortly after inheriting the property. He lived there until his death in 1962, along with his wife, Ann Hopewell Smoot, who donated the property to Virginia in 1974.

The Smoots' home replaced a burned two-story manor erected in 1759 by descendants of John Alexander, who had established Caledon

## DIRECTIONS

From Richmond, head north on I-95 to Exit 104. Follow VA 207 almost 12 miles to the town of Bowling Green, where it merges with US 301. Continue northeast on US 301 through Fort A. P. Hill and across the Rappahannock River. Drive 25 miles then turn left onto VA 218. After a quarter mile, a second left keeps you on VA 218, now running west parallel to VA 206. Follow the right fork when the two roads separate after 2.2 miles, and you'll find the park just over a mile ahead on the right. From Fredericksburg, simply follow VA 218 east from its junction with VA 3. Upon entering the park, continue past a parking lot on your left to the visitor center's lot. The trailhead, marked by a signboard, is in the northwestern corner of the lot.

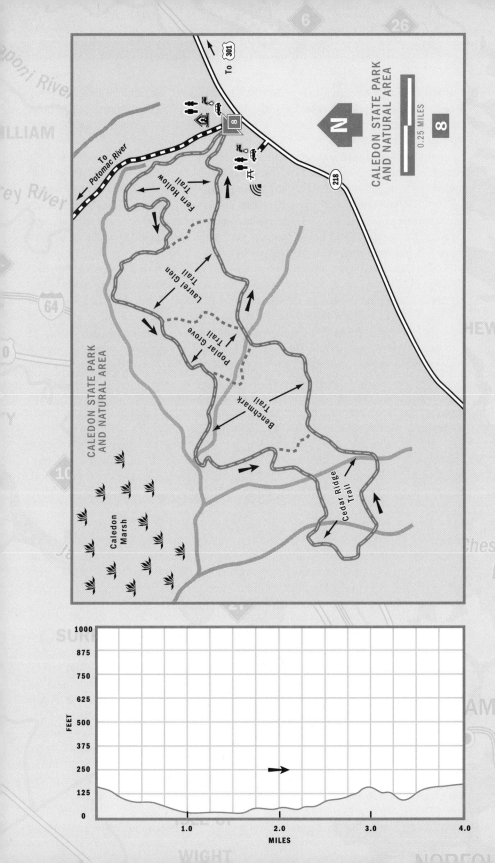

CALEDON STATE PARK
AND NATURAL AREA

8

0.25 MILES

N

To 301

To Potomac River

Fern Hollow Trail

Laurel Glen Trail

Poplar Grove Trail

Benchmark Trail

Cedar Ridge Trail

CALEDON STATE PARK
AND NATURAL AREA

Caledon Marsh

218

1000
875
750
625
500
375
250
125
0

FEET

1.0          2.0          3.0          4.0
MILES

Plantation exactly a century before. A Scottish immigrant, Alexander named his farmstead after the sweeping forest of Caledonia. Like many Virginia farmers of the Colonial era, Alexander and his sons grew tobacco. And it was tobacco that took him upriver to the city that would eventually bear his name, Alexandria.

In 1669 he traded 6,000 pounds of tobacco for as many acres north along the Potomac from Hunting Creek to Little Falls. Virginia governor William Berkley had awarded the territory to English ship captain Robert Howsing less than a month before. The seaman hauled his tobacco to market in London, while Alexander set about clearing the land. By 1749 the profitable crop blanketed northern Virginia, and farmers successfully petitioned Virginia's General Assembly to establish a town named in honor of the land's first real owner.

The intrepid settlers who transformed the forests of then-western Virginia into rolling fields were among the first wave of America's agrarian entrepreneurs. Their spiritual descendants would push west across the continent, but none did so without consequence. In Virginia the proliferation first of farms along the Potomac, then of suburbs, all but decimated the indigenous bald-eagle population. By 1977 only 33 pairs of eagles nested within the commonwealth. The population has rebounded thanks to a resurgent appreciation for our national symbol and growing support for wildlife conservation. Today the number of nesting pairs in the Old Dominion approaches 500, and up to 60 eagles roost in Caledon alone during the summer months. But to ensure that the shy eagles remain, many of Caledon's 2,579 acres are off-limits to visitors, as is the adjacent Choptank Creek State Natural Area Preserve.

Your best bet for eagle-watching is to join one of the park's guided tours along the Potomac. This trail, which has the distinct advantage of being open year-round, winds through forest a mile south of the shore. Eagles rarely venture so far inland, but you stand good odds of spotting pileated and red-bellied woodpeckers, as well as numerous songbirds.

Set out on the roomy single-track outlined in fallen limbs, and enter a glade of tall yellow poplars. Veer right when the Fern Hollow Trail forks. The red-blazed loop is the first of five interwoven loops that comprise Caledon's hiking-trail network. Curve left to a slight rise and pass an area of deadfall pines before making a 90-degree left to cross a rivulet on a footbridge. Climb through a collage of oaks: Southern and Northern red, scarlet, white, and chestnut. True to the trail's name, ferns make the forest floor green in warmer months.

Briefly double back, then make a distinct right to descend from the modest ridgeline. Even as you work your way steadily downhill to creekside bottomland, you establish a familiar pattern for this undulating loop. The hike dips through several draws, first along the winnowing ridges near an unnamed creek, then uphill, near the headwaters of its feeder branches. Before making a 90-degree right onto the Poplar Grove Trail, cross a culvert with steep, mossy banks, and veer briefly upstream.

The blue-blazed loop descends to cross a streamlet just upstream of its junction with another. The mossy, root-crossed trail then runs along that unnamed creek through beech and yellow poplar. It bends left to cross two deep-gullied feeder rivulets just upstream of their confluence. Crossing the second on a wooden bridge with handrails, you leave the Poplar Grove Trail for the Laurel Glen Trail.

This southwest-bound stretch of the trail begins its rise on wood-beam steps then bisects a ridgeline in a grove of holly shaded by beech and white oak. Ample yellow blazes guide you through a depression and across a second ridgeline before the trail curves left. Mountain laurel grows more abundantly on the western slope as you descend toward a stream valley and the Benchmark Trail.

Take the orange-blazed trail to the right, keeping the sandy-bottomed brook on your left as you round a knoll on the right. The eroded banks of the brook, up to 10-feet high and laced with tree roots, diminish as the valley floor widens. Cross the brook on a wooden footbridge just south of its confluence with the growing creek you first saw upstream. Briefly stroll beside the creek through a verdant bottomland forest. After passing a sign showing the footprints of various animals that reside in these woods, turn left to climb onto a ridgeline that heads south.

Move inland and uphill along the laurel-laden ridge top. Where it intersects the Cedar Ridge Trail, a sharp right takes you down the hillside. The trail bends left before finally descending to a footbridge. Mature beech trees dominate the forest surrounding Caledon's westernmost trail. The narrow single-track underfoot indicates that many visitors never traverse the entire trail network.

Following the Cedar Ridge Trail through the wide valley, you'll next cross another steep ridge to make the westernmost feeder branch of this hike. Crossing it on a bridge with handrails, follow the zigzagging trail downstream a short distance before it doubles back. Climb southwest through open forest before making a left at a bench. Now headed east, your path descends to recross the rivulet, noticeably shallower upstream.

Though the prongs and branches of this drainage are generally narrower on your return trip, its ridges are noticeably steeper. Take the opportunity to view these woods from a new perspective, looking north toward the low-lying forest you recently traveled. After the first of four successive climbs, descend to cross a rivulet, and then keep in to your left as you work your way downstream.

A winding ascent over the next ridgeline takes you through numerous holly trees. Just ahead, the path dips to meet the Benchmark Trail. Turn right and follow it uphill. A relatively long and level stint follows as you cross this wide knoll. The trail's sharp descent leads you across another feeder branch; the trail then rises up the opposite hillside. There, you'll find an enigmatic stone marker.

Crossing the ridgeline to rejoin the Laurel Glen Trail at a lengthy boardwalk, turn right to follow it upstream though a wide, grassy floodplain. The boardwalk makes a 90-degree left and crosses a small stream shortly before regaining single-track amid young beeches. Climbing away, you'll pass the thickets of mountain laurel that lend this trail its name.

A short distance on, turn right onto the Poplar Grove Trail, which briefly follows an old roadbed. Turn left off the wider path to continue on a fairly level stretch. Sycamores dot this forest, including a five-trunked specimen on trail right just before a sign devoted to the bird species of Caledon. A short distance on, cedars cluster on trail left, then Virginia pines prevail throughout the wood.

Shortly after passing within view of a private home visible uphill, veer right upon intersecting the Fern Hollow Trail. Hardwoods gradually reclaim the surrounding forest. Before completing your loop, pass the picnic shelter and amphitheater on trail right, then, after cresting a small hill, you'll see the trailhead just ahead.

# CANAL PARK TRAIL

## KEY AT-A-GLANCE INFORMATION

**LENGTH:** 3.6 miles

**CONFIGURATION:** Out-and-back

**DIFFICULTY:** Easy

**SCENERY:** Rappahannock Canal, pockets of wetlands amid suburban homes, small parcels of floral landscaping

**EXPOSURE:** Mostly open

**TRAFFIC:** Moderate

**TRAIL SURFACE:** Paved

**HIKING TIME:** 1.5 hours

**SEASON:** Open daily during daylight year-round

**ACCESS:** No fee; wheelchair accessible

**MAPS:** None available at trailhead or online, but the canal is depicted on most city maps

**FACILITIES:** Play fields, picnic tables, and restrooms in Old Mill Park

**SPECIAL COMMENTS:** In his copious reference work the *Trails of Virginia*, Allen de Hart proposes connecting Fredericksburg's Old Mill and Riverside Drive Parks with the canal trail to create a loop. This presently entails a road walk of almost a mile along Ford and Caroline Streets. For more information, contact City of Fredericksburg Parks at (540) 372-1086 or visit www.fredericksburgva.gov. More information on the canal's history is available from the Virginia Canals and Navigation Society (www.rockbridge.net/canal), which publishes William Trout's *Rappahannock Scenic River Atlas*.

**UTM Trailhead Coordinates for Canal Park Trail**

**UTM Zone (NAD27)  18S**

**Easting  282603**

**Northing  4243635**

## IN BRIEF

Understandably popular with area joggers, this paved, level out-and-back traces an important remnant of Fredericksburg's commercial past. Wetland parcels en route, home to swans and herons, are a welcome counterbalance to the concrete underbelly of US 1.

## DESCRIPTION

Constructed over two decades, the Rappahannock River canal system once stretched 50 miles upstream to Fauqier County. The notion of using canals to promote trade and industry along the river was first endorsed by Virginia legislators in 1811. Early proponents of canal navigation, including George Washington, had envisioned a system of controlled waterways lacing the commonwealth, ferrying goods to market and supplies upriver to farmers and settlers. That vision never came to pass, as most commerce moved from the canals to railroads. Nevertheless, canals were an integral component of commerce in Fall Line cities  like Fredericksburg and Richmond where they helped transfer cargo around waterfalls and rapids.

The private Rappahannock Navigation Company mustered sufficient capital to undertake

## DIRECTIONS

From Richmond head north on I-95 to Exit 130 (46 miles north of I-295). Head east on VA 3 for just over a mile, then turn left onto US 1. Continue 1.4 miles north then turn left onto VA 639 (Fall Hill Avenue). Drive 0.75 miles to reach the trailhead, a modest gravel lot on your left. Parking is available in small lots on both sides of the canal, which runs under Fall Hill Avenue. A steel bridge links the two lots, and the trail heads south on the western side of the canal.

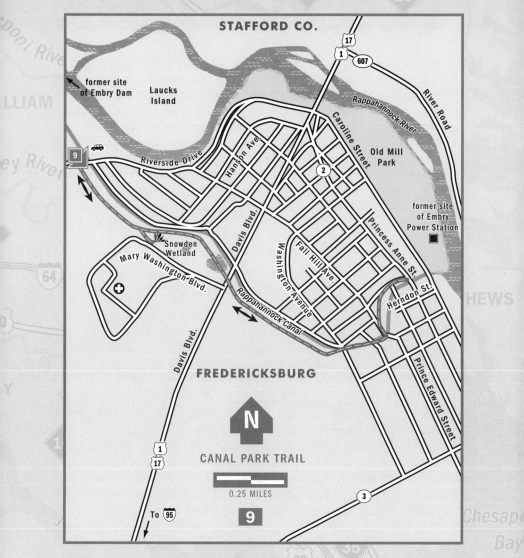

STAFFORD CO.

former site of Embry Dam

Laucks Island

Rappahannock River

River Road

Riverside Drive

Hanson Ave.

Caroline Street

Old Mill Park

former site of Embry Power Station

9

Davis Blvd.

Snowden Wetland

Mary Washington Blvd.

Rappahannock Canal

Washington Avenue

Fall Hill Ave.

Princess Anne St.

Herndon St.

Prince Edward Street

FREDERICKSBURG

Davis Blvd.

N

CANAL PARK TRAIL

0.25 MILES

9

To 95

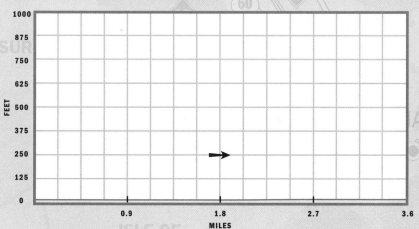

1000
875
750
625
500
375
250
125
0

FEET

0.9          1.8          2.7          3.6

MILES

construction of a canal stretching west from Fredericksburg in 1829. But 15 years later, when the cash-strapped company folded, the project remained incomplete. However, a short-lived gold-mining boom upriver hardened the city's resolve, and Fredericksburg assumed control of the project with state backing. The canal route was completed in 1849. However, as its turbulent creation presaged, the canal's heyday was fleeting. In 1852, railroad lines reached the upper Rappahannock Valley, and traffic along the canal network dwindled.

The enterprise was never sufficiently profitable to maintain its 47 locks and 20 dams. Enter entrepreneurship. Just six years after its completion, the Fredericksburg Water Power Company purchased the stretch of canal along which the city's Canal Park Trail now runs. The channel proved far more profitable, turning the turbines of flour, wool, and electricity mills, the remains of which lie just beyond the trail's terminus near Old Mill Park. In fact the conduit is often referred to as the VEPCO Canal, after the acronym for Virginia Electric and Power Company, which maintained the 1910 Embry Dam on the canal's west end and Embry Power Plant on its east end through the 1960s.

The Army Corps of Engineers is slated to dismantle Embry Dam by 2006, and afterward the trail may be extended along the canal northwest of Fall Hill Avenue to the Rappahannock River. At present, however, the trail begins southeastward, seemingly away from the river (the southbound canal curves to the east, and the eastbound river curves to the south before they rejoin). Setting out, the canal is visible below you on the left, a trickle of its former self. When it served to float barges, towed by horses treading this same path, the water level was kept higher, as evidenced by the sturdy stone walls that rise on opposite sides of the 20-foot-wide channel. Vegetation growing in the accumulated silt shades the present creek.

Power lines run concurrent with the path for the first quarter-mile, and a field on the right gives way to a buffer of trees, comprised most notably of river birch, red maple, sweetgum, and yellow poplar. Suburban back lawns are visible across the canal, and soon you come to a bridge that leads left to access the neighborhood. Turn right here, however, to visit a small natural gem tucked away among the trees.

The Snowden Wetland lies approximately 150 feet ahead on the left. Descend a few stairs to follow the boardwalk across the marsh to an observation platform with benches. A sign aids novice bird-watchers in identifying the waterfowl and songbirds that reside here. Shrouded by a wall of vine-draped ash trees, this shallow pond fringed with mallow and rush feels surprisingly serene.

Backtrack to the canal towpath, then turn right to continue eastward. A second wetland abuts the trail on the right a short distance ahead. It widens into a pond with buildings visible across it. Next, at roughly the halfway point, the trail's urban character is hard to ignore when it passes beneath busy US 1. The cavernous walkway beneath the overpass is scarcely inviting, but it is safer and more expedient than crossing the street above. Your imagination may conjure visions of bats, but rest assured those are barn swallows darting about in the dim passage.

As the road noise recedes behind you, a third, larger marsh of arrowhead plants appears on the right. A few leafless trees, some with trunks smoothed like driftwood by the wind and rain, remain standing at the periphery of the marsh. Here I spotted a heron, motionless as it awaited the approach of an unsuspecting fish. I figured if the bird didn't mind the proximity of homes and businesses, why should I? I felt my thought was validated when I spied a hummingbird feeding at a trailside trumpet-creeper vine just ahead.

Continuing along the canal on the paved path, there is yet another pond ahead on trail right, this one a rectangular impoundment built for the adjacent water-treatment facility. A field then opens on the right. Beyond it the trail curves left to cross Washington Avenue. Visible on your right up the street is the Mary Washington Monument, a worthwhile detour to the gravesite of George Washington's mother. She was interred beside Meditation Rock, said to be one of her favorite spots, near her daughter's home. An 1833 effort by President Andrew Jackson to have a shrine erected on the spot floundered, but 60 years later, Grover Cleveland commissioned the present obelisk.

Continuing along the Canal Park Trail, pass homes on the right to reach a second road, Canal Street. A small landscaped park graces this intersection with blooming coneflowers and black-eyed Susans. Traverse the street and park before taking a metal footbridge across the canal, continuing along the waterway. It's at this juncture that the canal turns left to head north toward the Rappahannock. Foliage screens the canal as the trail passes a medical office building on the left. The pathway again approaches the canal briefly before it disappears into an underground aqueduct. The trail veers left through a grassy field to its eastern terminus at Princess Anne Street, the turnaround for this out-and-back.

Intrepid hikers and Fredericksburg history buffs may wish to forge on, however, zigzagging across Princess Anne to walk a block north to Ford Street. Next, a left onto Caroline Street soon takes you to a marker describing the town's historic mill district. The brick remains of a wool-fabric mill, the foundation of a turn-of-the-century power plant used to illuminate street lights, and the ruins of a nineteenth-century flour mill are visible on the left side of the road as you continue northwest to reach Old Mill Park on the right. There you will find restrooms, a playground, picnic tables, and a stretch of Rappahannock shoreline.

The area's biggest attraction, of course, is Fredericksburg and Spotsylvania National Military Park. Civil War history buffs can tour four battlefields (five counting a tiny allotment on the site of the Battle of Salem Church), though the park's premier hiking trail, a 7-mile loop, is located at Spotsylvania Court House Battlefield (page 204).

# CHICKAHOMINY WILDLIFE MANAGEMENT AREA

 **KEY AT-A-GLANCE INFORMATION**

**LENGTH:** 3.3 miles plus options

**CONFIGURATION:** Out-and-back

**DIFFICULTY:** Easy

**SCENERY:** Chickahominy River, freshwater marsh on Morris Creek, mixed forest, waterfowl and other wildlife

**EXPOSURE:** Limited shade

**TRAFFIC:** Low

**TRAIL SURFACE:** Gravel-and-dirt double-track

**HIKING TIME:** 1.5 hours

**SEASON:** Trails are open daily during daylight year-round but best avoided during hunting seasons (see below).

**ACCESS:** No fee; mountain biking and horseback riding allowed; no ATVs; primitive camping allowed

**MAPS:** Available online at www.dgif.virginia.gov/hunting/wma/chickahominy.html

**FACILITIES:** Shooting range, fishing pier, and boat launch on Morris Creek; beach on Chickahominy River; informational signboards, resident staff

**SPECIAL COMMENTS:** All wildlife management areas are open to hunting. Check with the VDGIF to determine annual hunting seasons (call (804) 370-1000 or visit www.dgif.virginia.gov/hunting). It is recommended that you not hike during deer and wild turkey seasons, but if you do, wear blaze orange and hike only during peak daylight hours. For details, contact the VDGIF Williamsburg office at (757) 253-7072.

UTM Trailhead Coordinates for Chickahominy Wildlife Management Area

UTM Zone (NAD27)   18S

Easting   0331767

Northing   4132472

## IN BRIEF

The mostly flat 5,217 acres of Chickahominy do not include a loop trail along the namesake river. Nevertheless, a network of grassy double-track offers multiple out-and-back options, and gravel roads provide access to verdant Morris Creek to the southwest and the wide Chickahominy River to the east.

## DESCRIPTION

The Chickahominy River takes its name from a Native American tribe that still resides in the area. The correlation with hominy is no accident; the tribe was named for its dietary staple of pounded corn. Though not part of the Powhatan

## DIRECTIONS

From Richmond head east on I-64 to Exit 205. Make a brief southward stint on Old Stage Road to reach US 60 and follow the highway east for roughly 12.5 miles. Turn right (south) onto VA 155, zigzagging through the hamlet of Providence Forge. You will see brown signs for Chickahominy WMA and its boat launch. In 2.5 miles, turn left onto VA 614 and travel 4 miles. Make another left onto VA 615. Proceed 6.5 miles on this road, which bears right to become VA 623. The entrance road, VA 621, is your final signed left. Arriving from Richmond or Williamsburg via VA 5, take VA 623 north. Bypass peripheral parking areas on the right and turn right onto VA 621.

Once within the WMA, wind along blacktop past residences and fields to the trailhead parking area on your right about 75 feet off the road. To reach the Chickahominy River, follow VA 621 until the blacktop ends. Turn left onto a gravel road and proceed past a private residence to the water's edge. To reach the Morris Creek boat launch, turn right on a gravel road at the VA 621 terminus and right again when the road forks.

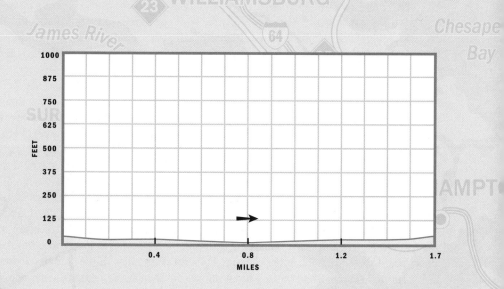

tribal confederacy with which they coexisted, members of the Chickahominy tribe relinquished English captain John Smith into the custody of Chief Powhatan, having captured him on an exploratory expedition up the Chickahominy River. Tradition holds that Chief Powhatan's daughter Pocahontas lobbied him to spare Smith, whom she had befriended. Alliances between natives and Englishmen were vital to the survival of colonists. Europeans often used indigenous names (particularly for waterways), evidence of at least limited coexistence and commerce.

The Wildlife Management Area's (WMA) access road ends at a small beach characterized by viscous, almost muddy, sand. Just upstream, a stand of bald cypress juts into the river, which is fringed by marsh grasses. Waves lap the shore, reminding you that the Chickahominy makes its confluence with the tidal James just 5 miles downstream.

Bird-watchers can look for bald eagles and osprey along the Chickahominy, while anglers can hope for striped bass and yellow perch. Smaller Morris Creek, which meets the Chickahominy at the WMA's peninsular southeastern tip, floods a wide, green marsh across the main channel. Herons stalk the marsh, while crappie, largemouth bass, and multiple catfish species lurk its waters. A rainbow of dragon- and damselflies darts among the cattails. Even if you don't venture to the creek, you'll find ample opportunities to test your knowledge of entomological taxonomy within Chickahominy WMA.

Take the opportunity to explore both the river and the creek, even though the WMA's only significant trails are located within its interior. There is a nice but short trail to an inlet of Morris Creek that leaves west from the next parking lot uphill of the boat launch. The trail traces a modest ridge to a popular campsite complete with a tire swing. Several feeder streams drain the WMA as they wind southward. These creeks form fingers of the marsh and make a trail along Morris Creek impractical. The WMA's east–west trail crosses their upper stretches and can be muddy as a result.

The route mapped here runs north–south along one of the area's older dirt roads without traversing any of the parcels of private land encompassed by the WMA. If you explore the other trails, be courteous of the half-dozen homes located within the WMA. From the most central parking area (located almost 2 miles from the entrance on the left), head west along an obvious double-track.

The double-track enters the woods through an area of young hardwoods, perhaps recovering farm or timberland, before reaching mature oaks on the left. Remnant gravel is visible underfoot, although sufficient earth has accumulated to allow for grassy ground cover. As the trail continues, the gravel thins beneath overgrowth. Expect the paths to be least overgrown in the winter and spring, not only because much of the growth is annual but also because the WMA sees the heaviest use during autumn and winter hunting seasons.

Of course hikers undaunted by summer humidity will find many rewards along the trail, not least of all blackberries, which grow in trailside thickets along the double-track after it bears southward. First the trail veers left at a fork marked by a cluster of sweetgum saplings. This is the only significant turn on the trail as mapped here. Not far ahead you'll pass through a small clearing. Look for dragonflies in the summer. It was here I spotted several white-tailed widow skimmers. Their white or translucent wings are black along the abdomen, making them resemble small moths or butterflies. Yellow-sided skimmers and reddish Needham's skimmers seemed likewise in abundance. As you continue along level ground, you may encounter downed trees, but aside from such obstacles the hiking is rather easy. The double-track undulates almost imperceptibly until the turnaround.

The blackberry brambles stretch out into the trail in search of sunlight and may claw at your pant legs. The bushes bloom with clusters of faintly pink flowers in the spring. In summer, honeysuckle and bright-orange trumpeter-vine blossoms dot the trailside, lending a sweet fragrance to the air. The most common wildflowers include black-eyed susans and purplish meadow beauty, also known as deergrass.

Though you may not be able to tell, this old roadbed follows what passes for a ridge in this flat terrain. Feeder streams descending to Morris Creek parallel it less than a quarter mile away on both sides. The path veers right after bypassing a spur trail on the left and in another half mile makes a short, steep descent to reach its terminus near Morris Creek. For views of the verdant creekside marsh, however, you may need to bushwack a short distance. As you near the water, listen for the croak of frogs. Or in the winter listen for wind rustling through the brown beech leaves; younger specimens of this riparian deciduous species retain their leaves until spring.

A fallen pine in the Morris Creek Marsh

After retracing your steps for about 3 miles total, you may opt to turn left and explore other trails within the Chickahominy network. Though the trails are wide, maintenance is sporadic; bring maps, but be ready to reconcile discrepancies between the park map and area topos.

History buffs will want to return west along VA 5 to see the centuries-old plantation homes that line the James River. Closest to Chicahominy Wildlife Management Area is Sherwood Forest, former home of President John Tyler. It is furnished with many of the Tyler's possessions and is open for tours; call (804) 282-1441.

# CHIPPOKES PLANTATION STATE PARK

## KEY AT-A-GLANCE INFORMATION

**LENGTH:** 5 miles

**CONFIGURATION:** Balloon with out-and-back spur

**DIFFICULTY:** Easy

**SCENERY:** Cobham Bay beach along the James River, cypress swamp, nineteenth-century plantation homes and buildings, cultivated fields, Chippokes Creek

**EXPOSURE:** Open with limited shade

**TRAFFIC:** Moderate

**TRAIL SURFACE:** Paved and dirt

**HIKING TIME:** 2 hours

**SEASON:** Trails open daily from 8 a.m. to dusk year-round; Jones-Stewart Mansion and Chippokes Farm and Forestry Museum are open weekends April–October and weekdays June–August (parking is $2–$3).

**ACCESS:** Parking: $2 weekdays and $3 weekends. The mansion, museum, visitor center, restrooms, some trails, cabins, and campsites are wheelchair accessible.

**MAPS:** Available at the park and online at www.dcr.virginia.gov/parks/chippoke.htm

**FACILITIES:** Visitor center, restrooms and-showers, picnic area, swimming pool, beach, campground with hook-ups, rental cabins, multiuse and equestrian trails.

**SPECIAL COMMENTS:** Wear shoes with sturdy soles that you don't mind getting wet for the 1-mile trudge down a shell-covered beach. Call the mansion and museum at (757) 294-3625 for hours and rates. Contact the park office at (757) 294-3625.

---

**UTM Trailhead Coordinates for Chippokes Plantation State Park**

**UTM Zone (NAD27)   18S**

**Easting   0345557**

**Northing   4112178**

## ▶ IN BRIEF

The pastoral environs of Chippokes Plantation State Park are positively evocative. It's easy to imagine Native Americans paddling a canoe through the lush wetlands where Chippokes Creek meets the James or to imagine early settlers tending the nearby fields of corn and wheat.

## ▶ DESCRIPTION

A wealth of history awaits visitors to Chippokes Plantation State Park. Nearby colonial- and American-history landmarks at Williamsburg, Jamestown, and Yorktown draw more than a million visitors annually. But here, just across the five-mile-wide James River, the pace is slower and the setting bucolic. And in addition to its human past, Chippokes highlights the region's natural history, including a fossil record that reaches back eons. To appreciate the park's diverse offerings, begin your trek at the visitor center, where centuries-old farming tools; fossils, shells, and bird nests; and a diorama detailing the plantation's early history all vie for attention.

## ▶ DIRECTIONS

From Richmond take I-95 south to Exit 61 or I-295 south to Exit 15 and head east on VA 10. Continue approximately 40 miles to the hamlet of Surry. Turn left at the intersection with VA 31, then turn right at the blinking light, remaining on VA 10 all the while. (If you're coming south from Williamsburg via VA 31 and the Jamestown-Scotland Ferry, turn left onto VA 10 here.) Turn left at VA 634 (Alliance Road) and follow it 4 miles to the park on the left. Drive through the park past the pool and campgrounds to park beside the visitor center at the road's terminus. The College Run Trail heads east out of a small roundabout in front of the visitor center.

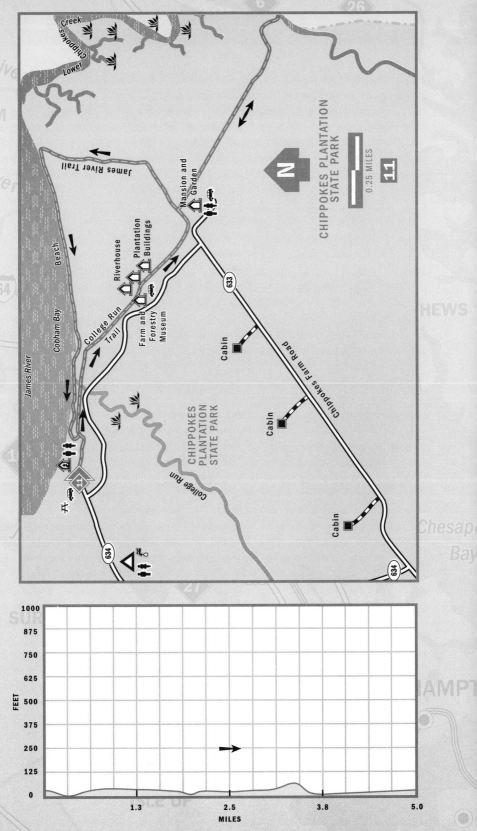

Peruse the brochure rack for maps and leaflets to augment your hike, then begin by heading east on the paved College Run Trail.

The path promptly descends to a cypress swamp on the right. Frogs chirp among the cypress knees; a short path on the left leads to the James River. Note the path, as it will later provide for your return from the beach. You may also note the buzz, and possibly bite, of deerflies, which will accompany you from this point on should you fail to use insect repellent. Cross College Run on a wooden bridge just ahead, and look for wild yellow iris blooming in the spring.

Lucas' Landing, the wide sandy shoal where College Run Creek meets the James, served as early as 1626 as a loading point for tobacco and other crops bound for England. The surrounding property had been granted to Captain William Powell in 1619. His plantation and Chippokes Creek, which borders it on the east, were named for a Native American chieftain who befriended colonial settlers. In 1646 Colonel Henry Bishop, having acquired the plantation, expanded it from 550 to 1,403 acres, an area slightly smaller than that of present-day Chippokes Plantation State Park.

The plantation's fields are among the oldest continuously cultivated cropland in North America, and demonstration fields of corn and wheat still surround the historic plantation structures. It is fitting that the park is home to Chippokes Farm and Forestry Museum, which showcases the agricultural implements of four centuries, including a Depression-era sawmill.

The path soon veers away from the James and uphill to pass the River House, the park's oldest structure, on the left. The Farm and Forestry Museum is visible across the road that parallels the trail on your right. Buildings along Quarter Lane, now part of the College Run Trail, are fronted by interpretive signs illuminating the workings of a nineteenth-century farm, including the hard labor done by slaves and sharecroppers. The lane was named for the slave and tenant quarters that dot the route. It also passes barns that were rebuilt in the 1930s.

On opposite ends of the lane stand the park's most notable structures: the River House, a Colonial-style clapboard built in 1830, and the stately brick Chippokes Mansion, also known as the Jones-Stewart Mansion. The latter was constructed in 1854 under the direction of Albert Jones, who had purchased the farm in 1837 and promptly enlarged the River House. The plantation prospered under Jones's ownership, and here operated one of few legal distilleries in Virginia. Legend holds that Chippokes Mansion and Plantation were spared the torch during the Civil War because Jones sold peach and apple brandy to both the North and South.

The Stewart name now associated with the mansion recognizes Victor Stewart and his wife, who capped a succession of owners when they obtained sole ownership of the plantation in 1925 (for a sum total of $52,000). The couple devoted time and resources to restoring the mansion (including purchasing the rare portable sawmill now displayed at the museum), and in 1967 Mrs. Stewart donated it to the people of Virginia as a memorial to her husband. Today, visitors can tour the mansion, stocked with antiques, for a small fee, and stroll its Paradise Garden for free. Be sure to pick up a "What's Blooming in Paradise" garden-guide leaflet at the visitor center.

You may incorporate the mansion and garden (or even the museum) into your hike or return by car afterward. To continue the hike, head northeast on the double-track path in front of the mansion. The path forks just beyond the grounds, with a pasture on the left and corn and wheat fields to the right. Turn right on the Lower Chippokes Creek Trail—there's a field to your left and a band of trees to your right. You can forgo this out-and-back if you're short on time, but the creekside dock at its terminus is an excellent spot for wildlife-watching. Brilliant green foliage surrounds the meandering channel, herons fish among the shallows, and crabs scurry along the shore. An outdoor class-room used for scheduled programs overlooks the dock.

From the creek, retrace your steps along the field then turn right onto the James River Trail. With a field on your right and forest to your left, curve gently left. Enter the woods to descend to the James River. You can elect to return by backtrack-ing on the James River and College Run

Stroll amid the seashells on the sandy beach at Chippokes Plantation.

Trails, but indulge your sense of adventure instead and return along the beach. You may have to scramble over a few deadfalls from the slowly eroding reddish-sand cliffs, but the scene is practically tropical. The sandy beach of Cobham Bay sweeps across the horizon.

The same slow erosion that has created the bay and beach has littered the shore with fossils. And the tide washes new shells ashore, its gentle lapping ever so slowly grinding them to sand. Be sure to grab a copy of the brochure "Picking Up the Past" at the visitor center. The pamphlet explains the various fossil types, generously including unaltered remains such as shells and bones. It also cites some of the fossils and shells commonly found along the beach. Visitors are asked not to dig any fossils from the bluff and are not permitted to keep the fossils they find.

You will know you are approaching the end of your walk along the beach when you come to College Run Creek. The creek fans out in a small delta with fingers too wide to leap. Plan to wade through the cool, clear shallows. Next, look for the short, narrow path on the left that returns you to the College Run Trail and thus back to your car. (You could trek farther down the beach to pick up the beach-access trail that leads back to the visitor-center parking lot, but the trail is not open in the winter.) Having completed your 5-mile round-trip, avail yourself of the park's other offerings.

# CHUBB SANDHILL STATE NATURAL AREA PRESERVE

## KEY AT-A-GLANCE INFORMATION

**LENGTH:** 3.2 miles

**CONFIGURATION:** Out-and-back

**DIFFICULTY:** Easy

**SCENERY:** Lush pine forests crisscrossed by blackwater creeks, the Nottoway River

**EXPOSURE:** Shaded on trails, exposed on road walk

**TRAFFIC:** Low

**TRAIL SURFACE:** Dirt, asphalt

**HIKING TIME:** 1.5 hours

**SEASON:** Open daily during daylight year-round

**ACCESS:** No fee; not recommended for wheelchairs

**MAPS:** Available online at www.dcr.virginia.gov/dnh/chub.htm

**FACILITIES:** Observation platform on the Nottoway River; interpretive signs; there is a public boat landing on the opposite side of the river at the VA 631 bridge

**SPECIAL COMMENTS:** The preserve is subject to closings for resource protection and prescribed burns. Call ahead. As a state-protected natural area, Chubb Sandhill is open only for low-impact activities. Bikes, horses, and ATVs are not allowed. Contact the Virginia Department of Conservation and Recreation Natural Heritage Program at (804) 786-7951.

**UTM Trailhead Coordinates for Chubb Sandhill State Natural Area Preserve**

**UTM Zone (NAD27)   18S**

**Easting   0305140**

**Northing   4081667**

## IN BRIEF

Bordered on the west by the Nottoway River, Chubb Sandhill State Natural Area Preserve is essentially flat and easily explored on wide fire lanes. Hikers must walk the one-third mile stretch of VA 631 between the two main trails. You may not see anyone else on this rural road, but stay to the shoulder—drivers don't expect to see you either.

## DESCRIPTION

Like other state-owned preserves profiled in this guide, Chubb Sandhill in rural Sussex County is open to low-impact recreation but managed for the benefit of rare plants and animals. The preserve protects two ecosystems rare in Virginia: a tupelo–bald cypress swamp grows in the bottomland along the Nottoway River, while a pine–scrub oak forest blankets most of the preserve's interior.

Among the uncommon species found growing here are several understory flowering plants, including pineland tick-trefoil, Virginia false-gromwell, golden puccoon, and hoary scurfpea. The latter is not known to occur in any other county of the commonwealth. A relative of Indian breadroot, its roots are edible too. Another rarity found on the site, Queen's delight, was long a staple of folk remedies. American Indians used the

## DIRECTIONS

From Richmond head south on I-95 to Exit 41 (33 miles south of the James River). Exit onto VA 35 and continue southeast for 19.5 miles, crossing VA 40 in the small town of Homeville. Fork right onto VA 631 and look for a small gravel parking area on your right 2.4 miles ahead. If you cross the Nottoway River, you've gone too far. Farther west, VA 631 does intersect I-95 at Exit 20, just north of Emporia, but it's a narrow, winding trip east to the preserve.

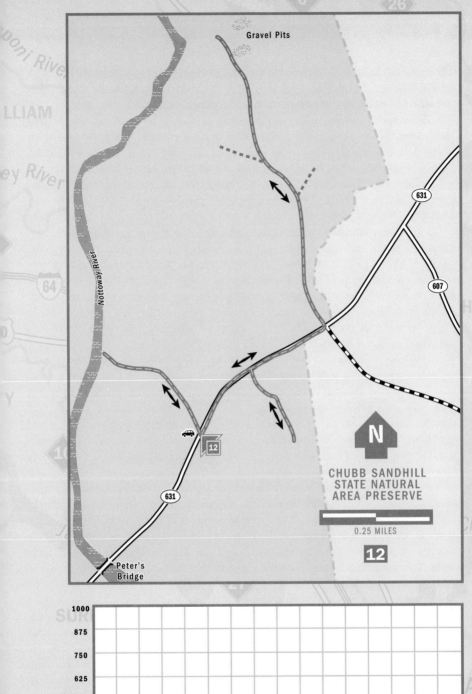

Gravel Pits

Nottoway River

631

607

N

CHUBB SANDHILL
STATE NATURAL
AREA PRESERVE

0.25 MILES

12

631

Peter's
Bridge

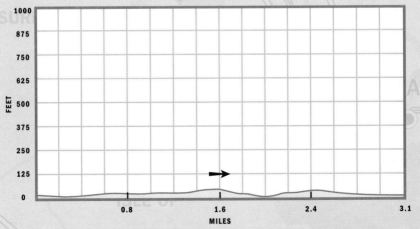

1000
875
750
625
500
375
250
125
0

FEET

0.8          1.6          2.4          3.1

MILES

astringent herb to treat digestive ailments and skin rashes. A perennial with slender, leathery leaves, it grows to four feet, and the root is traditionally dug in late summer—but not in the preserve, where collection is prohibited.

These species thrive in the sandy, acidic soil found in southeastern Virginia. Chubb Sandhill lies along the shoreline of an ancient estuary. When the prehistoric sea receded, it left a flat expanse of deep sand. The dry forest that took root was prone to wildfires sparked by lightning. Indigenous tribes also set fires, often to clear the underbrush. This enabled them to range farther, enhanced their hunting prospects, and promoted the growth of desirable plants—not just herbs but berries, which need sunlight to ripen.

Subsequent landowners found that some crops, like peanuts and cotton, grew well in this soil. They cleared much of the forest and, in the twentieth century, suppressed wildfires to protect homes and crops. At the Chubb Sandhill site, a past owner also found the sand itself was valuable as fill dirt. Shallow pits left dotting the land now fill with rainwater, creating a unique habitat for salamanders and toads. Tannins from fallen pine needles stain these pools a brownish black, so you'll have to look closely to spot shy amphibians like the dwarf waterdog. Simply stand patiently still, however, and the frogs will fill the air with a droning chorus.

This hike begins with a trip to the Nottoway. Head northwest from the parking area past a gate with a sign stating, "Foot travel is welcome." A dense forest dominated by loblolly pines has begun to encroach on this old double-track. A collage of moss, lichen, and clubmoss grows bright green along the seldom-trod trail. As you progress, the pines give way to parcels of blackwater swamp, with good views on trail right. Long, slender leaves of sawgrass arc into the water, and moss colors the surrounding tree trunks. Look for willow oak and water tupelo, the latter growing wide at the base like bald cypress.

Soon, you pass through a small clearing to approach the river. A wooden observation platform overlooks this bend in the Nottoway, where birch trees stretch out from the banks. Pause here for a bit of bird-watching if you like. Wood ducks hunker down in the riverbank foliage, while belted kingfishers eye their prey from the branches above. Rare, brightly colored dragon- and damselflies also haunt these waters. Yellow and black spine-crowned clubtails dart cautiously across the river, and slender, reddish duckweed firetails hover near the shore.

Retrace your steps to the parking area, then head north along VA 631. A short distance ahead, you'll find another gate on trail right. Though not depicted on the preserve brochure, this path is open to travel, according to the sign. Turn for a brief out-and-back through mixed woods. Trees now protrude from enigmatic trailside mounds, presumably reminders of sand mining. Sweetgum saplings line the path but give way to a cluster of pines before the trail rounds a bend. The trail may stretch to within view of the Nottoway, but I retreated at a cluster of deadfalls. In the summer, tall grass may also deter passage.

The preserve's longest trail lies just a short distance north on the left (northwest) side of VA 631. Also an out-and-back, it features a slight, almost imperceptible elevation gain, but this is sufficient to alter the surrounding forest. The boggy forest you found near the river is replaced by the pine–scrub oak sandhills for which the preserve was named. Loblollys and Southern red oaks tolerate this fast-draining, acidic soil, but you'll see few other hardwood species.

In spring and early summer, scan the forest floor for the yellow, lantana-like blossoms of golden puccoon and the small violet petals of hoary scrufpea. Look for these perennials in the open understory beneath maturing pines. Ongoing restoration efforts, including prescribed burns, aim to eventually re-create an airy pine savanna within the preserve.

Bear left at the first trail fork and right at the second. You can explore these prongs, but they soon dead-end. If you peer into the trailside woods between them, you can spot some of the former sandpits now teeming with tadpoles. Additional pits were dug near the end of the trail, just over half a mile from the road. A more riparian woodland extends west to a bend in the Nottoway. The path is easy to follow, and your prospects for spotting wildlife in these isolated woods are excellent. Linger quietly at the turnaround and you may spot a fox or bobcat slinking across the trail.

Northeast of Chubb Sandhill is the hamlet of Waverly, in the heart of Virginia's peanut-growing southeast. Located at the corner of VA 40 and US 460 is the 1890 Victorian house where folk artist Miles B. Carpenter lived for more than 70 years. It now serves as a folk-art museum, and there are two additional museums on the grounds. The Wood Products Museum tells the story of Sussex County's timber industry. Carpenter operated a sawmill on the site before he undertook woodcarving as art. The First Peanut Museum recounts the history of Sussex's main crop, from its introduction in the 1830s, to the first factory in the 1880s, to the twentieth century.

# COLD HARBOR BATTLEFIELDS
## Richmond National Battlefield Park

## IN BRIEF

Dug in at Cold Harbor, Confederate forces repulsed the Union advance toward Richmond in a protracted engagement that left 16,000 men dead. The victory amounted to a stay of execution for the besieged Confederate capital and prompted General Ulysses S. Grant to later confess, "I have always regretted that the last assault at Cold Harbor was ever made…no advantage was gained to compensate for the heavy loss." Today those somber words are emblazoned on the battlefield's visitor center. Earthen fortifications still wend their way through the now-silent woods, and an interpretive trail explains the grim reality of what in 1864 was a new phenomenon: trench warfare.

## DESCRIPTION

The Richmond National Battlefield Park encompasses ten units, a central visitor center at the Tredeger Iron Works, and the Chimborazo Medical Museum. The park's most notable trail, however, is here at tiny Cold Harbor, northeast of Richmond. A mere crossroads, Cold Harbor erupted in violence on May 31, 1864. General Robert E. Lee's Confederate troops made a decisive stand in order to protect their capital 9 miles to the south.

The initial Union assault was disastrous, claiming 6,000 troops from the federal ranks in a single day, June 3, 1864. The Union matched the entrenched Confederates by constructing

## DIRECTIONS

From I-295, Exit 34A, follow Creighton Road (VA 615) northeast. Turn right on VA 156 and drive 2.5 miles. The battlefield is located on your left; the visitor center and two cannons are visible from the road. Plenty of signs from the interstate will direct your route.

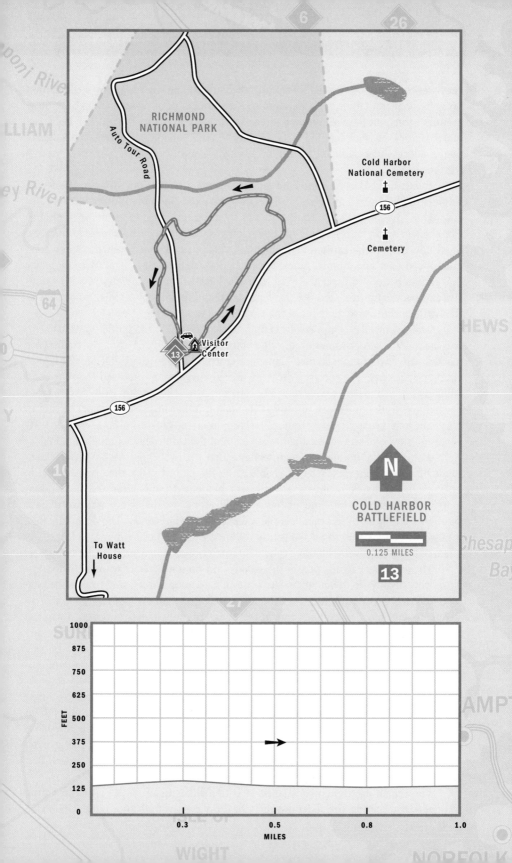

RICHMOND
NATIONAL PARK

Auto Tour Road

Cold Harbor
National Cemetery

156

Cemetery

13 Visitor
Center

156

N

COLD HARBOR
BATTLEFIELD

0.125 MILES

13

To Watt
House

1000

875

750

625

500

FEET

375

250

125

0

0.3        0.5        0.8        1.0

MILES

earthworks along the battle lines, but the subsequent fighting saw little Union progress. General Grant, who had assumed command of all federal units only three months earlier, on June 12 ordered a retreat, ending the battle. It would be Lee's last major victory. Lessons learned at Cold Harbor would shape not only Grant's subsequent, successful assault on Richmond from the south, but military tactics through the Great War.

Today, Cold Harbor Battlefield is an inauspicious park, one of many along the Virginia Civil War Trail auto-tour route. Drive the park's loop road to see territory not covered by the footpath. En route you will spy a recently placed granite memorial to Connecticut soldiers, testimony to the ongoing remembrance the battlefield inspires. Moss now carpets the earthen berms behind which soldiers once crouched, and trees, notably red oaks and loblolly pines, tower overhead. There is a solemnity to the place that cannot be fully appreciated from your car. Take the opportunity to view the extensive earthworks up close and read trail signage that illuminates both the importance of the battle and the miserable lot of the Civil War foot soldier.

Begin your hike at the visitor center with a primer on the battle. Walk beneath two mammoth oaks canopies on the side of the center nearest VA 156. The trailhead is marked with two cannons and an aging monument placed by the Confederate Memorial Literary Society. The society, whose all-female membership included the wives and daughters of Confederate veterans, was chartered in 1890, with Belle Bryan (who deeded Joseph Bryan Park to the city of Richmond in her husband's honor) serving as president for its first 20 years. Besides erecting numerous historical markers, the society established and still maintains the Museum of the Confederacy in Richmond.

Also near the trailhead, a sign explains that the battlefield encompassed thousands of acres, far beyond what is visible along the path. In fact, the opposing battle lines extended almost 7 miles. The present battlefield park is located in approximately the center of the line of battle. Walk along on the wide, well-worn path through a grassy field that parallels the road some 20 yards away. The decidedly pastoral scene visitors find today—a gently rolling meadow bounded by thick forest—is a marked contrast to the bloody scene recounted on park signs and in the literature.

The trail veers right to enter the woods and presents hikers with their first up-close view of an entrenchment. In this case, it's a Union zigzag, dug to provide passage between two trench lines. As the battle wore on, intense fighting gave way to stalemate, and most casualties came at the hands of trained sharpshooters. Despised by the infantrymen on both sides, these snipers imposed a lethal penalty upon any troop who dared leave the confines of the trenches. According to park signage, one infantryman said crawling through the trenches carrying rations and ammunition made him feel like "some unholy cross between a pack mule and a snake." Another lamented: "A man's life is often exacted as the price of a cup of water from the spring."

The trail crosses a string of earthworks on an elevated bridge that protects them from wear. The trenches and berms visitors see today are significantly weathered and would have afforded greater protection at their original size. Constructing such earthen fortifications was no easy task, done as it was under the threat of enemy fire, using bayonets and bare hands in lieu of shovels.

The remaining trenchworks form a battlefield map of sorts, with the Union trenches representing the federal army's farthest point of advancement. Unable to

A silent canon now guards the meadow at Cold Harbor. The woods beyond are laced with Civil War earthworks.

break through enemy lines, Union soldiers dug in under cover of night and remained for two grueling weeks. A park sign indicating a Union rifle pit notes that its Confederate likeness is situated a mere 50 yards away. In between is the gulf that would be dubbed no-man's-land.

For the soldiers confined for days to squalid trenches, the brief truce of June 7 must have seemed surreal. During the three days following the Union's first unsuccessful charge, Generals Lee and Grant, in a precursor to their meeting at Appomattox, negotiated a two-hour cease-fire. The halt to battle afforded Union medics the opportunity to attend to soldiers who lay wounded from the initial failed advance. Along one stretch of the battle line, a Union work party recovered 244 dead and only 3 survivors. A New Jersey soldier recalled, "During the truce the enemies were talking to each other and exchanging newspapers. The works were lined with unarmed men, all gazing upon the solemn scene. The two hours soon passed. The signal was given. The men rushed to their arms and the rattle of musketry was again commenced along the line."

Meandering through the woods, you will find that downed trees, holly thickets, and other brush intermittently disguise the earthworks, but the path remains obvious. The trail makes the most of the limited woodland area, winding beneath white oaks before passing numerous fire-scarred tree trunks. You'll cross the park road twice, but otherwise there are no intersections. As the trail approaches the road for the first time, you'll notice a gurgling brook on trail right, known as Bloody Run in memory of the violent hand-to-hand combat that occurred here.

After crossing a pair of wooden bridges and heading uphill into the forest, look for a particularly informative sign depicting the earthworks as they were used during the battle, with grooves for the soldiers' knees and elbows and wooden beams on which to steady rifles. A private home on trail right signals the trail's impending end. Soon it emerges from the woods in view of the parking lot.

# CRUMP PARK

## KEY AT-A-GLANCE INFORMATION

**LENGTH:** 0.9 miles with an additional 0.75-mile spur

**CONFIGURATION:** Figure eight

**DIFFICULTY:** Easy

**SCENERY:** Meadow Farm, circa 1860, complete with stable, pasture, and demonstration crops; suburban woods, duck pond

**EXPOSURE:** Open near farmstead, shaded on trails

**TRAFFIC:** Moderate

**TRAIL SURFACE:** Paved and dirt

**HIKING TIME:** 30 minutes–1 hour

**SEASON:** Open daily during daylight year-round, however, the demonstration farm is most active in the summer; the farmhouse is open March–November daily except Monday from 12-4 p.m. and only on weekends out of season

**ACCESS:** No fee to tour the grounds; a fee is charged for some programs; wooded trail is not recommened for wheelchairs

**MAPS:** Available online at www.co. henrico.va.us/rec

**FACILITIES:** Restrooms, playground, horseshoes, picnic area, short fitness trail, fishing pond, nineteenth-century farm museum; sports fields and additional facilities available in adjacent R. F. & P. County Park

**SPECIAL COMMENTS:** Additional dirt trails lead south from the main loop, North Run Creek Trail. You can explore without fear of getting lost in the relatively small wood. Call Henrico County Parks at (804) 501-5108.

---

**UTM Trailhead Coordinates for Crump Park**

**UTM Zone (NAD27)**  **18S**

**Easting**  0277984

**Northing**  4172658

## ▶ IN BRIEF

Crump Park is a window into Henrico County's past, often overshadowed by the county's ongoing suburban boom. Admittedly, the park's trails are secondary to its historical resources, but they are a welcome addition. You can step back to 1860 at Meadow Farm Museum and stretch your legs in the adjacent woods. And while you're in the neighborhood, take the opportunity to drop by other sites of historic interest just down the road.

## ▶ DESCRIPTION

Officially named General Sheppard Crump Memorial Park but typically truncated to Crump Park, this unique County of Henrico parcel is more than just a county park—though it works fine as such, complete with a duck pond (stocked biannually with channel catfish), playground, and an open meadow for kite flying. The park's showcase is Elizabeth A. Crump Manor, circa 1810, now part of the Meadow Farm Museum. The manor was the

## ▶ DIRECTIONS

Crump Park is located in Glen Allen. If you're coming from I-295, exit onto Staples Mill Road (VA 33, Exit 49) heading south, then take the first left onto Mountain Road. If you're coming from the city via Staples Mill, turn right onto Mountain. Heading east on Mountain, take the third left into the park. Entering the park through a wooded buffer, you'll soon pass restrooms and an elaborate playground on the left. A field opens before you, and the road curves around it. After passing a signed connector to neighboring R. F. & P. Park on the right, park in a lot on the left. The lot faces the Sheppard family homestead, now Meadow Farm Museum. (To exit the park, continue along the one-way park road, passing a pond on the right.)

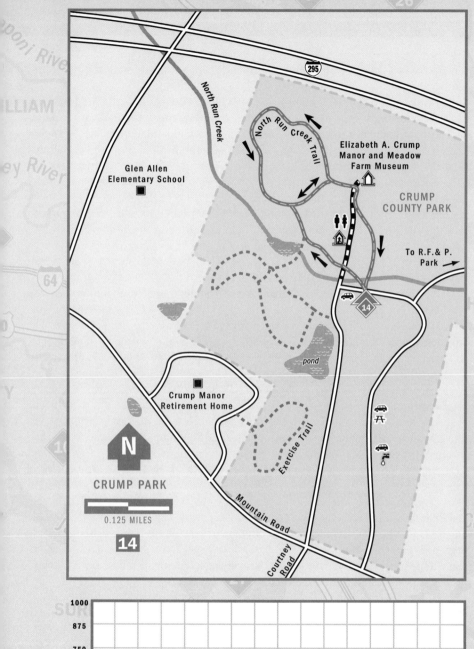

**295**

North Run Creek

North Run Creek Trail

Glen Allen Elementary School

Elizabeth A. Crump Manor and Meadow Farm Museum

CRUMP COUNTY PARK

To R.F.& P. Park →

**14**

pond

Crump Manor Retirement Home

**N**

CRUMP PARK

0.125 MILES

**14**

Exercise Trail

Mountain Road

Courtney Road

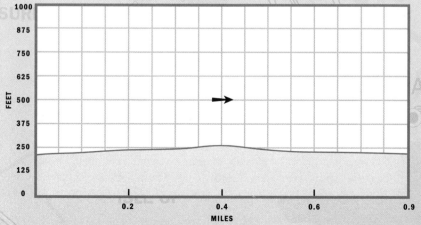

centerpiece of Meadow Farm, cultivated by the Sheppard family since the eighteenth century.

Part of a 400-acre land grant made to William Sheppard and Richard Baker in 1713, Meadow Farm was home to Sheppard's descendants until 1975, when Elizabeth Crump donated it to Henrico County in memory of her late husband, Sheppard Crump. Besides serving as the state's adjutant general (head of the Virginia National Guard), Sheppard Crump was a member of the First Caucus of the American Legion.

Costumed docents now operate the farm as a living-history museum. Some period buildings, including the tobacco barn, were relocated to the site to recreate its appearance in 1860, when the farm produced 6,000 pounds of tobacco. Although no slave quarters remain, the farm played an important role in the 1800 slave uprising known as Gabriel's Rebellion. Family slaves Tom and Pharoah warned then-patriarch Mosby Sheppard of the impending upheaval, which was orchestrated by a slave at Brookfield Plantation named Gabriel.

As a blacksmith, Gabriel was able to travel widely; this exposed him to the city's free-black community, then some 10 percent of the city's African American population. Literate, he was also aware of the successful 1791 slave uprising in Haiti. The rebellion's intricate plans (which involved killing plantation owners, burning bridges, and kidnapping the governor) were scuttled by heavy rain on August 30 and crushed when, tipped-off, Sheppard informed Governor James Monroe the following day.

Caught and imprisoned on September 23, then sent to the gallows on October 10, Gabriel was the last of 26 slaves executed for participation in the plot. In one of history's bitter ironies, the thwarted rebellion reversed a post–Revolutionary War trend toward autonomy for African Americans. Abolitionist societies, which had sprung up among Methodists and Quakers, were shut down, and freed slaves were required to vacate the commonwealth within six months under penalty of reenslavement.

Meadow Farm again played host to history on May 11, 1864, when Union general Philip Sheridan passed by, via Mountain Road, with 12,000 horsemen. (For more on the Union's 1864 advance toward Richmond, see North Anna Battlefield Park, page 150, and Cold Harbor National Battlefield, page 158.) Shortly thereafter, Sheridan's troops met J. E. B. Stuart's 3,000 soldiers at the Battle of Yellow Tavern, defeating the smaller Rebel force and mortally wounding Stuart.

A Virginia Civil War Trail sign near the parking lot explains that, during the war, Dr. John Sheppard, a physician and farmer, lived at Meadow Farm with his wife and nine children. The eldest son, Alexander Hamilton, was a guard at Libby Prison (see Belle Isle and Brown's Island, page 26), and the farm was required by an 1863 Confederate law to provide one-tenth of its crops and meat as a tax.

The sign also serves as the starting point for the route mapped here. Cross the park road onto a paved sidewalk, passing over the slender trickle of North Run Creek. A newer gravel path directs you to the left, just past a stone marker and toward the farm museum's Orientation Center. The path promptly meets a (gated) gravel road.

A sign bearing a hiker icon indicates a short trail that departs to the left. Although this spur passes an unsightly drainage pond en route, it does provide access first to the Sheppard family cemetery, now surrounded by a white picket fence, then

Historic Crump Manor, now part of the Meadow Farm Museum

to the site of a former icehouse near the park border. Though the icehouse structure is gone, a pit dug to keep ice cool remains. Ice cut from a small pond downhill from Crump Manor had to be transported to the icehouse by wagon. The path terminates at a parking lot for the adjacent Glen Allen Elementary School. It is also linked to the North Run Creek Trail loop by a north–south connector. Using that connector to access the cemetery and icehouse allows you to first examine the manor, stable, and demonstration fields.

Before heading uphill to Crump Manor, stop by the Orientation Center, where you can learn about life at Meadow Farm and arrange a tour. Proceeding to the farm, you will pass a fenced pasture, barn, and blacksmith forge on the left, and the house, flanked by great, aged holly trees, on the right. Don't overlook the field, garden, and 1860 doctor's office located behind the house.

There is a signed spur to the North Run Creek Trail loop that leaves westward from the house, between two fenced pastures. Bear right and circle the loop through former cropland now shaded by fragrant pines. Opposite the farmhouse, you will approach I-295, which, though not visible, is audible, and some adjacent homes. You will also pass the aforementioned spur trail heading south. Stay on North Run and you will circle back behind the barn before returning to the house. Head back to your vehicle on the paved walkway that passes in front of Crump Manor, and you will pass a tobacco barn and then a somewhat overgrown ice pond on the left.

Facing the park's exit is Courtney Road Service Station. Preserved by the county as it would have appeared in 1925, the station isn't open but is still worth a peek. A sign out front explains the evolution of the modern filling station.

In the opposite direction (west) along Mountain Road, Echo Lake Park merits a visit and possibly a quick stroll around the lake. Simply cross Staples Mill Road, turn right onto Springfield Road at a T intersection, and you will soon see the park on your left. Now graced by two fountains, Echo Lake was formed when residents dammed Meredith Branch in the mid-1800s.

# CUMBERLAND MARSH NATURAL AREA PRESERVE

## KEY AT-A-GLANCE INFORMATION

**LENGTH:** 4.5 miles

**CONFIGURATION:** Figure eight and balloon

**DIFFICULTY:** Easy

**SCENERY:** Bluffs overlooking marshy Holts Creek (a waterfowl haven), laurel-flanked ponds, mixed forest

**EXPOSURE:** Mostly shaded

**TRAFFIC:** Low

**TRAIL SURFACE:** Dirt

**HIKING TIME:** 2.5 hours

**SEASON:** Open daily February–October during daylight hours

**ACCESS:** No fee; bikes and pets not allowed; boardwalk is wheelchair accessible; trail not recommended for wheelchairs

**MAPS:** On signboard at trailhead

**FACILITIES:** Parking area with signboard

**SPECIAL COMMENTS:** Though part of Virginia's Natural Area Preserve network, Cumberland Marsh is owned by the Nature Conservancy and accessed through a private farm. Be respectful of rules established by these landowners, and tread lightly. Contact the Virginia Office of the Nature Conservancy at (434) 295-6106 or at www.nature.org/wherewework/northamerica/states/virginia/preserves/art1232.html. Call the Virginia Department of Conservation and Recreation Natural Heritage Program at (804) 786-7951 or visit www.dcr.virginia.gov/dnh/cumberland.htm.

**UTM Trailhead Coordinates for Cumberland Marsh Natural Area Preserve**

**UTM Zone (NAD27)  18S**

**Easting  0325020**

**Northing  4157226**

## IN BRIEF

The blufftop trail at 1,193-acre Cumberland Marsh is a bird-watcher's delight. The grassy islands and still waters of Holts Creek are a valuable stopover for migratory waterfowl traveling the Atlantic flyway and a year-round home for herons, egrets, and raptors. The level trails encircle a small pond and traverse a recovering forest.

## DESCRIPTION

Cumberland Marsh is home to the world's largest population of a rare plant called sensitive joint vetch and is one of only two preserves set aside for the plant (the other is in Cumberland County, New Jersey). Also known as Virginia joint vetch because its shrinking range is now primarily within the commonwealth, the annual legume grows to six feet and in the summer produces small, red-veined, yellow flowers. Its name derives from its reflexive fern-like leaves, which fold slightly when touched.

The plant favors the periphery of brackish tidal marshes where the soil is inundated twice

## DIRECTIONS

From Richmond take I-64 east to Exit 214. Exit onto VA 155, heading north for 2 miles. Turn right onto VA 249 and continue 2.25 miles, passing through the hamlet of New Kent before turning left onto VA 637 (look for signs for Cumberland Hospital for Children). Follow the road more than 2 miles, passing the signed end of state maintenance. Shortly beyond a white wooden fence on the right and with the hospital coming into view ahead, turn left onto a gravel road. A 20-foot cedar shades a sign for Cumberland Marsh Natural Area Preserve at this turn. Parking is available at the road's terminus near the trailhead signboard.

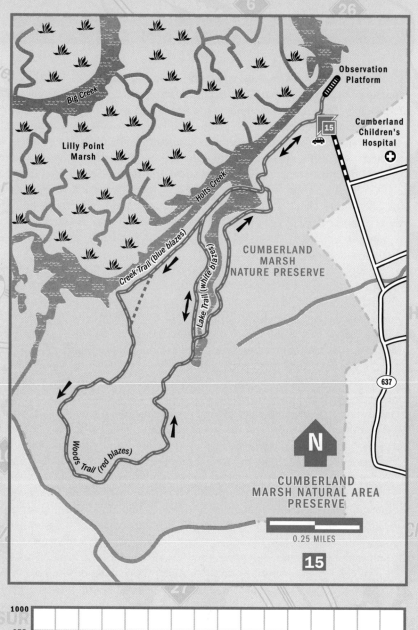

**Observation Platform**

**Cumberland Children's Hospital**

**15**

**Big Creek**

**Lilly Point Marsh**

**Holts Creek**

Creek Trail (blue blazes)

Lake Trail (white blazes)

**CUMBERLAND MARSH NATURE PRESERVE**

Woods Trail (red blazes)

**N**

**CUMBERLAND MARSH NATURAL AREA PRESERVE**

0.25 MILES

**15**

637

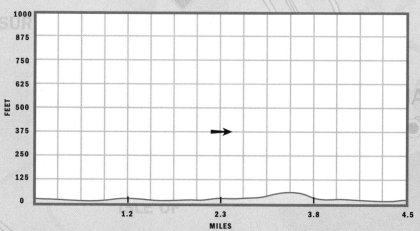

daily. Invasive reeds can overrun stands of vetch, but muskrats—like the one I saw swimming beside the pier at Cumberland Marsh—often clear the way for sensitive joint vetch by consuming perennial vegetation.

For a close-up glimpse of the plant and other native species thriving in this protected marsh, begin your hike with a brief out-and-back along the L-shaped boardwalk and pier northeast of the trailhead. Approach quietly to avoid startling the songbirds flitting among the buffer vegetation and the waterfowl bobbing about on Holts Creek. Big Creek runs beyond the flat, wooded peninsula visible before you, with Lilly Point Marsh beyond that. Holts Creek flows northeast, disappearing around a bend before its confluence with the Pamunkey River at Cumberland Thorofare, once an important shortcut for merchant vessels hauling goods downstream to the much wider York.

Though closed in the dead of winter, the preserve is open late into the fall and early in the spring, when patient visitors, armed with binoculars, can still spot wintering populations of canvasbacks, wood ducks, mallards, and of course chatty Canada geese. Springtime visitors will also find flowering mountain laurel overhanging the preserve's pond and crowding the interior double-track.

Begin your hike by heading southeast from the trailhead, passing a crop field to reach the single-track. A small sign indicates that the red-blazed Woods Trail, blue-blazed Creek Trail, and white-blazed Lake Trail initially share the same path. The field remains close at hand on your left, as the path works its way through a buffer of forest overlooking the marsh below. Though rustic, the trail remains level atop the bluff. Vines and thorn bushes thicken the surrounding forest—a collage of trees, including Northern red oak, hackberry, loblolly pine, river birch, and yellow poplar.

After curving left along an inlet, the trail intersects a dirt double-track. Turn right to approach the lower and larger of two ponds within the preserve. Originally dammed to provide water for irrigation and livestock, the pond now offers recreation and rehabilitation activities to patients at nearby Cumberland Hospital for Children.

Proceeding west with the pond on your left and a stand of pines on your right, soon come to a washout on trail right, where the soil was drastically eroded after two large pines were blown down. On my visit, one of the pines still lay atop a misshapen Old Town canoe no longer of use to the hospital. Depending on the pace of restoration, you may have to pick your way around the tree trunks and puddles here.

Ahead, the trail rises slightly to a modest ridge between the pond and marsh. After the initial stretch of winding, narrow trail, you'll welcome the airy feel of this bluff populated by chestnut oak and mountain laurel. You soon approach a trail intersection where the Lake Trail heads left. Follow this white-blazed path as it bends south and quickly rejoins the pond's shore on your left. Lofty poplars shade young beeches and holly on your right, with ferns sprouting amid the roots nearer the pond.

The still water remains close by as you progress southward, and mountain laurel crowds the shore. Gnawed stumps signal the presence of beavers. Below, on your left, the pond recedes to yield a valley of sandbars dotted with puddles. The stream running between the larger, lower pond and its uphill cousin has been reshaped by beaver activity. On my visit, a beaver dam was evident just where the stream emerges from the upper impoundment. As a sign indicates, the trail takes a sharp left here to cross the original, earthen dam. This rather narrow crossing requires careful footwork. Once across, turn left and head north.

A field extends beyond the screen of oaks on your right and continues as the pond reappears below on the right. Downed trees have been cleared here, opening the forest. Veer left with the short Yellow Trail to stay nearest the laurel and holly growing along the pond. The spur rejoins the White Trail ahead, beyond a bench shaded by a triple-trunked chestnut oak. As you near the northern edge of the pond, the trail veers right toward the field. Duck briefly back into the woods on your left to emerge at the pine-needled stretch of double-track you walked earlier. Retrace your steps, passing the washout, and regain the bluff overlooking Holts Creek.

This time, continue southwest, beyond the first trail junction, on the Creek Trail. Enjoy views of the marsh below, keeping an eye out for the spot where a lone single-track path bears right, away from the wide former roadbed. The blue-blazed trail forks from the red-blazed loop to afford a sweeping vista of the marsh. Follow the single-track as it winds through the trees along a mossy bank.

You'll soon reach a mossy promontory graced with an ancient white oak. A bench awaits just downhill. Holts Creek widens before you, with geese dotting its placid waters. From this vantage, I spotted a Northern harrier, or marsh hawk, flying low above the grassy islands. Distinguishable by the white spot on its back, the only harrier native to North America has an owl-like face and keen sense of hearing that enables it to hunt by flying near the ground.

When you're ready to continue, backtrack a few paces and look for the blue-blazed single-track that heads south (right) along an inlet of the marsh. It soon rejoins the wider Woods Trail and continues into the interior forest. Loblolly and Virginia pines shade younger hardwoods in the thicker forest ahead. Veer slightly left as you pass through a small clearing flanked by cedars, following the blazes as the path rounds its westernmost corner. Here, young laurel has sprung up in the center of the old dirt road, its forebearers pressing the double-track on either side.

The phenomenon recurs ahead, as the trail winds on to draw along a more open, forested hillside on the right. You'll soon reach a sign indicating that the path ahead is closed, and the Woods Trail makes a left onto another double-track. Follow this stretch through a more open forest, passing several sinewy hornbeams, to draw along a hill on the right. Another trail closure lies ahead, and the Woods Trail makes a second sharp left, this time onto a winding single-track. A smattering of laurel persists among the holly in this young forest, and fallen logs outline the twisting path.

Shortly after crossing a narrow water channel, proceed through a parcel of pines to approach the upper, smaller pond. The trail bends right to run nearer the water before reaching the aforementioned dam. Beyond the dam, the trail intersects the pondside path you've already trod. This time, follow the path north, back toward the marsh. Turn right upon reaching the bluff to retrace your steps back to the trailhead.

# CUMBERLAND STATE FOREST MULTIUSE TRAIL

## KEY AT-A-GLANCE INFORMATION

**LENGTH:** 8.4-mile main loop plus 3.4-mile optional loop and 4.5-mile (one-way) spur from Bear Creek Lake State Forest

**CONFIGURATION:** Loop that can be extended as a figure eight or balloon

**DIFFICULTY:** Moderate to hard (proportionate to length)

**SCENERY:** Hardwood and pine forests, creeks, Winston and Arrowhead Lakes

**EXPOSURE:** Shaded except in meadows and on roads

**TRAFFIC:** Low, but autos permitted on roads

**TRAIL SURFACE:** Dirt single-track and gravel forest roads

**HIKING TIME:** 4 hours, more with options

**SEASON:** Trails are open daily during daylight year-round; best avoided during hunting seasons (see below)

**ACCESS:** No fee to enter the forest; mountain biking and horseback riding allowed on multiuse trail; no ATVs

**MAPS:** Available at forest office and online at www.dof.virginia.gov/stforest/index-csf.shtml

**FACILITIES:** Grass parking area, forest office, picnic areas, lake boat launches, and shooting range; Bear Creek Lake State Park offers restrooms, a campground with showers, a lakeside beach, and a snack bar

**SPECIAL COMMENTS:** The state forest is open to hunting with the proper license and permission stamp. Contact the forest office at (804) 492-4121.

---

**UTM Trailhead Coordinates for Cumberland State Forest**

**UTM Zone (NAD27)  17S**

**Easting   0740089**

**Northing   4156367**

## IN BRIEF

Though it does rely on gravel forest roads to make a complete loop, the Cumberland Multiuse Trail, or CMT, features long stretches of single-track. A creekside picnic shelter near Winston Lake and subsequent stream crossings invite you to rest and refuel. Though the hiking-only Willis River Trail is also located within the forest, the CMT has the significant advantage of a loop configuration.

## DESCRIPTION

The bulk of Cumberland State Forest, like much of Virginia's state-forest system, was purchased from struggling farmers by the federal government under the New Deal–era Bankhead-Jones Farm Tenant Act. In accordance with the act, the federal government granted Virginia a 99-year lease to the land in 1939. However, in 1954 the U.S. government permanently deeded the land to the commonwealth.

Like all Virginia's state forests, Cumberland is self-sustaining, its income derived from timber and hunting-permit sales. The forest is subject to

## DIRECTIONS

From Richmond travel west on US 60. Continue through Midlothian and Powhatan to Cumberland. East of town you will pass VA 622 on the right; signs here point visitors toward Bear Creek Lake State Park. However, to reach the forest office and trailhead, continue 3 miles before turning right on VA 628. Wind along the road 3.3 miles, passing signs to indicate you've entered Cumberland State Forest. Just beyond an intersection with VA 629, the trailhead and office are straight ahead. The office, located in a brick house, is visible along the road, but trail users are advised to park in the grass outside the sometimes-locked gate. The trail leaves from the northwestern corner of the grassy area (on the left as you face the office).

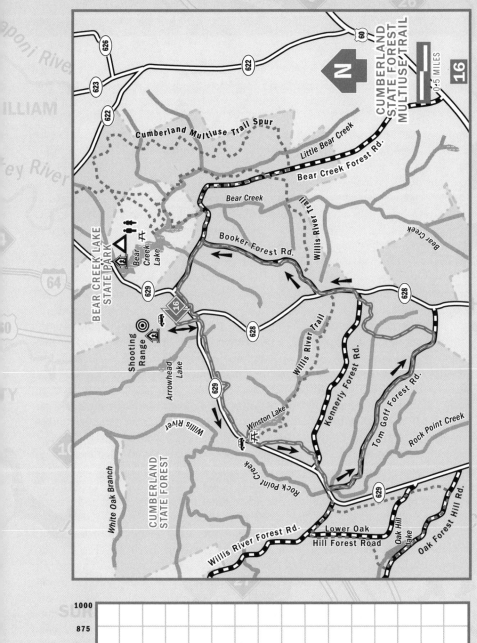

0.5 MILES

N

Saponi River

ILLIAM

rey River

64

60

Cumberland Multiuse Trail Spur

Little Bear Creek

Bear Creek Forest Rd.

Bear Creek

Booker Forest Rd.

Willis River Trail

Bear Creek

Bear Creek Lake

BEAR CREEK LAKE
STATE PARK

629

16

Shooting Range

Arrowhead Lake

629

628

628

Willis River Trail

Kennerly Forest Rd.

Tom Goff Forest Rd.

Rock Point Creek

HEWS

TY

Winston Lake

Willis River

White Oak Branch

CUMBERLAND
STATE FOREST

Rock Point Creek

629

Oak Hill Lake

Chesap

Bay

Willis River Forest Rd.

Lower Oak
Hill Forest Road

Oak Forest Hill Rd.

10

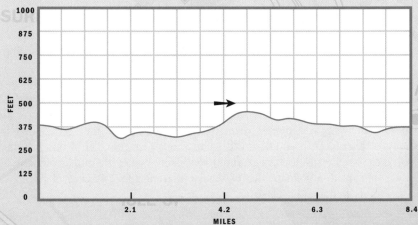

SU

WIGHT

AMPT

NORFOLK

| FEET | | | | |
|------|---|---|---|---|
| 1000 | | | | |
| 875 | | | | |
| 750 | | | | |
| 625 | | | | |
| 500 | | | | |
| 375 | | | | |
| 250 | | | | |
| 125 | | | | |
| 0 | 2.1 | 4.2 | 6.3 | 8.4 |

MILES

thinning, and even large-scale logging, but is also charged with education, watershed protection, and recreation. Cumberland's four lakes, Bonbrook, Arrowhead, Oak Hill, and Winston, offer anglers boat launches and the chance to vie for largemouth bass, sunfish, and channel catfish. The forest also operates a wheelchair-accessible sporting-clay range. The forest's 16-mile end-to-end Willis River Trail and the hiking trails in adjacent Bear Creek Lake State Park are profiled separately within this guide (see pages 235 and 18, respectively).

The area's variety of recreation makes it a good candidate for an extended visit. However, camping is allowed only within Bear Creek Lake State Park. Day hikers are advised to use the Cumberland Multiuse Trail's forestry-office trailhead, as they can pick up maps at the office and avoid the state park's fee. Campers should also consider using this trailhead, which is linked to the CMT's main loop by a mere 0.2-mile spur. The spur trail from the state park departs near the campground but connects to the CMT's main loop only after 4.5 miles, making for a 17.4-mile balloon hike. It is also possible to use the state park's Running Cedar, Lakeside, and Circumferential Trails to reach the CMT at Booker Forest Road after 2 miles.

When beginning from the forestry-office trailhead, leave southbound along a power-line clearing to reach VA 629. A thin barrier of trees separates this corridor from the grassy field on trail left. You'll spot the first of many light-blue blazes along this stretch. Combined with marked turns, these make the CMT relatively easy to follow. After crossing the road, the narrow spur path terminates at its junction with the Cumberland Multiuse Trail's main loop. Bearing right (west), follow the single-track as it parallels VA 629. The lightly trafficked road remains close for more than a mile, but hikers may not realize that after crossing a streamlet and curving up a modest rise.

After drawing within sight of the road again, the CMT makes a left onto an old logging road. The trail curves eastward before cutting right through young hardwoods. The route makes a 90-degree left for a short double-track segment. The CMT soon turns right, passing beneath yellow poplars to enter a pine thicket. I found the trail dishearteningly overgrown here, but it was an isolated problem.

The CMT winds slightly beneath mixed forest, heading steadily southwest toward Winston Lake. The trail emerges beside VA 629 just before the lake's gravel access road. Follow it left to enjoy a serene vista across placid waters, bordered by green lily pads in the summer. Walk the dam then turn right at the spillway to follow the stream that flows north toward the Willis River. Strewn with moss- and lichen-spotted boulders, this noisy brook appears relocated from Appalachia. You can enjoy a respite at the log-and-stone picnic shelter here before crossing a footbridge and ascending a stone stairway to rejoin the CMT. The trail continues briefly along the road before turning left and rising amid towering white pines.

Atop a mixed-pine ridgeline, the CMT follows a dirt road that eventually meets gravel Kennerly Forest Road. However, the CMT makes a right before the junction, heading west and downhill to cross Kennerly shortly before reaching VA 629 on a sharp curve. This is the westernmost point of the main loop and the access point for the CMT's smaller loop around Oak Hill Lake. Though roughly half of this 3.5-mile spur loop is on gravel roads, it offers charming views of the small lake and an old farm nearby. Hikers can make a balloon hike of the loop, using the 2.8 miles of the CMT just described as an out-and-back string.

To avail yourself of the optional loop, head west along VA 629, crossing over Rock Point Creek, then turn right onto Willis River Forest Road. After a gradual rise and descent, make a left onto Lower Oak Hill Forest Road. Meadows alternate with stands of pine beside this mostly level grade. Back on a dirt path, the trail heads southwest, eventually crossing the creek. The trail then rises to meet Oak Hill Forest Road. Turn left and follow the gravel road along the southwestern shore of the lake. Steadily climbing, the road passes meadows on the right, often dotted with wildflower blooms, then a pair of weathered barns on the left. Before the road's terminus at VA 629, the CMT departs to the left. This earthen stretch dips to traverse the drainage that feeds Oak Hill Lake, then rises again to cross Lower Oak Hill Forest Road. A long climb is rewarded with a leisurely descent as the trail heads north toward the main loop.

The CMT proper heads south from VA 629, soon reaching a wet crossing. Over the next 2 miles, the trail follows a ridge, joining a dirt double-track for much of the journey. In the midst of loblolly pines, the CMT bisects a meadow where hikers can expect to find Queen Anne's lace and goldenrod in the summer. The trail turns left after emerging onto earthen Goff Forest Road.

Pass a privately owned parcel on trail right, before the CMT turns left again, following a small ridge then descending through a tunnel of young pines. The CMT climbs out of the valley to turn right, heading toward Kennerly Forest Road. Upon meeting the road, turn right to cross VA 628. Fronting a logged expanse, look left for a power-line clearing. The CMT travels north through this corridor to meet Booker Forest Road, then turns right. Hikers can choose to avoid the sometimes soggy and overgrown clearing by following VA 628 then making the first right onto Booker.

Generally level, Booker is the first of two lengthy gravel-road walks. At the junction with Bear Creek Forest Road, there is a spur from the state park on the right. The CMT's main loop heads left, downhill, to bridge a small creek. At 7.5 miles, the trail begins its final climb beneath Virginia pines. Then, just as the walking levels, the CMT cuts left onto a single-track path, while the the forest road reaches VA 629. This final CMT segment parallels VA 629 before crossing VA 628. The forest office and trailhead are then visible to the right, with the loop's first junction just ahead.

Now, what to expect if you elect to reach the main loop via the 4.5-mile spur from Bear Creek Lake State Park: first, expect to trail blaze around downed trees and muddy patches—easily accomplished but annoying. The spur sets out on a well-trod, pine-needled path, but it is evident that the trail sees less use as it winds southward away from the park. As the pines recede, take note of the many species represented in this oak-dominated forest, including broad-leafed bear oaks, dark-trunked black oaks, and bottomland water oaks.

Following an old dirt road, the trail includes seasonal wet crossings and takes you across a final creek on a concrete bridge before turning right. Now on a single-track segment, descend to a birch glade before crossing Little Bear Creek. Just uphill, the route turns right again onto Bear Creek Forest Road, which heads north along a pine ridge before turning left and dipping into Bear Creek Valley. The road straddles the 15-foot-wide creek on a wooden bridge.

As noted above, the state forest envelops Bear Creek Lake State Park (see page 18), which features swimming, fishing, camping, and a network of shorter hiking trails. The 16-mile end-to-end Willis River Trail (page 235) also traverses Cumberland State Forest.

# DEEP RUN PARK

## KEY AT-A-GLANCE INFORMATION

**LENGTH:** 1.7 miles

**CONFIGURATION:** Loop

**DIFFICULTY:** Moderate

**SCENERY:** Suburban woods, duck pond

**EXPOSURE:** Mostly shaded, open around pond

**TRAFFIC:** Moderate (higher near pond)

**TRAIL SURFACE:** Paved

**HIKING TIME:** 1 hour

**SEASON:** Open daily during daylight year-round

**ACCESS:** No fee

**MAPS:** Available online at www.co.henrico.va.us/rec

**FACILITIES:** Restrooms, fitness trail, soccer fields, basketball courts, playgrounds, pond (fishing allowed), nature center with boardwalk, recreation center under construction

**SPECIAL COMMENTS:** In 2004 Henrico County began construction of a ´recreation center at Deep Run. The route mapped here remained passable initially, but construction will temporarily inhibit a complete circuit. Plans for the rec center permit the restoration of the necessary trails upon its completion. In the meantime, feel free to explore the additional dirt trails that zigzag between and around the paved routes. The park is relatively small, so you can't get lost for long. Contact Henrico County Parks at (804) 501-5108 for more information.

---

UTM Trailhead Coordinates for
Deep Run Park

UTM Zone (NAD27)   18S

Easting   0271648

Northing   4167150

## IN BRIEF

Shrouded in suburbs, Deep Run Park is a welcome retreat, and the throngs of families, dog walkers, and couples who flock here on sunny weekends attest to its popularity.

## DESCRIPTION

The centerpiece of Deep Run Park, nestled within Richmond's sprawling West End, is a bilevel pond encircled by a paved trail. Couples stroll by as youngsters timidly cast breadcrumbs to a gaggle of Canada geese that has made a permanent stopover of the small pond. Rambunctious schoolchildren frolic on the playground uphill, and teens play three-on-three on the adjacent basketball court after class. Fitness-conscious suburbanites tackle the exercise trail on their way home from work, and after-dinner dog-walkers make their daily rounds.

A forlorn bobber hanging from a limb on the bank testifies to the occasional angler; however, a sign forbids swimming, boating, and ice-skating. Another instructs those fishing that there is a two-catch limit. Most fishing on this small body of water is probably catch-and-release, although the nearby picnic shelter often hosts weekend barbecues, so no one goes hungry.

## DIRECTIONS

From Richmond take I-64 to Exit 180A and follow Gaskins Road south past Three Chopt Road to Ridgefield Parkway. Turn right and then right again into the park. You will pass one parking lot on the right upon entering. This lot is most convenient to the fitness trail, basketball court, playground, and pond. A second lot, also on the right, is closer to restrooms and the nature pavilion. This lot is the trailhead for the hike described here. A third lot provides access to soccer fields, restrooms, and a very elaborate playground.

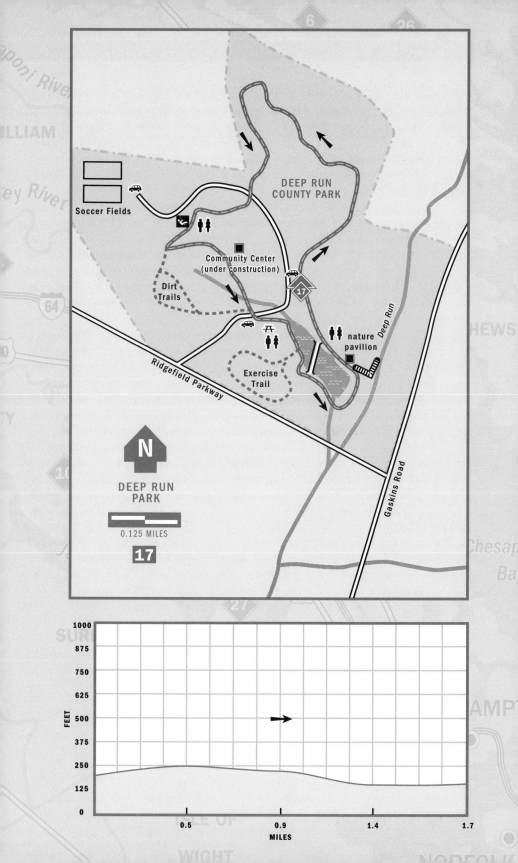

A wooden walkway bisects the pond atop the dam that splits it into two levels. A gazebo and a wooden deck allow for gazing out upon the pond's lower level, and wooden bridges cross the creek that flows from the pond to join the Deep Run in the marshland near Gaskins Road. The nature pavilion on the pond's northern shore is girded with extensive wooden decking, complete with a gazebo and lofty boardwalk leading northeast for perhaps 100 yards to a wildlife-viewing station overlooking Deep Run.

Fallen trees, chainsawed and moved aside, are evidence of ongoing maintenance. River birch, willow oak, and sweetgum dominate the forest. At the center of the nature pavilion is a small building, restricted to park staff, the walls of which feature several dioramas and posters. These educational displays describe the habitats and wildlife of the Mid-Atlantic; those depicting snakes and bats are sure to amuse curious schoolchildren. In addition to giving pro-conservation and anti-littering messages, the pavilion presents an outlook for the future of the Henrico County Parks Department.

Though the water side sees most of the action at Deep Run Park (excluding the soccer fields, which teem with participants and parents in spring and fall), the trail circumnavigating the park totals only 0.4 miles. Fortunately, additional trails will raise the total to a more respectable 2.3 miles. The 1.7-mile route mapped here, the most efficient circuit through Deep Run Park, begins from the top of the second parking lot, heading north (away from the entrance). No need to lace up your hiking boots; tennis shoes will do on the paved trails. In a few spots, seeps wet the trail, but they are easily avoided. Deep Run is a handy spot for joggers who would rather avoid the traffic of nearby modern suburbs, which seldom feature sidewalks. Note, however, that the fitness trail alone totals a meager 0.3 miles.

Affording up-close glimpses of nature, unofficial dirt trails crisscross the woods in the park's northern and western sections. You may well spy a band of mountain bikers tackling the latter. One can readily stray from the route described here with little fear of getting lost. You may well arrive in an apartment complex or someone's back yard, but you'll never have to backtrack too far to hit one of the paved loops. Through the winter-bare woods, hikers can glimpse the roofs of surrounding suburban homes on even the paved trails. Thick with summer vegetation, however, the forest becomes a verdant cloister, a delightful respite just a short drive from the much-vaunted shopper's paradise at Short Pump.

American holly is scattered throughout the understory of this relatively mature, largely red-oak forest. Trees en route are identified with signs to provide budding botanists a chance to test their tree-identifications skills. Labeled species include red and white oak, pignut hickory, loblolly pine, red maple, dogwood, red cedar, sweetgum, yellow poplar, and the less-common ironwood, so named for its hefty, solid wood. The relatively short (20 to 30 feet tall) ironwood is also referred to as the eastern hophornbeam owing to its hops-like seed pods. Real hops, which lend beer its aroma and bitterness, are grown on poles. The specie's scientific name, *Ostrya virginiana,* is one of many that early naturalists named for the commonwealth despite its presence throughout the eastern United States.

After tracing the park's border uphill, the trail bears sharply left and descends slightly. Cross the park road carefully and bear right. You'll soon pass the picnic shelter, restrooms, and elaborate playground that front the largest parking lot, which serves the soccer fields in the park's western corner. A gravel-and-dirt trail continues around the fields and accesses the neighboring apartments. Make a left turn, however, staying on the pavement. Bear right at the upcoming intersection and descend along a pretty, rocky rivulet flanked with cedars. It's here that construction of the rec center may interrupt your loop.

Dirt paths carved by cyclists west of the paved ones provide a temporary way to circumvent blocked trails and are well worth exploring. As is often the case with mountain-bike trails, the network defies cartography. However, it is sufficiently compact that you can't wander too far, and you're as likely to encounter pedestrians as cyclists. Presumably, upon the center's completion, the paved route will be more or less restored and you'll be able to descend from the park's westernmost trail toward the first parking area and the pond.

Upon doing so, cross the park road again and pass the parking lot on your right. By hiking the trails as described here, you save the pond and nature pavilion for last. The advantage is that you can take a load off on one of the benches overlooking the pond to watch the ducks and geese beg for handouts. If you're hiking with youngsters still full of vim and vigor, let them romp at the playground or, if they're older, perhaps make a quick loop of the fitness trail above the pond on the south. Numerous pathways diverge from, but quickly rejoin, the pond loop.

To return to your car, follow either the park road or the pathway just beyond the restrooms northwest of the nature center. The second parking lot is a short stroll from the pond through a primarily pine wood dappled with cedars.

# DOREY PARK

## KEY AT-A-GLANCE INFORMATION

**LENGTH:** 2.1 miles plus optional 2.6-mile adjacent mountain-bike trail

**CONFIGURATION:** Figure eight

**DIFFICULTY:** Easy

**SCENERY:** Woods, duck pond

**EXPOSURE:** Mostly shaded, open around pond

**TRAFFIC:** Moderate (higher near pond)

**TRAIL SURFACE:** Paved and gravel

**HIKING TIME:** 45 minutes

**SEASON:** Open daily during daylight year-round

**ACCESS:** No fee

**MAPS:** Available online at www.co.henrico.va.us/rec

**FACILITIES:** Restrooms, fitness trail, equestrian trail, disc-golf course, soccer fields, baseball and softball fields, tennis courts, playground, pond (fishing allowed), adjacent recreation center

**SPECIAL COMMENTS:** More than 2.6 miles of well-designed mountain-bike trails make the most of limited space at Dorey Park. These can be linked to the route mapped here and are suitable for hiking, except on crowded weekends. Equestrian trails on the opposite (eastern) half of the park exceed 3 miles. Contact Henrico County Parks at (804) 501-5108 for more information.

**UTM Trailhead Coordinates for Dorey Park**

**UTM Zone (NAD27)** 18S

**Easting** 0292956

**Northing** 4148331

## IN BRIEF

Just south of Richmond International Airport, Dorey Park is a model county park. The well-maintained facilities cater to a range of interests, from tee-ball to horseback riding. By combining a stroll around the pond, a brief jaunt into the woods, and a loop of the exercise trail, it's easy to string together a couple of miles on wide gravel paths. Elongate your hike by venturing onto the mountain-bike single-track, which connects to the hiking trail in the southern reaches of the park, near the disc-golf course, and extends northward past the ball fields.

## DESCRIPTION

Dorey Park offers the citizens of eastern Henrico County a veritable smorgasbord of recreational activities. Besides numerous sports, including tennis and disc (a.k.a. Frisbee) golf, the park accom-

## DIRECTIONS

From Richmond take I-64 to Exit 195 and travel south on South Laburnum Avenue to Darbytown Road. Turn left, and the park entrance will be on your right after you pass under VA 895 (Pocahontas Parkway). An open field and a Virginia Civil War Trail marker signal the upcoming turn. From I-295, take Exit 22, and then take VA 5 (New Market Road) northwest and make the third right onto Doran Road. Proceed north until the road terminates at Darbytown Road. Turn left, and the park entrance will soon be visible on your left. Once inside, follow the main road, passing soccer fields on the left and the Dorey Park Recreation Center, in a converted barn, on the right. Continue through a gate, passing ball fields and the equestrian center, then park in a lot on the left at the road's end. The lot fronts a large playground and picnic shelters; the pond is visible a short distance to the south.

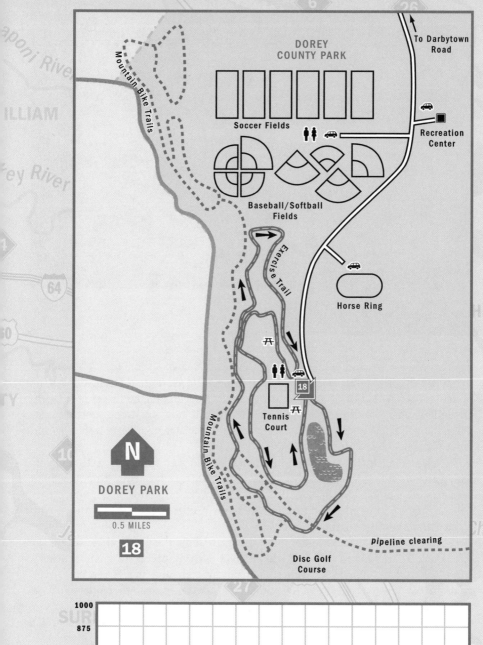

**DOREY COUNTY PARK**

Soccer Fields

Baseball/Softball Fields

Mountain Bike Trails

Exercise Trail

To Darbytown Road

Recreation Center

Horse Ring

Tennis Court

Mountain Bike Trails

**N**

**DOREY PARK**

0.5 MILES

18

Disc Golf Course

Pipeline clearing

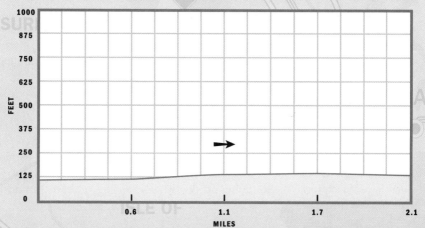

Take a stroll around Dorey Park, then enjoy a picnic beneath a pondside weeping willow.

modates equestrians and mountain bikers. You may even spot some fishermen around the park's five-acre pond as you head out. Though no more than ten feet deep, the pond has been part of the Virginia Department of Game and Inland Fisheries (VDGIF) Urban Program since its inception in 1993. The VDGIF now stocks the pond with catfish, although some anglers are lucky enough to land largemouth bass, bluegill, and redear sunfish.

Stay to the left along the pond's eastern edge and pass a wooden deck, complete with gazebo, jutting out over the water. Two fountains located within the pond enhance the park-like atmosphere. Pass beneath a weeping willow, under which park benches invite you to relax and toss crumbs to the resident geese. Soon turn left onto a gravel trail, heading southwest into the woods.

The park's designated hiking trail, this path abuts the disc-golf course on the left. Along its length you will find labeled trees such as sweetgum, pignut hickory, white oak, and red maple. In wintertime, spindly holly and shaggy red cedar lend color to the forest understory. An abundance of labeled species renders this an informative outing for the budding naturalist.

After passing through a pipeline clearing, bear right. The mountain-bike trail's switchbacks are visible downhill to the left. Ahead, a spur trail to the right recrosses the pipeline clearing to meet the hiking-trail loop on its return to the pond; however, you should continue downhill to cross the clearing and head north near the park's western border.

The single-track bike trail runs parallel to the gravel hiking loop and intermittently connects to it. The trail is a boon to area mountain bikers, clearly signed and well built, with an extensive boardwalk through boggy forest in its northern reaches. But the route is not so popular with bikers as to preclude foot traffic. If you have the time and ambition to extend your hike, it's a viable option. The twists, turns, and piled-log obstacles may be more fun on two wheels, but hikers have an easier time circumventing downed trees and muddy spots. On my visit, ongoing post-storm maintenance obscured the trail along the ball fields, but things looked to be on the mend.

The wide, level hiking loop is free of obstacles and conducive to both leisurely strolls and jogging. If you're out for exercise, the park's fitness trail, the northern loop of this figure-eight route, offers the chance to augment your run with pull-ups, sit-ups, and the like. Continue straight on where a trail heads to the right (this is the hiking loop doubling back), and soon a wooden post with metal handles will signal the start of the fitness trail. Bear left here—after making use of the wooden post if you can. Its instructional sign now missing, one can only guess what exercise the post facilitates.

After completing most of the fitness loop, you will cross a small gulch on a wooden footbridge. As you face the parking lot, the trail promptly doubles back to recross the gulch and veers left to pass along a small field and return to the intersection distinguished by the enigmatic post. Head south (left) here to retrace your steps along the connector trail. Next, turn left to traverse the remaining portion of the hiking loop, which emerges along the pond. Turn left to follow the pond's western shore and return to your vehicle.

While in the vicinity of Dorey Park, Civil War buffs may want to visit the Fort Harrison unit of Richmond National Battlefield Park, located southwest of the park. To reach it, take Darbytown Road out of the park, turn right onto Doran Road, then turn right on VA 5 (New Market Road). A final left onto Battlefield Park Road takes you through the battlefield before you reach a turnaround at the James River.

# DUTCH GAP CONSERVATION AREA

## KEY AT-A-GLANCE INFORMATION

**LENGTH:** 8 miles

**CONFIGURATION:** Out-and-back

**DIFFICULTY:** Moderate

**SCENERY:** Tidal flats along an old channel of the James River

**EXPOSURE:** Open with limited shade

**TRAFFIC:** Low

**TRAIL SURFACE:** Dirt-and-gravel double-track

**HIKING TIME:** 3.5 hours

**SEASON:** Open daily during daylight year-round

**ACCESS:** Fee for adjacent Henricus Historical Park only

**MAPS:** Available on park literature at visitor center

**FACILITIES:** Visitor center, restrooms, picnic tables, bird-identification trail, re-created Colonial Citie of Henricus

**SPECIAL COMMENTS:** Dutch Gap Conservation Area is owned and managed by Chesterfield County. It encompasses Henricus Historical Park, a re-creation of the 1611 Citie of Henricus settlement operated by the independent Henricus Foundation. Contact Chesterfield County Parks at (804) 748-1623 or visit www.co.chesterfield.va.us/tourism/d_gap.asp. Information is also available from the Henricus Visitor Center at (804) 706-1340.

---

**UTM Trailhead Coordinates for Dutch Gap Conservation Area**

**UTM Zone (NAD27)**   18S

**Easting**   0290763

**Northing**   4138850

## ▶ IN BRIEF

The 810-acre Dutch Gap Conservation Area abuts Henricus Historical Park (see page 106), site of an English settlement just four years younger than Jamestown. The area's present topography bears the scars of four centuries of human manipulation, beginning with the moat-building project for which it was named. Yet nature persists undaunted, and this hike, which traces a tidal inlet of the James that was formerly an oxbow bend in the river, affords you the chance to escape civilization into a marsh teeming with wildlife.

## ▶ DESCRIPTION

Dutch Gap Conservation Area is undergoing a resurgence. In partnership with the City of Richmond and Henrico and Chesterfield Counties, the Henricus Foundation has spearheaded the re-creation of the 1611 Citie of Henricus within the conservation area. The area has benefited from a new visitor center and, happily, new visitors. Many visitors are quite content to tour the historic sites and gawk at the widening James

## ▶ DIRECTIONS

From I-95 southeast of Richmond, take Exit 61 and follow VA 10 (Iron Bridge Road) east. Turn right at the first stoplight onto VA 732 (Old Stage Road). From I-295 take Exit 15 and follow VA 10 west for 3.5 miles before turning right onto VA 732. Head north on VA 732, and turn right upon reaching a T intersection with VA 615 (Coxendale Road). After passing Dominion Power's Chesterfield Power Station, turn right onto Henricus Road, and follow it 2 miles to Dutch Gap Conservation Area. North of the parking lot is the re-created Citie of Henricus, with a precipice overlooking the James beyond it. On the east is the visitor center. The Dutch Gap Trail, which this hike follows, starts behind it.

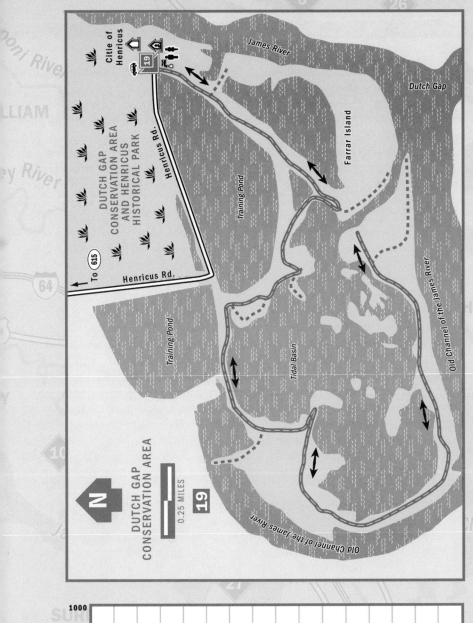

James River

Dutch Gap

Citie of Henricus

Farrar Island

DUTCH GAP
CONSERVATION AREA
AND HENRICUS
HISTORICAL PARK

Henricus Rd.

Training Pond

Old Channel of the James River

Training Pond

Tidal Basin

To 615

Henricus Rd.

64

19

N

DUTCH GAP
CONSERVATION AREA

0.25 MILES

Old Channel of the James River

Chesape
Bay

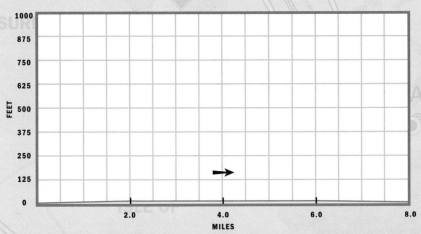

1000
875
750
625
500
375
250
125
0

FEET

2.0          4.0          6.0          8.0

MILES

from (renamed) Pocahontas Bluff, leaving the southern bulk of the conservation area to those with a few hours to spare—and some insect repellant.

Enthusiastic bird-watchers have long known about Dutch Gap's blue-heron rookery, and you may pass some enthusiasts, binoculars in hand, scanning the non-tidal marsh on the left of Henricus Road en route to the parking area. The 4-mile, one-way Dutch Gap Trail, your pathway for this hike, even has a ten-station ornithology trail, the work of an aspiring Eagle Scout. In addition to garden-variety species such as the tufted titmouse and the chickadee, the trail notes barred-owl and screech-owl habitats.

Dutch Gap Trail makes its out-and-back journey along a narrow spit of land that practically encircles a tidal lagoon dotted by small islands and the crumbling remains of old wooden barges. The present lagoon was formerly a sand-and-gravel quarry, and the channel cut to fill it now prevents the trail from connecting in a full circle. On its other, outer edge, the trail is ringed by an old channel of the James River. The antiquated nomenclature for this peninsula, Farrar's Island, recalls the river's eighteenth-century route. It was once an island, if only in times of high water.

Successive efforts have sought to manipulate and truncate the river's course. It was not long after English colonists established the Citie of Henricus, named for King James's son Henry, that Sir Thomas Dale orchestrated the construction of a moat to protect the settlement. He employed a Dutch technique and the resulting waterway was termed Dale's Dutch Gap. During the War Between the States, Union troops under the command of General Benjamin Butler began to excavate a canal across the Dutch Gap in order that the Union Navy might proceed upstream out of reach of Confederate cannon fire. The canal was completed with a bang—literally—when an explosion breached the dam in 1865. The James was redirected again to its present course in the 1930s. That final extension of the canal created Hatcher's Island to the north.

Though the quarry is flooded, industry remains close as you begin this hike. As the trail heads south, a fence looms uphill on the right. Behind it lies a flyash pond, part of the adjacent coal-fired Dominion Power plant. Such ponds are required by law as a means of collecting industrial pollutants. In some stretches, the trail passes directly beside this pond and its twin to the west. And while they mar the first third of the hike, it is fortuitous that they are fenced and quiet. If the birds don't mind, why should we? Simply focus your attention on the waterside woods.

Proceeding south on a roomy double-track, you will pass two spur trails on the left. The first leads to a fishing point, the second to a wildlife-viewing area. Beyond, veer left, away from the hillside, to pass a small freshwater pond, also the remnant of a 1920s mining operation. It's speculated that miners tapped into a spring, which keeps the pit flooded to this day. Continue southwest to the water's edge, where tables invite a picnic. On your left is a stand of bald cypress, and across the water your halfway point, mile 4. However, you've got to take the long way (unless you've brought a kayak).

Backtrack briefly then bear left before the freshwater pond to reach a small field with an inlet to the south (left). The trail then turns left into a wooded area—where I spotted several white-tailed deer bounding through the trees—before cutting sharply right. Pass along the edge of the lagoon before bearing right again for a short northward stint. The trail turns left and grazes the second flyash pond, with the terrain descending sharply to the lagoon.

You will soon see the end of the old river channel on the right of the narrow finger of land you are hiking. You will follow it with the lagoon to your left, until you reverse course. Visible on the lagoon side are the remains of wooden barges, which provide a sheltering habitat to aquatic life. You may spy anglers casting from small boats within the lagoon. Sadly, you will occasionally spot debris along the shore, a reminder that rubbish cast overboard eventually washes ashore.

Next, the trail cuts east onto a small peninsula within the lagoon, formerly the site of a hunting lodge and presently home to maintenance buildings. Upon reaching the water's edge, scan the lagoon for islands that dot its eastern half. These formed through silt accumulation, which put sandy flesh on the skeletons of discarded barges. Cattails and grasses took root, expediting the accumulation of soil.

Bear left as you leave the peninsula to trace the lagoon's southern rim. As the epicenter of activity recedes behind you, your odds for spotting wildlife increase. Besides blue herons, you'll likely spot black cormorants (whose name was derived from the Latin for "sea crow") bobbing on the water, distinguishable by the their long, periscope-like necks. Keep your eyes peeled not only for large waterfowl but also for long-billed kingfishers and hawk-like osprey, both of which dive underwater to grasp their prey.

After the trail bends to head eastward, you'll notice a change in the surrounding vegetative character. Sandy soil, scattered with pebbles, and slightly higher elevation produce a small glade of twisting, scrubby oaks. There are even a few cacti on the trailside. It was here that I spotted two black snakes intertwined. I gawked for a moment, then gave the couple a wide berth; they were more likely rat snakes than copperheads, but I didn't need to find out.

As the narrow ring of land about the lagoon widens, an L-shaped spur trail heads left into thick woods. Often, pools of black water glisten below tree trunks along this spur. The trail's terminus lies ahead, marked by a modest wooden railing. Of course, your hike is only half over. As you retrace your route along the semicircular peninsula, be mindful of details you may have overlooked before, and avail yourself of the spur trails you bypassed on the way out.

While at Dutch Gap, don't overlook the hike past Henricus Historical Park and west along the James (see page 106). The route couples an informative overview of the 1611 Citie of Henricus with a pleasant riparian stroll. It also passes north of Dutch Gap's great blue-heron rookery.

# FLUVANNA HERITAGE TRAIL

## KEY AT-A-GLANCE INFORMATION

**LENGTH:** 7.7 miles but can be hiked one-way with a shuttle

**CONFIGURATION:** Out-and-back

**DIFFICULTY:** Moderate

**SCENERY:** Hillside forest and bottomland along the Rivanna River

**EXPOSURE:** Mostly shaded, more open near trailheads

**TRAFFIC:** Low

**TRAIL SURFACE:** Dirt

**HIKING TIME:** 3.5 hours

**SEASON:** Open daily during daylight year-round

**ACCESS:** No fee; the full route is not recommended for wheelchairs, but the first 0.5 miles follows an accessible trail, made of crushed gravel, to the riverside

**MAPS:** Available at trailhead; a low-resolution version is available online at www.fluvannaheritage.org

**FACILITIES:** Eastern parking area has a signboard, trash cans, and portable toilets; western trailhead offers water and picnic tables at the Pole Barns and sports fields at Pleasant Grove

**SPECIAL COMMENTS:** The term Fluvanna Heritage Trail is collectively applied to a network of hiking and equestrian trails west of the Rivanna River. In 2004 the Fluvanna Heritage Trail Foundation opened a rail trail in Palmyra across the river. Contact Fluvanna County Parks at (431) 842-3150.

---

**UTM Trailhead Coordinates for Fluvanna Heritage Trail**

**UTM Zone (NAD27)  17S**

**Easting  0740099**

**Northing  4193662**

## ▶ IN BRIEF

A descent from the eastern trailhead to a pebbled shoal on the Rivanna River affords hikers an up-close encounter with the waterway they will only glimpse through the trees for most of this out-and-back. After running along hilly bluffs between recovering forest and a riparian floodplain, the route ventures to a second overlook at Burke Creek then uphill to the former Haden farmstead.

## ▶ DESCRIPTION

Fluvanna's history is inseparable from that of the Rivanna River, which bisects the county and meets the James on its eastern border. Besides providing water to farms, the river powered mills and carried crops to market. The Fluvanna Heritage Trail traces the river's western shore, opposite the hamlet of Palmyra, itself a tribute to the area's rich past.

The names Fluvanna County and Rivanna River are both vestiges of the reign of Queen Anne, for whom English colonists also named the North and South Anna Rivers. The name Fluvanna—the

## ▶ DIRECTIONS

From Richmond follow I-64 northwest to Exit 136. Take VA 15 south about 9 miles to Palmyra. Just beyond the small town and across the Rivanna River, make a right onto VA 53. The turn for the eastern trailhead is located 0.3 miles from VA 15 on the right. It is marked by a small sign, and there is a gravel parking area uphill. To reach the western trailhead, continue 1.5 miles on VA 53, then turn right. Parking is available at the Pleasant Grove athletic fields, on the right a quarter mile ahead. A sign beneath a large oak signals the trail, reached via the gravel double-track past the old Haden family farmhouse and Pole Barns picnic shelter. Charlottesville residents can reach the trail by following VA 53 southeast for 15 miles from its junction with VA 20.

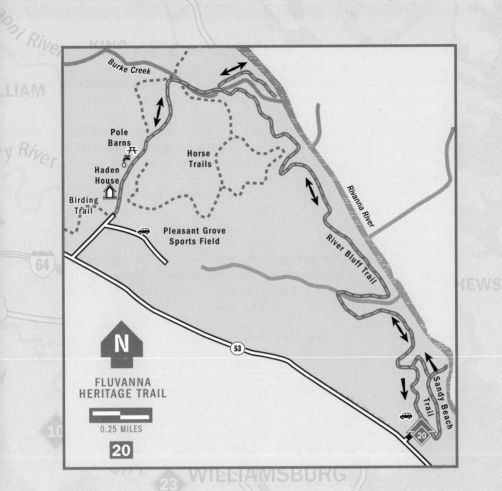

Burke Creek

Pole
Barns

Horse
Trails

Haden
House

Birding
Trail

Pleasant Grove
Sports Field

Rivanna River

River Bluff Trail

Sandy Beach
Trail

**N**

FLUVANNA
HERITAGE TRAIL

0.25 MILES

20

53

20

64

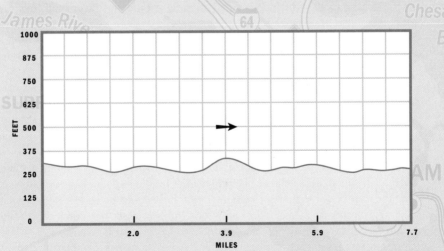

FEET

1000
875
750
625
500
375
250
125
0

2.0          3.9          5.9          7.7

MILES

Latin equivilant of Rivanna—was applied to the James west of its confluence with the Rivanna River. Its usage was later abandoned.

Fluvanna County was founded in 1777, in the midst of the Revolutionary War. Yet the fledgling county's population more than tripled, to 3,300, in its first five years. In 1824 Fluvanna's multi-denominational Brick Meetinghouse (present-day Brick Union Baptist) was built under the supervision of prominent landowner General John Hartwell Cocke, who like his friend Thomas Jefferson was a Renaissance yeoman. The citizenry found occasion to erect a jail in 1829, today the Old Stone Jail Museum. The brick courthouse, with a stone classical portico, remains a fixture of quaint Palmyra. Coke was also the catalyst behind construction of the courthouse two years later. The original courthouse is an architectural gem, largely because it never suffered the indignity of addition or modernization. The 1813 gristmill just south of town along the Rivanna wasn't so lucky. Union troops burned Palmyra Mills in 1865.

Rebuilt, the mill remained in use through the Depression and is now being converted to a park, with hopes that it will ultimately be linked by footpath to the Heritage Trail and half-mile Heritage Rail Trail. The latter is a pleasant, level stroll that begins opposite the new county offices on Main Street.

Pick up a map brochure from the signboard at the hilltop eastern trailhead before setting out on the gravel path that leaves westward past mile marker 0. You'll spy these markers frequently along the network's backbone path, the River Bluff Trail. Go straight on the Sandy Beach Trail when the grassy River Bluff Trail heads left. Follow the gravel switchbacks through a sloping meadow, where young cedars have pushed their way through a tangle of thorns and vines.

Before reaching the riverside, the path curves through a sycamore-dominated wood to reach another trail junction. You will return here to access the River Bluff Trail, but first follow the Sandy Beach Trail through a meadow brightened by goldenrod and orange jewelweed in the summer. The gravel terminates at two benches, but a sandy path leads downhill to the water's edge (an ideal picnic spot).

Return to the last junction and turn right onto the River Bluff Trail. Passing through a lush flat where birches, sweetgum, yellow poplar, and bitternut hickory grow draped with vines, the mowed path quickly gives way to earthen single-track. After crossing the first of many rivulets—some spanned by wooden walkways—the trail makes a sharp left, ascending from the floodplain.

Turn right upon meeting another mowed path to remain on the dirt trail. Along this hillside, you will pass through the first of many Virginia-pine thickets. Characterized by scaly bark, short needles, and small cones, this small-but-sturdy tree can survive in poor soils. Pine thickets promote soil accumulation and provide nutrients as their needles and fallen limbs decay.

Yellow blazes mark the trail, and scattered markers point to alternate equestrian paths. The hiking trail makes a sharp right after heading uphill, then curves left, following the river before regaining elevation along a finger ridge. A distinct right precedes the 0.8-mile marker. An area of older hardwoods with a brighter, open understory follows. A short descent then takes you across a wooden bridge over a marshy creek, where bottomland species thrive. The trail briefly follows this creek east, passing the 1-mile marker, before a left brings the Rivanna into view on your right.

The historic 1831 courthouse in quaint Palmyra, uphill from the Fluvanna Heritage Trail

As it progresses, the trail undulates with the terrain, dipping into a sizable drainage before cresting a knoll and descending to a second valley. Shortly after mile marker 1.8, the trail bears inland before curving north to cross a sturdy wooden bridge. The path bears right, running parallel to the stream you just crossed as it passes the 2-mile point. A steady ascent then leads to a hillside, where the trail bed turns to gravel.

Stay with the single-track, ignoring spurs to an equestrian area on your left. A steady descent takes you to a narrow streamlet before intersecting a mowed path. Continue forward, passing a no-horses sign. After traversing a beech grove, the trail turns left, running along a creek on the right. Pass through a birch glade with several picnic tables before fording Burke Creek, which averages ten feet wide but easily crossed on stones. Once across, turn right along a grassy clearing to head toward a river overlook.

After passing through a line of cedars, the trail bears right. Pass around a small island of trees to reach Burke Creek's confluence with the Rivanna. Retrace your steps to the last junction and head straight, following signs for the Pole Barns. Turn left, recrossing Burke Creek before heading right and uphill. Exposed, striated rock is visible in the trail bed as you head south through a tunnel of Virginia pines.

Finally, you will emerge into a meadow, still ascending as you pass mile marker 3. Continue forward to the western trailhead, enjoying the vista of rolling fields on your left before passing a chimney. Just ahead are the Pole Barns, open-sided shelters named for the tree-trunk poles that serve as support columns. A signboard trail map, a water spigot, and picnic tables are located here. The path continues westward as a gravel double-track. Beyond a gate, Haden house stands on trail right. To the left is Pleasant Grove, home to multiple sports fields and ample parking.

Birders may elect to follow the Fluvanna Heritage Birding Trail, a 1-mile series of connecting mowed loops through a meadow west of the Haden house. Out-and-back hikers should turn around to retrace the route, bypassing the overlook and beach, for a 7.7-mile round-trip.

# FREEDOM PARK

## KEY AT-A-GLANCE INFORMATION

**LENGTH:** 5 miles, plus 1 mile of old double-track

**CONFIGURATION:** Three interconnected loops

**DIFFICULTY:** Moderate

**SCENERY:** Recovering mixed forest; steep-sided, sandy-bottomed creeks

**EXPOSURE:** Well-shaded

**TRAFFIC:** Moderate

**TRAIL SURFACE:** Dirt

**HIKING TIME:** 2.5 hours

**SEASON:** Open daily 7 a.m.–dusk year-round

**ACCESS:** No entrance fee

**MAPS:** Available at trailhead

**FACILITIES:** Trashcan and mapboard at trailhead; additional facilities are planned for this park.

**SPECIAL COMMENTS:** The trails at James City County's Freedom Park—with the exception of the lackluster "multiuse trail" on old dirt roads—were created by mountain bikers and are identified with signs as bike trails. However, they've also proven a hit with trail runners. If you hike this route, please be mindful of cyclists and respectful of their trail-building efforts. Contact James City County Parks at (757) 259-3200 or visit www.jccegov.com/recreation.

**UTM Trailhead Coordinates for Freedom Park**

**UTM Zone (NAD27)** 18S

**Easting** 0340397

**Northing** 4131531

## IN BRIEF

The twists and turns along this trio of interconnected single-track loops nod to the mountain bikers who first blazed the trail. A predominantly double-track multiuse path stays to higher ground and encircles the parking area, but the longer trail explores both the recovering forest uplands and a stream valley that drains west to Colby Swamp.

## DESCRIPTION

James City County's newest park, 675-acre Freedom Park is still under development. A modicum of landscaping surrounds the recently paved parking lot, and a bridge links it to a level, open field where picnic shelters and other amenities may soon stand. The access road was sufficient, however, for the mountain bikers and trail runners who now frequent the park after work and on weekends. (The network is perfectly hospitable to hikers at all but the most crowded times. Still, you may want to take a rain check if you find the parking lot full and a bike rack on every vehicle.)

In the first planning stage for the park, James City County found evidence of a colonial

## DIRECTIONS

From Richmond take I-64 east to Exit 234 (34 miles beyond I-295). Follow VA 199 for 1.7 miles south, then exit onto US 60 westbound (toward Lightfoot). After 0.1 mile, turn left onto Centerville Road. Drive 3.1 miles southwest to the park entrance on your right.

Catty-corner to the entrance is VA 612 (Longhill Road), which provides easier access from downtown Williamsburg. From US 60 about 1 mile north of the College of William and Mary, turn left (south) onto VA 615 (Ironbound Road), then turn right onto VA 612 and head 4.4 miles west to arrive opposite the park entrance.

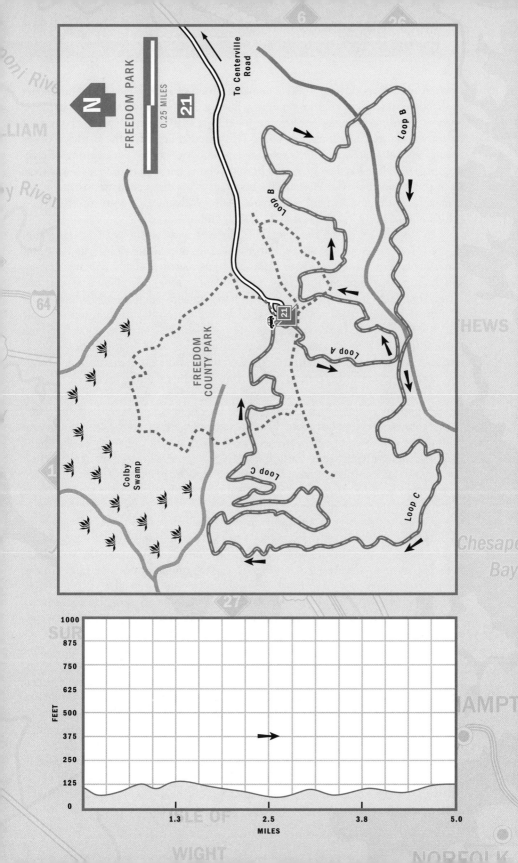

FREEDOM PARK

0.25 MILES

**21**

N

To Centerville Road

Loop B

Loop B

21

Loop A

FREEDOM COUNTY PARK

Loop C

Loop C

Colby Swamp

Chesape Bay

| | | | | | | | | | | | |
1000
875
750
625
500
375
250
125
0

FEET

1.3        2.5        3.8        5.0
MILES

farm on the site as early as 1680. The name Freedom Park, however, acknowledges the land's subsequent role in American history. The Revolutionary War Battle of Spencer's Ordinary was fought here on June 26, 1781 (presumably, the eponymous tavern was located hereabouts as well). The skirmish preceded the battle at Green Springs and ultimately the British surrender at Yorktown (see Greensprings Greenway, page 98). It marked an increased bravado on the part of a joint Franco-American force commanded by the Marquis de Lafayette, who dispatched troops under the command of Colonel Richard Butler and Major William McPherson to intercept a British raiding party led by Lieutenant Colonel John Simcoe.

In his 1881 history *The Yorktown Campaign and the Surrender of Cornwallis,* Henry Johnston wrote: "Simcoe's Rangers had been collecting cattle and burning stores above Williamsburg, where Cornwallis was halted… Major William McPherson, at sunrise, mounted fifty of the Light Infantry behind as many dragoons and pushed hard after him. Simcoe, meanwhile had gone into camp about six miles above Williamsburg, near Spencer's Ordinary, when McPherson dashed in upon his pickets. A brief hand-to-hand skirmish took place. McPherson was unhorsed, but escaped, and his dragoons scattered and retreated… Simcoe regarded the American attack as a serious one, and sent word to Cornwallis without delay, who immediately moved the whole army forward to his aid; but no farther fighting occurred."

After the war, shortly after the turn of the nineteenth century, the area was home to a community of free African American citizens. Census figures indicate that "Free Persons of Color" comprised more than 5 percent of the Commonwealth's population prior to the Civil War, of which whites were a scant majority. Many freed slaves and their descendants remained in the Tidewater region, continuing to work as field hands on the vast tobacco plantations. A few owned land or practiced a trade, but most rented sharecroppers' plots or lived as squatters on unfarmed land. Ostracized from white society and often discouraged from associating with slaves for fear they might sow discontent, free African Americans lived in small, close-knit communities.

Historical records on the settlement at today's Freedom Park are rare, but the county plans to present the story through interpretive displays in the completed park. On my visit, however, the only sign was at the trailhead, near the southern corner of the parking area. Map brochures are available in the mailbox beside it. The description below defers to the map and follows loops A, B, and C, in that order. However, you may elect to hike only one or two loops or to tack on the succinct multiuse trail, a pair of upland loops along former roadbeds.

Loop A is the shortest of the three loops signed for mountain-bike use, making it a good test run for the entire network. Proceed straight past an almost immediate fork to the right, then bisect a double-track, part of the short multiuse trail. The trail was clearly blazed with bikers in mind, and its many twists and turns seem a bit gratuitous on foot. Trail runners, however, will find an engaging course with relatively few rocks and roots. Look for one short, steep drop before winding downhill; a drainage appears on your right.

Ferns spring from the hillside, shaded by taller trees stretching up from the creek valley. Look for chestnut and white oak, birch, and red maple. The path curves left with a steep slope on the right and the creek below. It almost collides with another length of the trail network before turning left and uphill into piney woods.

Soon you'll double back to descend within view of the creek again before climbing away in earnest.

Upon intersecting an old fire road that's now part of the park's modest multi-use network, turn right. Loop B technically heads forward for a short stretch that involves elevated planks propped on fallen logs. This is the one section best left to bicyclists, but it is easily avoided on foot. Simply make another right when the single-track intersects the old road again up ahead.

Follow the path for a steady descent after which it bends to the left. After a brief level jaunt, you begin to climb steadily, with a draw on your right. Curve around the crown of the steep-sided drainage, then wind through a mix of pines and hardwoods with numerous storm-downed trees. Felled trees are scattered beside much of this westernmost length of trail. You'll descend to cross a wooden bridge over a low-lying muddy area. Yellow poplars shade this open wood, but dead pines abound along the trail ahead.

Ascending to the low bluff, proceed through pine forest, then veer right to reach a stretch with hardwoods on trail right and pines on the left. Beyond a mossy bank and smattering of mountain laurel on trail left, you'll cross a stream on another wooden bridge. Descend with streamlets on the left, then cross a sandy-bottomed tributary before curving left.

You'll soon intersect a cutoff trail leaving for the parking lot on trail right. Continue straight beneath the taller, hydrophilic hardwoods like sycamore and yellow poplar that thrive in this hard-to-log valley floor. Keep the creek, now about 4 feet wide, on your left before turning right, upstream along a feeder branch. Cross the laurel-flanked rivulet on a wooden bridge and continue with the creek discernable on your left.

The trail soon bears right, away from the tributary of Colby Swamp and into a parcel of Virginia pines. Longer-leafed loblolly pines dominate most of the trail network. After cresting a small hill, you'll dip through a drainage then enjoy a level stretch. Make a steady descent with a hillside sloping away beyond the trees on trail left. You'll again find scattered deadfalls in the forest ahead. You'll also notice signs indicating private property on trail left.

The mixed forest gives way to a bottomland tangle of sycamore, beech, red maple, and red oak stitched together with vines. Pines again overtake hardwoods on the gradual, winding climb that follows. However, the trail doubles back twice more ahead. You'll make a wide loop before heading north just below the tread you recently followed south. Then, you'll veer right and head south again along a seasonal stream before crossing it at the head of the draw.

Bear left to climb with the stream still on your left. You'll round the crest of a hilltop with views of another Colby Swamp tributary below. Again, hardwoods dominate the floodplain. Curving right to cross the hilltop, you'll find a dense wood of pines and spindly holly trees. A few more zigzags and you'll cross the double-track once more before again approaching the trailhead.

If you're still feeling spry, tack on the park's mile of multiuse pathway. Identified on some maps as the "hiking trail," the multiuse trail has two loops that stick to old forest roads except when dipping through a creek valley in the northwestern section. Watch for turns on this one.

# GEORGE WASHINGTON BIRTHPLACE
## National Monument

### KEY AT-A-GLANCE INFORMATION

**LENGTH:** 1-mile nature trail and 1-mile circuit around Memorial House

**CONFIGURATION:** Loops

**DIFFICULTY:** Easy

**SCENERY:** A wide bay on Popes Creek just south of the Potomac; the rebuilt Memorial House and grounds; the footprint of the home where Washington was born

**EXPOSURE:** Well-shaded along forested nature trail; exposed along Popes Creek and on the Memorial House grounds

**TRAFFIC:** High near Memorial House; moderate on nature trail

**TRAIL SURFACE:** Crushed gravel, crushed oyster shells, brick, dirt

**HIKING TIME:** 1 hour plus 1–2 hours sightseeing and driving between trailheads

**SEASON:** Open daily 8 a.m.–5 p.m year-round

**ACCESS:** $5 pass (good for one week) for adults; children ages 16 and under free; Memorial Home is wheelchair accessible

**MAPS:** Included on park brochure and online at www.nps.gov/gewa/ed/parkmap.htm

**FACILITIES:** Restrooms, visitor center, re-created colonial farm with costumed interpreters; picnic area, convention center, Washington family cemetery; ranger-led tours on the hour 10 a.m.–4 p.m.

**SPECIAL COMMENTS:** Contact the park office at (804) 224-1732 or visit www.nps.gov/gewa.

---

UTM Trailhead Coordinates for George Washington Birthplace National Monument

UTM Zone (NAD27) 18S

Easting 0331976

Northing 4227638

### ▶ IN BRIEF

Count on a mile's stroll through the re-created colonial home and farm at George Washington Birthplace National Monument. Though merely a mile long, the noncontiguous nature trail is a pleasant addition, especially if you plan a picnic.

### ▶ DESCRIPTION

America's first president was a fourth-generation Virginian, and much of his family's history unfolded here. John Washington, George's great-grandfather, left England for Virginia in 1656 and within two years was wed to Anne Pope, for whose family Popes Creek was named. The couple's eldest son Lawrence served as burgess and sheriff for Westmoreland County, cementing the Washington family's standing among the Virginia gentry. Nevertheless, his

### ▶ DIRECTIONS

From Richmond head north on I-95 to Exit 104. Follow VA 207 about 12 miles to Bowling Green, where it merges with US 301. Continue northeast on US 301 through Fort A. P. Hill and across the Rappahannock River. After 18 miles turn right onto VA 3 (from Fredericksburg you can arrive via VA 3). Drive 13 miles west to VA 204 and turn left, following signs for the monument. In 1.75 miles you will approach the obelisk. Turn right here to park in the visitor center lot and see the Memorial House.

To reach the nature trail, drive in the opposite direction 0.2 miles past the obelisk, then veer right toward the picnic area. The trail heads northwest from the picnic-area parking lot 0.6 miles ahead. To visit the Washington family cemetery, continue a mile beyond the obelisk rather than veering toward the picnic area. The cemetery is on the left side of the road, but a parking area precedes it on the right. The road terminates at the Potomac a half-mile on.

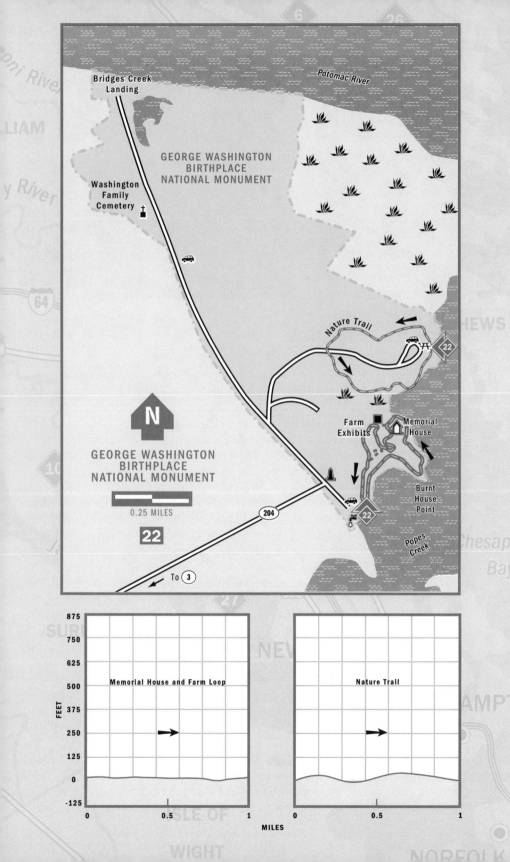

Potomac River

Bridges Creek
Landing

GEORGE WASHINGTON
BIRTHPLACE
NATIONAL MONUMENT

Washington
Family
Cemetery

Nature Trail

**N**

GEORGE WASHINGTON
BIRTHPLACE
NATIONAL MONUMENT

0.25 MILES

**22**

Farm
Exhibits

Memorial
House

Burnt
House
Point

Popes
Creek

Chesapeake
Bay

**204**

To ③

| | Memorial House and Farm Loop |
|---|---|

875
750
625
500
375
250
125
0
-125

FEET

0          0.5          1

| | Nature Trail |
|---|---|

0          0.5          1

MILES

The Washington family cemetery, where the first president's father and mother are buried.

widow, Mildred, left for England when she remarried, taking their young son Augustine Washington. Following Mildred's death in 1691, John Washington Jr. sent for Augustine, who came of age in King George County.

After marrying his first wife, Jane, in 1715, Augustine returned to his father's Bridges Creek farm, which he soon expanded eastward. In 1726 the family moved to a two-room house overlooking the wide mouth of Popes Creek. The Washingtons' tobacco plantation prospered, but in 1729 illness claimed Jane Washington.

A widower with three children, Augustine remarried to Mary Ball in 1731. Just under a year later, on February 22, 1732, their first child was born. George Washington spent only three years in the home of his birth. The Washingtons moved first to John Washington Sr.'s original farm on Hunting Creek, then on to Fredericksburg, where Augustine was invested in an iron-mining enterprise. Washington would come of age at Strother Plantation on the Rappahannock, later named Ferry Farm.

When George was 11 years old he lost his father and gained the burden of managing the estate. During his teen years, George frequently visited his stepbrother Augustine Jr. at Popes Creek Plantation. When Augustine Jr.'s son, William Augustine Washington, inherited the farm in 1762, he renamed it Wakefield. In 1779, however, he returned from a Christmas Day hunting expedition to find the roof ablaze. Hence the promontory west of Popes Creek was rechristened Burnt House Point.

In 1858 the homesite and the family cemetery to the west were granted to the Commonwealth of Virginia, but the Civil War aborted any plans to erect a monument. The land was passed on to the federal government in 1882. Fourteen years later, a 50-foot-tall stone obelisk was erected atop an old foundation erroneously assumed to be that of Washington's birth house.

In the 1920s public interest in the site skyrocketed. The Wakefield National Memorial Association raised a considerable sum, not least of all from John D. Rockefeller Jr., to construct what members deemed a more suitable homage to Washington: a replica of the mansion where he was born, the Memorial House, and a living-history farm. The group more accurately identified the location of the original home but mistakenly assumed its foundation was that of a barn and vice versa. The home they completed in 1931 more closely resembles the upper-class dwellings of Washington's later years than the cottage of his birth. Additional archaeology rectified the misperception, which had the unintended positive result of leaving the actual home's foundation visible to visitors.

Before visiting the historic area, be sure to examine the artifacts displayed in the visitor center, among them ceremonial swords Washington wore as a general. A 14-minute film examines Washington's agrarian roots. Exit the rear of the visitor center, following a gravel trail along Popes Creek. Look for herons and swans in the estuary. The path rises slightly to the 70-year-old cedar grove that envelops the Memorial House, which comes into view on your left. At a fork in the trail, bear right and continue beside Popes Creek. The path curves northward and passes the herb garden on the left before emerging from the cedars.

A wide lawn opens on your left. The trail turns left to approach the first of the re-created outbuildings, the weaving room. Ahead on the right is a pen in which you'll see numerous barnyard fowl. Turn left to approach the Memorial House. Costumed interpreters provide tours of the mansion and work in the surrounding farmyard. A virtual tour of the home is online at www.nps.gov/gewa/memorialhouse.htm.

After exploring the house, go straight from the entrance to pass the stand-alone kitchen on your left. Turn left just beyond this. First you will pass the brick foundation of a dairy on trail right. Then, on your left, you'll see white oyster shells outlining the U-shaped foundation of Washington's birth home. The wood-frame house where young George spent his infancy stood here. A sign devoted to archaeology at Popes Creek fronts the foundation, and an herb garden borders the site to the north.

You can stroll the garden using an access path just ahead. Afterward backtrack to the dairy site and turn left to approach the ox yard. Turn right to continue along the log fence to the farm workshop. There you will find informative displays on colonial-era farm tasks like spinning wool, dipping candles, and drying tobacco. Turn right upon exiting the workshop, then left at the hog pens. Continue south between crop fields and the ox yard, then bear right to return to the front of the visitor center.

To hike the nature trail, you must drive to the picnic area. From the picnic-area parking lot, head northwest on the nature trail, passing a marshy inlet of Popes Creek on the right before entering mixed forest of red oak, willow oak, loblolly pine, and holly. The loop trail is easy to follow and passes several signs explaining the importance of woodlands to colonial farmers, who relied on them for game and timber.

After the trail curves left and crosses the park road, it nears Dancing Marsh. Watch for muddy sags in the path. The grassy marsh stretches away on trail left. Water-tolerant willow oaks shade the path as it heads east. The marsh recedes and the shoreline squeezes the trail when it passes near a reconstructed log-beam-and-plaster house (used as a conference center).

The nature trail rises through a parcel of woods to emerge in the picnic flat, also dotted by cedars. The parking lot is visible ahead, just beyond the restrooms. After finishing the loop, be sure to visit the Washington family cemetery, where you will see the graves of several of Washington's family members and a sign marking the site of John Washington's Bridges Creek home.

# GREENSPRINGS GREENWAY

## KEY AT-A-GLANCE INFORMATION

**LENGTH:** 3.1 miles

**CONFIGURATION:** Figure eight

**DIFFICULTY:** Easy

**SCENERY:** Swampland, historic cropland, mostly hardwood forest

**EXPOSURE:** Well-shaded except on boardwalk and near parking area

**TRAFFIC:** Moderate

**TRAIL SURFACE:** Gravel, dirt, boardwalk, and sidewalk

**HIKING TIME:** 1.5 hours

**SEASON:** Open daily during daylight year-round

**ACCESS:** No entrance fee

**MAPS:** Available at signboard

**FACILITIES:** Signboard with maps. 30 interpretive signs en route

**SPECIAL COMMENTS:** Plans call for the creation of an additional trail west of Jamestown High. When complete, this path will allow hikers to make a figure eight without using the sidewalk that fronts the school. Contact James City County Parks at (757) 259-3200 or visit www.jccegov.com/recreation/greensprings_hiking.html.

**UTM Trailhead Coordinates for Greensprings Greenway**

**UTM Zone (NAD27) 18S**

**Easting 0341333**

**Northing 4123209**

## IN BRIEF

Popular with residents of the surrounding neighborhoods, Greensprings Greenway is equally inviting to after-work joggers and out-of-town history buffs. Interpretive signs highlight the ecosystem that English colonists found here and the centuries of agrarian heritage they established, as well as the Revolutionary War Battle of Green Springs.

## DESCRIPTION

Aside perhaps from the auspiciously named Jamestown High, the suburban surroundings of Greensprings Greenway belie the area's historic significance. The trail encircles a beaver pond where snowy egrets and red-headed woodpeckers nest. Virginia's earliest English colonists might have happened upon similar sights when first venturing beyond their haven at Jamestown Island, 2 miles to the south. In exploring the woodlands north of the James River, the colonists had agrarian ambitions foremost in mind. Their charge was to produce crops for export (they soon settled on tobacco). Bordering the trail to the south is Mainland Farm, under cultivation as long or longer than any farm in the nation.

## DIRECTIONS

From Richmond take I-64 east to Exit 234. Follow VA 199 south about 8 miles to VA 5, then turn right and continue 3 miles. You may also arrive via VA 5 (John Tyler Highway) from central Williamsburg, but mind the signs, as it isn't a straight shot. Turn left onto Eagle Way at a stoplight signed for Jamestown High School. You will pass the school on your right and may park in the school's lot (near the tennis courts), provided class is not in session. Limited spaces are also available straight ahead at the road's terminus. A green sign invites you to head south along the school's sports fields.

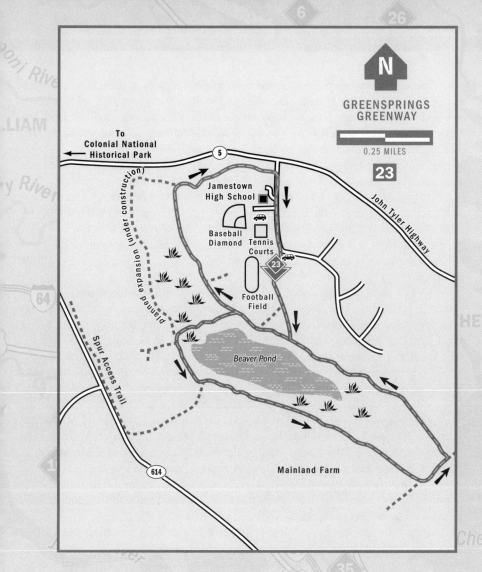

**N**

**GREENSPRINGS GREENWAY**

0.25 MILES

23

To Colonial National Historical Park

5

Jamestown High School

Baseball Diamond

Tennis Courts

23

Football Field

planned expansion (under construction)

John Tyler Highway

Spur Access Trail

Beaver Pond

614

Mainland Farm

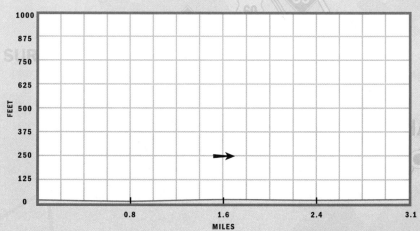

FEET

1000

875

750

625

500

375

250

125

0

0.8    1.6    2.4    3.1

MILES

The Greenway begins inconspicuously, marked only by a green sign. To reach the official trailhead, park in the school lot and look for that green sign, which directs you south. Pass between a piney wood on the left and the school's football field and track on the right. Bear left when you come upon a drainage pond to reach the trailhead signboard, where you can pick up a map that shows the location of 30 informational signs along the main loop. Although a spur leads right, follow the path that bends left into the woods if you plan to see the signs in their intended order.

As you enter the woods along a slight descent, willow oak, swamp chestnut oak, holly, and loblolly pines—the tallest of the lot—greet you. A granite marker commemorates Earth Day volunteers who helped develop the trail system. Nearby, the first interpretive signs recount the familiar story of the English arrival at Jamestown in 1607 and describe the ecology they encountered. Turn right at a T intersection and continue straight.

Shortly beyond a sign devoted to the Powhatan Creek watershed you'll pass the first of several modest boardwalks. A sign explaining the role of streams within the water cycle is situated nearby. You'll note ferns thriving in this lush environment. A path soon veers right, but the main, signed loop turns left, across one of two major boardwalks with railings. This one traverses the swamp. Approach quietly so as not to spook the herons, turtles, and songbirds frequently seen here. Alongside the boardwalk to the north, young sweet gums cling to purplish leaves, while to the south, the limbless trunks of their drowned predecessors tower precipitously above the water.

Resuming the pea-gravel trail, you'll soon arrive at another trail junction. Though at present it connects only to a nearby neighborhood, the trail departing to the right here will ultimately link to a northbound trail, making a loop around the northern reaches of the swamp feasible. The main loop, labeled Loop 3 on junction signposts, veers left again, passing beneath several maples. It soon reaches the second lengthy boardwalk, which traverses a peripheral, thickly vegetated area of the wetland. In the summer, look for cardinal flower blooming below.

After passing some homes on the right and a spur trail connecting them to the main loop, the trail draws along Mainland Farm. Many of the trees in this area, including several white oaks, are visibly more mature. Dogwoods fill out the forest beneath them. Eastbound, the trail passes several interpretive signs devoted to this land's agricultural heritage. Beyond a pine grove, an abandoned relic of early mechanized farming lies rusting on trail left.

Just ahead, an interpretive sign recounts the Revolutionary War Battle of Green Springs, in which British general George Cornwallis nearly ensnared 800 revolutionary troops under the command of Frenchman Marquis de Lafayette and American general "Mad" Anthony Wayne. Near the Main (of Mainland Farm), an American expeditionary force unexpectedly engaged the bulk of Cornwallis's Army, which was preparing to cross the James in a move toward Portsmouth. Drastically outmanned, Wayne nevertheless ordered a defiant charge. Though the revolutionaries suffered 140 casualties, twice those of their enemy, the counteroffensive stalled the advancing Royalists long enough for Wayne to orchestrate a successful retreat.

Aided by gathering darkness and marshy terrain such as you just traversed, the Americans were able to evade capture and rejoin their compatriots. The British subsequently crossed the James, meeting ships in Portsmouth that carried them on to Yorktown. They promptly set about constructing the batteries and redoubts in which they would weather a combined American–French siege until Cornwallis's famous surrender on October 19, 1871. That climactic event may have played out elsewhere—or differently—had Commander-in-Chief George Washington not received word that French reinforcements, commanded by Count de Grasse, were en route from Haiti to Virginia. Upon hearing the news, the first president cleverly maneuvered south from New York to assume command of the combined forces at Yorktown.

As you continue, you'll encounter a sign devoted to another kind of revolution, an agricultural one. Though inefficient by modern standards, the new fertilizers and horse-drawn plows of the nineteenth century allowed fewer farmers to produce more crops.

Along this southernmost stretch, the trail spans multiple seasonal streamlets on small boardwalks. Pass beneath a grove of tall tulip poplars and beside a maple with a partially horizontal trunk. If it's been raining, you will be forced to navigate around some muddy stretches after the raised pea-gravel trail bed gives way to dirt. Upon reaching a T intersection, turn left to head northeast through open, drier forest, passing an enigmatic concrete cylinder beside the trail. Tall grasses replace ferns along this forest floor, giving the odd appearance of a prairie sprung up in a wood.

Veering left at the next intersection keeps you on the main trail, which parallels a culvert on the right. Following another fork to the left, the main loop employs additional boardwalks in traversing a boggy area. As you again approach the spur that links the trailhead and main loop, additional signs highlight the larger oaks and gnarled holly trees along the trail—loggers spared the former to delineate property boundaries and the latter because their wood was undesirable.

Continue beyond the trailhead connector, briefly retracing your steps, then head straight, rather than left to the boardwalk, to begin the second loop of your figure eight. A slight right, away from the wetland, takes you past a mysterious pit on trail right, which may have been dug to store ice in an era without refrigeration. Today, noisy frogs are content to reside in the water accumulated here. Just ahead, the trail curves left, and the Greenway, now true to its name, passes along a wide grassy corridor. Drainage ponds and brier thickets alternate on trail right, while young pines grow densely on the left. Additional paths access Jamestown High to the right, and at one a left is required to stay on the loop, labeled Loop 2.

Gravel reappears in the foot bed as the trail bisects a pine-dominated forest to make a T intersection with a dirt double-track. According to development plans, a left here will ultimately connect to the aforementioned trail around the swamp's northern arm. At present, however, a right takes you uphill to earthen single-track. A slight left is required when the double-track seemingly veers toward the school's sports fields.

Traffic is audible on VA 5 as the narrowing path winds through a corridor of trees between the road and school. Turn right upon emerging onto the sidewalk in front of Jamestown High, and a brief amble will return you to your vehicle. Drive just a couple miles south to tour Colonial National Historic Park's Jamestown unit, which recounts the arrival of English colonists in Virginia. The National Park Service's Colonial Parkway links the Jamestown unit to Williamsburg and Yorktown.

# HARDWARE RIVER WILDLIFE MANAGEMENT AREA

## KEY AT-A-GLANCE INFORMATION

**LENGTH:** 2.6 miles, with two similar non-contiguous trails in park

**CONFIGURATION:** Out-and-back

**DIFFICULTY:** Moderate

**SCENERY:** The Hardware River, seen from the bluffs above Muleshoe Bend and from the floodplain downstream, and an old family cemetery near a former homesite

**EXPOSURE:** Limited shade

**TRAFFIC:** Low

**TRAIL SURFACE:** Gravel-and-dirt double-track

**HIKING TIME:** 1.5 hours

**SEASON:** Trails are open daily during daylight year-round but should be avoided during autumn and winter hunting seasons (see Special Comments below)

**ACCESS:** No fee; horseback riding and mountain biking allowed; no ATVs; not recommended for wheelchairs

**MAPS:** Available online at www.dgif. virginia.gov/hunting/wma/ hardware_river.html

**FACILITIES:** Parking-lot signboards

**SPECIAL COMMENTS:** All wildlife management areas are open to hunting. Check with the VDGIF to determine annual hunting seasons (call (804) 370-1000 or visit www.dgif.virginia.gov/hunting). It is recommended that you not hike during deer and wild turkey seasons, but if you do, wear blaze orange and hike only during peak daylight hours.

---

**UTM Trailhead Coordinates for Hardware River Wildlife Management Area**

**UTM Zone (NAD27) 17S**

**Easting 726290**

**Northing 4182512**

## ▶ IN BRIEF

The steep-sided, rocky Hardware River is something of an anomaly: a delayed-harvest trout stream in Virginia's Piedmont. Follow this mostly dirt double-track along a ridge overlooking the river's Muleshoe Bend, then make a twisting descent to pass an old family cemetery before reaching the river to fish. If you're not interested in fly-fishing, consider pairing this hike with a canoe trip to make for a full day. Outfitters in Scottsville will gladly facilitate your float down the James. A waterside picnic is another pleasant option.

## ▶ DESCRIPTION

There are four parking areas within Hardware River Wildlife Management Area (WMA), and an out-and-back stint of double-track leaves from each. Unfortunately, none of these old roadbeds meet. This hike begins along the now-gated southernmost stretch of Kidd's Mill Road, and is best for accessing the prime trout waters of the Hardware River. To the east, another dirt road

## ▶ DIRECTIONS

From Richmond follow I-64 northwest to Exit 136 (41 miles beyond I-295). Take VA 15 south, passing through Palmyra, Fluvanna's county seat. After 11.4 miles, veer right onto VA 649. Then, in 0.4 miles, make a hard right to stay with VA 649 westbound. After 3.5 miles, turn right onto VA 6 at a T intersection. Look for VA 611 on the left 6.6 miles beyond VA 15. Follow VA 611 south 1.3 miles, then turn left onto Kidd's Mill Road. Park in the cul-de-sac less than half a mile ahead.

Charlottesville residents can reach the trail by following VA 20 about 18.5 miles south of I-64 to Scottsville, then driving 3.75 miles east on VA 6 to turn right (south) onto VA 611. Follow directions from VA 611 above to reach the park.

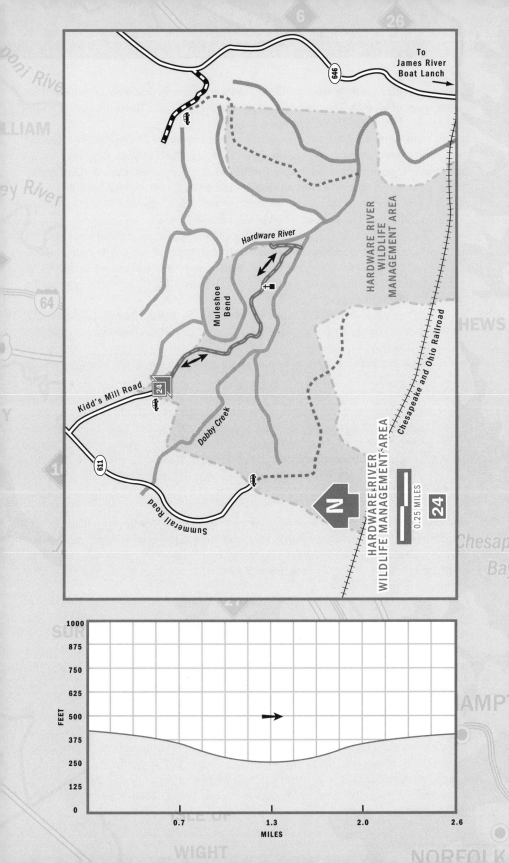

runs south along a ridge from a difficult-to-locate parking area on a gravel road that veers west off VA 646. This trail ends at the Hardware River's Horseshoe Bend, a mirror image of Muleshoe Bend upstream.

State-maintained VA 646 technically terminates at the Chesapeake & Ohio rail line, but an asphalt extension continues south across the Hardware River on a wood-on-steel bridge to reach a boat ramp on the James. This is Hardware WMA's largest, most popular parking area, wth a valued put-in and takeout for paddlers. A double-track leaves west from the signboard, running through a mowed corridor between a riparian buffer and the rail line's end at the James.

Lastly, on the WMA's western border, a gated dirt road heads southeast from VA 611, which first becomes Summerall Road. It terminates at the rail line, and pedestrians are not allowed through the rail right-of-way. Adventuresome amblers can tackle each of these but shouldn't bank on linking them up without some potentially confusing bushwacking.

The mere out-and-back mapped here makes for a leisurely stroll. Of the WMA's paths, it offers the best access to the 2.6-mile stretch of the Hardware designated a delayed-harvest trout stream.

From the parking area, continue south past the signboard through a wide grassy corridor. A steep slope wooded in white oak and yellow poplar descends on your left, while a dense stand of young pines buffers the trail to your right. The double-track underfoot was once the southernmost stretch of Kidd's Mill Road before it was graveled and gated off. The roadbed passes beside an old homesite and a family cemetery, then on to a flat plain along the Hardware River. Presumably, its namesake nineteenth-century gristmill was located thereabouts.

The mill's location was by no means arbitrary. Rather, it was a product of geography. The flat land south of Muleshoe Bend is a rarity along the steep-sided Hardware River. Farming these rugged hillsides with horse-drawn plows was scarcely an option. Even the road follows a tapering ridge to elongate its descent. Thus, it was feasible for horse-drawn carts laden with grain to reach the mill. When mechanization obviated the gristmill, the Kidd homestead, located on a knoll uphill, must have seemed needlessly isolated, both from nearby cities and the broad swaths of land common to the Piedmont.

The Kidd family's roots in Fluvanna County run deep, at least back to 1791, when Henry Kidd purchased 400 acres of land north of the James River. The deed indicates this property encompassed branches of Cunningham Creek, placing it north of the Hardware River Wildlife Management Area across VA 6. Many of Kidd's descendants remained in Fluvanna County, as Civil War muster rolls indicate. The crossroads of Kidd's Store (east of the Area on VA 6) and Kidd's Mill Road pay tribute to industrious members of the family.

Heading south toward the old homestead, you will pass a recovering meadow dotted with young pines on the right, but note older forest descending toward the river on trail left. The roadbed curves right to face an opposing hillside. Dobby Creek runs unseen toward the Hardware in the valley below. Just ahead, beyond a parcel of pines, views of the Hardware rounding Muleshoe bend await on trail left (east). Peer cautiously through the tree trunks and mountain laurel cascading down the steep hillside toward the river.

Descending on, the trail curves right to round a knoll, where young evergreens grow interspersed with birch trees, red maples, and hornbeams. The three hardwoods indicate moist soil underfoot on this brief level stretch of trail. A short distance ahead, the trail appears to fork. In fact, it merely encircles an island of vegetation. This dense pocket of scrub, with cedars at its core and surprising yucca plants on its fringe, marks the former homesite.

A short distance farther downhill, beyond a thickly vegetated meadow, the old family cemetery is shrouded in tall red cedars on trail right. Here, too, the sword-like leaves of low, round yucca plants abound; the nonnative species was commonly used to decorate homes and graves in the rural South during the nineteenth and early twentieth centuries. Several of the older tombstones, including a few wrapped in an iron fence, are now illegible. One marker, for Samuel Kidd, dates to 1888. The most recent headstone dates to 1947. A blanket of crawling evergreen covers the graves.

Continuing downhill along the trail, you will see a cedar-dotted meadow to the west and a wall of Virginia pines and other conifers bordering the trail to the left. The grassy corridor widens as the path makes its final descent toward the Hardware River. An out-and-back spur to the right leads through a small grassy field and along a short path to Dobby Creek. The larger path turns left to parallel the river for a short distance before disappearing into the forest—your turnaround point.

Multiple paths lead to the riverbank overlooking the Hardware and provide anglers with access to the boulder-strewn river. Across the water, a steep hillside rises, colored by gray stones and deep-green mountain laurel. The trout-fishing area begins here and continues downstream almost to the James. Avid anglers take note: the only similar stream within an hour of Richmond is Holliday Creek in Appomattox-Buckingham State Forest (see page 14). The VDGIF stocks the river October through May, and catch-and-release fishing is permitted here with artificial lures and a trout license. June through September, general state regulations apply. To complete this hike, simply make an about-face and walk uphill back to your vehicle.

# HENRICUS HISTORICAL PARK

## KEY AT-A-GLANCE INFORMATION

**LENGTH:** 2.6 miles

**CONFIGURATION:** Out-and-back

**DIFFICULTY:** Easy

**SCENERY:** Re-created seventeenth-century English settlement along the James River

**EXPOSURE:** Mostly shaded along river, limited shade at Citie of Henricus

**TRAFFIC:** High

**TRAIL SURFACE:** Dirt and boardwalks

**HIKING TIME:** 1 hour, more to tour the Citie of Henricus

**SEASON:** Trails open daily during daylight year-round

**ACCESS:** Citie of Henricus and visitor center open Tuesday–Friday 10 a.m.–4 p.m. and Saturday and Sunday 10 a.m.–5 p.m.; tours of Henricus Historical Park cost $5 for adults, $4 for children, and $3 for children enrolled in Chesterfield or Henrico County schools; school and group tours are available by reservation; contact the park or visit www.henricus.org for an interpretive-events schedule

**MAPS:** Available at visitor center

**FACILITIES:** Visitor center, restrooms, picnic tables, bird-identification trail, re-created colonial Citie of Henricus

**SPECIAL COMMENTS:** Dutch Gap Conservation Area is owned and managed by Chesterfield County. It encompasses Henricus Historical Park, operated by the Henricus Foundation. Contact the visitor center at (804) 706-1340.

### UTM Trailhead Coordinates for Henricus Historical Park

**UTM Zone (NAD27)  18S**

**Easting  0290763**

**Northing  4138850**

## IN BRIEF

Henricus Historical Park is home to the Citie of Henricus, a re-creation of an actual English settlement on the site circa 1611. The park preserves the colony's legacy, which included a spate of New World firsts: the first hospital, the first college, the first tobacco fields, and the first privately owned land. Owing to the latter, as well as to the colony's successful blacksmith and brick-making industries, park literature makes the auspicious but not wholly inaccurate claim that Henricus witnessed "the development of the American system of free enterprise." Indeed, the history of Richmond and its surrounding counties began here.

## DESCRIPTION

Perched on a promontory that overlooks the James River's Pocahontas Bluff, the first Citie of Henricus was established by Sir Thomas Dale in 1611 and named in honor of King James's eldest son Henry. On behalf of the Virginia Company of London, Dale led 350 settlers to the site, which was first explored by Sir Christopher Newport in 1607 and deemed more healthful than Jamestown downriver.

## DIRECTIONS

From I-95 southeast of Richmond, take Exit 61 and follow VA 10 (Iron Bridge Road) east. Turn right at the first stoplight onto VA 732 (Old Stage Road). From I-295 take Exit 15 and follow VA 10 west for 3.5 miles before turning right onto VA 732. Heading north on VA 732, turn right upon reaching a T intersection with VA 615 (Coxendale Road). After passing Dominion Power's Chesterfield Power Station, turn right onto Henricus Road and follow it 2 miles to Dutch Gap Conservation Area. North of the parking lot is the re-created Citie of Henricus. To the east are the visitor center and museum store.

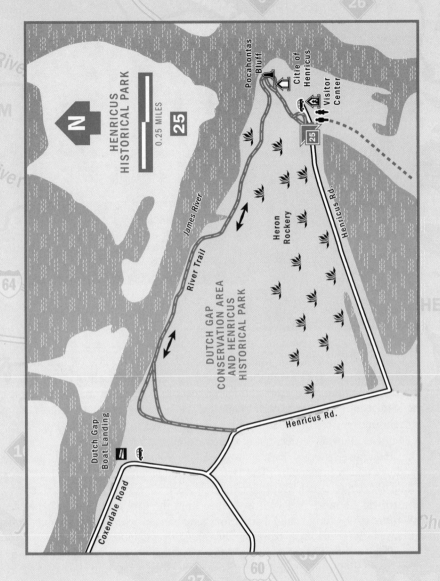

HENRICUS
HISTORICAL PARK

N

0.25 MILES

25

Pocahontas Bluff

Citie of Henricus

Visitor Center

25

Henricus Rd.

James River

River Trail

Heron Rockery

DUTCH GAP
CONSERVATION AREA
AND HENRICUS
HISTORICAL PARK

Henricus Rd.

Dutch Gap
Boat Landing

Coxendale Road

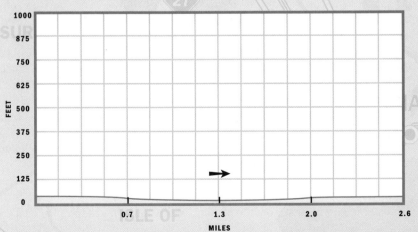

1000

875

750

625

500

375

FEET

250

125

0

0.7                 1.3                 2.0                 2.6

MILES

The marsh south of the James at Henricus State Park offers great bird- and wildlife-watching.

In order to protect the town, Dale orchestrated the excavation of a moat using Dutch techniques, and though the moat is gone, the name Dutch Gap remains. It was also here that John Rolfe crossbred Dutch tobacco with native strands, giving rise to the settlement's premier export. Ironically, the booming tobacco business, coupled with the introduction of private land ownership, served to diminish the English colony at Henricus, drawing settlers out of the city to nearby farms.

Henricus Historical Park now retells the colony's story through period-style buildings and reenactments. The Henricus Foundation operates the park, located within the larger Dutch Gap Conservation Area, in partnership with Henrico and Chesterfield Counties and with assistance from the City of Richmond. Unveiled in 2004, the park's early colonial structures simultaneously evoke Elizabethan cottages and a Wild West stockade. However, they are not yet complete.

Plans call for the rebuilding of Mount Malady, the first English hospital in the New World and a processing point for new arrivals. Rock Hall, home of Reverend Alexander Whitaker, will also be re-erected. In 1613 it was Whitaker who converted the Native American princess Pocahontas, a prisoner at the time, to Christianity and taught her English; he may have introduced her to her future husband, John Rolfe.

In 1622 an attack by native Indians halted construction on the Colledge of Henricus, which had won support from the first Virginia Assembly three years earlier. Both the re-created school and a Virginia Native American village will be added to the park. Re-creations of a tavern and trading post will round out its offerings.

Presently, chickens and geese roam among the thatched-roof cottages, kept from the garden plot at John Rolfe's Farm by log fences. Reenactors go about their farming chores, and craftsmen demonstrate period blacksmithing and pottery techniques. A 2.6-mile stroll along the James makes the park even more worthy of a visit.

The route follows the out-and-back River Trail from Pocahontas Bluff, the northernmost point in the park. It is also accessible by a trail that bypasses the settlement on the west (left from the parking lot). In addition to a few picnic tables, several monuments stand on the bluff. A stone cross recalls Whitaker's church and the establishment of the Anglican Parish of Henricus (alternately called Henricopolis). A stone obelisk commemorates the founding of the Colledge of Henricus. Standing nearby like a monument is a brick chimney, all that remains of a former lightkeeper's residence. The keeper was charged with maintaining oil lamps on either end of Dutch Gap Canal, between 1875 and 1910, before electricity displaced him.

Overlooking the James from this high point, you will see the modern I-295 bridge on the horizon. Approaching Dutch Gap from downstream, the river forks in three directions: north around Hatcher Island, straight through the Dutch Gap Canal cutoff, and south to the river's old channel, which once rejoined the river near your hike's terminus but has since been blocked, silted over, and built upon. Leaving the bluff to the west, descend wooden stairs to reach a large gazebo. Within it, signs detail the centuries of canal digging that reshaped the James River at Dutch Gap, including the Civil War canal dug to advance Federal gunships out of line of Confederate fire. Other signs describe the various boats that have plied these waters, most commercial rather than military.

Descend additional stairs to reach a boardwalk beneath large sycamore and hackberry trees. The path bears right to cross directly above a beaver dam. To your left is a wide wetland expanse. Look for great blue herons tiptoeing among the marsh grass; the birds nest in a rookery to the southwest. You're equally likely to spy other waterfowl bobbing about, tadpoles darting through the water, turtles sunning on logs, and, in the spring, yellow wild-iris blossoms. The irises, which even appear on park brochures, are not a native species but—appropriately for the setting—a European import.

The boardwalk zigzags west to meet a dirt-and-gravel trail, which heads generally west. You will approach the river, then veer into lowland forest thick with vines. At the base of the tree trunks you'll see debris washed ashore by the swollen James. Benches along the way invite you to rest a moment. One can only imagine how alien the verdant, marshy banks of the James must have seemed to early colonists accustomed to the rolling fields of Shropshire or the narrow, medieval streets of London. Next, the trail trends north to reach a mud flat along the James. You may see pleasure craft, from deluxe motorboats to canoes, or even commercial vessels in the river.

Not far ahead, the path veers inland again. The park's map shows a small balloon at the western end of the trail, but this is not apparent on the ground. A spur trail heads to a fishing spot on the right as the trail approaches its terminus at a stairway. These stairs lead to the county's Dutch Gap Boat Landing, which can serve as an alternate trailhead (simply veer left instead of turning right from Coxendale Road onto Henricus Park Road). As you retrace the trail, accompanied by chirping birds and croaking frogs, take note of flora and fauna you may have overlooked on your first pass.

Departing from the same trailhead as this hike is an 8-mile out-and-back exploration of Dutch Gap Conservation Area (see page 82). The longer hike wraps around a tidal lagoon south of the parking area, and because it is traveled less, it offers excellent bird-watching. Allot time for both hikes, and you'll enjoy a day infused with history and natural splendor.

# HICKORY HOLLOW STATE NATURAL AREA PRESERVE

## KEY AT-A-GLANCE INFORMATION

**LENGTH:** 3.4 miles

**CONFIGURATION:** Loop

**DIFFICULTY:** Moderate

**SCENERY:** Forested ridges, rhododendron thickets, small streamlets, and Cabin Swamp on the upper Western Branch of Corrotoman River

**EXPOSURE:** Well-shaded

**TRAFFIC:** Moderate

**TRAIL SURFACE:** Dirt

**HIKING TIME:** 1.5 hours

**SEASON:** Open daily during daylight year-round

**ACCESS:** No fee; not recommended for wheelchairs

**MAPS:** Available online at www.northern neckaudobon.org and on signboard at trailhead; key to numbered trees and sites along the trail also available online

**FACILITIES:** Limited to parking and trail signage

**SPECIAL COMMENTS:** As a state-protected natural area, Hickory Hollow is open only for low-impact activities. Bikes, horses, and ATVs are not allowed. Contact the Virginia Department of Conservation and Recreation Natural Heritage Program at (804) 684-7557 or (804) 786-7951; or visit www.dcr.virginia.gov/dnh/hickory.htm.

---

**UTM Trailhead Coordinates for Hickory Hollow State Natural Area Preserve**

**UTM Zone (NAD27)   18S**

**Easting   0372786**

**Northing   4181271**

## IN BRIEF

The interlaced trails at Hickory Hollow traverse a hilltop pine-hardwood forest, descend to marshy Cabin Swamp along the Corrotoman River drainage, and trace a gurgling brook though tunnels of laurel. You may find the latter stint reminiscent of the mountains—appropriate given that botanists have identified plants here found nowhere outside the Blue Ridge.

## DESCRIPTION

Since 1971, when County Forester Henry Bashore began carving a trail network through woodland overlooking the Western Branch Corrotoman River, Lancaster residents have valued Hickory Hollow as both an environmental and recreational resource. When in 1997 the county contemplated constructing an industrial park on the site, the public outcry soon dissuaded the board of supervisors. Instead,

## DIRECTIONS

From Richmond follow US 360 northeast across the Rappahannock to the small town of Warsaw (approximately 45 miles beyond I-295). Turn right onto VA 3 and drive 23 miles southeast to the town of Lancaster. Turn left onto VA 604 (Regina Road) just beyond Lancaster High School. The parking area is a quarter mile down the road on the right.

From Fredericksburg, take winding VA 3 the full 80 miles southeast or take US 17 for 47 miles to Tappahannock, then follow US 360 for 7 miles to Warsaw before accessing VA 3. Follow the directions from VA 3 above.

From Newport News and points south, take US 17 north 30 miles beyond Yorktown. Turn right onto VA 33, continuing 7 miles east to VA 3. Take VA 3 north for 17 miles to Lancaster, making a right onto VA 604 while still on the east side of town.

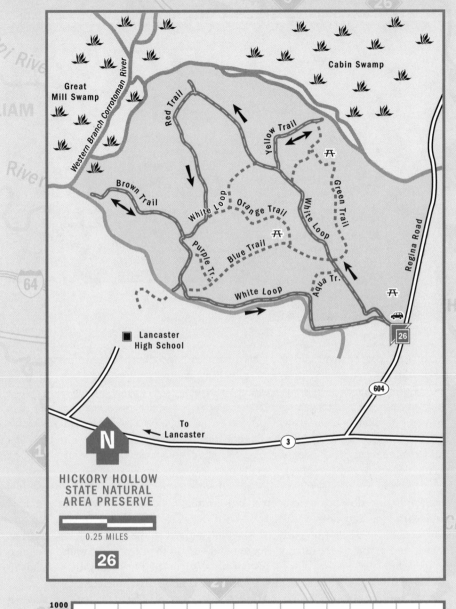

Cabin Swamp

Great
Mill Swamp

Western Branch Corrotoman River

Red Trail

Yellow Trail

Green Trail

Brown Trail

White Loop

Orange Trail

White Loop

Purple Tr.

Blue Trail

White Loop

Aqua Tr.

Regina Road

Lancaster
High School

64

604

26

To
Lancaster

3

N

HICKORY HOLLOW
STATE NATURAL
AREA PRESERVE

0.25 MILES

26

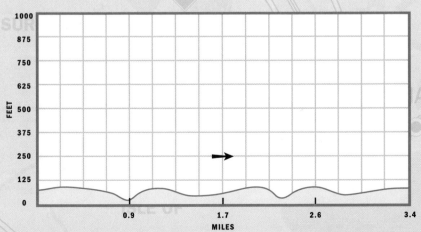

| FEET | | | | |
|---|---|---|---|---|
| 1000 | | | | |
| 875 | | | | |
| 750 | | | | |
| 625 | | | | |
| 500 | | | | |
| 375 | | | | |
| 250 | | | | |
| 125 | | | | |
| 0 | 0.9 | 1.7 | 2.6 | 3.4 |

MILES

A bench invites hikers to rest on
the bluff above a winding creek.

the 254-acre property was sold to the Northern Neck Audubon Society, which later partnered with the commonwealth to establish a state natural-area preserve.

Fittingly, Hickory Hollow is a featured stop along the Virginia Birding and Wildlife
Trail, and diligent birders can spy Acadian flycatchers and hooded warblers here. The
keen eyes of budding botanists will likewise be rewarded, because more than 500 plants
thrive in Cabin Swamp and its diverse environs. Novices can hone their tree-naming
skills at numbered posts along the route, which denote such Virginia natives as black
cherry, dogwood, and hornbeam.

Begin at the official trailhead, where there is a picnic shelter and informational
signboard. Just after setting out on a single-track connector, you will join a graded
double-track heading northwest (right). This is the white-blazed Main Loop, which provides access to a rainbow of trails: green, yellow, and red on the outside; and aqua, blue,
orange, and purple on the interior. (An out-and-back to the Great Mill Swamp is named
for its destination, not by color.) Trails outside the loop lead to streamside wetlands or
river-bluff overlooks, while those inside traverse the mostly level upland forest.

Shortly after joining the old roadbed, you will pass the first of the park's numbered
trees, a persimmon. As the signpost key notes, the tree owes its name to Algonquian-
speaking Indians who dried the autumn-ripening fruit for cold-weather sustenance. Just
ahead is a labeled loblolly pine, a common reforestation species that hints at the age of
this predominantly hardwood forest. A sawmill operated in what is now the preserve
during the 1960s. Continue straight when the white-blazed loop forks to the left, and
you will pass a stand of Virginia pine then a pair of borrow pits on trail right. These, too,
recall a bygone logging operation. Earth was "borrowed" from these holes in order to
level the old road on which the trail was subsequently grafted.

Proceed forward on the Main Loop through three junctions: first the aqua-blazed
Short Loop meets your trail on the left, then the green-blazed Picnic Trail makes a T
junction on the right, and finally the blue-blazed Ridge Trail forks left. As of publication,

the green trail was blockaded by windblown trees and consequently overgrown. Investigate this option on your visit, as it may be cleared. If it's passable, note that an unmapped red-blazed spur links it to the yellow-blazed Swamp Trail.

Beyond a stretch of forest carpeted in the clubmoss known as ground cedar due to its obvious resemblance to cedar branches, the path passes more borrow pits and the old saw-mill site, distinguished by an earthen mound that originated as sawdust. Soon after the Picnic Trail rejoins the Main Loop, turn right onto the Swamp Trail, an out-and-back to the small boardwalk abutting Cabin Swamp. Along an initial level stretch, red maples, beech, and sycamore trees foretell the presence of water, and then the trail bends right for a steep descent to a marshy tributary of the Western Branch Corrotoman River.

Having retraced your steps to the white-blazed loop, continue right and then right again at the red-blazed Overlook Trail. The needle-carpeted trail passes through a coniferous wood of predominantly Virginia and loblolly pines to emerge on a beech-dominated hillside with a thick mountain-laurel understory. Passing a junction on the left, continue ahead a short distance to reach the overlook, where a bench graces the bluff above a meandering creek dotted with fern islands. Retrace your steps to the junction and make a sharp right.

This leg of the Overlook Trail passes through a younger beech forest and briefly leads you along a small seasonal-stream gully. A segment of the trail was rerouted here, but it is easy to follow. As the trail rises, a valley widens on the right. A modest trickle runs through the gully, but steep banks testify to the heavy runoff that follows downpours. Upon regaining the Main Loop, make a right to continue your circuit. Clubmoss and ferns carpet the floor of a diverse hardwood forest here. The Great Mill Swamp Trail out-and-back turns right off the white-blazed loop then traverses a level ridge thick with young pines and ironwoods before making a descent to its soggy namesake. This isolated spot is promising for wildlife watchers.

After retracing the path to the Main Loop and continuing right, veer right again at a junction with the short purple-blazed trail. A descent into an open beech glade follows, with a rivulet running along the hillside on trail left. Shortly beyond a junction on the left, the feeder branch joins a small, sandy-bottomed creek. Here the Main Loop turns left before reaching the creek.

The blue-blazed Ridge Trail promptly forks left from the Main Loop. A wide, mostly level path, it provides pleasant walking back to the trailhead. The white-blazed Main Loop, however, offers the natural climax to your hike. As it parallels the creek heading upstream, the root-laced trail bed narrows to single-track to squeeze through thickets of laurel and holly. As you wind around a few deadfalls and through feeder gullies, the streamlet below narrows. The constricting valley cloisters the trail, creating a wild and almost mountainous scene. Heading east to complete its loop, the white-blazed path passes the aqua-blazed Short Loop connector on the left. After heading a short way south, the trail then emerges onto double-track. The parking area lies a short distance to the right.

# HOG ISLAND WILDLIFE MANAGEMENT AREA

## KEY AT-A-GLANCE INFORMATION

**LENGTH:** 3.8 miles plus options

**CONFIGURATION:** Loop

**DIFFICULTY:** Easy

**SCENERY:** James River, tidewater marsh, pine forest, waterfowl and other wildlife

**EXPOSURE:** Open with little shade

**TRAFFIC:** Low

**TRAIL SURFACE:** Gravel double-track

**HIKING TIME:** 1.5 hours

**SEASON:** Open daily during daylight year-round, but best avoided during hunting seasons (see below)

**ACCESS:** No fee but ID required (see below); mountain biking allowed; no ATVs

**MAPS:** Available online at www.dgif.virginia.gov/hunting/wma/hog_island.html

**FACILITIES:** Office, two wildlife-viewing towers, designated fishing area, boat launch on noncontiguous Carlisle Track; informational signboards, resident staff

**SPECIAL COMMENTS:** This Hog Island is not to be confused with the one on Virginia's Eastern Shore. Admittance to the WMA requires passage through the Surry Nuclear Power Station, where security guards will need to see your ID and inspect your vehicle. All WMAs are open to hunting or fishing, but much of Hog Island is closed to both. Check with the VDGIF to determine annual hunting seasons and regulations; call (757) 253-7072 or visit www.dgif.virginia.gov/hunting).

---

**UTM Trailhead Coordinates for Hog Island Wildlife Management Area**

**UTM Zone (NAD27)   18S**

**Easting   0350681**

**Northing   4117310**

## IN BRIEF

To reach the main tract of Hog Island Wildlife Management Area (WMA), you must first pass through a perfunctory security screening at Dominion Power's Surry Nuclear Power Station. However, once inside, you're surrounded by tidewater marsh teeming with wildlife, and the civilized world seems miles and miles away.

## DESCRIPTION

The Virginia Department of Game and Inland Fisheries manages Hog Island Wildlife Management Area primarily for the benefit of migratory waterfowl, though a host of birds and other animals benefit from the managed habitat and resultant hunting restrictions. Even fishing is limited to the James River along the western shore of the peninsula. That's correct: Hog Island is an island no more. Construction of earthen levees (atop which you will enter and hike through the WMA) linked Hog Island to the peninsula known as Gravel Neck. No longer truly tidal, the marshes

## DIRECTIONS

From Richmond take I-95 south to Exit 61 or I-295 south to Exit 15, and head east on VA 10. Continue about 40 miles to the hamlet of Surry. Turn left at the intersection with VA 31, then turn right at the blinking light, remaining on VA 10 all the while. (If you're coming south from Williamsburg via VA 31 and the Jamestown Scotland–Ferry, you'll turn left onto VA 10 here.) Head east on VA 10 for another 6.5 miles before turning left (east) onto VA 617 at Bacon's Castle. In 1.5 miles, the road reaches a T intersection with VA 650 (Hog Island Road, which also intersects VA 10, to the south). Turn left (north) onto VA 650 to reach Hog Island in less than 5 miles, passing through the power-plant security check en route.

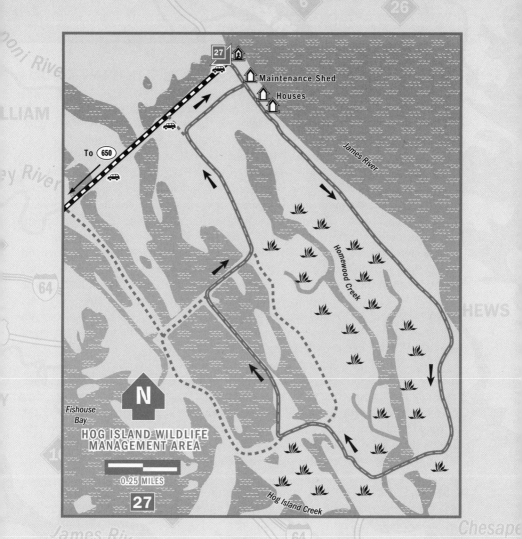

**HOG ISLAND WILDLIFE MANAGEMENT AREA**

Maintenance Shed

Houses

James River

Homewood Creek

To 650

N

Fishouse Bay

0.25 MILES

27

Hog Island Creek

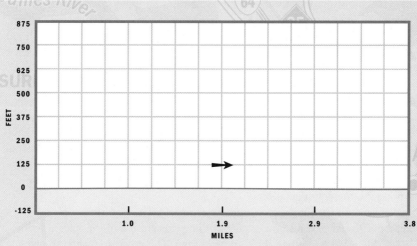

| FEET | | | | | |
|---|---|---|---|---|---|
| 875 | | | | | |
| 750 | | | | | |
| 625 | | | | | |
| 500 | | | | | |
| 375 | | | | | |
| 250 | | | | | |
| 125 | | | | | |
| 0 | | | | | |
| -125 | 1.0 | 1.9 | 2.9 | 3.8 | |

MILES

within the WMA are now filled and drained through dikes. This allows the VDGIF staff to create optimum conditions for specific species.

During the colonial era Hog Island was separated from the mainland, at least in high water, since it is scarcely above sea level. Its name harks back to the bygone farming practice of allowing swine to wander and forage freely on islands. You won't find any wild boars on modern-day Hog Island, but there remains a great diversity of wildlife. In a single afternoon I spotted two herds of deer, numerous white herons and nesting ospreys, a bald eagle, a pair of foxes, and some very large fish I took for carp. I also spied commonplace songbirds, raptors, and the seemingly ubiquitous flocks of Canada geese. It's no wonder bird-watchers are among this off-the-beaten-path WMA's repeat visitors.

Anglers, too, frequent the area's western shore, but aside from passing them on the way in, you won't find any on this route. In fact, apart from the gravel double-track underfoot, the only sign of civilization I saw in the area's eastern half was the "Ghost Fleet," a string of defunct ships moored on the horizon. The James River is 3 miles wide east of Hog Island and passable by such oceangoing vessels. However, no paths lead to the WMA's easternmost Walnut Point or along the winding ribbon of Hog Island Creek, in its southeastern corner.

Begin your hike along the James, heading southeast from the park office at the entrance road's terminus. First scan the field, brilliant green in the springtime, stretching northwest of the office to northernmost Hog Point. Look for grazing deer and for raptors nesting in the still-standing skeletons of dead trees that border the cultivated field. Proceed past the maintenance shed and two residences on the right to draw along a sandy beach on the James River.

You may be lucky enough to spy an eagle swooping down to snatch a fish from the water. White-chested ospreys, or "fish hawks," also nest on Hog Island, and, unlike eagles, these catch fish by diving underwater. According to the *National Audubon Society Field Guide* for the Eastern United States, in places where the two species co-exist, "eagles obtain much of their food by stealing it from the smaller fish hawk." This is not exactly model behavior for a national symbol, but Americans can take pride in conservation measures that have produced a resurgence in both species since pesticides decimated their numbers in the 1960s. But, as the Audubon guide notes, the bald eagle "is still not as numerous as it was in Colonial times, when it was a familiar sight along almost every coastline."

Continuing southeast, you will next pass through an area forested with pines, where you may spot a heard of deer bounding through the underbrush. On my springtime visit a band of still-spotted youngsters was on the move. The trail then bears right to circle Homewood Creek, now impounded to regulate water levels in the marsh you first passed on the right. It was here that the sound of fish splashing about the trunks of pine trees lured me to the edge of a seasonal pool. Most likely the fish were carp, which splash about as they spawn in shallow areas, leaving their eggs among the marshy vegetation.

Views of the James soon open to your left. The trail then curves right again to head northwest past a stand of pines. Along this stretch of the hike, a red fox trotted out of the grass and along the trail before me. The creature turned to give me a puzzled look, as if rethinking its famous timidity, before slinking back into the brush.

You'll soon reach an intersection on the left. It's possible to continue straight here for a shorter loop, but bear left to pass a northern arm of Hog Island Creek, where white herons tiptoe among the marsh grass in vibrant contrast to the surrounding browns and greens. Patient birders will find numerous other species in abundance as well. More than 30 types of waterfowl and 35 shorebirds have been identified within this wildlife management area, prompting its inclusion on the state birding trail. You may wish to walk beyond the next turn to better approach the creek. A vital connector was closed for habitat restoration on my visit, but if it's open on yours, you may elongate your loop and pass north of Fishouse Bay by bearing right at the next three intersections.

To follow the mapped route, however, make the next right, which leads to a narrow spit of land bordered by marsh-ringed ponds. Along this strip you can scan the water on both sides. The path reaches a T intersection, where you should turn right to continue along another narrow earthen ridge overlooking a wetland expanse to the east. You will soon encounter a second T intersection. Bear left this time, and head northwest though a low-lying plain where Canada geese are often found foraging.

The staff residences and maintenance shed you passed earlier are visible on the horizon, as is the main park road. Rather than returning to the road, turn right at your next opportunity, then go left to pass the maintenance building and return to your car. You may find yourself not yet ready to head home, however. There is, after all, negligible elevation gain or loss on this hike, and, as long as you're wearing insect repellent, Hog Island Wildlife Management Area is a fascinating place. The vibrant ecosystem teems with life, so you will never make the same hike twice.

# HOLLIDAY LAKE STATE PARK

## IN BRIEF

Traverse the bottomland valley along Holliday Creek and scan the marsh north of Holliday Lake for herons and swans. Then, walk beside lichen-spotted rock outcroppings on a narrow, hillside single-track above the lake. Finish your loop by climbing away from the water and into mixed forest before returning eastward.

## DESCRIPTION

It may seem unlikely that these forested hills were rolling farms at the turn of the last century. The steep slope punctuated by rock outcroppings on the lake's eastern shore contrasts sharply with the bucolic countryside you'll drive through en route from Richmond. It wasn't until the 1930s that the federal Resettlement Administration (later the Farm Security Administration) bought out local farmers hit hard by the Depression and allowed the land to revert to its former forested state.

Some of those ex-farmers signed on with the Works Progress Administration (later the Works

## DIRECTIONS

From Richmond travel west on US 60 (Midlothian Turnpike). Continue through Midlothian, Powhatan, and Cumberland to the crossroads of Sprouses Corner (just east of Buckingham). Turn left onto VA 640, which you will follow generally southwest for 10.7 twisting miles. Turn left after 2.1 miles to stay with VA 640 when it joins VA 633, then veer right to stay with VA 640. After passing through tiny Andersonville, make a left onto VA 636. After a mile, turn right onto VA 614 and travel 2.5 miles. A left onto VA 692 leads into the park. Drive to the trailhead 1.5 miles ahead at the road's end, paying your vehicle-entrance fee and passing the campground en route.

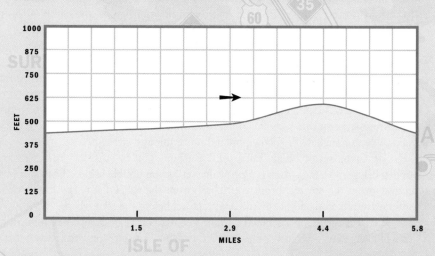

**Carter-Taylor Multiuse Trail**

**Holliday Creek**

**APPOMATTOX-BUCKINGHAM STATE FOREST**

692

**HOLLIDAY LAKE STATE PARK**

Carter-Taylor Multiuse Trail Spur

Saunder's Creek

Saunder's Creek Tr.

**Lakeshore Trail**

**Dogwood Ridge Tr.**

Northridge Tr.

**James Cemetery**

28

N

**HOLLIDAY LAKE STATE PARK**

0.25 MILES

28

723

**4-H Camp**

**Lakeshore Trail**

**Cemetery Creek**

**Holliday Lake**

**Holliday Creek**

**APPOMATTOX-BUCKINGHAM STATE FOREST**

| | | | | | | | | | | |
|---|---|---|---|---|---|---|---|---|---|---|
| 1000 | | | | | | | | | | |
| 875 | | | | | | | | | | |
| 750 | | | | | | | | | | |
| 625 | | | | | | | | | | |
| 500 | | | | | | | | | | |
| 375 | | | | | | | | | | |
| 250 | | | | | | | | | | |
| 125 | | | | | | | | | | |
| 0 | | | | | | | | | | |

**FEET**

1.5    2.9    4.4    5.8

**MILES**

*Projects* Administration) to plant trees and build recreational facilities on the land. Their rustic handiwork remains an integral part of the park, as you'll see in the log-beam Shelter 1, the trailhead for this loop. The trail also passes over the New Deal–era dam that created the lake in 1938. Originally the government planned to dam Fish Pond Creek, a mile west. However, Holliday Creek won out because its deep valley could be transformed into a larger, 150-acre reservoir. Shortly after the lake was complete, the federal government transferred the land to state control. But only in 1972 did Virginia establish Holliday Lake State Park as such, and the campground was added at that time.

The loop mapped here begins north of the concessions building. Approaching Shelter 1 from the road, the path is visible heading along the lake downhill on your left. Just up the hill (west), the 0.3-mile Northridge Trail accesses the loop by running—true to its name—north along a ridge. There is generally ample parking for these trailheads in the midst of the park road's wide cul-de-sac. On the busiest summer days, however, you may find it easier to avoid the crowded beach and picnic area by beginning on the access spur path for the Carter-Taylor Trail (see Appomattox-Buckingham State Forest, page 14). Leaving from a lot north of the park road, the connector joins the Lakeside Trail near Holliday Creek.

Setting out along the shore on the Lakeside Trail, you'll notice numerous deadfalls, both on the hillside rising on your left and at the water's edge. A wooden fishing platform on trail right invites anglers to tempt the largemouth bass, sunfish, and chain pickerel that hide among decaying branches. The trail rises briefly then descends through a mixed forest of beech, red maple, Southern red oak, and cedar, among others. The trail runs along the lake's edge and rounds a peninsula before again veering inland, up a pine-studded hill to meet the Northridge Trail that appears on your left.

The trail, flanked by bright-green moss, maintains its elevation while winding above an inlet and over a peninsular knoll, then drops again to the water's edge. Beyond a signed spur to the campground, 0.1 mile west, the steepening hillside squeezes your path nearer the lake. Large stones dot the surrounding forest as you approach a long pier on the left. Its twin stretches toward it from the opposite shore to give the appearance of a partially dismantled bridge.

Ahead, a small footbridge crosses a deep culvert before the path again veers left. The marshy northern arm of Holliday Lake opens to your right as you climb. A short distance ahead, in a power-line clearing, the Carter-Taylor Trail connector joins your footpath to continue north along the right-of-way. Holliday Creek, screened by foliage, flows toward the reservoir in the valley on trail right.

Descend toward the waterway and bear right as the Carter-Taylor Trail continues ahead. The Lakeshore Trail now takes you upstream, along Holliday Creek, which riffles over rocky shoals. Vibrant clubmoss abounds on the forest floor in this moist floodplain, and disease-stricken pines lay fallen about as well. The blight spared a few of the evergreens, which mingle with yellow poplar, hornbeam, and river birch.

The Carter-Taylor briefly joins the Lakeshore Trail to cross Holliday Creek on a wooden bridge. The trails then promptly diverge as you double back to head south. Veering away from the stream, begin your climb from the valley floor. The Lakeshore Trail continues south along a hillside thick with laurel before the lake returns to view.

The path again approaches the water's edge to curve eastward, passing through a stand of evergreens—Virginia pines and red cedars. Continue forward when a dirt road meets the trail on your left. Cross a small footbridge then a larger, zigzagging boardwalk. Here, Forbes Creek drains into the northeastern arm of the lake. Upon ascending a set of wooden stairs, turn right to begin a mile-long stint southbound.

After curving into a damp drainage, the familiar red oaks and pines recede where chestnut oak and laurel thrive. Fringed in vibrant moss, the narrow single-track twists to navigate the numerous rock outcroppings. The park's beach and picnic areas come into view across the water before the trail curves left. Descend toward the dam on a lengthy wooden staircase.

Cross the dam on a railed walkway, pausing to admire Holliday Creek, flowing untamed again toward the Appomattox River. Once across the dam, bear right and look for a trail climbing away to the left; a deceptive path continues forward but terminates at a lakeside bench. Climb the rooty, rocky path to proceed along a bluff overlooking the southernmost arm of Holliday Lake.

The mossy-banked single-track at Holliday Lake

The lake winnows to a stream, which the path traces briefly before turning right to cross a pair of footbridges. Now presented with an intersection, follow the signed Lakeshore Trail as it veers left. Bypass the 4-H camp on your right and the Appomattox-Buckingham State Forest arboretum on your left. Instead, keep Cemetery Creek on your left. A parking lot and basketball court visible on trail right soon give way to a meadow. Shortly thereafter, cross the creek on a footbridge, and continue upstream through the bottomland forest.

Cross the creek once more before ascending into a stand of pines. The juncture of these two forest types presents the odd sight of ferns sprouting through pine needles on the forest floor. Rising away from the creek valley, you will traverse a grassy flat before reaching a gravel road. Proceed across the road to ascend a set of wooden stairs signed for the Lakeshore Trail. Momentarily, a second sign directs you left at a T intersection.

Follow the level single-track path as it winds through trees, keeping the road within view on the left for almost a quarter-mile. Turn right when your path meets a double-track on a small knoll. It's all downhill from here, but keep an eye out for the next intersection. In a thick pine forest, the double-track forks. The Lakeshore Trail veers left at this junction. Make another left on the single-track just ahead.

Maturing hardwood forest signals that you are again approaching the state park; the path draws along a rivulet on the left. This branch feeds into Sanders Creek, which in turn empties into Holliday Lake. Winding downstream through white oaks and hornbeams, cross two small tributaries before curving left to cross the creek on a wooden footbridge. The lake is just a short distance ahead.

# IVY CREEK NATURAL AREA

## IN BRIEF

Much of the land now protected by Ivy Creek Natural Area was farmed by freed slaves and their descendants for nearly a century. A then-modern barn built in the 1930s remains as testament to the land's agricultural heritage. It now hosts environmental-education exhibits, and the surrounding 215 acres, largely reforested, are home to a host of native wildlife.

## DESCRIPTION

Established three decades ago, Ivy Creek Natural Area is a model of environmental conservation and education in a growing city. An exemplary partnership between the natural area's eponymous foundation, the City of Charlottesville, and Albemarle County ensures the land will escape encroaching suburban development. Pedestrian-only trails crisscross the hillsides above the Ivy Creek arm of the South Fork Rivanna Reservoir, and an education building hosts programs for schoolchildren.

Located across the park-like, quiet observation area from the trailhead signboard, the education building was designed in the style of the larger Depression-era barn that stands just to the north. Erected by Farm Bureau extension agent Conly

## DIRECTIONS

From Richmond follow I-64 northwest to Exit 118 (59 miles beyond I-295). Exit northbound on US 29/250 Bypass. After 4 miles, exit northbound to remain on US 29 (which rejoins Business 29). In 0.4 miles, turn left onto VA 743 (Hydraulic Road) at the first traffic light. Turn left again 1.75 miles on, staying on VA 743 (now Earlysville Road). Just over half a mile ahead, the entrance to Ivy Creek Natural Area is on the left. Pass a private dwelling on the right to park in the gravel lot just south of the trailhead signboard, restrooms, and education building.

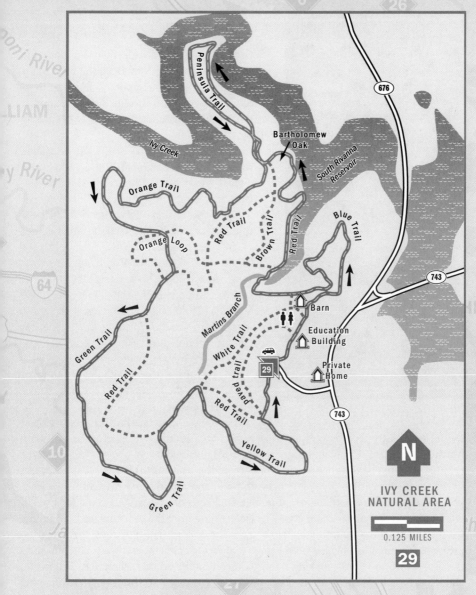

Peninsula Trail

Ivy Creek

Bartholomew Oak

South Rivanna Reservoir

676

Orange Trail

Red Trail

Brown Trail

Red Trail

Blue Trail

Orange Loop

743

Martins Branch

Green Trail

Red Trail

White Trail

paved trail

Barn

Education Building

29

Private Home

Red Trail

Green Trail

Yellow Trail

743

N

IVY CREEK
NATURAL AREA

0.125 MILES

29

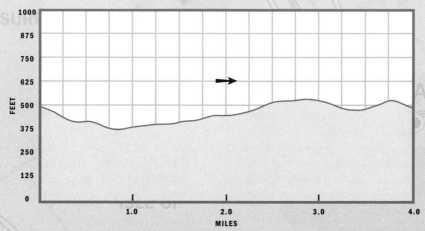

1000
875
750
625
500
375
250
125
0

FEET

1.0        2.0        3.0        4.0
MILES

Shaded Martin's Branch gurgles past boulders before emptying into the South Rivanna River Reservoir.

Greer during the decade that saw both the Dust Bowl and the New Deal, the barn was a showplace for contemporary farming techniques. If you wish to tour the barn, contact the Ivy Creek Foundation, as it is open only by arrangement.

Today the barn is the most visible reminder of a century of African American–owned enterprise at River View Farm, as the land was long known before a dam on the South Fork Rivanna River flooded the surrounding valley. Conly Greer's father-in-law, Hugh Carr, was born a slave. A sharecropper in the wake of the Civil War, he and his wife, Texie, managed to scrape together sufficient savings to purchase the farm piecemeal between 1870 and 1889. Their daughter, Mary Carr Greer, served as an Albemarle County school principal, and a nearby elementary school was named in her honor.

Leaving northwest from the parking area you will pass the cemetery on the right before reaching a covered signboard, from which you can pick up a map brochure. Stay straight on the paved trail to pass between the observation area on the right and an area of thick brush on the left. Upon approaching the barn, bear right to encircle the adjacent meadow, passing beneath a broad red oak. From the rear (north) of the barn, turn right to set out on the earthen Blue Trail beneath hackberry and hickory trees.

Named for its colored blazes, the Blue Trail runs northwest between a field of tall grass on the right and woods on the left. Descending from the old farmstead, a connector heads left to the returning leg of the peninsular Blue Trail. But continue along the meadow, looking for songbirds in the grass and raptors circling overhead. The trail soon ducks left into the forest, making a rocky descent and a second, sharp left. Follow the single-track path downhill through yellow poplar, red oak, and thickets of Virginia pine toward an arm of the South Rivanna River Reservoir.

Hornbeam and beech trees dominate the forest nearer the water's edge and line the root-laced path that veers left and uphill beside a feeder streamlet on the right. Look for a rocked-in spring at the head of the rivulet. Nearing the hilltop, turn right at an intersection. This level stint of the Blue Trail leads to the Central Red Trail, which, as the name suggests, is a sort of backbone loop from which most other trails spur. The route mapped here uses several trails to make a wider loop but traverses the Red Trail intermittently, allowing you to shorten your venture by returning via the interior loop should daylight fade or muscles flag.

Turning right, follow the Red Trail west as it descends to meet Martin's Branch. The stream pours over rocks to meet the reservoir at a still inlet shaded by yellow poplars. Crossing a footbridge, look to the left for an old stone wall that runs along the creek valley. The trail curves briefly uphill, passing a gnarled black oak and a junction with the Brown Trail before veering back toward the water. The path ultimately turns left to rise away from the inlet past the signed Bartholomew Oak. At two centuries, it is the oldest tree in the park and was named for a former park steward.

Just beyond an intersection with the Brown Trail on the left, the Red Trail veers left, the purple-blazed Peninsula Trail continues straight ahead, and the Orange Trail leaves right. Follow the Orange Trail a short distance through young hornbeams and then hickories to an intersection with the Peninsula Trail. Now turn right onto the path, which forks just ahead to circle a spit of land jutting into the marshy Ivy Creek arm of South Rivanna River Reservoir. The path is one of the natural area's least traveled, so look closely to remain on track. From the western length of the Peninsula Trail's loop, sycamore-shaded islands are visible in widening Ivy Creek.

After briefly retracing your steps to regain the Orange Trail, turn right to follow it in and out of drainages on the hillside above Ivy Creek. The wide trail bed traverses a mature beech wood with minimal undergrowth before mountain-laurel thickets reappear trailside. Reentering hardwoods, the path curves past the first of several rock piles. Additional rock piles are visible along the trail ahead, which heads south and uphill past shagbark hickory and red maple.

The trail bends east before an optional looped spur leaves right. Follow the spur to descend through a meadow now growing over in pines and cedars. The more obvious path is the eastern half of this minor loop, but the segments soon rejoin before breaching an old stone wall to meet the Red Trail. Turn right on the park's main loop, and follow it downhill to cross a tributary of Martin's Branch on a footbridge. Ferns grow from a foot-high bank above the angular stones scattered in the streambed, and a mammoth beech stands nearby. A brief forested stretch follows before the trail emerges into a pipeline right-of-way approximately 30 feet wide.

The Red Trail turns left with the clearing, but follow the Green Trail straight ahead. The Green Trail gets off to a lackluster start, passing through pine-dominated recovering forest then bisecting a power-line clearing. A more open beech glade follows, then a mix of hardwoods characterized by chestnut and white oaks. The path descends to cross a small streamlet just as it passes underground, then continues to span another stream-fed creek on a modest bridge. Beyond a hedge of paw-paw a private home is visible off trail right as the path turns from south- to eastbound.

It soon turns again, heading northward to recross the creek just upstream of its junction with Martin's Branch, which is visible in a wide culvert on the right. The Green Trail promptly terminates at the Red, and a right turn takes you northwest along Martin's Branch. The trail curves right to cross the stream, channeled under a stone bridge through a pipe. Soon thereafter, bypass the Yellow Trail as it leaves right, beneath the right-of-way. A slow-moving, rocky streamlet runs in the valley on trail left. Though dotted with young beech trees, this is relatively mature forest, with red maples interspersed among the more-common beech and chestnut oak. Cross the streamlet on a footbridge before the trail curves around a smaller drainage.

A short distance ahead lies the aforementioned power-line clearing, and the Yellow Trail makes a hard left to run along it briefly before meeting the Red Trail. Turn right at this intersection, the last of your hike, bypassing a spur designed for school groups, on the left just ahead. Passing beneath the power lines, the Red Trail descends along then crosses a meadow to return to the parking area.

# JAMES RIVER PARK
## MAIN SECTION

## KEY AT-A-GLANCE INFORMATION

**LENGTH:** 4 miles, plus 2-plus miles of optional trails

**CONFIGURATION:** Figure eight

**DIFFICULTY:** Easy

**SCENERY:** James River, boulder garden, Richmond skyline, Boulevard Bridge

**EXPOSURE:** Shaded to the south, open along the river

**TRAFFIC:** High

**TRAIL SURFACE:** Gravel and dirt

**HIKING TIME:** 1.5 hours

**SEASON:** Open daily during daylight year-round; best avoided after rainfall

**ACCESS:** No fee; not recommended for wheelchairs

**MAPS:** Available at visitor center and online at www.jamesriverpark.org/location.htm

**FACILITIES:** Restrooms, park headquarters and visitor center, picnic shelters, canoe-and-kayak put-in, small clothes-changing station, mountain-bike trail; bridges doubling as observation decks

**SPECIAL COMMENTS:** Dogs are not allowed in the Main Section of James River Park. Picnicking is permitted, but glass containers are not. Paddlers can phone (804) 646-8228 for river-level information. Call the park at (804) 646 8911 or visit www.ci.richmond.va.us/department/parks_rec/james for more informatio. on the park or the annual James River Days.

UTM Trailhead Coordinates for
James River Park Main Section

UTM Zone (NAD27)   18S

Easting   0281644

Northing   4155561

## IN BRIEF

Bisected lengthwise by a railroad track, the Main Section of James River Park retains a distinctly urban character. In addition to providing up-close views of boulders and islands along the banks of the James, this route passes under the Boulevard Bridge at its western terminus and crosses two lofty walkways that double as observation decks, offering views of the river and the city skyline.

## DESCRIPTION

Richmond's James River Park is comprised of ten noncontiguous parcels, which together significantly multiply the outdoor-recreation options of Richmond residents. Besides providing water access to anglers and paddlers, the almost 450-acre park offers waterside trails for walking, jogging, and cycling and is home to a surprising

## DIRECTIONS

From downtown Richmond cross the James River on the Robert E. Lee Bridge (US 1/301). To reach the bridge from I-95/I-64, take Exit 76, and head south on Belvidere Street, which merges with 2nd Street just before crossing the Lee Bridge. Immediately upon reaching the southern end of the bridge, exit onto Riverside Drive, heading west (right). You will pass a parking lot (often gated) on your right near the eastern terminus of the trail. The trailhead lot is the next right and is signed for the park's visitor center. A third parking area farther west along Riverside is an optional trailhead.

From the south via US 1/301 (Jefferson Davis Highway), turn left onto Semmes Avenue. It will become Forest Hill Avenue just before passing Forest Hill Park on the right. Turn right onto 42nd Street and proceed to a T intersection. Turn right onto Riverside Drive and the lot is just ahead on your left.

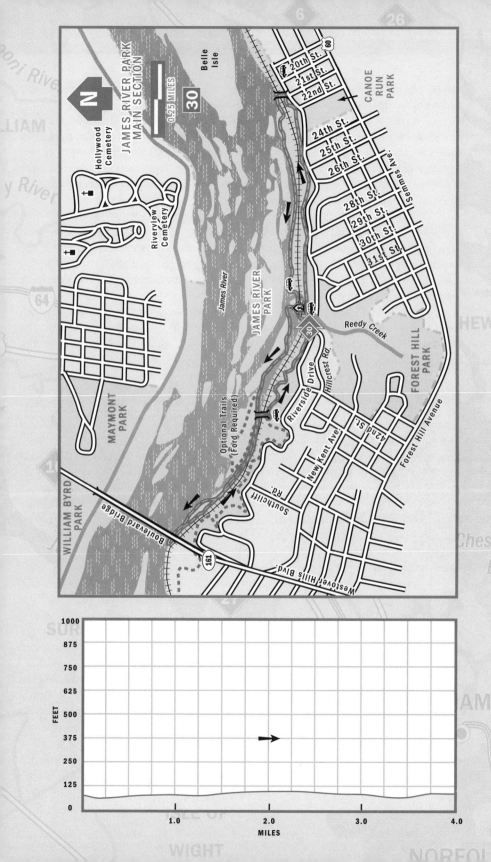

diversity of wildlife—a testament both to nature's persistence within the modern city and an urbanite desire to escape into the outdoors.

This is particularly true of James River Park's Main Section, where the park headquarters stands a short distance from railroad tracks still in use. The tracks run east–west through the Main Section and have necessitated the construction of two concrete footbridges over them. Yet the river frontage remains popular despite the occasional rumble of freight passing beneath, and some visitors come primarily to gawk at the skyline from atop the walkways.

Within the Main Section, a band of single-track known as the Buttermilk Trail is pressed against the hillside below Riverside Drive, while a wide gravel path north of the railroad tracks provides spur paths to the James. Mountain bikers frequent the winding dirt single-track, while walkers and joggers gravitate toward the river. By making use of the single-track, this route minimizes backtracking, but you should be mindful of approaching cyclists.

It's possible to begin this hike from the western or eastern parking areas, which are linked to the river via the aforementioned walkways. However, it is mapped as starting at the central gravel lot. Here, the entry road passes parking spaces on the right, crosses the tracks, then turns right toward the visitor center.

Head north from the parking spaces or west from the headquarters to the park's canoe-and-kayak access. It's possible to head west past a small meadow on the park's wide, gravel main path, but it is preferable to begin at the canoe launch then proceed along the river on a dirt trail. The trail soon joins the gravel path but first passes a narrow river channel sprinkled with boulders. In the summer, sunlight filters through trees at the water's edge, and the river splashes over minute waterfalls to create a serene setting distinctly removed from the surrounding city.

What you see is merely a side channel of the river, most of which lies opposite the rocky islands before you. Though it widens considerably before reaching the Chesapeake, the James is almost half a mile wide by the time it reaches Richmond. The city is located on the fall line, where the rolling Piedmont meets the flatter coastal plain, and the James's boulder-dappled rapids signal its swift descent. The river's watershed, 10,099 square miles, drains a quarter of the state.

In periods of heavy rainfall, the James swells over its banks. Look closely and you will see debris and detritus wrapped about tree trunks and lodged amid rock formations in the channel. You'll find hydrophilic species such beech, sycamore, and birch growing along the shore, often entwined with vines. In periods of drought, the river recedes to reveal rocks and pebbles, the remnants of larger stones churned to bits by torrential waters then smoothed by the river's continuous flow.

As you head west along the shore, you'll rejoin the gravel path then be tempted to break away again on the spurs that approach the shore. Be cautious at the river's edge, especially in high water, but allow yourself to gravitate toward the river. You will soon pass a large, concrete staircase on the left, which leads over the railroad to the westernmost parking lot. On the right, across the channel, there are trails on two of the larger islands. In periods of low water, it's possible to rock-hop to these islands without getting wet. However, the risk of falling, or even drowning, is greatly magnified by high water, hence their exclusion from this hike.

Continue west along the main path, then veer right to pass a picnic shelter and return to the water's edge. This spur rejoins the main path just before it passes under the Boulevard Bridge. Turn around after admiring the steel span set on concrete pilings and perhaps the lofty Carillon, Richmond's WWI memorial, visible on the opposite shore. Follow the main path back to the walkway to the western parking lot and climb the stairs. Admire the view as you catch your breath, then pass over the railroad tracks. Next, look for an earthen trail on your right and follow it as it loops through the woods and under the bridge.

At 1.75 miles, you're now on the southern single-track, which twists and turns with the topography. Continue generally east through the towering trees and dense vegetation. Descending to meet the middle parking lot, cross it to continue on the opposite side. You'll soon pass Reedy Creek, one of the river's many tributaries, on a footbridge. There are additional boardwalks along this stretch, where water seeping downhill tends to muddy the trail. Rising along the hillside, the railroad tracks come into view on your left.

You'll soon reach Buttermilk Spring, a highlight of this dirt trail, which was nicknamed the Buttermilk Trail for it. The bricked-over spring, a trickle of its former self, served as a nineteenth-century refrigerator. Farmers stored milk cans in the spring's waters to keep them cool before hauling the milk to market in town.

Next, the trail descends to meet the eastern parking lot. Traverse the paved lot to ascend granite steps in the opposite corner. After a short stretch of dirt trail, cross the railroad tracks again via the eastern walkway at approximately 3 miles. Before descending the stairs to reach the eastern portion of the main path, take in the far-reaching views of Belle Isle and downtown Richmond across the river. Once down the steps, head west back to the park headquarters via the main trail. It is possible to walk farther east along a cement-encased pipe, which provides access to the boulder garden south of Belle Isle. However, venture onto the rocks at your own risk, and be very mindful of the current.

As you return, you'll again be tempted to veer away from the unsightly railroad track toward the river on your right. Doing so, you'll pass another picnic shelter on the left before reaching the headquarters. Ascend the stairs at the rear of the building and follow the walkway around the building and back to the gravel lot that fronts its southern entrance. The entrance and parking spaces are a short distance west and across the railroad tracks.

Though scarred by heavy use and periodic flooding, the riparian woods along this hike retain their allure for many Richmonders. And while the park is worn, the river is now significantly cleaner than it was three decades ago, when municipal and industrial pollution kept residents away. A sewer project, prompted by the Clean Water Act and completed in 1972, not only diverted polluted runoff, but also provided the park's first land acquisition—originally the project right-of-way. Water quality remains dependent on activity upstream, as the James has made almost three-quarters of its 340-mile run by the time it hits Richmond. Contemplate, when enjoying the river, the long journey that Appalachian snowmelt has made to reach the city, and keep in mind the ecologically rich Tidewater downstream.

# JOSEPH BRYAN PARK

## IN BRIEF

Abutting Henrico County in north Richmond, Joseph Bryan Park offers wide-ranging amenities, from tennis courts to state park–style group-picnic shelters. Its streamside woods are pleasantly rustic, despite the roaring interstate nearby.

## DESCRIPTION

Joseph Bryan never resided on, or even owned, the land that was to become his namesake park. The end-of-the-century publisher of the *Richmond Times,* which he merged with its main competitor to form the *Times-Dispatch* in 1903, lived instead at two of North Richmond's most famous addresses. A Confederate veteran, Bryan wed Isobel "Belle" Stewart in 1871 and moved into her family's posh estate, Brook Hill, which had served as a Confederate hospital and inn during the Civil War. Although his father-in-law added a gothic-revival wing to better accommodate the young couple, the Bryans purchased the Laburnum estate, 2 miles east, in 1883. Perhaps Joseph Bryan was inspired by his close friend Lewis Ginter's success as a real estate developer. It was Ginter who gave Bryan, his personal attorney, the then-struggling *Richmond Times* in 1887.

## DIRECTIONS

Joseph Bryan Park lies at the crux of I-64 and I-95, hemmed in by I-64 and I-95. The main entrance is on Hermitage Road (which is Lakeshore Avenue north of the park), at the park's northeast corner. If you're coming from I-64, follow the signs for I-95 North before exiting at Hermitage (Exit 80) and heading a short distance north. Dumbarton Avenue runs parallel to the park's northern border and intersects Hermitage—just head south half a mile to reach the entrance from Dumbarton.

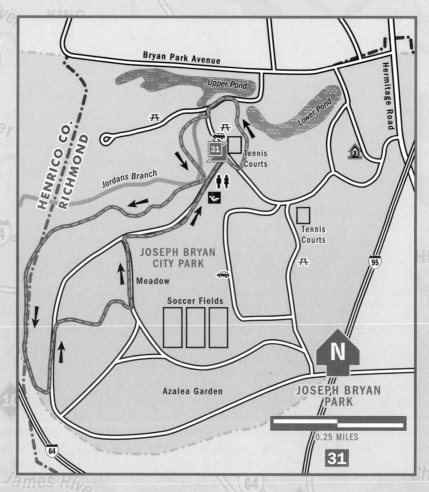

Bryan Park Avenue

Upper Pond

Lower Pond

Hermitage Road

HENRICO CO.
RICHMOND

Jordans Branch

**31**

Tennis
Courts

Tennis
Courts

**JOSEPH BRYAN
CITY PARK**

Meadow

Soccer Fields

Azalea Garden

**N**

**JOSEPH BRYAN
PARK**

0.25 MILES

**31**

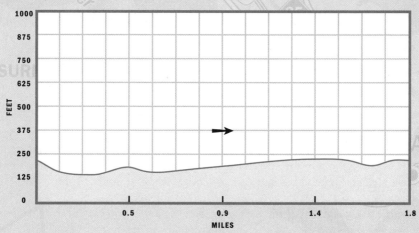

| FEET | | | | | |
|---|---|---|---|---|---|
| 1000 | | | | | |
| 875 | | | | | |
| 750 | | | | | |
| 625 | | | | | |
| 500 | | | | | |
| 375 | | | | | |
| 250 | | | | | |
| 125 | | | | | |
| 0 | | | | | |

0.5          0.9          1.4          1.8
MILES

The original Laburnum, a many-gabled brick Victorian featuring elaborate ironwork and gas lighting, burned in 1906. The Bryans resolutely set about constructing a 50-room Colonial-style mansion with towering limestone columns that stands to this day. Bryan died in 1908, shortly after the house was completed.

Soon thereafter, his wife purchased the Rosewood estate at a public auction. (The land was acquired by William Young in the 1700s and bequeathed to his daughter Rosina in 1832.) In 1909 Belle Stewart Bryan donated the Rosewood land to the City of Richmond in honor of her late husband, specifying that it remain "a free park for the use and benefits of all its citizens." Over the next few decades, the city reshaped what was a large tract of farmland into the wooded, rolling hills and duck pond visitors see today. The rustic shelters, bridges, and stonework were constructed during the Depression by the Works Progress Administration (WPA).

Of the 262-acre park, some 175 acres are forested. The pond and adjacent marsh (on its northern, upper portion) offer welcome respite to migratory waterfowl, although ducks and geese, fattened by bread crumbs, maintain a presence year-round. Contemporary visitors will also find a playground, tennis courts, and soccer fields, as well as an azalea garden. Those seeking to stretch their legs will want to head past the pond, garden, soccer fields, and playground to park near Shelter #1. The signboard near the parking lot features a map, but not all trails are included. The intrepid need not worry: stick to well-worn paths and you'll soon reemerge on pavement.

Begin by walking past the shelter and continuing downhill on the road to the right of the shelter. At the base of the hill, you can walk across the dam bisecting the two-tiered pond. For longer trails, however, head left to the bridge, which evokes a Parisian pont with its wrought-iron lampposts. Across the bridge a short trail bears right along the pond then uphill to Shelter # 2; a road returns to the bridge. A worthwhile side trip for those interested in Depression-era park construction, this small loop suffers from infrequent maintenance.

For the trail mapped here, bear left (facing the bridge) into the woods. Follow the earthen path as it drops to parallel Jordans Branch, which feeds into the pond. Grills along the stream will beckon you to return with the family for a picnic. The path rises to meet a road, but bear right and you'll find it quickly dives back into the woods near a sign reading "Jordans Branch Trail." Meander through woods of white oak and water-loving birch trees. Towering oaks felled by Hurricane Isabel in 2003 may still force hikers around them.

Upon reaching a T intersection with a wider path, turn right then left again. Enjoy this lengthy stretch of woodland walking. In winter the deep-green American holly interspersed among taller deciduous trees lends life and color to the forest. Soon the trail draws near I-64, and the drone of traffic temporarily overpowers birdsong. The trail emerges onto a paved road, one of several in the park rarely opened to vehicles. Turn left and continue on the road until reaching a trail on your right. Follow the trail through vine-strewn woods to emerge on another road. Bear left onto the pavement and right at the subsequent T intersection to return to your vehicle via the blacktop.

If you wish to visit the park's meadow, however, you may bear right soon after emerging onto this second stretch of pavement. A path leads past the concrete rem-

Azaleas and dogwoods burst into bloom every spring at Joseph Bryan Park.

nants of a forgotten structure and alongside a grassy clearing on the left. Formerly a city stump-dumping sight, the undulating surface of the meadow is now mowed annually. In the summer its tall grasses teem with birds and insects. Up a short, steep hill are the more neatly manicured soccer fields. Bear left across the fields toward the playground to return to your vehicle from the meadow.

When done with your hike, take the park tour described on the Friends of Bryan Park Web site, www.friendsofbryanpark.com. It includes several points of historic interest in the park's western half, removed from the trails described here. Then you can drive down Brook Road to gawk at Joseph and Belle Bryan's former residences, historic Brook Hill and Laburnum.

# LAKE ANNA STATE PARK

## KEY AT-A-GLANCE INFORMATION

**LENGTH:** 6.25 miles (9 with optional spur)

**CONFIGURATION:** Loop with optional balloon spur

**DIFFICULTY:** Moderate

**SCENERY:** Mostly hardwood forest, fingers of Lake Anna, creeks in the park's interior

**EXPOSURE:** Mostly shaded but open on optional Powerline Trail

**TRAFFIC:** Low (higher in summer)

**TRAIL SURFACE:** Dirt

**HIKING TIME:** 3 hours

**SEASON:** Trails open daily 8 a.m. to dusk year-round; main season runs April–October, with staffed beachfront facilities

**ACCESS:** Parking costs $3 on weekdays and $4 on weekends or $2 off-season. Beach swimming costs $2 for children ages 3–12 and $3 for adults, $1 more per guest on weekends; boat-launch usage costs $4 daily. Visitor center, restrooms, picnic areas, and fishing pier are wheelchair accessible.

**MAPS:** Available at the park and online at www.dcr.virginia.gov/parks/lakeanna.htm

**FACILITIES:** Visitor center, restrooms, showers, swimming beach, boat launch, fishing pier, playground; in-season canoe, pedal boat, and rowboat rentals available (prices vary with craft and time of day)

**SPECIAL COMMENTS:** As of publication, cabins were about to open at Lake Anna. Call the park office at (540) 854-5503.

---

UTM Trailhead Coordinates for
Lake Anna State Park

UTM Zone (NAD27)   18S

Easting     0252824

Northing    4222344

## IN BRIEF

Escape the crowds along the shore of Lake Anna, the park's main draw, by following this loop through mostly hardwood forest, past scenic rivulets, and alongside an inlet of the lake. Take the optional balloon spur, and you'll cover 9 of the park's 13 trail miles. Most are multiuse, so expect a foot bed scarred by horse hooves in wet spots.

## DESCRIPTION

The gold rush in the land that is today Lake Anna State Park preceded its famous California counterpart by 20 years. Mining continued in the area, known as Gold Hill, through the 1940s, though prospecting peaked some sixty years earlier. The last gold found was discovered in a zinc mine.

The foundation of the Goodwin Gold Mine now crumbles within the state park, opened in 1983. Lake Anna itself was formed in 1971 to provide cooling water for the North Anna Nuclear Power Station. A sign at the park entrance reminds visitors of the facility's proximity, but, fortunately, traces of industry are scarce within the park's 2,300 acres. Instead, a sandy beach and pedal-boat rentals help kids wile away sunny, school-free days. On summer weekends, throngs of youngsters frolic on the beach, parents tend their barbecue grills, and motorboats roar across the lake.

On a winter's day, however, a profound silence enshrouds Lake Anna State Park. The

## DIRECTIONS

From I-95 take Exit 118 and head west on VA 606, which merges with VA 208. After 16 miles, turn right on VA 601 then left into the park after 3 miles. The necessary turns are marked with brown signs from the interstate. The park is about a 20-minute drive from the interstate though rolling hills and rural farms.

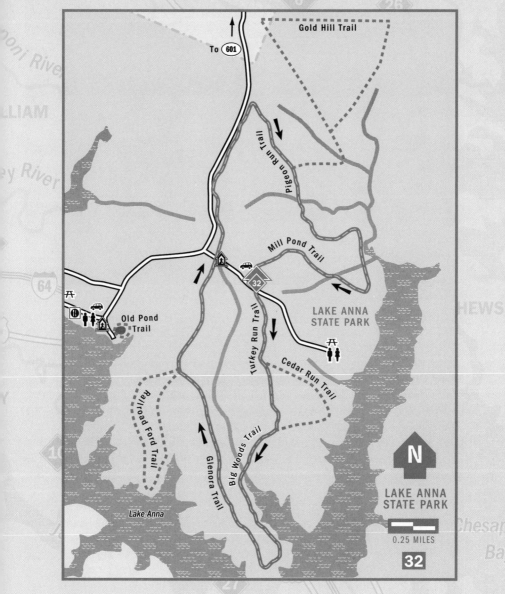

Gold Hill Trail

To 601

Pigeon Run Trail

Mill Pond Trail

32

LAKE ANNA
STATE PARK

Old Pond
Trail

Turkey Run Trail

Cedar Run Trail

Railroad Ford Trail

Big Woods Trail

Glenora Trail

Lake Anna

N

LAKE ANNA
STATE PARK

0.25 MILES

32

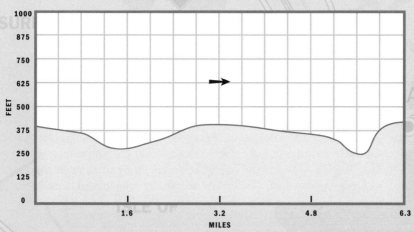

A pier juts out over glistening Lake Anna.

breeze passes inaudibly through leafless trees and the waves dare not lap at the shore. On one February weekday visit, I had the park to myself.

Overlooking the swimming beach are showers, rest rooms, a concession stand, and a playground. Downhill to the east stands the visitor center, behind which is the fishing pond—a startlingly modest impoundment relative to it's 13, 000-acre neighbor a few yards away. A former landowner dammed a stream to create the pond, and the park subsequently encircled it with the Old Pond Trail. A leaflet highlights the plants and animals visible from nine stations along the route. Although brief, the path is an informative primer for a more serious hike at Lake Anna State Park.

West of the beach are the boat launch, picnic tables, and a fishing pier. The Fisherman's Trail, a brief lakeside stroll, leaves from this area. Those opting to cast a line in Lake Anna can hope to catch walleye, channel catfish, sunfish, and striped bass.

To hike the route mapped here, turn left off the main road after passing the park office, also to your left. You'll spy the small trailhead parking lot ahead on the right. Farther down this side road is a picnic area with restrooms.

To begin your venture, briefly walk along the road, away from the park office, before ducking right into the woods on the Turkey Run Trail (erroneously labeled Turtle Run on some maps), heading southeast. Pass through a predominantly oak forest, in which deep-green American holly is particularly evident during the winter.

You'll soon arrive at a fork in the mostly level trail; the fork is marked by an unusual white oak with a secondary trunk jutting first horizontally then vertically. Veer left on the 0.8-mile Cedar Run Trail, which approaches the lake before rejoining Turkey Run to form the Big Woods Trail. Of the 8.5 miles of lake frontage at Lake Anna State Park, the beach area covers but a portion. This route periodically traces a finger of the lake where Pigeon Run once descended to meet the North Anna River.

After veering left onto the Big Woods Trail, descend through a young forest thick with pines and cedars. The forest is recovering from logging done in the 1950s.

The entire area was selectively logged during the first half of the twentieth century, hence it was dubbed "Big Woods."

Cross a wooden footbridge over a small stream winding on its way to Lake Anna. Nearby a streamside boulder beckons picnickers. Horseback riders are diverted from the trail to ford the rivulet, but the two paths soon rejoin. The trail does not diverge at a second bridge, and horse hooves have chopped up the nearby soil. In general, the wet earth nearer the lake is more easily scarred by equine passage.

A thoughtfully placed bench, courtesy of the Friends of Lake Anna State Park, affords hikers a place to rest and gaze across the lake. The woods grow thick with vines, and red cedars begin to replace holly in the understory before the Big Woods Trail intersects the Glenora Trail, which bears right. Moving upland, the trail turns briefly to red clay, recalling the hills of Georgia. You'll pass a section of trail where bricks were used in vain to rip-rap the path; they are now scarcely visible in the worn soil.

Next, the 1.6-mile Railroad Ford Trail departs to the left. This balloon path offers an undulating tour of another lake peninsula and is mercifully off-limits to all but pedestrians. The trail follows a 1916 railroad grade built to transport lead and zinc for ammunition production during the Great War. The waters of Lake Anna subsequently submerged a short, but nevertheless vital, stretch of track. Heading north from the Railroad Ford Trail, now on the Sawtooth Trail, the abandoned railroad grade is visible on trail left.

You will ultimately draw within sight of the park office. If you're tuckered out, now is your chance to retreat to your car, down the road to the right. Otherwise continue straight across the road and in front of the office. The Sawtooth Trail parallels the park's main road for a significant stretch; it also crosses the driveway of a park staffer's residence. The footpath is in better shape here, north of the trailhead, and this helps compensate for the nearby asphalt.

The path eventually cuts a sharp right back into the forest. You're now on the Pigeon Run Trail. The optional Gold Hill Trail balloon departs from the left. If you're feeling frisky, you can add another 2.8 miles to your total by taking this trail, which passes the remains of a nineteenth-century gold mine. However, note that the trail relies for half its length on a power-line right-of-way. Though the power lines detract somewhat from the woodland experience, the relatively wide clearing provides an excellent vantage for bird-watching.

The Pigeon Run Trail, dipping southwest then northwest, fords not its namesake (according to my topo map) but a scenic feeder stream. The stream sparkles with quartzite and fills the glade with its gurgling before ascending a steep hill cloaked in mountain laurel. In the late 1800s, Hailey's Mill, a gristmill, operated on hydraulic power from Pigeon Run. As the park brochure notes, the dam broke in an 1889 storm. Also gone now are the passenger pigeons from which the stream took its name.

The Pigeon Run Trail veers right for a hill-and-vale stretch on the aforementioned right-of-way before turning right onto the Mill Pond Trail. After the junction you'll pass through an area of recently cut pines. A rivulet again meanders along the footpath. As you pass under mature forest, a pine beam in the trail signals your impending completion of the loop. Emerging onto the road, turn left, and follow it back to your vehicle.

# MARINERS' MUSEUM PARK

## IN BRIEF

The Maury Trail encircles its namesake lake on the grounds of the Mariners' Museum Park. Fittingly located in Newport News, America's shipbuilding capital, the museum explores maritime history, from the Age of Exploration to modern naval warfare. However, no admission is required to explore the grounds on this 5-mile loop, which presents a sweeping view of the James River.

## DESCRIPTION

Archer Huntington, heir to the Newport News Shipbuilding and Drydock Company, established the Mariners' Museum in 1930 with the goal of amassing America's foremost collection of maritime art and artifacts. Before most of the collection was purchased, Huntington had reshaped the 800-acre parcel on which he chose to build. From the outset he envisioned wooded grounds adjacent to the museum and its library. In 1931 he had Waters Creek dammed at its confluence with the James, flooding the swampy valley floor to create Lake Maury. Its name honors the "Pathfinder of the Seas," Virginia-born Matthew Fontaine Maury, the nineteenth-century naval commander whose pioneering work in oceanography also earned him homage on Richmond's Monument Avenue.

In 1932, the Lion's Bridge, so-named for the larger-than-life stone lions standing sentinel on its

## DIRECTIONS

From Richmond take I-64 southeast to Exit 258 (58 miles east of I-295), then exit onto US 17 southbound. The museum is 3 miles southwest of the exit. Upon crossing VA 143 continue straight on VA 312. Upon intersecting US 60, continue straight again, onto Museum Drive. A grass overflow-parking area for trail users is located on the right side of the road before you reach the larger lot adjacent to the museum.

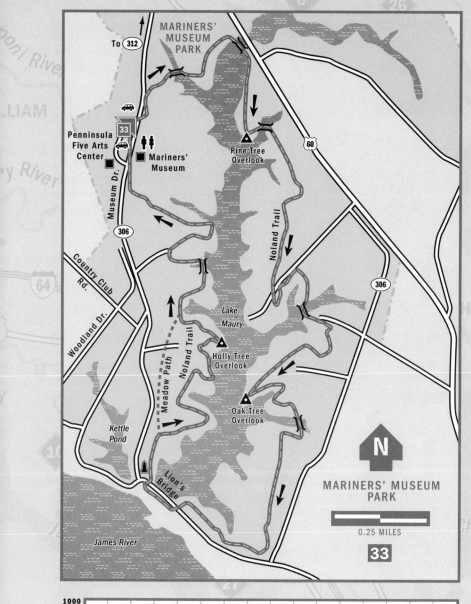

MARINERS'
MUSEUM
PARK

To (312)

Penninsula
Five Arts
Center

Mariners'
Museum

Museum Dr.

(33)

(306)

Pine Tree
Overlook

(60)

Noland Trail

(306)

Country Club
Rd.

Woodland Dr.

Meadow Path

Noland Trail

Lake
Maury

Holly Tree
Overlook

Oak Tree
Overlook

Kettle
Pond

Lion's
Bridge

James River

(64)

N

MARINERS' MUSEUM
PARK

0.25 MILES

(33)

Chesape
Bay

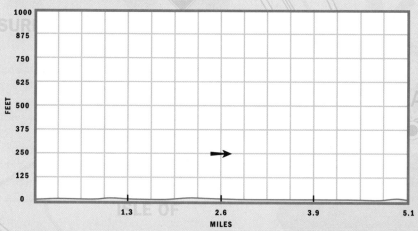

1000
875
750
625
500
375
250
125
0

FEET

1.3          2.6          3.9          5.1
MILES

A seagull rests atop the statuary at the Lion's Gate between Lake Maury and the James River.

four corners, was completed atop the dam. The sculptures were designed by Archer's wife, Anna Hyatt Huntington, who also crafted the larger monument mounted uphill. Named "Conquering the Wild," the uphill sculpture depicts a man wrestling to subdue a horse, with four figures (representing science, art, learning, and history) looking on. The area around the bridge remains a focal point for visitors, who relish views of the lake, statuary, and tidal flats along the widening James.

Though its grounds have always been an integral element of the Mariners' Museum, the Noland Trail, your route for this hike, wasn't opened until 1991. Named for a beneficent local family, the path incorporates 14 numbered boardwalk-like bridges over various creeks and inlets. Four overlook piers provide vistas of the lake.

Once you've gawked at the large propeller in the garden opposite the museum's office entrance, look for a stone marker that directs visitors toward twin trailheads north and south of the museum. Similar markers designate the numbered bridges en route and mark the trail mileage in half-mile intervals. To follow the loop as described here, begin just north of the museum's main entrance, which is bedecked with nautical flags and a ship-shaped weathervane.

Set out downhill through a white oak and yellow poplar forest decorated with a smattering of deep-green holly. Almost immediately, you approach the first bridge, modest by this trail's standards. A short distance on, a spur to the grassy overflow-parking area intersects the loop on your left before a slightly longer span crosses a finger of the lake.

After ascending a pine-forested peninsula, you'll approach a lengthy boardwalk paralleling US 60, under which the northernmost arm of the lake extends. The road briefly remains visible on your left before the trail rises to enter pines and poplars cloaked in ivy. Shortly beyond the 0.5-mile marker, pass a parcel of black birches as you approach the Pine Tree Overlook, a T-shaped pier on trail right.

The path then rises to run south through a hardwood forest of black and red oaks above the lake. After bisecting an old roadbed, the path descends left to cross a soggy drainage and comes again upon the water. Look for a low brick wall on trail right before you reach a lengthy bridge, which extends from the tip of one small peninsula to another. The triangular wall cordons off an old cemetery.

Ascending above the water, continue paralleling the curving lakeshore. The Noland Trail now clearly bears right as an old roadbed stretches away to the left. Beyond a parcel of young hardwoods, a meadow-like green space stretches away atop the hill on your left. The trail passes briefly along a wooden fence next to an old gravel road on Curtis Point. Where the road makes a cul-de-sac, pass through a metal gate and beneath a broad white oak to descend to Oak Tree Overlook. From the wooden platform, the glimmering waters of the James are visible beyond Lion's Bridge.

Resume winding generally south along Lake Maury's eastern shore. Dogwoods, red maples, and mountain laurel are scattered in the woods here. After crossing two more bridges on either side of a small finger of land, make another uphill climb to the halfway point, mile 2.5. The Noland Trail then crosses three smaller bridges in succession as it curves around a wet hillside to head west. Note sweet bay magnolias growing amid the vine-filled woods before you emerge within sight of Lion's Bridge. Continue straight, mindful of auto traffic on the bridge.

The trail's east and west entrances are signed on either side of the bridge. Cross the bridge on the left to examine the sandy tidal flats of the James River. Look north and imagine how this valley once appeared: not the shimmering lake before you but a muddy saltgrass marsh. So it was when Captain Edward Waters, for whom the dammed creek was named, was granted the property in 1624. There were likely crop fields overlooking the valley floor by 1781, when American militiamen led by another Captain Edward—Edward Mallory—gave chase to a party of plundering redcoats they encountered at the mouth of Waters Creek.

Beyond the bridge the Noland Trail veers north and uphill to pass beneath the "Conquering the Wild" sculpture. Just ahead is the first real trail junction of your hike. The Meadow Path continues straight through a grassy flat as the main trail curves right to trace a peninsula. The Meadow Path shortens the hike slightly but is worth considering in the spring, when wildflowers carpet the field.

The Noland Trail takes a more winding route along the lakeshore, passing an open forest that was thinned in the wake of storm damage. Just beyond the loop's twelfth bridge is the Holly Tree Overlook, braced atop a steep bank on trail right. A wheelchair-accessible path links it west to Museum Drive. Beyond it, the path wends its way downhill to mile 4, positioned between two more bridges.

You'll note more pines in the forest in the last mile. After passing a holly-clad drainage, the trail bends inland for the final time. The boathouse is visible across an inlet of the lake and a connector to it heads right shortly before the Meadow Path rejoins the trail from the left. Here, with suburban homes visible across Museum Drive, is the trail's southern entrance. Turn right to return to the parking area.

# MOTTS RUN RESERVOIR

## KEY AT-A-GLANCE INFORMATION

**LENGTH:** 3 miles plus 1.5-mile optional spur

**CONFIGURATION:** Figure eight

**DIFFICULTY:** Moderate

**SCENERY:** Hardwood-forested hillsides overlooking Motts Run Reservoir, mountain-laurel thickets above rocky streams

Exposure: Well-shaded except along the lake

**TRAFFIC:** High in summer, low otherwise

**TRAIL SURFACE:** Dirt single-track

**HIKING TIME:** 1.5 hours

**SEASON:** Park facilities open daily 6 a.m.–sunset April–October

**ACCESS:** No fee; trails are not recommended for wheelchairs, but there is a wheelchair-accessible fishing pier; no bikes, horses, ATVs, or swimming allowed

**MAPS:** Available at park office and on signboard at trailhead

**FACILITIES:** Park office, nature center, restrooms, concessions, picnic tables, grills, boat launch, three fishing piers, orienteering course

**SPECIAL COMMENTS:** The facilities at Motts Run, including the entrance road and parking lots, are closed November–March, except by special arrangement. However, hikers may park outside the entrance gate (without blocking it) and access the trails on foot. Contact the City of Fredericksburg Parks at (540) 372-1086 or visit www.fredericksburgva.gov.

UTM Trailhead Coordinates for
Motts Run Reservoir

UTM Zone (NAD27)  18S

Easting    0276404

Northing   4243843

## IN BRIEF

North of Motts Run Reservoir, trails lace the hillside, looking out across the lake. Undulating terrain and towering forest belie the tight-knit nature of the trail system, which can be customized to different lengths.

## DESCRIPTION

The trail network at Motts Run Reservoir serves the threefold aim of this 860-acre city park, which fuses outdoor recreation with environmental education and habitat preservation. In a scenario familiar to Virginia hikers (see Beaverdam and Walnut Creek Parks, among others), the City of Fredericksburg elected to open a nature park on the shores of its recently completed reservoir in 1974. The park's initial appeal was lake fishing, which remains a significant draw. However, the newly built nature center is testament to an increased focus on education.

Though cool weather banishes first the throngs of picnickers, then the anglers, and, finally, the park's seasonal staff, the nature center remains open to school and civic groups for prescheduled programs. Also during the off-season, local scouting troops help maintain the trail bed and bridges. An Eagle Scout even helped

## DIRECTIONS

From Richmond, head north on I-95 to Exit 130 (46 miles north of I-295). Head west on VA 3 for less than a mile, then turn right onto VA 639 (Bragg Road). Having continued almost a mile north, turn left onto VA 618 (River Road). The park entrance is on the left, 2.4 miles ahead. From Fredericksburg, it's possible to arrive from the east on VA 639 (Fall Hill Avenue north of VA 618) then turn right onto VA 618. There is an alternate parking area uphill, but this route begins from the road's lakeside terminus.

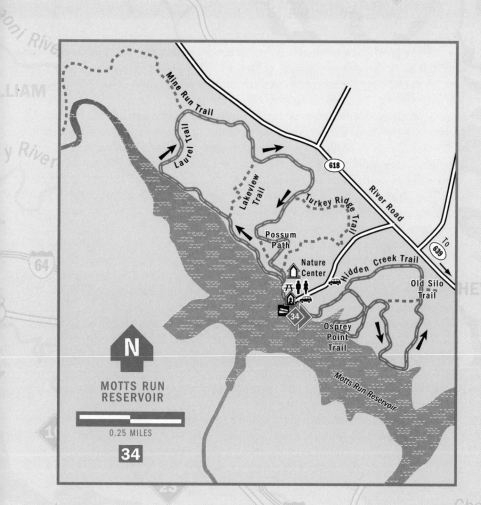

N

MOTTS RUN
RESERVOIR

0.25 MILES

34

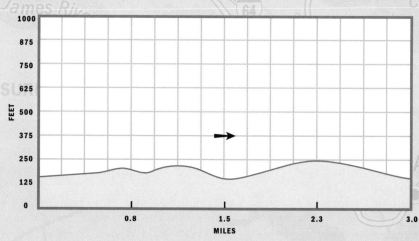

develop the park's new orienteering course. Armed with a compass and instructions obtained from the office or nature center, would-be trailblazers can crisscross the park on one of eight routes, which vary in difficulty and distance. Numbered posts at key points along the course help keep hikers on track.

A relatively mature forest and open understory help make off-trail orienteering feasible at Motts Run, though navigating around a thicket of mountain laurel or stand of beech saplings is no doubt occasionally required. Those abundant species share the forest with holly, white oak, Northern red oak, and dogwood, among others. Trails wind beneath them in two parcels of land separated by the park's entrance road. The route outlined here makes a figure eight, using both halves of the network but not all trails. To shorten your hike simply choose one of this hike's two loops; to elongate it, follow the bypassed spur trails.

Beginning from the lower, lakeside parking lot, head east, opposite the park office, on the signed Hidden Creek Trail. After a brief stride along the lake, blue blazes guide you upland to run northeast along a hillside above an inlet, with the stream that feeds it visible just ahead. Upon reaching a fork in the trail, turn right and descend to cross the rivulet on a wooden footbridge just above a mossy rock slide.

The path rises steeply away, promptly gaining 60 feet in elevation. As it levels, look for a T intersection ahead. Here, the Osprey Point Trail heads right. Follow this balloon spur for views of the lake beyond the waterside foliage. The trail rises slightly then drops dramatically to approach the shore. Fallen limbs and logs outline the path as benches invite you to relax and enjoy the vista. Upon completing the loop, proceed north along a finger ridgeline.

Approach an intersection just beyond a tree with a rotund burl protruding from its trunk, as noted on the park map. Bend right with the proper Hidden Creek Trail, bypassing a cutoff trail that veers left. Descending southeast through maturing hardwood forest dotted with laurel and cedars, the path again nears the water as it rounds a point. A steady climb follows as the trail curves left, away from the lakeshore and along an inlet on the right.

A parcel of downed pines crowns the hilltop. Exposed to strong winds, the shallow-rooted conifers were toppled by a storm. Though cleared from the trail, they remain scattered about. The cutoff trail rejoins the main loop here as the main loop bends right, off the hilltop, to pass a spur, the Old Silo Trail, on the right. This brief out-and-back leads to the remains of an old granary. Beyond it, the Hidden Creek Trail widens as it approaches River Road, screened by the woods to your right.

Making a distinct left beside a mossy mound, however, the path retreats from the noise of traffic and down a draw. The stream you previously crossed emerges from a small spring on trail left, and it grows to a steady trickle as it descends. The path runs along the stream gully, twice crossing feeder-runoff channels on wooden footbridges. Mountain laurel proliferates on either side of the stream but particularly on the steep bank opposite.

The lake comes into view shortly before the trail rejoins the access path to the parking lot, the first bridge of your hike now visible on the left. Briefly retrace your steps across the bridge to the Hidden Creek trailhead, then continue through the parking lot and past the office toward the picnic area. Beyond a parcel of landscaping, begin following the lake's edge near a cluster of picnic tables shaded by cedars and yellow poplars. The nature center and a storage shed stand inland on your right.

Just beyond here the Turkey Ridge Trail heads uphill, but bypass it and continue through the picnic area along the lake. This well-worn waterside single-track also serves for bank fishing. Beyond the picnic tables, a pipeline clearing perpendicular to the trail precedes a footbridge over a small rivulet. Soon thereafter, the green-blazed Lakeview Trail heads uphill. Continue forward however, squeezed between the water and encroaching vegetation. Beyond another footbridge, the path you're on curves sharply right and uphill.

This is the aptly named Laurel Trail. It ascends from the lake with a small rivulet on the right. A few sweetgums mingle with the preponderance of oaks in the surrounding wood. Curving slightly westward as it rises northbound, the trail enters younger forest on the reaches of drier upland bluff. Lichen grows on low banks beside the trail as it approaches a junction. Here an old farm road gives the appearance that the trail continues straight to meet River Road, but it makes a T intersection with the Mine Run Trail. A left takes you along an optional 1.5-mile out-and-back to rocky-bottomed Mine Run. This is the best way to extend your hike at Motts Run Reservoir; the path curves southwest to its terminus amid ferns along the brook.

If you elect not to take this extension, bear right from the Laurel Trail onto the red-blazed Mine Run Trail, following the wide path east. In the autumn scattered scarlet oaks brighten this stretch of trail with their purplish leaves. Enjoy level walking for half a mile, bypassing the Lakeview Trail on the right before the path veers closer to the road, visible through a screen of trees on your left. Mercifully, the trail soon makes a wide curve away from the road to head briefly southward and meet the yellow-blazed Turkey Ridge Trail.

To the east, just before heading downhill to the nature center, the Turkey Ridge Trail passes a spur to the entrance road. A left onto this spur may be advisable if you've come during the off-season and parked outside the gate. Note that this is the easiest trail by which to access the network to and from the gate.

Following the route as mapped, however, take the Turkey Ridge Trail downhill through increasingly numerous beeches, hornbeams, and red maples. After making a distinct left, take a second left onto the Possum Path, a small subloop that wends its way along the hillside toward a deep-gullied streamlet.

Drawing parallel to the streamlet on the left, the path descends to rejoin the Turkey Ridge Trail, turning left. That trail completes its loop with a steep ascent behind the nature center through enclaves of running cedar, clubmoss, and Virginia pine. To complete the figure eight, however, you need to veer right away from Turkey Ridge Trail and return through the picnic area to your starting point.

# NEWPORT NEWS PARK

## KEY AT-A-GLANCE INFORMATION

**LENGTH:** 4.5 miles, with significant additional double-track mileage in park

**CONFIGURATION:** Loop

**DIFFICULTY:** Easy

**SCENERY:** Lee Hall Reservoir, reforested Civil War trenches, marshy Beaverdam Creek

Exposure: Well-shaded except on boardwalks and bridges

**TRAFFIC:** Moderate, high in summer

**TRAIL SURFACE:** Dirt, lengthy wooden bridge across lake

**HIKING TIME:** 2 hours

**SEASON:** Open daily during daylight year-round

**ACCESS:** No entrance fee. Restrooms, snack bar, and some campsites are wheelchair accessible; trails not recommended for wheelchairs.

**MAPS:** Available at signboard, visitor information building, and Discovery Center

**FACILITIES:** Restrooms, picnic tables, grills, playground, boat launch, campground, 5-mile Bikeway loop, 5.5-mile mountain-bike single-track, amphitheater, wildflower garden, archery range, ropes course, adjacent golf course. Boat and bike rentals available. Campsites, with optional hookups, cost $15–$18 per night.

**SPECIAL COMMENTS:** The hike outlined here is a single-track loop, but old fire roads increase your options. Contact the park office at (757) 888-3333 or visit www.newport-news.va.us/parks/park1.htm.

---

**UTM Trailhead Coordinates for Newport News Park**

**UTM Zone (NAD27)** 18S

**Easting** 0363518

**Northing** 4115952

## IN BRIEF

At 8,000-plus acres, Newport News Park is the largest municipal park east of the Mississippi, though large swaths are essentially untrammeled. The loop described here takes in both historical and ecological landmarks. It works well as an introduction for campers—or anyone else—looking to explore the outlying trail network.

## DESCRIPTION

Before setting out take a moment to visit the park's Discovery Center, where you will find aquariums, terrariums, and related displays on park wildlife. In addition to maps you can pick up a trail guide that corresponds to numbered posts along the way. Then begin your hike beside a historic marker noting the now-submerged Warwick River's role in the Civil War. The first trail of this loop, the Twin Forts Loop, tells that story in detail.

A short wooded stint and small bridge follow before you cross the park road to reach the Dam Number 1 Bridge. The long wooden walkway across Lee Hall Reservoir is named for the first of three dams hastily erected here during the war. On the eastern edge of the bridge beside a granite monument is the first of several interpretive signs devoted to the the 1862 Peninsula Campaign.

## DIRECTIONS

From Richmond take I-64 east to Exit 250. Take VA 105 (Fort Eustis Boulevard) 0.35 miles northeast (left off the exit ramp). Then turn left to take VA 143 (Jefferson Avenue) roughly the same distance northwest. Make a right-hand turn to enter the park, passing a visitor information building on your left. Proceed 0.85 miles to park at the Discovery Center on your right. The trail departs just north of the center near a historical marker, and maps are available at a nearby signboard or inside the center.

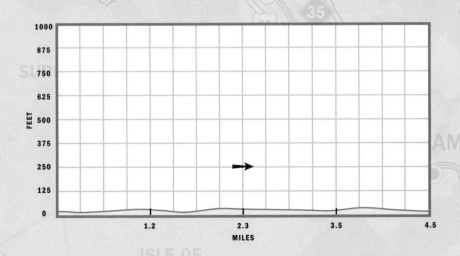

That spring, Confederate general John Bankhead Magruder determined to dam the Warwick River at the present location of Lee Hall Reservoir. The resulting water obstacles initially deterred Union soldiers from advancing against Confederate positions. Finally, on April 16, members of the Vermont Infantry, known as the Green Mountain Boys, stormed the entrenched Southerners. They met with initial success, but, pinned down and soaked, could not endure the reprisal by a Georgia brigade.

The standoff ultimately proved anticlimactic. The Union Army spent 17 more days arraying cannons in preparation for an assault. They stormed the line only to find that the Confederates had fled two days earlier in order to prepare Richmond for an impending siege. The remains of an extensive network of Confederate trenches—and a few Union rifle pits—are visible at numerous points along this hike, some of the best-preserved Civil War earthworks anywhere.

After crossing the reservoir, bear left with the Twin Forts Loop, forestalling your walk along the White Oak Trail, which departs to the right. Along the lakeshore grow water-tupelo trees, which have trunks swollen at the base like their bald-cypress neighbors. Earthworks are visible on your right, shaded by a forest of white oak, red maple, holly, and loblolly pines.

Beyond a sign marking the Green Mountain Boys' initial attack, veer right, away from the lake, to bisect a trenchline. Headed slightly uphill, the trail turns left to cross a streamlet on a footbridge. It then intersects a double-track and makes two successive right-hand turns: first onto the roadbed then back into the woods. Continuing northeast along the double-track provides access to the Bikeway and campground.

This hike, however, recrosses the aforementioned rivulet to encircle the wall of Confederate earthworks here. After rounding the defenses, the path passes a sign devoted to their original appearance, explaining that they were braced by logs and supported cannons trained on the opposite shore. The bridge by which you arrived lies just ahead, but you'll want to turn left onto the White Oak Trail.

A marshy stretch of lakeshore borders the trail on its right as you head north across a stream toward a junction with the Sycamore Creek Trail, another connector to the Bikeway. Remain on the well-trod White Oak Trail. Downed trees were cleared from the forest ahead, giving it a bright, open quality. Holly grows more thickly beneath the forest canopy, however, as the trail curves left. An inlet of the lake fed by Sycamore Creek stretches inland on trail right. A wooden overlook allows you to scan the swamp, dotted with yellow poplars.

A low-lying, often-muddy expanse of forest extends beyond the creek on trail right, then the path rises to enter a mixture of shortleaf and loblolly pines. The evergreens accompany you until the path veers left, entering forest thick with young beech trees. After crossing Greenbrier Creek the White Oak Trail approaches its junction with the Wynn's Mill Loop. Turn left onto the latter, promptly crossing the Swamp Fire Trail, yet another link to the Bikeway.

Ahead, a footbridge crosses a trench, indicating that you've entered the remains of a second earthen battery. After crossing a marshy drainage on a boardwalk, you'll note a trench that runs along trail right. The path you're walking briefly joins an older roadbed; look for an easy-to-miss right-hand turn ahead (reach Beaverdam Creek and you've gone too far). At the only unsigned junction on this loop, the Wynn's Mill Loop makes a wide turn beside a double-trunked yellow poplar. The path immediately bisects one trenchline and soon cuts through a second between two pines.

Follow the trail as it winds through earthworks that, though eroded, remain up to ten feet tall and are arrayed in complex formations rather than straight lines. A pier on trail left also affords you a view of the cattail marsh along Beaverdam Creek, which feeds the reservoir. Rounding earthworks on the right, the swamp is visible on trail left just beyond the gnawed tree trunks that prove the creek's name was no accident.

Turn left to cross the lengthy wooden Swamp Bridge, also part of the the White Oak Trail, which arrives from the opposite direction. An observation deck built into the bridge invites you to pause and scan the marsh northeast of Lee Hall Reservoir for wintering tundra swans or resident mallards. Once across, turn right onto a narrow single-track against a mossy bank.

A great blue heron stands on a tree stump in a shallow inlet formed by Sycamore Creek.

The city's Deer Run Golf Course is visible uphill and through the mature hardwoods on your left. As it proceeds along the widening lake, your path repeatedly approaches the course. The path curves slightly inland to cross Deer Run Creek on a bridge with sycamore and beech growing nearby. The path then runs along the lake to reach its final boardwalk, a zigzagging affair that deposits you within a short walk of the Dam Number 1 Bridge and the Discovery Center.

Bordering the park to the north is Colonial National Historic Park's Yorktown unit. A walkway runs from the visitor center past the Yorktown Victory Monument to the hamlet of Yorktown proper, where a short, pleasant stroll takes in the home of Thomas Nelson, successor to Thomas Jefferson as governor of Virginia, the excavated remains of a colonial-era pottery factory, and the circa 1697 Grace Church.

# NORTH ANNA
# BATTLEFIELD PARK

## IN BRIEF

The site of a Civil War battle between May 23 and 26, 1864, this park retains well-preserved earthworks. Ten interpretive signs along what was once Ox Road recount the battle. Under the command of Robert E. Lee, who was ill during the battle, Confederate troops halted the Union advance but failed to give chase, thereby allowing the Union to regroup and move toward Richmond.

## DESCRIPTION

The Battle of Ox Ford unfolds as you hike through this Hanover County park. Interpretive signs describe the events of the battle in chronological order, highlighting the personalities, tactical strategies, and logistical constraints that shaped the conflagration. In many ways, this hike serves as a precursor to Cold Harbor Battlefield (page 58), because the Confederate Army's successful use of earthen defenses along North Anna informed the subsequent strategy of entrenchment.

Rarely crowded, the park stimulates contemplation. The soft rustling of wind in the trees overhead is in marked contrast to the shouts and explosions of battle evoked en route. Yet the pleasant woodland setting alone is worth the trip (or a

## DIRECTIONS

From I-95 take Exit 98 and go west on VA 30 for 0.7 miles to US 1 (Washington Road). Turn right, drive 1.5 miles, and turn left onto Vernon Road (VA 684). Continue for 2.5 miles along a railroad track and a string of power lines on your left. A small brown park sign and a Virginia Civil War Trails sign indicate the entrance on your right. Enter along a gravel road, promptly passing a historical marker titled "Attack at Ox Ford," and then veer right through a wooden gate hung on stone posts as you pass a quarry to your left.

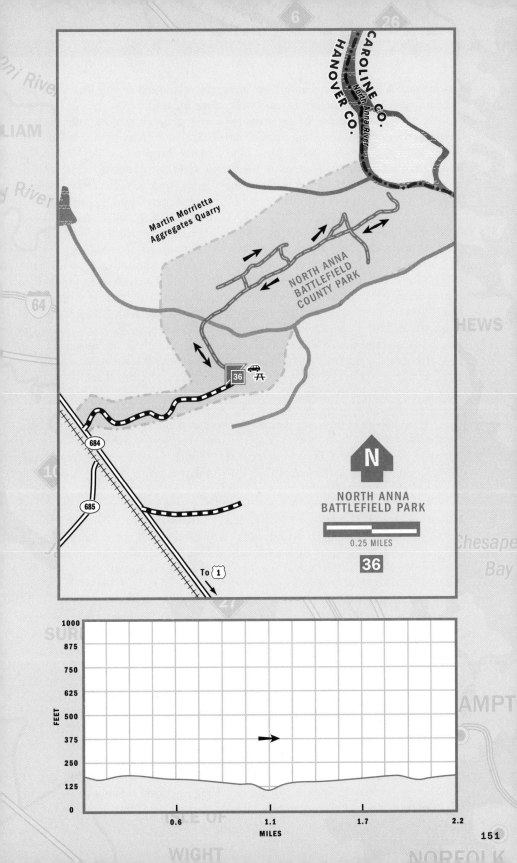

Martin Morrietta
Aggregates Quarry

CAROLINE CO.
HANOVER CO.

North Anna River

NORTH ANNA
BATTLEFIELD
COUNTY PARK

684

685

36

To 1

**N**

NORTH ANNA
BATTLEFIELD PARK

0.25 MILES

36

repeat visit). A few tables and a trash can at the gravel trailhead parking lot invite a picnic, and numerous benches invite you to relax along the way.

A covered stone-and-wood signboard at the edge of the parking lot marks the trailhead. Along a painting depicting the 57th Massachusetts Infantry rallying before their initial, ill-fated charge is a brief explanation of events that preceded the battle of Ox Ford, including Confederate stands at Wilderness and Spotsylvania Court House (see page 204). On May 21, Ulysses S. Grant ordered his Army of the Potomac south to Hanover Junction, present-day Doswell, which held strategic value as the intersection of the Virginia Central Railroad and the Richmond, Fredericksburg, and Potomac Railroad. Subsequent interpretive signs pick up the saga, explaining the battle as it played out. Next to the trailhead sign, a granite memorial honors the fallen of both sides.

From the parking area, head northwest through a primarily pine wood, with diminutive Virginia pines, characterized by small 1.5- to 2.5-inch cones and short 1- to 3-inch needles, interspersed among loblolly pines that can easily double them in size. The well-maintained gravel trail, on average five feet wide, traces the route of Ox Ford Road, which formed one side of Lee's much-vaunted "hog snout line," also known as the inverted (upside-down) V. The hike illuminates the strength of this formation.

The quarry property is approximately 50 yards to your left and is visible intermittently along the hike on the park's western border. The first remnant of earthworks soon appears on trail right, then the path descends a series of steps made of wooden beams with a wooden rail. Atop the stairs is the first of several benches.

At the bottom of the stairs, the trail draws parallel to a rivulet then crosses it on a wooden footbridge. This wet lowland is dotted with birch trees and ferns; the latter were unfurling new fronds on my springtime visit. Though many trees had yet to leaf, monarch butterflies floated intermittently across the trail before me. The surrounding forest includes white oak, holly, and pignut-hickory.

Ascend to approach the first interpretive sign, which describes the events that transpired between 11 a.m. and 8 p.m. on May 23, 1864—primarily the positioning of Confederate cannons along Ox Ford Road in the wake of a Confederate retreat from the Telegraph Road bridge upstream. Pass a large double-trunked white oak on trail right before approaching the first fork in the trail. Don't be fooled by a misplaced sign, as I was; markers two, three, and four are to your left, not straight ahead. You've gone too far if you pass a log bench.

Up the trail, the next interpretive sign explains that Virginians under the command of Colonel David A. Weisiger began construction of earthen trenchworks here on May 24 following orders from Lieutenant General A. P. Hill. Turn left to trace a short spur for a close-up examination of the earthworks. Note that the hillside visible to the north through the trees is a product of modern industry; the entrenched rebels surveyed very different terrain in search of a Federal advance.

Confederate earthen defenses remain clearly visible throughout this portion of the park, despite the works sesquicentennial. Many are cloaked in moss, and trees have risen up through them. Yet the eroded trench lines remain, with ditches averaging three feet deep and berms up to four feet high.

Continue northwest to the third sign, which says that Grant, having misjudged the Confederates, ordered his men to rout any remaining rebels and continue to Richmond. He instructed Major General Ambrose Burnside to cross the North Anna River at Ox

Ford, but the general found it too well defended. The next sign describes the initial Union advance by Brigadier General James H. Ledlie's brigade, forthrightly denouncing Ledlie as one of the Union's least-qualified generals. Having commanded the Massachusetts infantrymen for merely a week, the drunken general ordered a foolhardy charge. His troops were exposed to the fire of entrenched Confederates led by Brigadier General William H. Mahone, and a bloodbath ensued.

A mossy stretch of trail with a rivulet flowing beneath it precedes the fifth sign, found beside a cul-de-sac in the trail. It details the deployment of Confederate brigades from Mississippi and Alabama that fought in the trenches visible here. Descend past another mossy patch in the trail to rejoin the main path and continue northeast. A small rivulet has eroded a sizable gully on trail right.

Turn left at the next intersection to reach a marker that recounts the repulse of Ledlie's charge, ordered in defiance of his division commander, on the evening of May 24. A quote from Captain John Anderson of the 57th Massachusetts Infantry recounts the scene: "It was just a wild tumultuous rush where the more reckless were far to the front and the cautious scattered along the back but still coming on. Many of the Confederate soldiers stood upon their breastworks and called out in a tantalizing manner, 'Come on Yank. Come on to Richmond.'"

Winding through the woods, the trail approaches a wooden deck worthy of a suburban backyard. On it you'll find a bench facing a marker that describes the countercharge made by the 12th Mississippi Infantry, from which the Federals beat a hasty retreat. Perhaps the lone Union hero to emerge from the battle, in stark contrast to Ledlie, was Lieutenant Colonel Charles Chandler. He valiantly rallied the 57th, but the infantry fell back when he was struck down.

Had Union generals appreciated the strength of General Robert E. Lee's position, they may have reshaped their tactics (it's been suggested that want of a topographic map cost Grant the battle). The park's next sign, approached on a small out-and-back spur, marks the tip of Lee's so-called inverted V. Perhaps an A better represents the Confederate position, with the crossbar representing the easy exchange of men and material between flanks. Union forces, on the other hand, had to break ranks in order to assault the rebel positions. Gazing downhill through the trees, one appreciates the literal uphill battle Grant's men faced.

After returning to the main trail, turn left. After passing another gulch on the right, the trail veers left. Juniper bushes dot both sides of the trail as you approach another sizable wooden deck, from which the North Anna River is visible below. A steep descent separates you from the river, and there is no approved trail down. The ninth marker explains that on the night of May 24, when Grant's scattered army was most vulnerable, the sickly General Lee "lay in his tent repeating over and over again, 'We must strike them a blow. We must never let them pass us again. We must strike them a blow.'"

Failure to do so, however, allowed the Union army to dig in. A two-day siege followed, costing each side 2,000 lives and merely forestalling Grant's approach to Richmond. The final park sign, which designates the trench line of the 10th Georgia Battalion, notes the extensive use of heavy artillery during the battle. To reach it, retrace your steps to an out-and-back spur on the left (the path coming from marker eight enters on the right at this intersection). To complete your hike, return to the main path and follow it back to the trailhead.

# OBSERVATORY HILL

## KEY AT-A-GLANCE INFORMATION

**LENGTH:** 2.25 miles plus numerous options in a compact network

**CONFIGURATION:** A balloon hike that ends with a flattened figure eight

**DIFFICULTY:** Difficult on the climb up, easy on the way down

**SCENERY:** McCormick Observatory, hillside hardwood forest

Exposure: Well-shaded except at peak of Jefferson Mountain

**TRAFFIC:** High

**TRAIL SURFACE:** Dirt single- and double-track

**HIKING TIME:** 1.5 hours

**SEASON:** Open daily during daylight year-round

**ACCESS:** No fee; trails not recommended for wheelchairs.

**MAPS:** A topo version is available via www.virginiatrails.org; there is no official map.

**FACILITIES:** Limited to small roadside parking areas

**SPECIAL COMMENTS:** To view the night sky through the telescope's 26-inch lens, attend one of the UVA Astronomy Department's bimonthly public nights. These free events are held the first and third Friday night of each month (visit www.astro. virginia.edu/pubnite for details). Contact the University of Virginia Community Relations for information about the observatory or its trails at (434) 924-1321.

---

**UTM Trailhead Coordinates for Observatory Hill**

**UTM Zone (NAD27)** 17S

**Easting** 0723328

**Northing** 4210929

## IN BRIEF

Located on the University of Virginia campus, this dense trail network makes the most of limited acreage on the slope below McCormick Observatory, for which the trail is named. The trail lures dog walkers and hardcore mountain bikers alike and is understandably popular with students. The knot of unblazed trails on Observatory Hill offers many permutations, so use this hike as a starting point.

## DESCRIPTION

How apropos: scaling Jefferson Mountain while on a visit to UVA. Though our third president designed this campus, its observatory was not constructed until 50 years after his death. However, he certainly knew this prominent mountain even before it became his namesake. It looms above the main campus to the east.

The mountain rises north from this hike's starting point across the street from Fontaine Research Park. Once across, turn left and follow a single-track path up the small hill (this is the Rivanna River Trail). Atop the slope, turn left on a dirt trail leaving north. Set off uphill on one of the

## DIRECTIONS

From Richmond follow I-64 northwest to Exit 118 (59 miles beyond I-295). Exit northbound on US 29. Drive 0.7 miles before turning right onto Fontaine Avenue (US 29 Business). After 0.2 miles, you will pass a gated dirt road on the left. This leads a short distance uphill to a water tower, which is visible from the trail. The gravel area outside the gate is sometimes used as a trailhead. However, to avoid blocking the gate, turn right at the first traffic light and park in the large lot of the Fontaine Research Park office development. Exit the office park on foot, and cross Fontaine Avenue at the light.

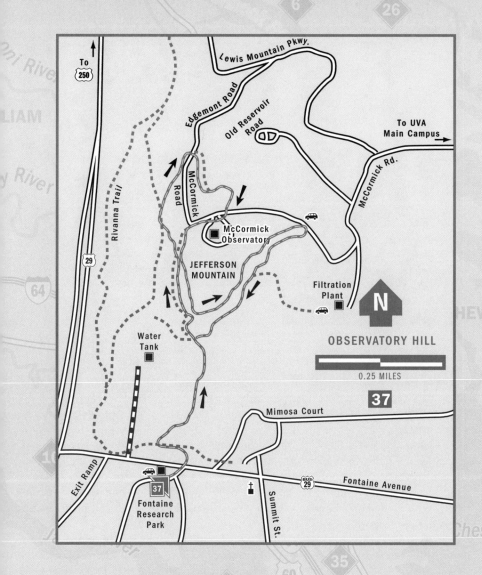

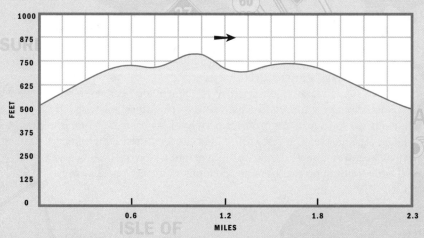

Metal-domed McCormick Observatory crowns Jefferson Mountain.

mountain's gentler slopes. The trail curves slightly to the right, avoiding the large
body of water visible through the forest on trail left. Chestnut and northern red oaks
dominate this hillside, which is spotted with white pines. Also look for a smattering
of cucumber trees, a deciduous relative of the magnolia easily distinguished by its
large leaves.

Climbing above the water tank, you reach a wide dirt roadbed. The old road,
along which you will soon return, leads right (east) to a gate at McCormick Road,
which serves as an optional trailhead. For now, proceed across the double-track and
veer slightly left to resume your single-track climb northward. White oaks and mountain laurel grow more abundantly along this loftier stretch of trail, and modest boulders dot the forest floor.

As you near the peak, make a second left rather than forging on to the observatory. Follow a level stretch of trail as it curves around the hillside, bypassing the
paths that fork off downhill. This trail eventually emerges onto paved Edgemont Road
below the observatory, which is uphill on your right. You can elect to walk along the
lightly trafficked road if you wish. The route mapped here, however, crosses the street
at a power-line clearing. Bear right and continue on a single-track that curves southeast, first running level then climbing steadily southward to crest Jefferson Mountain,
with the observatory just across the street.

UVA's mountaintop observatory is named for Leander McCormick, who in
1877 donated to the university what was then the largest telescope in America. Leander made his fortune as the business partner of his brother Cyrus, who perfected the
scheme for a mechanical reaper first conceived by their father, Robert. The Virginia
Reaper, as it was known, dramatically increased a farm's efficiency and is widely cred-
ited with spurring on the agrarian development of the American West.

Another tycoon, Cornelius "Commodore" Vanderbilt (who built his fortune on a New York ferry route) helped fund construction of a metal-domed brick building to house the telescope. It was completed in 1884 along with a residence for the observatory director. Now known as the Alden House after a former keeper of the telescope, that brick abode stands a short distance south of the observatory.

Though the site was chosen for its vertical rather than horizontal views, today's persistent hiker is rewarded with far-reaching views of the surrounding Appalachian foothills. Obstructed by treetop foliage in the summer, views are best in the winter, particularly after a dusting of snow. Consider a return visit to the observatory to gaze through the university's telescope (see "Special Comments" section). To return from the peak, follow the paved road west and downhill. Look for a trail on your left, opposite a small gravel lot (there may be a tractor-trailer parked here for storage). Reenter a dense and vine-strewn parcel of woods, then descend to the southwest. You will soon reach the intersection where you turned left; this is the final portion of your climb. Turn left again, this time making a generally level run to the northeast.

Curving around the hillside past sizable stones, you may find the trunks of windblown chestnut oaks still lying near the trail. You'll notice the old dirt road running below you on the right and a pair of bluish water tanks beyond it. Above you on the left, the Alden House is visible. Beyond a power-line clearing your path will meet the roadbed at its gated junction with McCormick Road. Loop around to follow the double-track on its steady descent.

The rocky roadbed passes the enigmatic remains of a small brick structure pressed against the red-earth wall on trail right. Spur trails drop sharply away on your left, but stick with the double-track until you reach the trail on which you arrived. A left onto that familiar single-track leads back downhill to Fontaine Avenue.

Of course, east of UVA is Jefferson's famed Monticello estate, accessible via the Saunders-Monticello Trail (page 196). Tours of the restored manse and grounds leave from the western trailhead. The trail passes above Michie Tavern, a late eighteenth-century inn that still offers a daily lunch buffet, as well as tours led by interpreters in period garb. About a mile from Monticello stands Ash Lawn Highland, where guests now tour the former home and garden of President James Monroe.

# PETERSBURG NATIONAL BATTLEFIELD PARK

## IN BRIEF

In many ways the Union siege of Petersburg was the climactic battle of the American Civil War, and the subsequent Confederate surrender merely the denouement. Today, more than 150,000 visitors tour Petersburg National Battlefield Park annually. However, many never set foot on the multiuse national recreation trail that rings the park. A mandatory visit for residents and tourists with even passing interest in U.S. history, the battlefield park doubles as an outdoor escape for locals.

## DESCRIPTION

Sight of the longest siege in the annals of American warfare, Petersburg National Battlefield includes four Confederate forts northeast of the city. Here, on June 15, 1864, federal troops commanded by General Ulysses S. Grant began their onslaught against entrenched Confederates. After more than ten months and a combined 70,000 deaths, General Robert E. Lee's Army of Northern Virginia could no longer weather the assault. On April 2, 1865, Lee evacuated the city under cover of night. The defeat precipitated the Confederate surrender at Appomattox one week later.

This route follows the park's national recreation trail, an almost 7-mile loop with a 0.4-mile connector that allows you to shorten the hike to 3.8 miles. Those wishing to see the park's forts and displays may use the trail instead of the main road.

## DIRECTIONS

Leave Richmond heading south on I-95 and drive (22 miles from downtown) to Exit 52 in Petersburg. Take Wythe Street east and merge onto VA 36 as the road curves northward. The entrance lies ahead on the right, approximately 2.5 miles from the interstate, and you will spot signs en route.

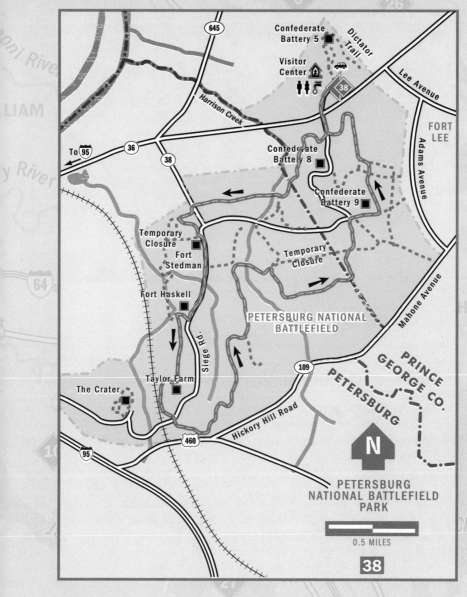

Confederate
Battery 5

Dictator
Trail

Visitor
Center

FORT
LEE

Lee Avenue

38

645

Harrison Creek

To 95

36

38

Confederate
Battery 8

Confederate
Battery 9

Adams Avenue

Temporary
Closure

Fort
Stedman

Temporary
Closure

Mahone Avenue

Fort Haskell

PETERSBURG NATIONAL
BATTLEFIELD

Siege Rd.

The Crater

Taylor Farm

109

PETERSBURG

PRINCE
GEORGE CO.

Hickory Hill Road

460

95

N

PETERSBURG
NATIONAL BATTLEFIELD
PARK

0.5 MILES

38

Chesape
Bay

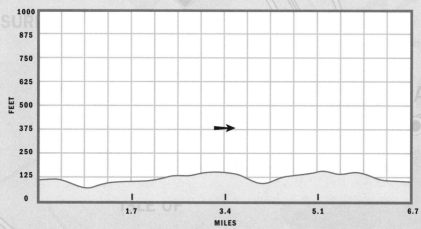

The entrance to the tunnel used by Union troops to plant explosives at what is now The Crater.

Doing so, however, makes for a full, 10-mile hiking day. Those making a return visit can make a circuit, omitting the spurs, with few reminders of the park's Civil War past—or its modern-day popularity.

Begin your first visit at the visitor center, where you can pick up both a brochure and a park map. While there, examine the artifacts and displays, which explain both the battlefield tactics and day-to-day drudgery of the siege. A film outlines the chronology of the city's defense and ultimate capture.

The Dictator Trail, named for a squat, round Union mortar, departs from the visitor center. Along the interpretive path, the park has marshaled the full range of cannons employed during the battle. Made of brass or iron, these armaments range from four to eight feet long. Those guarding Confederate Battery 5 just ahead retain their wheeled mounts. The trail continues beyond the fort and down a few stairs before looping back to the parking area, from which the hike itself begins.

A brief road walk leads you to the multiuse trail. Be mindful of vehicles as you cross above VA 36 on the park road, and look for the earthen trail that intersects it shortly after entering the woods. By hiking the loop counterclockwise (right), you save most of the optional spurs for the return trip and can explore them as you desire. After ducking into the woods, bear right along the single-track, switchbacking toward a tributary of Harrison Creek.

The trail heads south through a creekside plain, where maturing trees shade a thick carpet of grasses and ferns. Yellow blazes on trailside trees indicate the multiuse loop.

Shortly after the trail turns right onto a wider path, the connector trail heads left. Accessible via the connector is a meadow dotted with cannons to mark the farthest advancement of Lee's troops in their final, assault, the Battle of Fort Stedman. The Confederates were halted at Harrison Creek, which you cross on a wooden bridge. From the creek, continue through a pine wood, crossing an asphalt maintenance road. Ahead, at a T intersection, bear left and then take your first right. The single-track trail crosses a clearing, through which Fort Stedman is visible uphill.

At the next intersection, you may find the trail closed. Retreating from the trail closure, this route passes Fort Stedman and heads toward the park road. Continue south to Fort Haskell, which is still surrounded by a modest moat. The stopping point of the Confederate advance during the Battle of Fort Stedman, Fort Haskell was crowded so tightly with Union soldiers that most could merely load weapons and pass them forward to those stationed at the walls.

Just beyond the site, a trail to the right runs alongside the fort and rejoins the multiuse trail at mile 2.2. If the entire multiuse trail is open on your visit, instead of walking along the road, you'll cross a tributary of Poor Creek before the trail parallels the stream.

The trail continues on a level, winding single-track through thick woods. Then as the path curves right, it draws along the meadow that descends from the Taylor Farm site. A brick foundation and chimney are all that remain of the Taylor family farmstead. The trail curves left to pass through an open field below the chimney.

The trail then crosses the park road ahead. However, if you're incorporating the park's historic sites into your hike, turn right and follow the road 0.4 miles to reach The Crater, the battlefield's most famous, and infamous, landmark. On July 30, 1864, Union troops detonated gunpowder buried beneath the Confederate fort at Ellicott's Salient, killing 300. Soldiers in Pennsylvania's 48th Infantry, coal miners by trade, had secretly tunneled more than 500 feet to place the explosives. The Crater is an indentation roughly 30 feet deep and 60 feet wide. Following the spectacular explosion, Federal troops charged the destroyed battery, but many were so awestruck that they paused to gawk at the hole. For more than 4,000, this proved a fatal mistake. They were unprepared to meet an ensuing Confederate counter advance, which trapped them inside the rift.

Backtracking to the multiuse trail, head south of the park road on a double-track that curves left then curves right to cross a seasonal stream. Veer left at an intersection uphill. Continue north along a level stretch of trail flanked by pines.

A pipeline clearing soon precedes a trail crossing. Turn right and make a quick descent to cross Harrison Creek on a wooden bridge. The trail rises to yet another intersection, where the multiuse connector heads left and another trail leads forward. Turn right onto the official multiuse trail, which soon makes a distinct left to head east into a shady pine forest.

Turn left at the next T intersection, and you will soon come to a four-way junction. Go straight (north) to follow the route as mapped, bypassing the easternmost stretch of the multiuse path. Continuing north, you'll soon reach Confederate Battery 9.

Re-created wooden portions of this fort include sharpened stakes protruding from the earthen walls. The site also includes a soldier's winter hut and a store that merchants established to hock canned goods and other small comforts. A Union regiment of African Americans took this position early in the siege. To the north, free African Americans also captured Confederate Battery 8.

Head east from Battery 9 to reach a trail junction and turn left, crossing a stream ahead. If you wish to see Battery 8 turn left at the next two intersections and cross the park road. Otherwise, veer right at the first intersection to make a prompt left, continuing north. Turn left at the next T intersection to rejoin the multiuse loop, which passes a spur on the left then wends its way north near VA 36. Following the curving path southward, cross two wooden bridges through gullied terrain to rejoin the park road. A right takes you back to the visitor center.

# POCAHONTAS STATE PARK

## KEY AT-A-GLANCE INFORMATION

**LENGTH:** 3 miles around Beaver Lake plus 2 or more on the Forest Exploration Trail

**CONFIGURATION:** Loops

**DIFFICULTY:** Moderate

**SCENERY:** Stone spillway; beech forest, creeks surrounding Beaver Lake; Swift Creek and mixed hardwood-pine woods

**EXPOSURE:** Shaded

**TRAFFIC:** Moderate

**TRAIL SURFACE:** Dirt (short paved start)

**HIKING TIME:** 1.5 hours around Beaver Lake, 1 hour on the Forest Exploration Trail

**SEASON:** Trails open daily from 8 a.m. to dusk year-round; main season runs April–October

**ACCESS:** Parking costs $3 on weekdays and $4 on weekends or $2 off-season. Swimming costs $5 for children ages 3–12 and $6 for adults, $2 more per guest on weekends. Visitor center, museum, amphitheater, and some trails are wheelchair accessible. Campsites with hookups cost $20 per night.

**MAPS:** Available at the park and online at www.dcr.virginia.gov/parks/pocahont.htm

**FACILITIES:** Swimming pool, campground, conference center, CCC Museum, amphitheater, Algonquian Ecology Camp, and Heritage Conference Center. In-season canoe, kayak, and rowboat rentals (prices vary).

**SPECIAL COMMENTS:** To find out about concerts and museum hours, call (804) 796-4255.

---

**UTM Trailhead Coordinates for Pocahontas State Park**

**UTM Zone (NAD27)   18S**

**Easting   0271385**

**Northing   4140669**

## IN BRIEF

The premier hiking trail at Pocahontas State Park encircles Beaver Lake. Misleadingly named, the lake was actually the work of the Civilian Conservation Corps, and this route descends from the park's CCC Museum to pass the Depression-era stone spillway before circling the lake. The Forest Exploration Trail, the park's newest, crosses Swift Creek just where it begins to widen north of Swift Creek Lake. Though not connected (except by pavement) the two loops together highlight the park's cultural and ecological heritage.

## DESCRIPTION

The first park of its kind in the Richmond environs, Pocahontas State Park was created as federally owned Swift Creek Recreational Area by the New Deal–era Civilian Conservation Corps. That

## DIRECTIONS

Pocahontas State Park is in Chesterfield County about 20 miles south of downtown Richmond. From I-95 take Exit 62, or, from the roughly parallel US 1/301, take VA 288 west. Exit onto Iron Bridge Road (VA 10) headed south, then turn left onto Beach Road (VA 655). The main park entrance is ahead on the right. Proceed into the park, pay your vehicle-entrance fee, and continue toward the CCC Museum and amphitheater, passing the campground on your right. Turn left then left again to park in front of the CCC Museum. The trail departs to the right of the museum as you face it. To reach the Forest Exploration Trail, continue past the museum and amphitheater on the main park road. You will pass a large parking lot on the right. Turn right to follow the parking lot's northern border then veer left at the lot's northeast corner. Just downhill is a boat launch with a smaller parking area. A footbridge crosses Swift Creek to begin the trail.

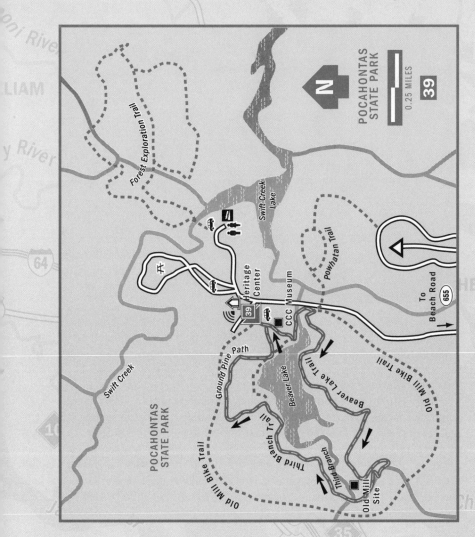

Water cascades over the stonework spillway built by the CCC to create Beaver Lake.

legacy is today enshrined at the park's CCC Museum, which commemorates the men of CCC Company 2386 who lived in camps nearby while constructing dams, cabins, and other park infrastructure. The National Park Service donated the 7,600 acres of parkland to the commonwealth in 1946.

It was split between a state park and state forest until a 1989 planning study suggested placing the entire acreage under Department of Conservation and Recreation auspices with a mandate to upgrade and expand Pocahontas State Park to better serve the growing population of the Richmond-Petersburg area. One recent expansion is the Forest Exploration Trail, which is included here along with a circuit around Beaver Lake that follows portions of the Spillway Trail, Beaver Lake Trail, and Ground Pine Path. Additional miles are available on the 2.5-mile Powhatan Trail and on a 25-mile network of forest roads and mountain-bike trails. The park's "Bike Trails Guide," depicts all forest roads.

Before setting out, drop by the modest CCC Museum for a primer on the Corps' history and its work within the park in particular. Franklin Roosevelt established the CCC during the first weeks of his administration. It was open to single men between ages 18 and 25, who served a maximum of 2 years in 6-month enlistment increments. They pocketed just 5 dollars a month, with $25 more sent home to their families. In all, more than 3 million young men passed through the Corps' ranks between 1933 and 1942. They built 40,000 bridges, created 800 state parks, and planted 2 billion trees. The pictures and stories of the men who labored here will lend you a greater appreciation for their sturdy handiwork.

Begin the lake loop at the signboard in the museum parking lot. Promptly veer left behind the museum, descending to Beaver Lake on the paved Spillway Trail. As the path switches back down the hillside, the lake vista stretches out before you. The path curves left at the lakeshore then crosses Third Branch on a footbridge just below its reemergence from the spillway dam. Perhaps the CCC workmen who built the spillway referred to the impoundment they created as Third Branch Lake, the name given it on some topo maps. By any name, the 24-acre lake pales in comparison to its neighbor to the east. A quarter-mile downstream of the spillway, Third Branch joins Swift Creek only to be stalled again in 150-acre Swift Creek Lake.

After admiring the spillway cascade and the handiwork of the stonemasons who built it, turn right immediately across the bridge and ascend into the forest on earthen Beaver Lake Trail (veering left from the footbridge will take you to the Old Mill Bicycle Path). The earthen path undulates over small ridges and traces inlets of the lake, intermittently drawing near to water before rising away through the towering beech forest. It is inspiring to fathom that the 100-foot-tall beech trees now shading Beaver Lake were planted as saplings by the grandfathers of modern-day visitors.

Before veering south and uphill, the path traverses a lakeside glade where a sign gives a sampling of the wildlife you may see: deer, rabbits, and raccoons among them. The Beaver Lake Trail crosses some small ravines on wooden footbridges as it twists away from the lake toward a former mill site on Third Branch. The path rounds a corner and descends to meet Third Branch; a stone foundation—now all that remains of the mill—is on your left.

Cross the babbling stream on a cement footbridge and bear right. Continue along the pebbly banks of Third Branch as it widens into a swampy delta. Beavers are in fact active in this area; you may spot one gliding through the water, but the stumps of felled trees are sufficient proof of their residence. As you reapproach Beaver Lake, a boardwalk affords dry passage through swamp-like terrain. A sign describes vegetation common to this boggy landscape, including jack-in-the-pulpit and pawpaw.

The trail continues, encircling the lake's western edge, which is blanketed in lily pads, and passing repeatedly through muddy stretches. A second boardwalk will help keep your shoes dry, but may not be enough. As you progress along the lake's northern shore, look for the Ground Pine Path, which departs to the left. Look on the forest floor for specimens of the trail's namesake. Ground pine, a variant of clubmoss, resembles a tiny evergreen, no more than five inches tall. The plant spreads through lateral underground branches and favors cool, moist forest. The wee clubmosses are descendants of ancient species that stood 40 feet high.

Turn right at an intersection to return to the Beaver Lake Trail for a brief stint back to the Spillway Trail. Here, downhill from the museum, a waterside bench beckons you to catch your breath and scan the lake for waterfowl.

Now if you've the time and energy to continue hiking, head to the park's northeasternmost parking area near the boat launch. A bridge across widening Swift Creek signals the trailhead for the Forest Exploration Trail. Bearing left across the bridge, the trail ascends with a meandering rivulet visible downhill on your left. Mature forest and mossy boulders lend this stretch a wilderness air. Ahead, you'll see evidence of bygone logging operations, including stands of young pine.

A forest road bisects the 2.5-mile loop, allowing you to make a 2-mile loop by turning right and returning with the road. Otherwise turn right after emerging onto the forest road, then turn left back onto single-track. You will again intersect the road, turning left onto it to return to the trailhead. This easy-to-follow loop is a fine cap to the day, affording an up-close view of the park's ongoing stewardship.

# PONY PASTURE RAPIDS

## KEY AT-A-GLANCE INFORMATION

**LENGTH:** 2.25 miles, plus optional trails

**CONFIGURATION:** Figure eight, plus multiple side and spur trails

**DIFFICULTY:** Easy

**SCENERY:** James River, hardwood swamp, marsh

Exposure: Well-shaded

**TRAFFIC:** Moderate (highest along river)

**TRAIL SURFACE:** Gravel with optional dirt trails and boardwalk

**HIKING TIME:** 1–1.5 hours

**SEASON:** Open daily during daylight year-round; best avoided after rainfall

**ACCESS:** No fee

**MAPS:** See signboard in main parking lot; also available at the visitor center in James River State Park.

**FACILITIES:** Restrooms, wildlife-viewing area

**SPECIAL COMMENTS:** Don't let the name or the promise of gravel trails fool you: unless there is a drought, this is a swampland hike. Paddlers interested in using the park as a put-in or take-out can phone (804) 646-8228 for river-level information. Call James River Park at (804) 646-8911.

UTM Trailhead Coordinates for Pony Pasture Rapids

UTM Zone (NAD27)    18S

Easting    0277365

Northing    4158695

## IN BRIEF

Despite the swampy nature of its ragtag woods, Pony Pasture Rapids remains a popular outing for Richmonders. A central, Southside location and well-marked trails attract dog-walkers, joggers, and families. Crickets drown the sound of traffic, and riparian wildlife thrives among the vine-swathed trees.

## DESCRIPTION

There are two main trails at Pony Pasture Rapids. The River Trail parallels the James, and Pleasants Creek Trail follows its namesake as it grows from a bubbling stream on the park's western edge to a 20-foot-wide creek where it enters the James. The two paths converge before a bridge across Pleasants Creek. On the opposite side is an additional gravel loop, the Wetlands Trail, that accesses the wildlife-viewing area.

## DIRECTIONS

From the southern terminus of the Huguenot Road Bridge (VA 147), follow Riverside Drive east. At 2 miles, the main Pony Pasture parking lot is on your left just after the road curves away from the river. It's equally feasible to access the park via Forest Hill Avenue, which intersects Chippenham Parkway (VA 150) to the southwest and Powhite Parkway (VA 76) to the southeast. Turn north from Forest Hill onto Hathaway Road, which is roughly equidistant from the parkways. Proceed to a Y intersection and veer left. The road (now Scottview Drive) makes a sharp left to become Riverside Drive. Turn right again to remain on Riverside, and the parking area will be your next right. A smaller eastern parking lot is also accessible from Forest Hill by turning right from Hathaway Road onto Wallowa Road. Take the second left onto Landria Drive, which dead-ends adjacent to the park.

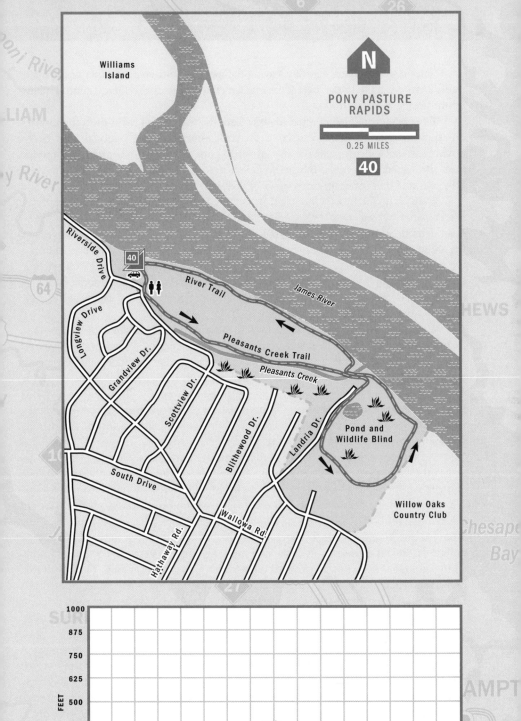

Williams
Island

Riverside Drive

40

River Trail

James River

Longview Drive

Grandview Dr.

Scottview Dr.

Pleasants Creek Trail

Pleasants Creek

Blithewood Dr.

Landria Dr.

Pond and
Wildlife Blind

South Drive

Hathaway Rd.

Wallowa Rd.

Willow Oaks
Country Club

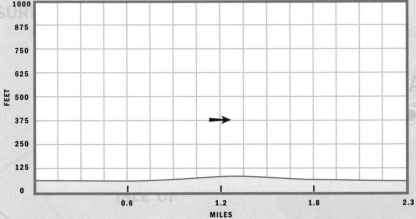

Trace a simple figure eight by leaving the main parking area on either of the main trails. Then cross the bridge over Pleasants Creek to follow the wetland circuit. Finally, return via the as-yet-untrod trail.

Of course, you'll be tempted to stray from the wide gravel paths onto the numerous spur and side trails that crisscross the park's interior. These optional trails easily double the trail mileage, and the risk of getting lost is minimal—you're never too far from the signed main trails. Budget sufficient time to wander. Besides extending your hike, the side trails offer up-close views of flora and fauna. Dress to get muddy.

Even along the heavily trafficked River Trail, mud puddles dot the gravel pathway for days after any substantial rain. Likewise, fluctuations in the water level of the James River determine its proximity to the trail, which can range from 20 to 50 feet. Waves lap the shore along the route, but the rushing rapids about 100 feet away are ever audible. On weekends you'll likely catch a glimpse of canoeists or kayakers darting downstream through the Class II rapids. Piles of trailside logs and debris testify to periodic flooding, and downed trees throughout the park are lingering reminders of Hurricane Isabel, which hit the city with unexpected force in 2003.

Most visitors stick to the River Trail, a solitary path into the park's interior and eastern wetlands acreage. In the eastern section, wooden blinds—facades with short, wide windows and animal- and plant-identification placards—facilitate wildlife viewing across a small pond. Bird-watching is particularly good here. I was fortunate to spot a downy woodpecker on one trip and a pileated woodpecker, its telltale red crest visible from its treetop perch, on another. On both visits a beaver slid from the bank of Pleasants Creek as I passed, gliding slowly away, cautious but hardly alarmed. All visitors will appreciate the serenity of this wetland area.

No visitor should miss sunset at Pony Pasture. But don't look west. The show is across the James, particularly in autumn, where the sinking sun sets the trees aglow and glints from the windows of riverside estates. A full harvest moonrise completes the scene. Some of the best river (and swamp) views are from spur trails, so give yourself time to explore—and wear appropriate attire. Follow Pleasants Creek from its wide mouth at the James riverbank upstream to where it dwindles to a mere trickle. Dragonflies dart about in warmer months, and honking Canada geese pass overhead in the spring and fall. The park's wet soil accommodates a host of vegetation, but few of the mid-Atlantic's more common hardwoods. Here sycamores tower over a deciduous mix thick with underbrush; shaggy-bark birches and ivy ground cover are common.

If you're going to flout the city's leash law, know that thick vegetation makes it easy to lose sight of your pet. I confess to letting Lucile, my rambunctious basset hound, tear through the woods in the park's eastern end. While I can't recommend you do the same, she came when called, emerging muddied but content. Many visitors bring dogs to Pony Pasture, but only a few are brave enough to slog through the park on a mountain bike. Tire tracks, however, testify to their persistence. The unkempt naturalness of Pony Pasture Rapids might seem a deterrent on first blush—it's hardly a well-manicured city park—but as it happens, the park's ruggedness is its biggest draw.

Huguenot Flatwater, the westernmost portion of the James River Park and a popular canoe and kayak put-in, offers another mile or so of trail easily linked to Pony Pasture via Riverside Drive.

# POOR FARM PARK

## ▶ IN BRIEF

Renowned among mountain bikers—as an old bicycle chained in the crux of a trailside tree attests—the dirt trails of Poor Farm Park are nevertheless also great for hiking and technical trail running.

## ▶ DESCRIPTION

It may have made a poor farmstead, but the land along Stagg Creek, approximately 4 miles west of Ashland, makes a fine Hanover County park. No doubt plowing the steep terrain that rises east from the creek would be difficult, especially using traditional methods. However, the county found the hillside ideal for the construction of an amphitheater and created one without clear-cutting the surrounding hardwood forest. Mountain bikers and trail runners did the rest, carving a spiderweb of single-track in the woods.

Entering the park, you'll pass level sports fields. The road veers right to reach the playground and popular picnic shelters with horseshoe pits, a volleyball court, and an open playfield adjacent. It's easy to see why area residents flock to this park for family gatherings, church picnics, and the like. The trail network lies beyond the fields, in the northwest reaches of the park, and the official trailhead is to the right of the horseshoe pits as you face the field. The gravel road off to the left and just

## ▶ DIRECTIONS

From Richmond follow I-95 north to Exit 92, and take VA 54 west. Drive through the city of Ashland, and, in approximately 5 miles, turn left onto VA 810 (Liberty School Road). There is a sign for the park at this intersection. Drive past Liberty Middle School on the left to enter Poor Farm Park. Continue on the entry road, veering right, and park in a gravel lot on the right at the road's terminus.

## KEY AT-A-GLANCE INFORMATION

**LENGTH:** 2.1 miles plus numerous options

**CONFIGURATION:** Loop

**DIFFICULTY:** Moderate

**SCENERY:** Hardwood forest, Stagg Creek

Exposure: Well-shaded

**TRAFFIC:** Moderate

**TRAIL SURFACE:** Dirt

**HIKING TIME:** 1 hour

**SEASON:** Open daily during daylight year-round

**ACCESS:** No fee

**MAPS:** See signboard at parking lot

**FACILITIES:** Baseball, softball, football, and soccer fields; archery range, volleyball court, horseshoe pits, picnic shelter, amphitheater, portable toilets

**SPECIAL COMMENTS:** Occasional "No Trespassing" signs separate the park from adjacent private land, but there is no fence, and some trails freely cross the boundary. Avoid crossing Stagg Creek and you will stay within the park. For more information call Hanover County Parks, (804) 365-4695.

**UTM Trailhead Coordinates for Poor Farm Park**

**UTM Zone (NAD27)    18S**

**Easting    0276281**

**Northing    4184347**

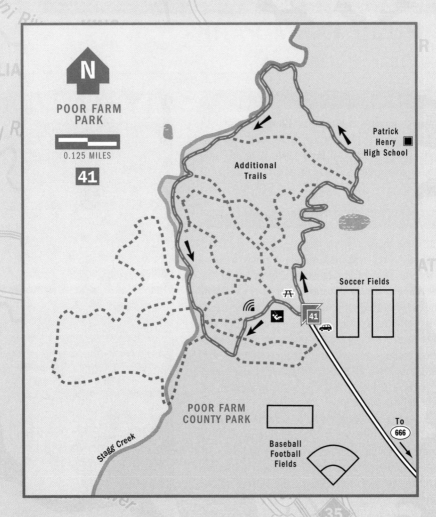

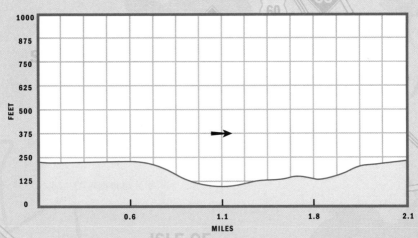

past the playground serves as a secondary trailhead, and the route mapped here returns from that direction to make a loop.

The park's own maps are lacking, and the trail network is simply too extensive and too compact to render completely, even with the aid of a GPS receiver. But, precisely because the trails are packed into a relatively small area, your risk of getting lost—at least for long—is minimized. In summer, vegetation fills the woods, creating a forested serenity but obscuring landmarks and nearby trails. Make the loop described here first in order to grasp the lay of the land, then take another pass, giving yourself leave to wander onto the numerous side trails. Think twice about fording Stagg Creek, however. It's not that the meandering stream poses a threat, but the park boundary lies just beyond it. (Some users have blazed trails on the adjacent land, and an uninformed visitor might reasonably infer that the park stretches farther west.)

Leaving from the primary trailhead, descend a wide gravel trail past the playing field on your left and archery range on your right. Turn right at the first intersection onto a narrower earthen trail. The path dips to cross a ravine and then switches back several times, heading generally north. Stay right to ensure you make a wider loop. You'll soon pass a drainage pond on the right, and then a bend ahead to the left.

Follow the trail northwest as it descends to Stagg Creek. Turn southwest (left) to trace the creek, heading upstream. The path undulates, occasionally overlooking Stagg Creek on small bluffs, but stick to the waterside when side trails beckon you left into the park's interior. Stagg Creek flows northeast to meet the South Anna River about 1.5 miles from Poor Farm Park. Within the park the swift-moving creek gurgles over rocky shoals, some of which recall an American Southwest canyon when viewed from above. About halfway along your riparian jaunt, the creek forks to pass around an island in narrow channels, with earthen banks a foot or more high fringed in moss. You then begin trekking southeast.

The woods along the creek are home to river birch, pawpaw, and beech, while holly thickets, oaks, hickories, and some pines fill the upland forest. In the springtime, white dogwood blossoms dot the woods, and brilliant red maples catch your eye in the autumn. You may also notice the preponderance of mayapple growing on the forest floor. The foot-tall plants have umbrella-like leaves with five to seven prongs. Those with only one leaf will not flower; those with two produce a small white flower, growing where the stem forks, in or around May. A yellow berry follows in the summer. A known laxative, the berry is sometimes still used today. Other parts of the plant are toxic, however, and it's said that native Indians sometimes consumed the roots and stems to commit suicide. Mayapple was later incorporated into folk remedies for digestive ailments and warts, and even today it is used to produce anticancer medication.

Soon the trail will veer away from the creek and enter a wide clearing where several trails intersect. Continue and take the final left uphill before returning to the creek. At this point you've hiked approximately 1.75 miles. If you reach a point where crossing the creek is your only option, you've gone too far south.

Heading eastward uphill, emerge along a fence and should turn left again. After a dip in the trail, go straight through a trail intersection to emerge onto a gravel road behind the amphitheater. Turn right to follow it back to the picnic area. Then having circumnavigated the bulk of Poor Farm Park's trail network, feel free to dive back in.

# POWHATAN WILDLIFE MANAGEMENT AREA

 **KEY AT-A-GLANCE INFORMATION**

**LENGTH:** 10.2 miles (with shorter and longer options

**CONFIGURATION:** Figure eight

**DIFFICULTY:** Hard

**SCENERY:** Mostly hardwood forest, fishing lakes, creeks, fields and hedgerows

**EXPOSURE:** Open along fields, shaded on some forested trails

**TRAFFIC:** Low

**TRAIL SURFACE:** Dirt and gravel double-track

**HIKING TIME:** 4 hours

**SEASON:** Open daily during daylight year-round, but trails should be avoided during autumn and winter hunting seasons (see Special Comments below).

**ACCESS:** No fee; horseback riding and mountain biking allowed; no ATVs; wheelchair access is very limited. Primitive camping is permitted, but do not leave campfires unattended.

**MAPS:** Available online at www.dgif. virginia.gov/hunting/wma/powhatan.html

**FACILITIES:** Fishing lakes with boat launch; information boards

**SPECIAL COMMENTS:** All wildlife management areas are open to hunting. Check with VDGIF to determine annual hunting seasons (call (804) 370-1000 or visit www.dgif.virginia.gov/hunting). Hiking during deer and wild turkey seasons is not recommended. If you do, wear blaze orange and hike only during peak daylight hours.

**UTM Trailhead Coordinates for Powhatan Wildlife Management Area**

**UTM Zone (NAD27)** 18S

**Easting** 0238324

**Northing** 4160923

## IN BRIEF

As Richmond's bedroom communities sprawl southward, rural Powhatan County seems closer and closer to home. Just west of its namesake county seat, Powhatan Wildlife Management Area (WMA) offers more than a dozen trail miles. This route takes in most of them, passing through low-lying wetlands, hillside hardwood forest, and fields buffered by hedgerows. As you would expect, your prospects for spotting wildlife are good, but you'll also see rusting machinery and an old cemetery, reminders of the area's past as timberland and farmland.

## DESCRIPTION

Maintained by the Virginia Department of Game and Inland Fisheries, Virginia's wildlife management areas are a boon to outdoor lovers in Central Virginia, where public land is in short supply. Though open for hunting in season and for fishing

## DIRECTIONS

From Richmond travel west on US 60 (the Midlothian Turnpike). Continue through Midlothian and then through Powhatan. One mile after US 60 narrows from four lanes to two, turn left onto VA 601. Proceed southeast for approximately half a mile to a small parking area on the right, identified by a Department of Game and Inland Fisheries sign.

Other parking areas border the wildlife management area on all sides. To drive to the fishing ponds within the WMA, continue past VA 601 on US 60, and turn left (south) onto VA 627. After about 1.5 miles, turn left again onto VA 662, which turns to gravel and dead-ends at Sunfish Pond, passing Bass and Bullhead Ponds en route. The Powhatan Lakes, located within the smaller portion of the WMA north of US 60, were closed to visitors as of publication.

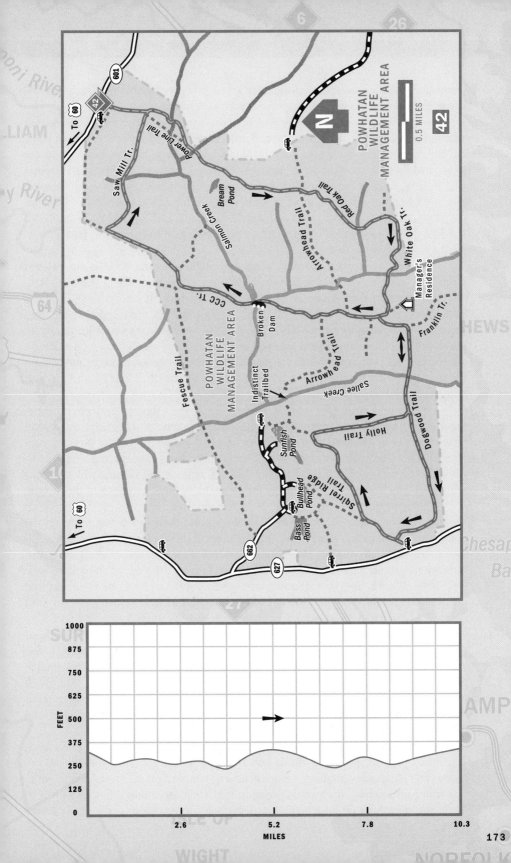

year-round, the state's wildlife management areas also encourage hiking—and, as you'll notice at Powhatan, they are quite popular with equestrians as well.

In addition to deer hunters, Powhatan draws hunters in search of woodland fowl: wild turkey, woodcock, dove, and quail. (Unfortunately for hikers anxious about being out with the hunters, these seasons coincide with fall foliage, but Powhatan is equally scenic blanketed in snow or dotted with wildflowers.) Powhatan may be most popular with anglers. Besides the twin Powhatan Lakes north of US 60, which total 58 acres, this WMA has four smaller lakes (2 to 9 acres) named for a prospective catch. Depending on what you hope to land, cast your line in Bass, Bullhead, Sunfish, or Bream Pond. The first three are clustered off the park's main gravel road in its western half; the latter stands alone to the east.

It's worth noting that a sizable wetland in the heart of the WMA is absent from official maps, which only show Beaver Swamp on the opposite side of the CCC Trail. Also missing from those maps is mention of the washed-out bridge along the CCC Trail. Water from the unmapped marsh now streams over the fractured concrete, rendering a wet crossing inevitable. The route mapped here assumes you want to take in most of the wildlife management area and don't mind soggy shoes. However, it doesn't ask you to blaze your way through the marsh near the intersection of Sallee and Salmon Creeks. Maps show the Arrowhead Trail passing through this area, but I found the path disappeared into the marsh.

Nevertheless, you have several options for longer, shorter, and drier routes, thanks in part to parking areas that dot Powhatan's perimeter. The 4,462-acre parcel includes areas of cropland that have been retained as fields, though they are now planted with wild game in mind. You'll see slender hedgerows between the fields, which host a variety of woodland mammals, such as mice and rabbits, which in turn bring predators like foxes, owls, and snakes. A wealth of birds also nests in the hedges.

Unlike nearby Amelia Wildlife Management Area, where such rolling fields abound, Powhatan also encompasses dense woods and more varied terrain. At several points the trail descends sharply to a stream crossing then promptly climbs away. Following heavy rainfall, you may find it difficult to ford these streams without getting wet, but they are generally narrow and shallow enough to cross unaided, or on rocks or logs. Near some, horse hooves have churned muddy spots in the trail bed, and you may find it easiest to stray into the woods to circumvent them. Though some are gravel, most of the trails at Powhatan are grassy passages through wide clearings.

Departing from the trailhead off VA 601 on the Richmond side of the WMA, head west past a pipeline clearing and into an area of reemerging forest. Stay to the left to follow a scenic side trail that rejoins the Power Line Trail after crossing an upper branch of Salmon Creek. Be on the lookout for rusting mechanical equipment on trail left. A metal wheel juts from the earth beside a shaggy red cedar. This enigmatic contraption may be old farming equipment, but more likely was part of the sawmill for which the Saw Mill Trail, on which you will return, was named.

The path fords gurgling Salmon Creek in a pleasant glade-like setting just ahead. To the east (left) the stream is visible bubbling from below ground. Downstream, the frothy creek descends crumbling rocky shoals en route to Beaver Swamp and its junction with Sallee Creek. Northward-flowing Sallee Creek bisects the WMA on its way to the James River. After cresting a hill, bear left when you emerge onto the grassy Power

Line Trail and you'll soon descend to a small feeder branch. After passing Bream Pond on the right, the pathway bears south, becoming the Red Oak Trail. Look for an an old family cemetery in a clearing to the left. The intricate ironwork of the small cemetery's fence now pokes through a blanket of honeysuckle.

Head south through maintained fields bordered by forest. Continue on the Red Oak Trail through its intersection with the Arrowhead Trail and into a hardwood forest. The trail descends to a stream crossing, advances uphill, and bears west (right) to become the White Oak Trail. You'll wind through the woods toward another stream, then ascend to intersect the gravel CCC Trail behind a cluster of barns adjacent to the manager's residence. Proceed north (right) a short distance before turning left to double back around the buildings and head south. The Dogwood Trail is on the right in less than a quarter mile.

Follow the gravel-based Dogwood Trail downhill to ford Sallee Creek, then begin an undulating ascent to the WMA's western border, where the trail curves north. The path continues through a wide corridor with more redbud trees than dogwoods and along mostly deciduous woods. As it circles back to head northeast, the path becomes the Arrowhead Trail at an intersection where the Squirrel Ridge Trail heads north. Portions of the latter have been incorporated into a brief nature trail that ascends a tiered path from the southwest corner of Bass Pond. As of my visit, few interpretive signs were in place, and it scarcely rivaled other nature trails included in this guide. However, if you'd like to traverse Powhatan without backtracking, you could leave a shuttle vehicle at Bass Pond and make this your terminus.

Otherwise, continue atop a ridge on the Arrowhead Trail. You'll descend to meet the Holly Trail, which heads to the right before Arrowhead reaches Sunfish Pond (another shuttle-placement option). Follow the Holly Trail southward to cross another stream and ultimately return to the Dogwood Trail. Retrace your steps to the maintenance buildings and head north (left) on the CCC Trail.

You will descend to reach the unnamed, unmapped body of water on trail right and its spillway over the CCC Trail. Depending on water levels, you may be able to pick your way across the rocks and concrete, but be cautious: it's better to have wet shoes than a twisted ankle. Once past, continue uphill through the forested corridor before you reach the Fescue Trail.

Turn right onto the Fescue Trail, which follows a grassy pipeline clearing, and proceed northeast for approximately half a mile, past more fields and hedgerows on the right, before turning right onto the Saw Mill Trail. You'll pass one more seasonal stream before regaining, through a young, vine-draped wood, the Power Line Trail at mile 10. From here turn left for a short walk back to your vehicle.

On the way home, why not stop at Midlothian Mines Park just south of US 60 via North Woolridge Road? Unveiled in 2004 and not complete as of publication, the park pays homage to this area's coal-mining and railroading heritage. Mines operated as early as 1730 in what is now Chesterfield County, and coal from Midlothian powered arms factories during the American Revolution. The second commercial rail line laid in the United States linked Chesterfield's mines to Richmond in 1831. Midlothian Coal was again a vital wartime resource during the 1860s, but production fell sharply during Reconstruction. Portions of the park are still under development but will feature historical interpretation, a gravity rail line, and a pedestrian tunnel.

# PRINCE EDWARD–GALLION STATE FOREST

## KEY AT-A-GLANCE INFORMATION

**LENGTH:** 7.4 miles one way with shorter options and spurs, as well as a 2.2-mile out-and-back option at trail's end

**CONFIGURATION:** End-to-end

**DIFFICULTY:** Moderate

**SCENERY:** Pine and hardwood forests, roadside wildflowers, small creeks

**EXPOSURE:** Shaded except on wide roads

**TRAFFIC:** Low; autos permitted on forest roads

**TRAIL SURFACE:** Gravel forest roads and dirt trails

**HIKING TIME:** 3.5 hours

**SEASON:** Trails are open daily during daylight year-round

**ACCESS:** There is no fee to enter the forest; mountain biking and horseback riding allowed on multiuse trail; trail not recommended for wheelchairs

**MAPS:** A low-resolution map is available online at www.vdof.virginia.gov/stforest/index-pesf.shtml

**FACILITIES:** Limited to parking, however adjacent Twin Lakes State Park offers restrooms, a campground, a lakeside beach, and a snack bar

**SPECIAL COMMENTS:** Portions of the state forest are open to hunting with a license. Call the forest office (434) 983-2175 for details. Check with VDGIF to determine annual hunting seasons; call (804) 370-1000 or visit www.dgif.virginia.gov/hunting).

---

**UTM Trailhead Coordinates for Prince Edward-Gallion State Forest**

**UTM Zone (NAD27)   17S**

**Easting   0741481**

**Northing   4117307**

## IN BRIEF

South of Farmville in Prince Edward County, the 6,496-acre Prince Edward–Gallion State Forest is one of three in Virginia's rolling Piedmont, each of which envelops a state park with camping (here it's Twin Lakes). The designated multiuse trail makes extensive use of gravel forest roads, but miles of earthen double-track crisscrossing the forest expand options for the intrepid.

## DESCRIPTION

In 1919 Emmett O. Gallion planted the seed that sprouted into Virginia's state-forest system. He bequeathed 588 acres in Prince Edward County to the commonwealth, stipulating that it be preserved undeveloped. That tract is today a wildlife sanctuary within Prince Edward–Gallion State Forest. The adjacent acreage, like most in the state-forest system, was purchased from struggling farmers by the federal government during the Depression then deeded to Virginia in 1954.

## DIRECTIONS

From Richmond take US 360 west (Hull Street Road in the city). Stay on US 360 through Burkeville, where it briefly meets US 460 then dips southward. Pass the first signed turn for Twin Lakes State Park, then turn right at signed VA 613, about 4.25 miles beyond Burkeville. Drive north 2 miles to turn right on VA 689 (beyond a park sign). Just over a mile ahead, the road forks. Massie Forest Road heads left, but bear right with Stony Knoll Forest Road. Grassy clearings beside the road serve as trailhead parking. This hike is 7.4 miles from one end to the other, so you may want to place a shuttle vehicle along the trail's final leg. Take US 360 west to Green Bay then turn right on VA 696. Turn right on Weaver Forest Road about a mile ahead and park on the shoulder.

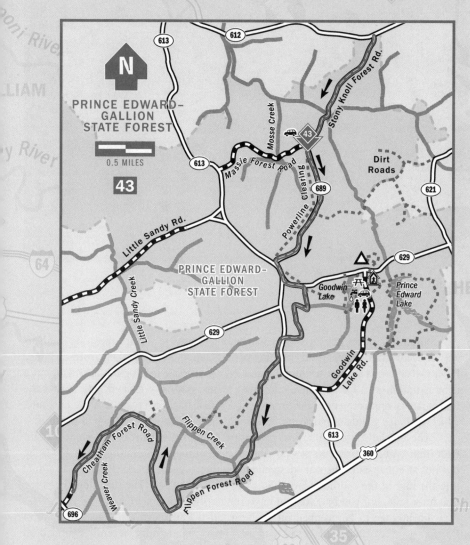

PRINCE EDWARD–
GALLION
STATE FOREST

N

0.5 MILES

43

613
612
Mosse Creek
43
Stony Knoll Forest Rd.
Massie Forest Road
613
Powerline Clearing
689
Dirt
Roads
621
Little Sandy Rd.
64
PRINCE EDWARD–
GALLION
STATE FOREST
Little Sandy Creek
629
629
Goodwin
Lake
Prince
Edward
Lake
Goodwin Lake Rd.
Cheatham Forest Road
Flippen Creek
Weaver Creek
Flippen Forest Road
613
360
696
Chesape
Bay

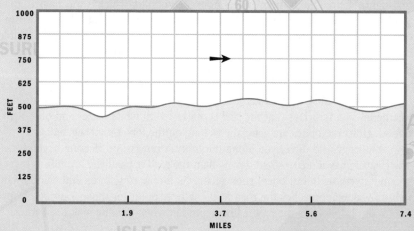

| | | | |
|---|---|---|---|
| 1000 | | | |
| 875 | | | |
| 750 | ➜ | | |
| 625 | | | |
| 500 | | | |
| 375 | | | |
| 250 | | | |
| 125 | | | |
| 0 | | | |

FEET

1.9    3.7    5.6    7.4
MILES

177

Much of the trail at Prince Edward–Gallion State Forest travels quiet forest roads.

Virginia's state forests are self-sustaining entities. Their operating budgets are derived from timber and hunting-permit sales. As a working forest, Prince Edward–Gallion is subject to thinning and even wholesale logging but also serves as a demonstration area for sustainable forestry. While swaths of cleared land border the trail near its opposite ends, they represent a small fraction of the scenery en route, which includes stands of pines and hardwoods in just about every stage of maturity.

The official route of the Prince Edward–Gallion Multiuse Trail stretches southwest from VA 612 to VA 696. It's possible to park in roadside clearings along the route but not at either end. The only designated parking, signed "Trailer Parking," is a mile into the hike at the southern end of Stony Knoll Forest Road. The road doubles as the trail for a mile, but you may wish to forgo the northernmost stretch.

Or arrange to be dropped off at the wooden forest sign on Stony Knoll Forest Road at VA 612. Follow the gravel road as it traces a pine ridge, recently denuded on trail right. The road dips, presumably from the knoll for which it was named, to serene Sandy River. The river is shaded by sycamore and river birch, and the confluence of its north fork with the unnamed stream flowing from Prince Edward Lake is visible just upstream of the wood-on-steel bridge. Uphill, summer-blooming black-eyed Susans flank the rising trail.

A house is visible on trail right before you reach the parking clearing. A sign for the forest's multiuse trail stands beside a trailer used as a part-time forest office. The weathered sign indicates that the trail is marked with white blazes and blue signs with arrows. However, blazes are generally lacking on the forest-road segments.

Blue signs do direct you along the modest power-line clearing beyond the sign. The clearing has more ups and downs than the road it parallels, VA 689. It is prone to summer overgrowth but offers good prospects for spotting birds and wildflowers. The right-of-way reapproaches the road at its halfway point for those wanting to opt for a road walk. If following the power lines, turn left when the line makes a T intersection.

If you choose to stay on the roads, turn left from VA 689 onto VA 613. Asphalt underfoot proceeds the turn. Follow the blacktop for just 0.4 miles, veering left on VA 629. Turn right into the woods at a trail crossing signed with an equestrian symbol. The power-line path emerges at this same crossing, which makes a good alternate starting point for those camping at nearby Twin Lakes State Park.

Once in the woods south of VA 629, the trail promptly veers right. Avoid another trail that continues straight through the hardwood forest. The multiuse path descends to meet a seasonal stream, passing tall white oaks and sweet gums. This muddy ford is the first of three moist sags that tend to be overgrown. Next, the trail widens as it bends right and heads uphill. After climbing 50 feet the multiuse trail makes a sharp left at one of the few blazed intersections along its length.

A brief descent takes you to another often-muddy sag in the trail. After navigating any puddles, continue southward over a small knoll where chestnut oaks have taken root in the drier upland soil. Identifiable by oblong leaves with wavy edges, the species attains neither the height nor girth of its namesake. Sadly, any 100-foot-tall specimens of American chestnut remaining at the outset of the twentieth century were decimated by an Asian fungal blight. The great trees, prized for their lumber, once grew along the Appalachians from Mississippi to Maine.

The trail soon descends to the third muddy stretch, though this is the least sloppy. It then curves right as it rises to meet a double-track before crossing VA 613. Having reentered woods, take a left onto the narrower track at an almost-immediate fork. The trail bears south through a stand of short Virginia pines, keeping the road in view for 0.2 miles before veering right. The path, alternately mossy and grassy, soon meets gravel Flippen Forest Road to wind through the Flippen Creek drainage.

Turn right and walk down the gravel road. As you round a corner to head south, a wide, level dirt road splits right from the gravel road. This 0.8-mile dirt road is closed to vehicles but is open to hikers. It follows a ridge, dips to cross a feeder stream of Flippen Creek, then rises to a dead end to create an alternate 4-mile out-and-back from the VA 629 crossing near Twin Lakes State Park.

The multiuse trail follows Flippen Forest Road on a steady descent though primarily pine forest to ford a stream. The road crests a hill once cloaked in hardwoods before dropping to cross its namesake creek on a bridge. Look for a blackberry thicket on trail left before the bridge. The pattern repeats with another bridged crossing before the road makes a distinct left.

Ahead, pastureland is visible through a metal gate on trail left. A second gate on the left at a T intersection forces you to turn right onto Weaver Forest Road. The forest here reverts to pines, many of which were recently clear-cut on trail right. The multiuse route continues on a lengthy northwestward ridge walk before the road turns left and dips to ford Weaver Creek.

Complete the end-to-end with a climb out of the valley drainage to meet VA 696. Those ardent hikers looking to tack on a few more miles can elongate the trip to almost 9 miles by tacking on a road walk along Gallion Forest Road. Turn left (south) on VA 696, and walk 0.3 miles before turning right onto Gallion Forest Road, which follows a ridge before descending to cross two feeder streams just east of their confluence to form Medley Creek.

# R. GARLAND DODD PARK
# AT POINT OF ROCKS

## KEY AT-A-GLANCE INFORMATION

**LENGTH:** 1.8

**CONFIGURATION:** Loop

**DIFFICULTY:** Easy

**SCENERY:** Ashton Creek Marsh, the Appomattox River, bottomland forest

Exposure: Well-shaded but open on marsh boardwalks

**TRAFFIC:** Low

**TRAIL SURFACE:** Dirt and gravel

**HIKING TIME:** 1 hour

**SEASON:** Open daily during daylight year-round

**ACCESS:** No fee

**MAPS:** Available from signboard at nature center and www.co.chesterfield.va.us/HumanServices/ParksandRecreation/p_rhome.asp

**FACILITIES:** Restrooms; playground, baseball, softball, soccer, and football fields; tennis courts, basketball court, picnic shelters

**SPECIAL COMMENTS:** Storm damage from 2003's Hurricane Isabel remains visible within the park. Although the route mapped here has been cleared, the park's boardwalk, formerly more than 500 feet, was damaged and subsequently dismantled. Downed trees also hampered access to the northernmost loop of the trail network (the Woodthrush Trail on the park signboard). Contact Chesterfield County Parks at (804) 748-1623.

UTM Trailhead Coordinates for
R. Garland Dodd Park at Point of Rocks

UTM Zone (NAD27)  18S

Easting  0291345

Northing  4132942

## IN BRIEF

This short, well-trod loop passes diverse terrain: hillsides forested in mature hardwoods, the cattail-and-cordgrass marsh along Ashton Creek, and the wide Appomattox River on its way to meet the James. Located near Hopewell, the park is as convenient to Petersburg as to Richmond's Southside.

## DESCRIPTION

Almost a quarter-century old, the trail system at R. Garland Dodd Park at Point of Rocks (formerly just Point of Rocks Park) bears the signs of wear and tear. At least one wooden footbridge is dated 1980, the year the park opened, as are a few of the many, many carvings in beech trees along the trail. These names, initials, and professions of love suggest a popular weekending spot. Yet trailside growth crowds the hard-packed single-track, so the trails at Point of Rocks feel broken-in but slightly past their prime, which isn't a bad thing. For instance, they haven't been "upgraded" to asphalt. Plus, if you come on a weekday, you'll likely have the network to yourself—a particular incentive to bird-watchers drawn by the park's multiple habitats.

Unfortunately, the system's newest extension, a long boardwalk over Ashton Creek Marsh, was dismantled in the wake of 2003 storm

## DIRECTIONS

From Richmond take I-95 south to Exit 61. Take VA 10 east for 5 miles, passing under I-295's Exit 15 en route. Turn right from VA 10 onto VA 746 (Enon Church Road), which reaches the park in about 2 miles, after first passing under an I-295 overpass. The park entrance is on the left, with a popular basketball court nearest the street. The trailhead is located to the right of the re-created homestead cabin if your back is to the baseball fields.

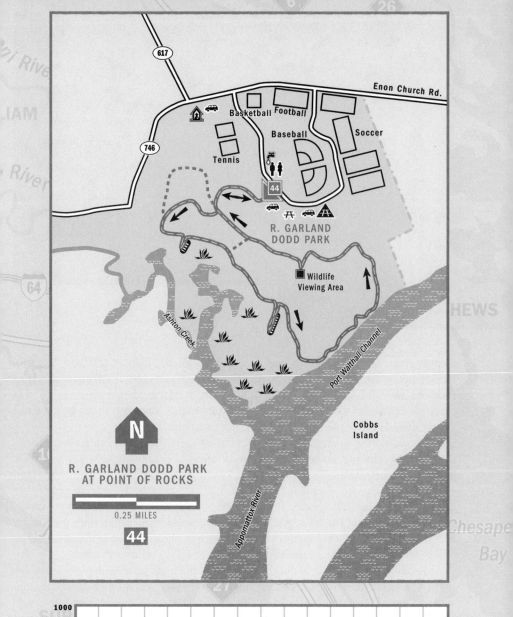

R. GARLAND DODD PARK
AT POINT OF ROCKS

0.25 MILES

44

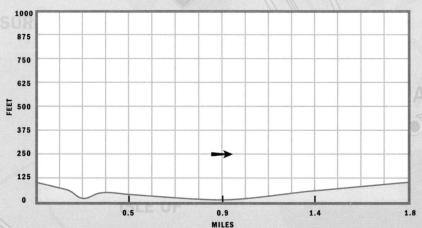

Settler-style cabins in a grove
near the trailhead at R. Garland
Dodd Park

damage, just two years after it was completed with the help of the local Sheriff's
Work Force units. Perhaps it will be restored before your visit; in any case, there are
excellent views of the marsh from the wooden overlooks that remain. You'll also
enjoy the chance to spot wildlife along the Appomattox River and in the bottomland
forest between the marsh and the park facilities uphill.

In addition to the herons, egrets, and kingfishers that attract amateur ornithol-
ogists, the freshwater marsh is home to an array of colorful dragonflies and their
daintier cousins, damselflies. Budding entomologists may identify the long-legged
green darter, Eastern pondhawk, Needham's skimmer, and Eastern amberwing
species. Some dragonfly species are territorial, staking small claims within a swamp,
and some make long annual migrations. Though much smaller than their prehistoric
ancestors, which had wing spans of up to 30 inches, these predatory members of the
order Odonata still serve a valuable purpose by snacking on mosquitoes.

Begin your hike west of the ball fields, at the parking area that is signed for
shelters 1 and 2 and abuts a shaded field on the west, site of a re-created home-
steader's cabin. The trail begins from the corner nearest the entrance and descends
wood-beam steps onto a sandy trail bed. The path curves left down a heavily wooded
slope, with concrete parking-lot barriers lining the downhill edge of the trail, a novel
recycling scheme to prevent erosion. Look for twisting mountain laurel growing on
trail left beneath a mixture of oaks, then scout for a wooden footbridge spanning the
rivulet running on your right.

A nondescript path veers right to cross the bridge; pause on the walkway to
admire the clear-running stream and the rounded pebbles it has smoothed over time.
Turn left, following signs for the marsh. (A spur loop through the forest, the
Woodthrush Trail, heads right.) Take note of a verdant glade on the left before entering an area heavily damaged by storms. A host of vegetation has sprung up in the
ample sunlight, a result of the downed trees scattered beside the trail. The slightly
rerouted trail soon intersects a wider gravel path. (The aforementioned spur loop

arrives at this junction.) Turn left again at a sign to the marsh and boardwalk. A sandy road leads right but soon terminates at the park border.

The overlook, just ahead on the right, is a small wooden platform with a bench that offers clear views of Ashton Creek Marsh, which is obscured by wetland flora for most of the hike. Wooden stairs lead to a larger wooden deck just a few feet above the marsh. This was formerly one end of a lengthy boardwalk that traversed Ashton Creek Marsh. On my visit, the dismantled boardwalk's former route was still visible, because the younger grasses along the way were a lighter shade of green that the surrounding cattails, swamp milkweed, and cordgrass.

Return to the trail via wooden stairs that fork, and bear right, heading east along the shore. The path undulates slightly, with dark, still water visible just downhill. Ahead is an arboreal oddity: a tall holly has enwrapped the towering sweet gum beside it. You'll notice a few orange blazes painted on trailside trees, indicating this is Cobbs Wharf Trail. The infrequency of blazes along this trail network diminishes their worth, but color corelations are given on the trailhead signboard.

Look for the granite-brick remains of a forgotten structure lying ignominiously on trail left before a fork in the trail. A double-track shortcut veers slightly left, but follow the single-track to the right. Continue past the charred remnants of a fire, perhaps the product of a lightning strike. Fortunately, the larger trees survived. Numerous beech trees, many victims of pocket-knife graffiti, populate the woods here, and just beyond a bench, one of the larger beech trees I've seen (and that's saying a lot in this part of Virginia) appears on trail left about 30 feet away. This specimen has developed a broad, leafy crown.

Catch your first glimpses of a field inland on the left as you approach the second overlook. A slightly longer section of the former boardwalk juts out over the marsh on this end. From the peninsular decking, Ashton Creek's confluence with the Appomattox River is faintly visible to your left. Return to the trail and continue past a closed trail spur, now blockaded with logs, which once led onto a spit of land on the right. If you're looking for a unique vantage point, you can still avail yourself of an elevated platform that lies ahead on trail left.

The main path soon turns northeast to run along the Appomattox River, with the reedy shore of Cobbs Island visible across Port Walthall Channel. The Appomattox reaches its confluence with the James at Hopewell, roughly 4 miles east. Occasionally, the trail abuts an open field inland. At other points, it dips to provide access to the river's narrow, sandy shore scattered with rocks.

The trail veers inland, uphill along the park boundary. In the midst of a wood thick with vines and underbrush, pass the remains of a metal gate on trail right along a path with numerous exposed roots and rocks. The trail bears left again to head west. You're now on the path back to the trailhead, so ignore the access trails that descend to meet it from the picnic shelters above.

After traversing a wooden bridge with chain-link sides over a seasonal-stream gully, you'll note a trail marked by wood-beam steps that intersects your path. This well-defined spur leads left, then left again, in about 25 feet, to reach a wildlife-viewing blind. A wide, grassy maintenance road heads east from this blind and is later visible along the main trail in a sweet gum glade on trail left. The main trail soon rises and rounds a corner, and the trailhead is recognizable ahead.

# RAGGED MOUNTAIN
# NATURAL AREA

## KEY AT-A-GLANCE INFORMATION

**LENGTH:** 5.9 miles, optional 3.5-mile short loop

**CONFIGURATION:** Loop

**DIFFICULTY:** Difficult

**SCENERY:** Charlottesville Reservoir, old pump house, water flume, hardwood-forested hillsides, creek-fed marsh

Exposure: Well-shaded

**TRAFFIC:** Moderate, highest near education building

**TRAIL SURFACE:** Dirt, plus optional paved trail

**HIKING TIME:** 3 hours

**SEASON:** Open daily during daylight year-round

**ACCESS:** No fee; not recommended for wheelchairs

**MAPS:** Available at park signboard and online at www.avenue.org/icf/RMNA

**FACILITIES:** Limited to gravel parking area with trailhead signboard

**SPECIAL COMMENTS:** Owned by the City of Charlottesville, Ragged Mountain is managed by the Ivy Creek Foundation for wildlife viewing and preservation only. Dog walking, jogging, cycling, swimming, camping, and, of course, hunting and fishing are prohibited. Contact the Ivy Creek Foundation at (434) 973-7772.

---

UTM Trailhead Coordinates for
Ragged Mountain Natural Area

UTM Zone (NAD27)   17S

Easting   0714511

Northing   4211375

## IN BRIEF

Before encircling Charlottesville Reservoir, the trail at Ragged Mountain Natural Area gets off to a rough start, gaining more than 300 feet in the first half-mile. After descending from the rocky peak of Round Top, however, the trail is largely level. Seemingly remote despite the proximity of I-64, the natural area protects both boulder-studded slopes and a creek-fed marsh.

## DESCRIPTION

A string of peaks reaching south and west from Charlottesville, the Ragged Mountains remain true to their name: boulders jut from the hillsides, and roots crisscross the earth. Cloaked in mature forest, the hillsides must appear today much as they did when Edgar Allen Poe hiked them as respite from his studies at the University of Virginia—woodland ambles that inspired his *Tale of the Ragged Mountains*.

In the 1820s Poe could have explored a steep-sided stream valley where modern visitors find Charlottesville Reservoir. In 1885 Charlottesville partnered with the university to dam the creek flowing southeast below Round Top, creating a public water supply. Twenty-three years later, the impoundment was tripled in size. Then in the 1920s a 13-mile-long, cast-iron aqueduct was laid underground to siphon water from Sugar Hollow Reservoir. The pipe still carries 4 million gallons

## DIRECTIONS

From Richmond follow I-64 northwest to Exit 118. Exit northbound on US 29/250 Bypass. In approximately half a mile, turn left onto Fontaine Avenue (US 29 Business in the opposite direction). Proceed a quarter of a mile, then turn right onto VA 202 (Reservoir Road). The road soon turns gravel and winds 2 miles to the trailhead on the right, shortly before the road's terminus.

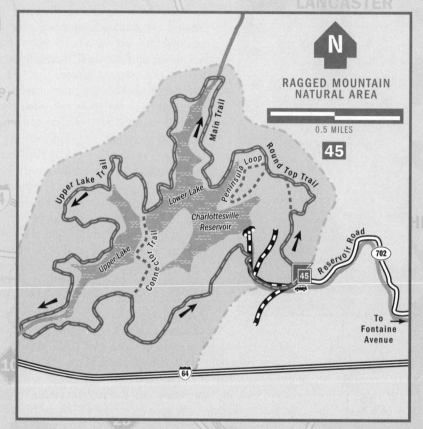

**N**

**RAGGED MOUNTAIN NATURAL AREA**

0.5 MILES

**45**

Main Trail

Upper Lake Trail

Lower Lake

Peninsula Loop

Round Top Trail

Charlottesville Reservoir

Upper Lake

Connector Trail

Reservoir Road

**702**

**45**

To Fontaine Avenue

**64**

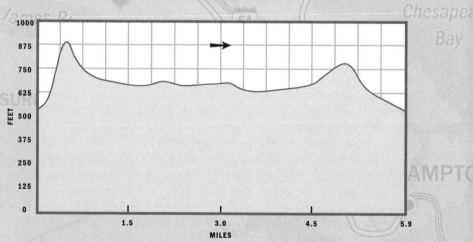

A flume emerging from beneath the trail carries a noisy torrent of water to the lake below.

daily, and this hike crosses the stone flume that channels that torrent toward its final cascade into the reservoir.

The route departs uphill, northbound, beyond the trailhead signboard. The rock-studded trail weaves beneath yellow poplar, red maple, and dogwood, ascending steadily toward the crest of Round Top. The surrounding vegetation indicates moist soil due to runoff from the rocky hill. After passing through a modest boulder garden and beside a mammoth chestnut oak, the trail forks. It's possible to avoid the final push by veering left with the Main Trail as the Round Top Trail heads right, but go ahead and make the peak—you're almost there.

Storm damage has exposed the upper hillsides, and downed logs were used to outline the path. Atop Round Top, look for a roofless, circular stone wall—a young boy's ideal play fort. Beyond a sign reading "Round Top Mountain, elevation 919 feet," look for a trail departing left. The path is somewhat obscure, so look for red-paint blazes to verify you're on the path back to the Main Trail.

Upon rejoining the loop, turn right, now following blue blazes. An old dirt road enters from the left, and the Main Trail enjoys a wide, level treadway as it heads gently downhill to the lakeshore. Soon the trail passes a short connector on the left for the half-mile Peninsula Loop. True to its name, the spur loop circles a low, wide ridge that juts into the reservoir's lower lake. Ahead along the Main Trail, continue through white, Northern red, and chestnut oaks to reach a stream. One of numerous tributaries that empty into the reservoir, the trickle has worn a deep gully into the hillside. After crossing on a footbridge, bear left and follow the fern-clad rivulet to the lake.

The trail follows the shore as it curves from west to north. Depending on the water level, granite walls may be visible across the water. Cross a small runoff culvert with the aid of railroad-tie steps after passing through a stand of Virginia pines. Not far ahead, mountain-laurel thickets crowd the path. Descend a slope before rounding the northernmost arm of the reservoir, fed by two small creeks. Look for shagbark and bitternut hickory growing in the moist soil here.

As the path turns south, it leaves the water's edge to pass beside rock walls about 10 feet high. Across a seasonal stream, the trail rises on wood-beam stairs through a boulder-strewn stretch of forest. Large rocks abut the lake ahead and invite sunbathing or picnicking. A series of three wooden bridges over small gullies brings you to an area of younger forest now thick with sumac and thorny brambles.

Upon reaching an intersection with the Upper Lake Trail, turn left for a brief out-and-back onto the earthen dam between the reservoir's upper and lower lakes. This detour lets you see the old pump house, which is detached from the earthen dam before it by a gulf that was, presumably, once spanned by a bridge. The weathered and rotting wooden building stands in odd contrast to its sturdy rough-cut stone pediment, which projects well clear of the water. By continuing across the dam, you may make a shorter, 3.5-mile loop on the Main Trail. But backtrack and head north, uphill, to circle both lakes.

Rising along an old roadbed, you will soon hear and then see the aforementioned flume channeling foamy white water from a pipe below the trail bed. Just beyond it, the trail turns left, leaving the roadbed to descend along a wide single-track. Approaching a deep-channeled rivulet on trail right, the path crosses it to enter a wide grassy floodplain. Beyond a smaller second culvert that is sometimes muddy, the trail begins to rise. Push ahead to enjoy an understory dogwood glade.

After crossing yet another drainage, the trail bends inland, drawing within sight of a brook on trail left. A pleasant stint along a wooded ridge follows. Gazing through the trees and across the lake, you can make out the misty cascade where water leaps from the flume into the reservoir.

Traversing a creek-fed marsh on the southwestern tip of the lake, look for sourwood trees growing along the water's edge. Tread lightly through this marsh, and you may spot waterfowl, otters, and turtles before they spot you. The trail turns away from the lake and up the creek valley, where riparian grasses and vines grow beneath young hardwoods, including vibrant red maples in the autumn. Step over a small rivulet, then rock-hop across the larger creek. A tall river birch shades a third small feeder, while a fern-dappled hillside rises opposite a fourth.

Briefly follow the trail parallel to the streamlet before rising away on a rocky path. Turn right on the ridgetop when the Upper Lake Trail terminates at the Mail Trail. Continue south along the ridge, with mature, oak-dominated forest descending on either side. An older path soon meets the trail but has been blockaded with logs to keep hikers on the Main Trail, which heads on, curving left against a peak. Make a lengthy ridge run northeast, passing mountain-laurel thickets and dense white pines.

The trail eventually descends to near the lakeshore for the last time just before it makes a sharp right. The dam that forms the reservoir's lower lake is visible through the woods. Several switchbacks then carry you downhill to cross a stone bridge over the creek draining from the lake. The trail promptly joins a gravel access road, turning right, away from the restricted area below the dam. Running briefly parallel to the creek, the double-track soon joins Reservoir Road, itself tapering out. Turn left and continue past a horse pasture on the right. A short road walk returns you to your vehicle.

# RIVANNA TRAIL

## KEY AT-A-GLANCE INFORMATION

**LENGTH:** 19.5 miles, with recommended 3-, 5.9-, and 6.2-mile out-and-backs

**CONFIGURATION:** A loop around the city, divisible into shorter hikes

**DIFFICULTY:** Easy to moderate depending on length and condition of trail

**SCENERY:** Riparian bottomland along Rivanna River, Meadow Creek, and Moore's Creek; hillside hardwoods and recovering forests; some city parks

**EXPOSURE:** Mostly shaded

**TRAFFIC:** Moderate

**TRAIL SURFACE:** Crushed gravel along 1.5-mile Rivanna Greenbelt, dirt elsewhere

**HIKING TIME:** Varies with segment

**SEASON:** Open daily during daylight year-round

**ACCESS:** No fee; only the Rivanna Greenbelt section is wheelchair accessible

**MAPS:** Official brochure provided at major access points; available online at www.avenue.org/rivanna/trail_maps.htm

**FACILITIES:** Limited to small roadside parking areas, with additional facilities in some city parks along the route

**SPECIAL COMMENTS:** To hike the circuit, you must incorporate detours on city streets totaling 1 mile. For more information, contact the Rivanna Trails Foundation at (434) 923-9022 or visit www.rivanna-trails.org; or, contact the City of Charlottesville Parks at (434) 970-3589 or www.charlottesville.org/parks.

---

**UTM Trailhead Coordinates for Rivanna Trail**

**UTM Zone (NAD27)** 17S

**Easting** 0723255

**Northing** 4211671

## IN BRIEF

The Rivanna Trail is a valued recreational resource for Charlottesville residents, but it's somewhat doubtful that many make the complete 20-mile loop. Fortunately, the ring trail passes numerous access points as it wends its way through parks and suburbs, so it's easy to customize an end-to-end or out-and-back that suits you. Three such hikes are recommended here.

## DESCRIPTION

More than a decade ago, Charlottesville hikers founded the Rivanna Trails Foundation with an auspicious goal: to encircle the city with a footpath 20 miles long. They chose primarily riparian corridors—along the Rivanna River and Moore's and Meadow Creeks—although on the city's western edge, the trail runs nearer roadways.

Having secured landowners' permission, cleared brush, built bridges, and blazed more than 19 trail miles, the foundation's volunteers have almost realized their vision. In only four short stretches along the southern portion of its loop does the trail require road walks.

## DIRECTIONS

From Richmond follow I-64 northwest to Exit 121. Exit northbound onto Monticello Avenue. Drive 0.7 miles before turning right onto Carlton Road. Continue another 0.7 miles, staying with Meade Avenue when Carlton veers left. Take a right onto Chesapeake Street, which terminates at Riverview Park in 0.6 miles. There you will find a trailhead for the Rivanna Greenbelt, the initial segment of the Rivanna Trail. Numerous additional access points dot the route. Cited below are the trail crossing at Park Street, near its intersection with Melbourne Road, and the crossing at the Virginia Department of Forestry office, at the back of Fontaine Research Park.

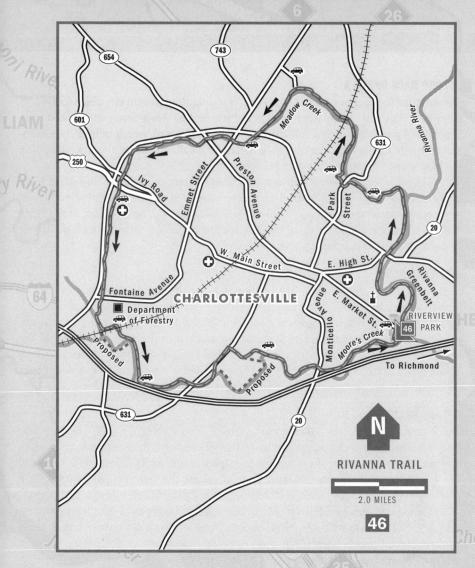

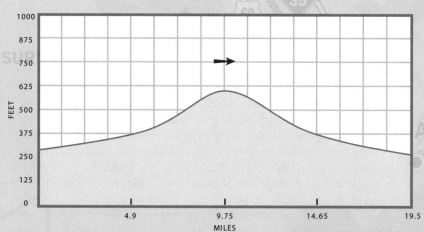

## OUT-AND-BACK OPTION A

The Rivanna Trail began with the city-owned Rivanna River Greenbelt, which follows its namesake waterway north from Riverview Park to East High Street at US 250. The Greenbelt's popularity fueled construction of the longer trail, which utilizes the Greenbelt footpath. On its own, the Greenbelt makes for a balloon hike of about 3 miles, with the loop section located in the park proper.

The wide, crushed-gravel surface is more conducive to casual strolling than most of the Rivanna Trail and is marked in quarter-mile increments. Additional numbered posts refer you to an interpretive booklet (available from the park section of the city's Web site) that identifies almost 20 tree species growing along the trail. Trailside fishing in the Rivanna is also a popular draw.

## BETWEEN A AND B

North of US 250 the Rivanna Trail continues along the Rivanna for about a mile to Meadow Creek then veers left along the tributary. A section as far as the Veterans of Foreign Wars (VFW) on River Road was recently upgraded by the city. However, as of publication, the trail was rerouted by construction and required a road walk between the VFW and Holmes Avenue (check the Rivanna Trail Foundation's Web site for updates). The trail bed north of Holmes is prone to flooding and is often muddy, so you're better off skipping this section outright and picking up the trail near McIntire Park.

## OUT-AND-BACK OPTION B

The Rivanna Trail offers a 5.6-mile out-and-back from Park Street to Brandywine and Hydraulic Roads. You can access the trail where it crosses Park Street near its intersection with Melbourne Road, with parking just uphill in the park. This segment begins in vine-laced riparian bottomland—quite common along the Rivanna Trail—with a thick perennial understory.

Setting out with Meadow Creek on your right, you will pass a broadcast tower on your left. Sycamores, yellow poplars, and red maples shade an oxbow with steeply eroded banks. Cross Schneck Branch on stepping stones near its confluence with the creek, then veer right, avoiding the spur to Melbourne Road on the left.

A curve to the north brings you to an open bottomland plain studded with mature silver maples. To the left, a dense recovering forest borders the glade-like flat, and you may spot a deer or raccoon darting back from a drink at the stream.

The trail bends left to approach the Norfolk-Southern Railroad underpass, where it crosses above the spillway then passes through the viaduct atop a metal pipe. Similar viaduct crossings occur elsewhere along the Rivanna Trail. Most are simply alternatives to crossing roads, but in this case the railroad track is off-limits. Be cautious in these sometimes-dark passages and avoid them at dusk or after heavy rain.

Across the railroad the Rivanna Trail heads northwest to enter Greenbrier Park, first winding with the boulder-dotted creek and passing a small swampy parcel. This wooded flat is a popular retreat for residents of the nearby suburbs, and you'll find a picnic table near an access bridge over Meadow Creek. The Rivanna Trail, however, keeps the stream on its left, leaving the park to cross Brandywine Drive.

You'll rock-hop across the dwindling creek with the aid of a metallic rope strung between two trees. Recross the creek by footbridge and the trail rounds its northernmost bend to head southwest against a hillside on the left. This slight elevation keeps the trail dry as it passes through a pleasant stretch of relatively mature, oak-dominated hardwood forest. Dense, soggy woods surround the trail again, however, on its approach to Hydraulic Road, the turnaround for the aforementioned out-and-back.

## BETWEEN B AND C

Through-hikers cross beneath Hydraulic Road in a viaduct, then do the same at US 250 Bypass and US 29. The Rivanna Trail passes the city's former fairgrounds, now a thick, young forest rather grandly dubbed Meadowcreek Gardens. A short road walk is required to reach Barracks Road, and then the trail wends its way west along the headwaters of Meadow Creek just south of US 250. However, at the time of publication, this stretch was closed due to road construction. An on-street detour led to Ivy Road, one end of the third out-and-back option along the Rivanna.

## OUT-AND-BACK OPTION C

The trail heads south from the Univeristy of Virginia Visitor Center on Ivy Road to run south, parallel to US 29. Pine needles carpet the trail as it sets out, with hardwood forest ahead. Chestnut oaks prevail on the twin slopes of Lewis and Jefferson Mountains, which tower over the trail on the left. You'll find several spurs ascending the latter, which is better known as Observatory Hill (see page 154). Stay with the well-blazed Rivanna Trail by generally veering right rather than left.

This western length of the trail has significantly fewer muddy sags than the rest, since it doesn't follow a floodplain. Short wooden bridges span perennial streams, and the trail bed is relatively free of roots and rocks. Lichen-spotted boulders and clusters of mountain laurel dot the open, hillside forest. However, there is a drawback: US 29 remains visible—and audible—on trail right until you cross Fontaine Avenue. Consider saving this stretch for summer, when leaves thicken the forest, and try to hike on a Sunday or holiday, when there is less traffic.

Across Fontaine Avenue, the Rivanna Trail reenters pines and bisects a fence line. It descends, uses a road bridge to cross Morey Creek, and then bears left. After a second creek crossing on stepping stones, look for a spur trail leading west to the Virginia Department of Forestry nature trail. This 1-mile loop threads through the remains of a Depression-era tree nursery. When combined with the Rivanna Trail, it makes for an almost 5-mile out-and-back between Ivy Road and Stribling Avenue. You may find it easiest to park at the forestry office in Fontaine Research Park and begin on the nature trail.

## BETWEEN C AND A

Before completing its loop, the Rivanna Trail works its way east on the southern edge of Charlottesville. This is the least appealing stretch, as it requires several road walks. However, proposed sections would link the existing stretches of trail into a seamless path. For now, there is limited single-track between Stribling Avenue and Azalea Park or between Azalea and Jordan Parks. The stretch along Moore's Creek that begins in Azalea Park is scenic but proximal to I-64. The stretch that begins in Jordan Park traverses younger forest and bluffs overlooking Moore's Creek. It descends to run along the creek, briefly running beside the interstate as well. The trail continues through a ragtag floodplain to approach the Rivanna River at the aforementioned Woolen Mills.

# ROCKWOOD PARK

## IN BRIEF

The paved balloon at Rockwood Park is popular with Southsiders out for a walk or jog, but the park's web of dirt paths—some of which are maintained and mapped—is surprisingly extensive. Trails trace the park's border with Gregory's Pond and crisscross its woodland interior. There's even a boardwalk for wetland-wildlife viewing.

## DESCRIPTION

By parking in and leaving from the area for shelter 4, you can hike the park's paved trails as a balloon (as mapped here). However, you may prefer parking in the nature-center lot if you're primarily interested in the park's web of dirt trails or, naturally, if you wish to visit the center.

The route mapped here is a good first go-round and will give you a feel for the lay of the land. To follow it, begin northbound from Shelter 4. Follow the path past the archery range and continue straight through an intersection with a dirt trail as you descend slightly toward the lake

## DIRECTIONS

Rockwood Park lies near the intersection of Courthouse Road (Huguenot Road farther north) and Hull Street Road (US 360), with entrances on both (although you can only exit the park from Courthouse Road). From Chippenham Parkway, exit onto Hull Street Road going southwest. Look for a wooden sign on the right. From Midlothian Turnpike (US 60) or the Powhite Parkway (VA 76), exit right onto Courthouse Road, heading south; signs indicate the approaching entrance, on the left. Pass the nature center and the official trailhead on your left and continue past another lot to the parking area for shelter 4 and the archery range. From Hull Street Road, bear right past the arboretum, and park in the lot on the right.

Gregory's Pond

Nature Center

Baseball

Basketball

Tennis

653

47

ROCKWOOD COUNTY PARK

Courthouse Road

Hull Street Road

360

**N**

ROCKWOOD PARK

0.25 MILES

47

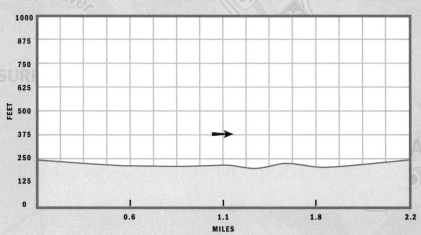

FEET

1000
875
750
625
500
375
250
125
0

0.6    1.1    1.8    2.2
MILES

The zigzagging boardwalk through the bottomland at Rockwood Park

(a right here takes you along the shore on a dirt trail.) You'll soon intersect the asphalt fitness loop. Turn right and follow it counterclockwise. Numerous earthen trails tempt you on either side, including a right turn toward the boardwalk along the northernmost stretch of the loop.

Note that the accompanying map does not show all the trails at Rockwood Park. The paved fitness trail, complete with pull-up bars and other exercise stops, rings a veritable nest of dirt trails. That paved loop, in turn, is partially ringed by an orange-blazed earthen path around the lake. Several of the dirt trails are maintained (some have wooden footbridges) and depicted on the park map. The system of blazes, however, is terribly unreliable owing to faded paint, unmarked intersections, and unofficial shortcut trails, which make it surprisingly easy to find you've inadvertently walked in a circle. But, as long as you have time to spare, you can wander with little fear of getting lost because the park's woods are hemmed in by Gregory's Pond (a private, no-fishing pond) and the creek that feeds it, as well as by the park's numerous sports fields.

A shortage of blazes aside, Chesterfield County does a thorough job of maintaining this 163-acre gem. The county's oldest park, opened in 1975, Rockwood has something for everyone, including community garden plots. (By the way, should you stumble out of the woods upon them, double back. A trail does cross into the opposite wood but leads only to the Courthouse Road entrance a short distance away.) An outdoor koi pond greets visitors to the nature center, which was closed for renovation for much of 2004. A paved trail departs from behind the center (on the left as you face it), and if you're lucky, you'll find an interpretive pamphlet in a mailbox near the start.

Also closed due to storm damage was the boardwalk leading across marshland in the northern reaches of the park west of Gregory's Pond. Assuming it's open on your visit, make the quick out-and-back hike for an up-close glimpse of the wetland habitat that exists along the park's primarily hardwood forest. A sign at the entrance reads "Gateway to Another World" and names some of the wildlife you may spy in the marsh, including dragonflies and muskrats. A deck at the boardwalk's end provides an excellent vantage for waterfowl watching, notwithstanding the suburban homes visible across a finger of the pond.

In fact, if you follow the outermost dirt loop over a markedly sturdy wood-and-metal bridge, you'll pass within a stone's throw (that's a metaphor, not a suggestion) of more houses opposite the creek that feeds the pond and forms the park's northwest boundary. Such reminders of Rockwood's suburban locale are not infrequent, but the park retains a pleasantly rustic feel, particularly in summer, when these woods, full of white oak, sweet gum, beech, and river birch, are flush with verdant summer foliage. Even along the stream, mossy banks and lichen-blotched boulders, not to mention a foot bed rough with roots, lay in contrast with the nearby toy-strewn backyards. It's a lucky youngster who can rock-hop to the park from his backdoor.

Indulge your own inner child with an afternoon visit to Rockwood. Hike the paved trails, or jog them if you prefer, but don't miss your chance to wander—in this case, along the beaten path(s).

# SAUNDERS-MONTICELLO TRAIL

## IN BRIEF

The well-built Saunders-Monticello Trail allows Monticello visitors to augment a trip to Thomas Jefferson's famous home with an amble along the hillside of Carters Mountain. However, the path's wide gravel surface and winding boardwalks are most frequented by locals out for a pleasant stroll or invigorating jog.

## DESCRIPTION

Today no American home save the White House is more widely recognized than Jefferson's Monticello; however, few people recall that the home fell into periodic neglect during the nineteenth century. Though Thomas Jefferson himself designed Monticello and oversaw its construction—an ongoing exercise in perfectionism that spanned four decades—it remained in his family just five years after his death in 1826.

It was at Monticello that Jefferson likely romanced his slave Sally Hemmings (and verifiably freed her offspring), yet he also consented to slavery there, because it gave a plantation at the rocky periphery of Virginia's Piedmont some prospects for economic viability. Nevertheless, upon his demise, Jefferson left his estate $100,000 in debt. The 1,000-acre plantation acquired in 1735 by

## DIRECTIONS

From Richmond follow I-64 northwest to Exit 12. Exit southbound on VA 20, following signs for Monticello. After half a mile, passing the Monticello Visitor Center on your right, turn left onto VA 53 (Thomas Jefferson Parkway). The parking lot fronting Kemper Park (the western trailhead) is a short distance ahead, just off the road to your right. To reach the Monticello lot (the eastern trailhead), continue on VA 53 for 1.5 miles, then exit the parkway north into the Monticello grounds at the stone Saunders Bridge.

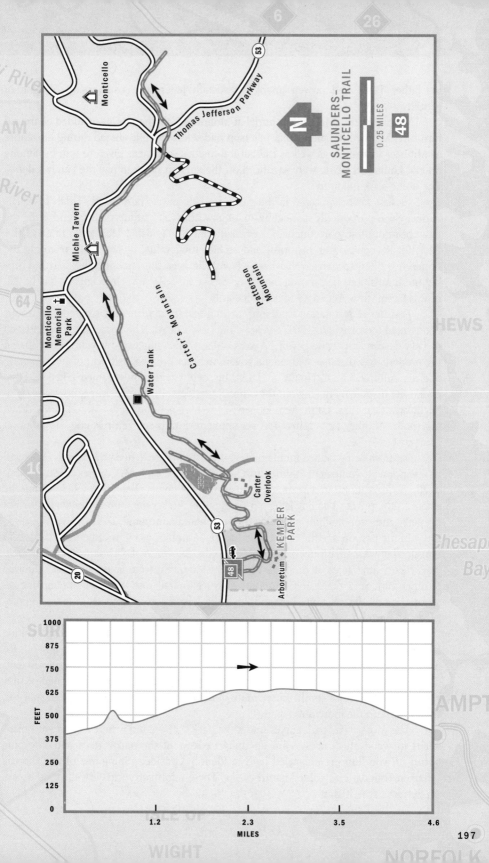

SAUNDERS–
MONTICELLO TRAIL

**48**

0.25 MILES

his father, Peter, had proven unable to sustain Jefferson's costly vision of agrarian gentility.

Within a year of Jefferson's burial at Monticello, the home was denuded of art and furniture. Many of the pieces that Jefferson had selected while abroad during his tenure as Minister to France, as well as the natural-history specimens given to him by, among others, Louis and Clark, were sacrificed on the auction block to pay the family's debts. The home soon followed.

Its first savior appeared in the garb of a U.S. naval commodore, Uriah Levy. His curiosity was purportedly sparked by an inquiry from the Marquis de Lafayette as to "the most beautiful house in America." Levy acquired a dilapidated Monticello in 1833 (for $2,700). Recognizing its historical and architectural value, he set about restoring the home. It is often speculated that Levy's Jewish heritage (his ancestors fled Portugal during the Inquisition) had moved him to reverence for Jefferson, chief agitator for the Bill of Rights and thus America's official secularity.

Decades of restoration were undone in a few short years after Confederate troops confiscated Monticello in 1861, a year before Levy's death. The home was later returned to Levy descendants, who began 17 years of legal wrangling over his will, which offered the property to a disinterested federal government for the establishment of an orphanage and agricultural school. Finally, in 1879, his nephew, the aptly named Jefferson Levy, ended the dispute by buying out the other contenders. In the meantime, however, Monticello was near ruin. Cattle were lodged in the basement and grain stored in the drawing room. Another Levy generation set about restoring and refurbishing the home at great cost.

Far from being lauded for his preservationist impulse, Jefferson Levy was subjected to a nationwide campaign, at times anti-Semitic in tone, to have Congress acquire Monticello by legislation. After years of intransigence, he finally relented in 1923, selling the estate to the private Thomas Jefferson Foundation. Today the foundation maintains the property and supports Jefferson-related research and education.

In the past decade the foundation has made ambitious improvements to the VA 53 corridor between Charlottesville and Monticello, known as the Thomas Jefferson Parkway. Eighty-nine acres at the base of Carters Mountain were landscaped and dubbed Kemper Park, and the 2-mile Saunders-Monticello Trail rose up the mountainside on sturdy boardwalks. A stone bridge linking the forested corridor with Monticello completed the project.

The finished greenway has proven popular with tourists as well as locals looking to stretch their legs. Whether you're augmenting a visit to Monticello or simply out for an afternoon stroll, this hike offers a steady but invigorating elevation change (300 feet) along its simple route. Beginning in Kemper Park, two paths leave the parking lot; they rejoin a short distance south. To see more of the park, head right (west) as you start out then return on the more direct path.

The wide, gravel path curves under the park's arboretum, where a short spur blanketed in wood chips allows you an up-close view of the native trees and flowering shrubs. If you find the unlabeled hard to identify, consider joining one of the Thomas Jefferson Foundation's guided nature walks. These informative trips leave from the park on Sundays at 9:30 a.m.

As the Saunders-Monticello Trail rises eastward away from the park, it passes through a thick stand of white pines, recognizable by their long cones and branches that typically grow in rings around the trunk. Ahead on trail left, numerous oak species—white, scarlet, willow, chestnut—were planted to one day shade the trail. Beyond those, black locust border the path, distinguishable by small leaves growing on long fronds, modest thorns, and legume-like seedpods.

A spur trail to the Carter Overlook departs to the right, curving as it climbs 50 feet. An alternate "rustic" dirt spur also leads to this hilltop; it leaves the main route farther ahead, just before the first boardwalk. After your brisk jaunt up the knoll, rest a moment at the stone wall and gaze northward. You can't see Monticello from here—or much besides the treetops in summertime. However, at the peak of autumn or after a winter snowfall, inspiring vista opens on the surrounding hilltops.

Downhill, views of the park's pond appear on your left as the main trail winds around the knoll. The sometimes-busy parkway borders the pond on the north, but fringed with cattails and flanked by river birches, it nevertheless makes for a pleasant scene. Follow the out-and-back trail along the water's southeastern shore, where benches invite visitors to relax (but not fish).

After returning to the main path, turn left onto the first of several boardwalks elevated by trestlework supports. Built against the hillside, these curving boardwalks, complete with handrails, provide both a level walking surface and a unique perspective of the surrounding forest. From these lofty walkways, you'll see rocky streamlets cutting small valleys beneath you, and you can stare out among the branches of young dogwoods.

Hugging Carters Mountain, the path soon passes a water tank visible in the woods below. The parkway is audible and intermittently visible through the trees on trail left. At roughly its halfway point, the trail bisects an old gravel road but continues forward to pass above Michie Tavern. Though the tavern was constructed in 1774, it was moved to its present location in 1928. Prior to that, the two-story, wood-frame structure stood in northern Albemarle County.

As it continues west, the Saunders-Monticello Trail alternately employs gravel tread and wide boardwalks. Chestnut oaks thrive on this steep hillside and buffer the trail before it emerges into a clearing. The stone Saunders Bridge is visible ahead and links the trail's longest stretch with its final stretch to Monticello. Note that the bridge is also used by vehicular traffic. Once across, bear right back into the forest. The trail wends a short distance farther, along Monticello's entrance road, to reach its eastern trailhead. Nearby are the Monticello gift shop and café. Don't expect to catch a distant glimpse of Jefferson's landscaped estate, however. For that, you'll have to take the tour.

History and architecture aficionados will find plenty more to see in the immediate vicinity. The Saunders-Monticello Trail passes above Michie Tavern, one of the commonwealth's oldest homes. Today the Tavern's Ordinary serves a daily lunch buffet between 11:30 a.m. and 3 p.m., as well as seasonal dinners. More than a restaurant, however, the tavern doubles as a museum of eighteenth-century life, complete with costumed docents and rotating exhibits. The grounds also include a gristmill, wine museum, and gift shop. (Tours cost $8 for adults, but locals are offered complimentary admission.) President James Monroe's one-time home, Ash Lawn-Highland, circa 1799, is just a mile south on VA 53 and is open for home and garden tours.

# SCHEIER NATURAL AREA

## KEY AT-A-GLANCE INFORMATION

**LENGTH:** 2.9 miles, 3.5 miles total in park

**CONFIGURATION:** Figure eight plus out-and-back spur

**DIFFICULTY:** Easy

**SCENERY:** Tributary of Cunningham Creek, cluster of small ponds, wooded ridges

Exposure: Well-shaded

**TRAFFIC:** Low

**TRAIL SURFACE:** Dirt

**HIKING TIME:** 3 hours

**SEASON:** Open daily during daylight year-round

**ACCESS:** No fee; not recommended for wheelchairs

**MAPS:** Available at park signboard and online at www.rivannariver.org/RCSscheier

**FACILITIES:** Limited to parking area with trailhead signboard

**SPECIAL COMMENTS:** Scheier Natural Area is managed the Rivanna Conservation Society for wildlife-viewing and preservation. Dog walking, jogging, cycling, swimming, camping, and, of course, hunting and fishing are prohibited. Contact the Rivanna Conservation Society at (434) 589-7576.

**UTM Trailhead Coordinates for Scheier Natural Area**

**UTM Zone (NAD27)** 17S

**Easting** 0730383

**Northing** 4191544

## ▶ IN BRIEF

Threading through reforested pasture and cropland, the trails at Scheier Natural Area descend well-drained hillsides to a northbound creek. Rising away on tapering ridges, and twice bisecting a feeder stream, it's easy to see how hydrology shapes topography in these Appalachian foothills.

## ▶ DESCRIPTION

The bulk of Scheier Natural Area is located west of the parking area; however, a cluster of ponds, created as a fish hatchery, lies east of VA 639. Today the ponds are fringed with bullrush and home to amphibians such as frogs. A brief out-and-back to reach them serves as a warm-up to your hike at Scheier, so begin by crossing the road to follow the Green Trail southeast through mixed forest. The double-track path is blazed in its namesake color, as are most at Scheier (though

## ▶ DIRECTIONS

From Richmond follow I-64 northwest to Exit 136. Take VA 15 south about 9 miles to Palmyra. Just beyond the small town, VA 15 crosses the Rivanna River. Three-quarters of a mile on, turn right onto VA 640 and drive for 3.6 miles. Turn right again onto VA 639 at an intersection guarded by a weathered clapboard church. Follow the narrow road, which makes one sharp bend left, for 3.7 miles to Scheier Natural Area, marked by a granite roadside sign. Parking spaces lie on the outside of the gravel drive that encircles the park signboard.

From Charlottesville take VA 53 for 13.5 miles past Monticello. Turn right onto VA 660/619, promptly veering left to stay with VA 660 for 3.2 miles. Make a right onto VA 640, then a quick second right onto VA 639 at the aforementioned church; from there, follow the directions above.

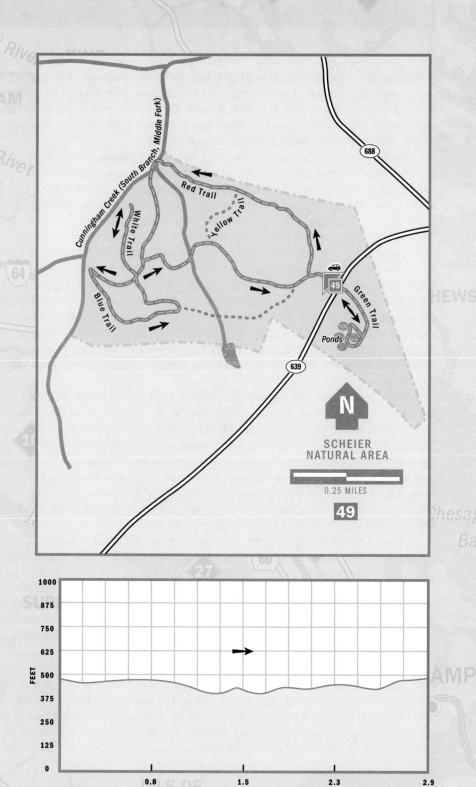

SCHEIER
NATURAL AREA

0.25 MILES

some share treadway, complicating matters). Appropriately named, as it is carpeted in bright green moss and pale gray-green lichen, the path curves right after passing a five-trunked chestnut oak. Upon reaching the tiered pools, trace a few of the earthen berms, just three or four feet wide, that separate them. These ponds, fed by springs and rainfall, stairstep down so that when one overflows it fills another. They ultimately drain east to the South Fork of Cunningham Creek.

Retrace your steps across the street and through the parking area to begin your hike in earnest. An orange-blazed connector heads westbound opposite the road. The trail begins on level ground, part of a broad ridgetop along which VA 639 runs. In the winter, pine saplings and cedars color an otherwise deciduous wood dominated by Southern and Northern red, chestnut, and post oaks. Mockernut hickories, red maples, and young beeches fill out this maturing second-growth forest.

Turn right at a T-intersection with the Yellow Trail and follow it as it bends from north to west. Logs line some stretches of the path, a sort of deadfall recycling, and a field is discernable through a veil of younger pines on trail right. Join an older, wider path by veering slightly left, then pass a thicket of young cedars guarded by an old barbwire fence on trail right. Passing through a smattering of young white pines, continue straight on the Red Trail when the Yellow Trail departs left. Young beech trees then signal a weaving descent. The path departs the finger ridge it has traveled to descend toward a northbound creek, a feeder streamlet running in the small valley on trail left.

Identified on the park map as the South Branch of the Middle Fork of Cunningham Creek, the larger stream is a tributary of the Rivanna River. The Rivanna Conservation Society (RCS) maintains this natural area not merely for watershed protection but largely as an educational forum. A map of the Rivanna River watershed at the trailhead signboard reinforces the notion that this small drainage is interwoven into a much larger ecological tapestry. Formed in 1990 and based in Fluvanna County, RCS is a not-for-profit group charged with citizen action and environmental education on behalf of the Rivanna River. Contact the group to learn more, and consider volunteering for their annual autumn river cleanup.

From a bench facing the creek, you can see mountain laurel clinging to a bluff upstream. Mossy, water-smoothed stones lie below, while a pebble-strewn sandy shoal waits downstream. Stepping over the feeder rivulet, look left to see ferns clinging to the striated-rock channel it has eroded. Then follow the trail on its short-but-steep rise to a pine-dotted ridge, the laurel now cascading downhill on your right. Continuing upland beyond a series of windblown trees, continue straight as the Blue Trail intersects your path on the left. Just ahead, take the White Trail as it heads right to curve north and runs out-and-back along a finger ridge above the creek.

Numerous white pines crown the ridge, most descendants of a lofty parent still watching over the grove. The trail terminates just before the bluffline, offering no vista of the creek below. However, in the springtime, hikers are rewarded with a cluster of blooming dogwoods here. After retracing the White Trail, turn right on the combined White and Blue Trails. Soon after the path curves west, the White Trail heads left. Continue on, however, to take in one more view of the creek.

After descending the hillside, the Blue Trail makes a sharp left. A brook is visible downhill, and if you go a short distance beyond the junction, you will see its junction with another. From here the creek flows northeast toward the spot where you first encountered it. The rock-bottomed stream runs against an eroded rock bank on the west, with sandy, beech-studded bottomland stretching eastward. Be aware that venturing to the water's edge entails leaving the natural-area boundary.

Beyond the sharp turn, the Blue Trail heads south, running gradually uphill and away from the brook. Mountain laurel abounds downhill then gives way to a stand of Virginia pines. A potentially muddy spot where runoff crosses the trail precedes another hard left. The single-track path then continues rising through a forest of white oak and red maple. The latter brighten the forest with red and yellow displays each fall. Barbwire was long ago strung along cedar posts on trail right. Upon reaching a junction with the White Trail, turn left to follow the stretch of it you earlier bypassed. Note that by veering right on the Blue Trail through a break in the barbwire fence, you can opt for a shorter loop along the periphery of the preserve rather than the interior figure eight described here.

The White Trail runs level through more maples before reaching a T intersection. Turn right and retrace your steps past the other half of the White Trail on the left. Next, make a right onto the combined Blue and Red Trail, which tacks east as it descends past a dense cluster of young beeches. Young hardwoods and slightly taller pines soon border the trail on either side, indicating a past fire or timber harvest here. Ground pine grows along the trail as it curves left. Then a small rivulet briefly runs along the trail on your right before meeting a larger branch—the first you crossed. The water is channeled through a pipe beneath the trail, which ascends away past piney, young forest on the right and more open, mature woods on the left.

The path soon meets the Yellow Trail. Turn right for this hike's return leg. Continue ascending, sandwiched between old and young trees, on grassy double-track studded with granite. The recovering wood on trail left momentarily yields to older trees, which then give way to a meadow of tall grasses. A dilapidated building, perhaps a barn, stands in the field, one wall covered in climbing vines. Yellow blazes guide you past a junction with an old roadbed before the blue trail meets the path to curve left and back toward the connector. Make a right at the next junction to return to the parking area.

# SPOTSYLVANIA COURT HOUSE BATTLEFIELD

## KEY AT-A-GLANCE INFORMATION

**LENGTH:** 5.7 miles

**CONFIGURATION:** Loop

**DIFFICULTY:** Easy

**SCENERY:** Recovering hardwood forest, Civil War trenches, the remains of Civil War-era houses, monuments

**EXPOSURE:** Some sun, some shade

**TRAFFIC:** Moderate, higher along roads

**TRAIL SURFACE:** Single-track along park roads and through forests and fields

**HIKING TIME:** 2.5 hours plus time spent at tour stops

**SEASON:** Open daily during daylight year-round; visitor center open 9 a.m.–5 p.m.

**ACCESS:** Vehicle admission $4 per week or $20 annually; audio vehicle tour $5 plus $20 deposit; visitor-center film $2, $1 for children under age 10 or seniors over age 61. Fees must be paid at the Fredericksburg or Chancellorsville Visitor Centers. Facilities and some interpretive trails are wheelchair accessible.

**MAPS:** Available at park office and on signboard at trailhead

**FACILITIES:** Visitor centers, restrooms at Fredericksburg and Chancellorsville Battlefields, Stonewall Jackson Shrine (south of Fredericksburg), Chatham Manor Museum (north of Fredericksburg), driving tour through all battlefields

**SPECIAL COMMENTS:** For more informtion, contact the Fredericksburg Visitor Center at (540) 373-6122, or visit www.nps.gov/frsp.

---

**UTM Trailhead Coordinates for Spotsylvania Court House Battlefield**

**UTM Zone (NAD27)   18S**

**Easting   0271156**

**Northing   4233175**

## IN BRIEF

Weaving through Spotsylvania Battlefield, this national recreation trail intermittently runs along park auto-tour roads before ducking back into woods. In addition to numerous earthen trenches, the circuit passes the Bloody Angle, scene of a 20-hour, rain-soaked battle, and the ruins of the Harrison House, Robert E. Lee's battlefield headquarters.

## DESCRIPTION

Fredericksburg and Spotsylvania National Military Park encompasses four Civil War battlefields—Fredericksburg, Chancellorsville, the Wilderness, and Spotsylvania Court House—where more than 100,000 soldiers perished. For a year and a half, Fredericksburg and farms to the west served as a linchpin in the Confederate defense of Richmond.

Union soldiers first attempted to cross the Rappahannock at Fredericksburg late in 1862 but were repulsed. A second crossing attempt upstream in Chancellorsville was thwarted the following spring. A year later, Federal soldiers crossed still farther upriver and met Confederate resistance at the Battle of the Wilderness. Indecisive struggles there and at Spotsylvania Court House to the south

## DIRECTIONS

From Richmond head north on I-95 to Exit 118 (34 miles north of I-295). Head west on VA 606 for 5.1 miles, then turn right onto VA 208. Continue 3.9 miles north before veering left onto VA 606. After half a mile, veer right onto VA 613 (Brock Road). Look for Grant Drive 1.4 miles ahead on the right. Bear right, then park in the lot on your left at the Spotsylvania Battlefield Exhibit Shelter. Facing the shelter, a trailhead signboard stands to your left. The shelter provides historical background on the battle at Spottsylvania Court House.

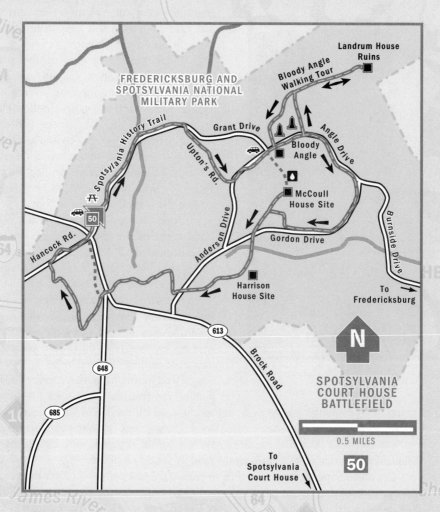

FREDERICKSBURG AND SPOTSYLVANIA NATIONAL MILITARY PARK

Landrum House Ruins

Bloody Angle Walking Tour

Grant Drive

Spotsylvania History Trail

Upton's Rd.

Bloody Angle

Angle Drive

McCoull House Site

Anderson Drive

Gordon Drive

Burnside Drive

Hancock Rd.

Harrison House Site

To Fredericksburg

613

648

Brock Road

685

To Spotsylvania Court House

N

SPOTSYLVANIA COURT HOUSE BATTLEFIELD

0.5 MILES

50

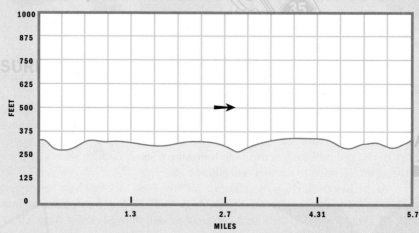

205

A cannon trained on vacant fields at
Spotsylvania Court House Battlefield

amounted to a Union victory: Grant's troops had made it across the Rappahannock and would press on to Richmond.

Today most visitors tour the park's 7,600 acres by car. Short walking tours serve as leg-stretchers along the route. Noteworthy among these is the 2-mile Gordon Flank Attack Trail at the Wilderness Battlefield Exhibit Shelter. The Spotsylvania History Trail—your route for this hike—is different, however. Rather than supplementing the park auto tour with up-close views, it lets you explore the entire battlefield on foot.

Begin your trek with an overview of the battle at the exhibit shelter near the trailhead. An illustrated aerial view of the area during the May 8–21, 1864, battle depicts the positions held by each side. Pick up a trail guide at the nearby trailhead signboard, but ignore a small sign indicating that the trail begins southbound toward VA 613. Instead, follow the route clockwise as described here; thus you approach the tour stops in their intended order.

Head north from the parking area to pick up the roadside single-track just beyond a group of picnic tables on the right. Across the road runs a line of Union earthworks. Tall oaks now dominate the surrounding wood. During the Civil War most of the battlefield was cropland. Many of the fields you see within the park were cleared by the National Park Service so as to present the land as soldiers found it.

Continue along the road as it dips to cross a tributary of the Ni River then curves to the east. Look for Upton's Road on the right, then cross the pavement to follow it southeast. Named for Union colonel Emory Upton, this wide single-track path was used by his troops to assault the Georgia brigade ensconced in earthworks at Dole's Salient. The surprise attack allowed the Federal soldiers to take 1,000 prisoners before losing an equal number of their own men to a counterattack.

The path emerges into a field at a stout granite obelisk, a monument to the soldiers who fought in Upton's charge. You bisect Dole's Salient just before reaching Anderson Drive ahead. Turn left to follow the road, crossing to the right side as you approach the epicenter of the fighting at Spotsylvania Court House, the Bloody Angle. Continue forward beyond the parking area, noting a side trail leaving right at the lot's southeast corner. If, after touring the Angle, you wish to forgo the loop's easternmost roadside stretch, you can backtrack to this trail. Following it south through woods, you will pass a spring before rising to the McCoull House ruins.

At the Bloody Angle, pass monuments to the New York and New Jersey regiments on trail left. The first stop on the Bloody Angle Walking Tour fronts these monuments. Pick up a trail pamphlet, then head northeast toward Burnside Drive. Turn left to cross the earthworks on a bridge. A solitary cannon guards this junction, and a reproduced painting depicts the gruesome conflagration that occurred here at the apex of the Confederate fortification known as The Muleshoe.

Continuing the tour, cross a meadow dotted with cedar and black-cherry trees to reach a gravel road at a three-way intersection. General Ulysses S. Grant's troops amassed in the woods before you in preparation for their assault on Lee's Muleshoe. Turn right and follow the path out and back to the Landrum House ruins. Two opposing stone chimneys are all that remain of this manor, which survived the battle only to burn in 1905. Returning from the ruin, veer left onto the trail that runs west of that by which you arrived. It guides you through the meadow and past several monuments to complete the Bloody Angle Walking Tour.

To continue on the Spotsylvania History Trail, briefly retrace your steps. The trail continues as a roadside path on the right-hand side of Burnside Drive. Across the road, Confederate trenches run parallel to your trail bed. Shortly after the woods on your right yield to a meadow, turn right at a three-road junction. Next, a roadside stretch along Gordon Drive brings the route's most noticeable change in elevation as it descends to the headwaters of a creek then rises steeply away.

Just as you begin to feel winded, the path grants a reprieve, turning right onto a forested single-track. Wind through the young woods, marked by numerous deadfalls, to emerge into an evergreen-dotted meadow facing the McCoull House site. Proceed to the foundation, bypassing a hard left in the History Trail. The stone rectangle is all that remains of Confederate general Edward Johnson's headquarters. Downhill to the north is the aforementioned shortcut trail to the Bloody Angle.

From the McCoull House, follow the History Trail as it runs along a paved access road back to Gordon Drive. Cross Gordon Drive and climb a gentle grassy slope to the stone-and-earth remains of the Harrison House. The home served as Confederate general Richard Ewell's headquarters, where Robert E. Lee pitched his tent on the lawn.

Follow the trail southeast to enter a forest of mixed oak, Virginia pine, and holly. The path emerges at the terminus of Anderson Drive. On your left are reconstructed earthworks. The short stretch of trench is braced by logs. Soldiers propped their muskets atop those wooden walls to fire, then crouched behind them to reload. The surrounding trenches of Lee's Last Line were built by General Martin Smith, who also oversaw the fortification of Confederate positions at Vicksburg and New Orleans.

After examining the re-created earthworks, proceed west on the trail with the original trench line on your left. Cross a wooden footbridge to weave through a dense wood. A second footbridge crosses the headwaters of another creek just ahead. Leaving the western trench of Lee's Last Line, the path emerges from the pines near Brock Road.

Cross the road and bear left on a path that runs along a wide field punctuated by a double-trunk sycamore. Briefly enter the adjacent forest of Virginia pines and red oaks to approach a turn-of-the-century monument. Placed by a judge wounded in the fighting, it honors the Maryland regiment that opened the battle with a charge across the field.

Emerging from the woods, head north across the field, bisecting an old farm road. Ahead, the trail runs beside a band of trees then enters woods to cross a streamlet on a footbridge. After a short, winding ascent across a Union trench line, take Hancock Road and turn right. Follow the road a short distance, turning right onto a path that briefly traces then crosses Brock Road. It runs along Grant Drive back to the trailhead.

# THREE LAKES PARK

**LENGTH:** 1.3 miles

**CONFIGURATION:** Figure eight

**DIFFICULTY:** Easy

**SCENERY:** Ponds and surrounding woodlands and wetlands, ponds

**EXPOSURE:** Mostly shaded

**TRAFFIC:** Moderate to heavy

**TRAIL SURFACE:** Paved, crushed gravel

**HIKING TIME:** 30-60 minutes

**SEASON:** Open daily during daylight year-round

**ACCESS:** No fee

**MAPS:** Available online at www.co.henrico.va.us/rec

**FACILITIES:** Restrooms, playground, picnic tables, pond fishing, nature center with deck

**SPECIAL COMMENTS:** The playground and picnic area are sometimes crowded with weekend revelers, though not all will stroll the waterside trails. Fishing is a popular pastime here, particularly in the easternmost impoundment. Contact Henrico County Parks at (804) 501-5108 and the Three Lakes Nature Center at (804) 261-8230.

UTM Trailhead Coordinates for

Three Lakes Park

UTM Zone (NAD27)   18S

Easting   0285451

Northing   4166026

## IN BRIEF

Just north of Richmond proper, the generously named Three Lakes Park is home to a trio of modest ponds and Henrico County's premier nature center. Popular for summer barbecues and close-to-home fishing, the park offers more than a mile of trail encircling its impoundments.

## DESCRIPTION

Upon entering Three Lakes you will pass parking on your right, then more spaces on your left. The parking lot is bounded to the north by the observation deck (an earthen mound, not a tower) and play area, which, if you come on a warm spring weekend, will be rife with frolicking youngsters; the nature center, complete with aquarium, is located near the lot's southeast corner.

Outside the nature center, an exhibit details various species that comprise the meadow-bog ecology evident within the park. Adjacent to the center, a large wooden deck overlooks what the park map affectionately calls Lake 2. Signage depicts some turtle species that visitors may spy basking at the shoreline. Between the decking and nature center is

## DIRECTIONS

Follow I-95 north of Richmond to Chamberlayne Road (US 301), Exit 82. Exit and drive north on Chamberlayne approximately three-quarters of a mile. Turn right on Wilkinson Road just past a sign for the park. Continue half a mile and turn right again at Sausiluta Drive, the access road to Three Lakes Park. If arriving from the north on Chamberlayne, you may turn left onto Diane Road then left on Wilkinson. Alternately, if coming from the Richmond-Henrico Turnpike (VA 627), turn west onto Azalea Avenue and make the first right onto Wilkinson. Follow it north to turn left on Sausiluta. Park near the nature center at the road's terminus.

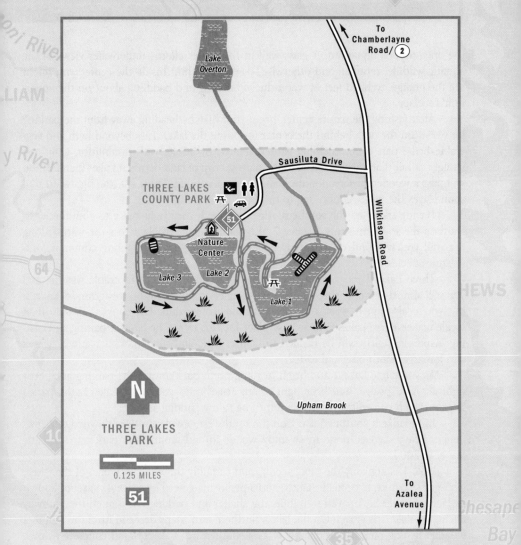

Lake Overton

To Chamberlayne Road / 2

Sausiluta Drive

Wilkinson Road

THREE LAKES COUNTY PARK

Nature Center

Lake 3

Lake 2

Lake 1

N

THREE LAKES PARK

0.125 MILES

51

Upham Brook

To Azalea Avenue

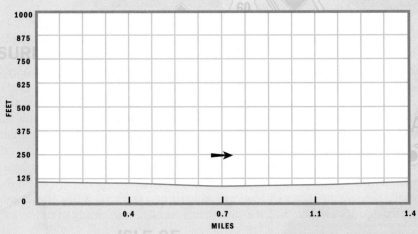

the open-topped aquarium. A glass wall in the center affords underwater views of the aquatic wildlife, reptilian and otherwise, dwelling within. Inside the center, you might see the orange, webbed feet of wood ducks bobbing and paddling about on the aquarium's surface.

After visiting the nature center, begin your hike by heading away from the parking lot (west) on the path behind the center (opposite the lake). Pass beyond herb and vegetable beds, part of an enabling garden tended by adults with disabilities. Continue straight rather than turning left onto the narrow strip of land between Lakes 2 and 3. You will pass a wooden observation deck and then a footbridge. Turn left (the rightward trail soon leaves the park), continuing to trace the water's edge.

Having traversed the southern edge of Lake 3, turn right twice to continue eastward on the southern shore of Lake 2, the nature center visible across the water. Along the trail you will find numerous tree-identification signs, highlighting common Mid-Atlantic species.

Three Lakes Park is a popular fishing destination. Visit in favorable weathe, and you will almost certainly spot some serious anglers camped out on westernmost Lake 3, but you're also apt to spot a parent-and-child fishing duo. The convenient suburban locale makes Three Lakes Park an easy place for kids to get the hang of baiting and casting. Aspirant anglers will be thrilled to land crappie and sunfish, while serious fishers aim for largemouth bass and catfish.

As you circle Lake 2 and begin heading north back toward the parking area, bear right across a bridge, and bear right again. This brings you along Lake 1, the park's largest, which you will circle before returning to the parking area.

In the marsh abutting Lake 1 on the southwest, a wide swath of downed trees evidences heavy damage done to swampy woods in and around the park by Hurricane Isabel in 2003.

Lake 1 is arguably the most scenic, and certainly the most park-like, of the three, with grassy banks, two small islands, and a peninsula graced by a sizable gazebo, known as Picnic Shelter 2. A paved trail links the shelter and parking lot, though the pathway encircling Lake 1 is gravel. On the lake's northern arm, steps descend from the trail to a wooden fishing pier. In the marshy woods southeast of Lake 1 stand concrete pylons, remnants of a now-forgotten structure.

Complete your circuit around Lake 1 and recross the bridge to Lake 2. Hang a right to return to the parking lot. If it's summertime, keep an eye out for bluebirds nesting in the wooden houses placed on poles around the park. It is fitting that Three Lakes Park should host Henrico County's Earth Day celebration, given the happy coexistence of playground, picnic tables, nature center, trails, and wildlife here.

However, the careful development evidenced in most of the park is compromised in the woods northwest of the lakes and playground, which are scattered with old tires and similar refuse. There are some short trails here—with links to Lake 3, the enabling garden, and the parking lot—but they are seldom trod. The scenery hardly justifies a venture. Suggesting a period of bygone maintenance is an identification sign on a mimosa tree—appropriately enough, an opportunistic nonnative species. Perhaps it would behoove the county to stage a cleanup for next year's Earth Day. Higher and drier than the park's southern half, the area, though small, is imminently worthy of a trail.

# TWIN LAKES STATE PARK

As its name suggests, water-based recreation is the main draw at Twin Lakes State Park. The smaller of the two lakes at 15 acres, Goodwin Lake is the epicenter of activity, with a swimming beach, floating deck, pedal-boat rentals, and onshore amenities. But this hike encircles the larger of the aquatic siblings, 36-acre Prince Edward Lake, a quiet fishing lake save when a particularly boisterous group rents the adjacent conference center.

▶ **DESCRIPTION**

How did Twin Lakes State Park come to have two modest man-made lakes a stone's throw apart? For decades the two were operated as separate parks. The surrounding land was purchased by the federal government during the Great Depression and subsequently deeded to Virginia. The smaller twin, Goodwin Lake, was the centerpiece of a recreation area established in 1939. But Twin Lake's larger impoundment, Prince Edward Lake, did not open until 1950, following a rather sad episode in the commonwealth's history.

▶ **DIRECTIONS**

Twin Lakes State Park is located in Prince Edward County south of Farmville. From Richmond take US 360 west (Hull Street Road). Stay on US 360 through Burkeville, where it briefly meets US 460 then dips southward. Pass the first signed turn for Twin Lakes State Park (this leads to the conference center), then turn right at VA 613 for 4.25 miles beyond Burkeville. Drive north 1.5 miles to VA 629 and turn right at the park-entrance sign. Head downhill on a road lined with kudzu to pass Goodwin Lake on your right. Make the first right onto Goodwin Lake Road (the park office lies at this intersection), then pay your fee and proceed to the opposite end of the parking area on the right.

▶ **KEY AT-A-GLANCE INFORMATION**

**LENGTH:** 2.6 miles with 0.5-mile spur

**CONFIGURATION:** Balloon

**DIFFICULTY:** Moderate

**SCENERY:** Upland woods, riparian bottomland, Prince Edward Lake

**EXPOSURE:** Mostly shaded, sometimes open along lakeshore

**TRAFFIC:** Low, high near Goodwin Lake beach

**TRAIL SURFACE:** Dirt

**HIKING TIME:** 2 hours

**SEASON:** Trails daily from 8 a.m. to dusk year-round; main season runs April–October

**ACCESS:** Parking costs $2 daily, $3 weekends in season. Swimming costs $2 for children ages 3–12 and $3 for adults. In-season canoe, kayak, and rowboat rentals available (prices vary). Campsites with hookups cost $20 per night. Restrooms, snack bar, and conference center are wheelchair accessible.

**MAPS:** Available at the park and online at www.dcr.state.va.us/parks/twinlake.htm

**FACILITIES:** Visitor center, campground, restrooms, showers, beach on Goodwin Lake, boat launches on both lakes, playground, snack bar, Cedar Crest Conference Center (available by reservation only)

**SPECIAL COMMENTS:** The Twin Lakes State Park brochure overstates the trail mileage within the park. However, there are two more short loops within the park. Contact the park office at (434) 392-3435.

**UTM Trailhead Coordinates for Twin Lakes State Park**

**UTM Zone (NAD27)** 17S

**Easting** 0741481

**Northing** 4117307

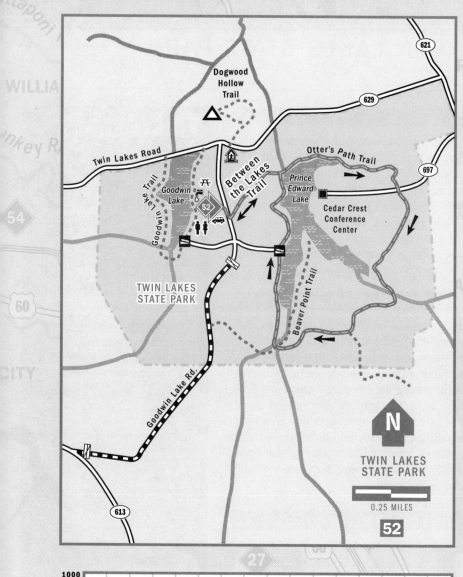

Dogwood Hollow Trail

621

629

WILLIA

Otter's Path Trail

697

Twin Lakes Road

Prince Edward Lake

Goodwin Lake

Between the Lakes Trail

Cedar Crest Conference Center

Goodwin Lake Trail

52

Beaver Point Trail

TWIN LAKES STATE PARK

Goodwin Lake Rd.

**N**

TWIN LAKES
STATE PARK

0.25 MILES

52

613

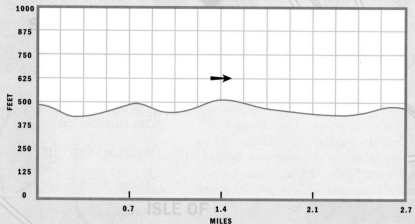

In 1948 an African American banker named Maceo Conrad Martin sued after being denied access to Staunton River State Park (located on Buggs Island Lake). In response, Governor William Tuck approved the construction of Prince Edward Lake Recreation Area for Negroes along the white's-only Goodwin Lake Recreation Area. The parks remained segregated, with a black superintendent and staff at Prince Edward Lake, until passage of the Civil Rights Act of 1964. The two parks were merged to form Twin Lakes State Park in 1986.

Though established under the auspices of providing "similar and equal facilities in lieu of access," it's noteworthy that Prince Edward Lake is twice as far from Mr. Martin's hometown as Staunton River State Park. Family, church, and civic groups hold cookouts in the shaded picnic area, and parents sunbathe on the sandy beach. The formerly "colored-only" facilities on Prince Edward Lake are today part of Cedar Crest Conference Center, which includes displays on the park's history but is open by reservation only. Following the route set out here, you'll see the center across the lake but will bypass it on an upland stretch of the otherwise lakeside loop.

Begin your hike southbound on the gravel entry road toward the boat launches, but turn left into the woods before the intersection that provides access to them. The wide, aptly named Between the Lakes Trail is distinguishable by a timber barrier that prevents vehicular access. Small moss- and lichen-covered boulders lie among the trailside cedars, Virginia pines, and post oak and black oaks, both of which favor dry, sandy soil. White oaks tower over the lakeshore as the trail bears right.

Just beyond a bench overlooking the water is a T intersection. This is the orange-blazed Otter's Path, which encircles the lake. Turning left to hike the loop clockwise will take you over the dam and into the forest, saving the scenic lakeside section for last. Pass over the sycamore-shaded concrete spillway on a boardwalk approximately 20 feet long. The rocky streambed below leads north to join the Sandy River, which in turn wends its way to the Appomattox.

Continue east across the grassy earthen dam, then bear slightly right to bypass a wider trail heading uphill in favor of a sandy single-track. Roots show through the path as it traces an arm of the lake, crossing feeder streamlets on concrete planks. You'll immediately note a different character to the woods here, which include river birch and red maple. In low-lying plains and on shaded hillsides, the forest floor is carpeted in ferns, sometimes interspersed with the round, lobed leaves of mayapples.

Turn left at the upcoming trail intersection, as the path leading straight ahead enters the conference-center grounds. The trail parallels a meandering stream with eroded banks then bears right to wind uphill. After cresting the hill, the path crosses an asphalt road into a glade of pines. An orange Otter's Path marker is visible ahead. Pass under a power-line clearing to enter a forest of hardwoods.

As the trail descends, swaths of the forest floor grow lush with ground cedar. True to its name, the verdant ground cover resembles a stand of four-inch-tall evergreens. This variant of club moss, often associated with ferns, favors moist, middle-growth forest. Reproducing by spores, club mosses spread along the ground through lateral underground branches. The fossil record shows that their ancient ancestors towered 40 feet high. The club moss bogs of the Carboniferous era 300 million years ago are the oil fields and coal mines of today.

Ahead, the trail skims the trunk of a sizable yellow poplar. More are visible down the trail, where a seasonal rivulet running on your right turns to briefly join the path. If you find yourself navigating a muddy trail bed here, take care to avoid trailside poison ivy. The path soon arrives at a T intersection, with a wooden beam obstructing the trail that heads right to the conference center. The Otter's Path turns left to trace a finger of Prince Edward Lake after passing through an airy stand of pine.

Boardwalks augment the trail as it bears right (south) around this marshy lake inlet fed by a small brook, itself draining from a pond upstream. This far end of the loop sees less traffic than the lakeside path, and grass and weeds growing in the moist soil may crowd the trail. Bearing right, the trail soon makes a steady ascent. As the small marsh recedes from view, hardwoods give way to pines, their needles blanketing the trail. Crest the hill, having ascended 90 feet in 0.1 mile, to join an old roadbed.

Begin tracing an oak ridge. The roadbed soon descends to cross a brook. Your route, however, bears right to reach another intersection. Here, the Beaver Point Trail, an out-and-back spur totaling half a mile, heads right. The Otter's Path crosses the brook before curving right itself. The shallow water is easily forded in an inviting glade where a bridge would merely be an intrusion. In the summer, look for the small flowers of orange jewelweed growing here.

Proceed along the clear-running, gurgling brook. The trail zigzags, rerouted by downed trees, before the southernmost arm of Prince Edward Lake comes into view. Ahead, the trail ascends steps made from the sawed limbs of another past windfall. At first glance one might mistake them for fortuitously located tree roots. As the lake widens on the right, the path undulates along the shore, occasionally drawing along the water. During the summer, insects skimming about in small coves may be so numerous that they give the illusion of falling raindrops.

Shortly after crossing a small feeder stream on wooden planks, the trail passes the boat launch. From here the conference center is visible on the opposite shore. The Otter's Path continues across the gravel vehicle-turnaround area, just slightly uphill. Pass small inlets in which decaying vegetation provides cover for the fish that lure anglers to this lake. The final leg of the loop continues along the lakeshore, traversing some small, seasonal streamlets and numerous tree roots to reach the Between the Lakes Trail on which you first set out (signed Connection Trail here). Turn to retrace your steps to the parking area, perhaps opting to cool off in Goodwin Lake.

The state park is enveloped by Prince Edward-Gallion State Forest (page 176), which offers a designated multi-use trail and a network of forest roads. Venturing into the forest is easy with Twin Lakes as your base camp. Twin Lakes State Park also manages Sailor's Creek Battlefield State Park, accessible from US 360 east of Twin Lakes via VA 307 and VA 617. Amenities at the latter are limited to picnic tables and grills, with the Overton-Hillsman House, a Civil War field hospital, open for tours June through August. At Sayler's Creek—which was corrupted to "Sailor's Creek" by troops who merely had heard it spoken—General Robert E. Lee's Army of Northern Virginia suffered 7,700 casualties on April 6, 1865, known as the Black Thursday of the Confederacy. The defeat precipitated Lee's surrender to General Ulysses S. Grant three days later. The site of that surrender, Appomattox Court House National Historic Park, is located northwest of Twin Lakes via US 460. Though just outside the range of this guide, it offers a 6-mile trail through a history-rich landscape.

# VOORHEES NATURE PRESERVE

## IN BRIEF

A visit to Voorhees Nature Preserve entails a visit to Westmoreland Berry Farm. So why not pick a bushel of strawberries, raspberries, or blueberries to snack on en route? Pause for a repast at the hike's turnaround overlook, and a bald eagle may swoop by to inspect your picnic. Or you can dine al fresco at the farm store, watching the resident goats traverse their wooden trapeze.

## DESCRIPTION

Owned by The Nature Conservancy, Voorhees Nature Preserve is accessible only through the privately owned Westmoreland Berry Farm. Guests are asked to register their visit in a trail log at the farm store, where seasonal produce and homemade desserts are sold most of the year. Across the street is the farm's goat pen, where a wooden apparatus called a goat walk allows the nimble, cloven-hoofed residents to display their surefootedness some 20 feet above the ground.

The preserve was donated to The Nature Conservancy in 1994 by Mr. and Mrs. Alan

## DIRECTIONS

From Richmond head north on I-95 to Exit 104. Follow VA 207 almost 12 miles to the town of Bowling Green, where 207 merges with US 301. Continue northeast on US 301 through Fort A. P. Hill, and across the Rappahannock River. After almost 18 miles, turn right onto VA 3. Drive 7.5 miles west before turning right onto VA 634. Signs point the way to Westmoreland Berry Farm from this junction on. After just under a mile, turn right onto VA 637. Make a final right onto Berry Farm Road after 1.6 miles, and the farm store is on your left 1.25 miles ahead. Check in there before beginning your hike. From Fredericksburg, simply follow VA 3 for 20 miles to its junction with US 301 and proceed as above.

## KEY AT-A-GLANCE INFORMATION

**LENGTH:** 4.1 miles, or 5.22 miles with optional extension

**CONFIGURATION:** Balloon with optional second loop

**DIFFICULTY:** Moderate

**SCENERY:** Orchards and fields, creek-fed marsh in Owl Hollow, hardwood-forested bluffs overlooking the Potomac

Exposure: Well-shaded except along the road and field

**TRAFFIC:** Low

**TRAIL SURFACE:** Dirt single-track

**HIKING TIME:** 2 hours

**SEASON:** Open daily 8 a.m.–6 p.m, May–December

**ACCESS:** No fee, no pets, trails not recommended for wheelchairs

**MAPS:** Available at Westmoreland Berry Farm store

**FACILITIES:** Restrooms and refreshments at farm store, pick-your-own fruits and vegetables, picnic tables

**SPECIAL COMMENTS:** Before hiking the preserve, sign in at the farm store. The preserve is closed during the winter and early spring, when bald eagles may be nesting. For details, call The Nature Conservancy Virginia State Office, (434) 295-6106, or visit http://nature.org/wherewework/northamerica/states/virginia/preserves/art1245.html. Contact Westmoreland Berry Farm at (804) 224-9171 or www.westmorelandberryfarm.com

---

**UTM Trailhead Coordinates for Voorhees Nature Preserve**

**UTM Zone (NAD27)** 18S

**Easting** 0320673

**Northing** 4223240

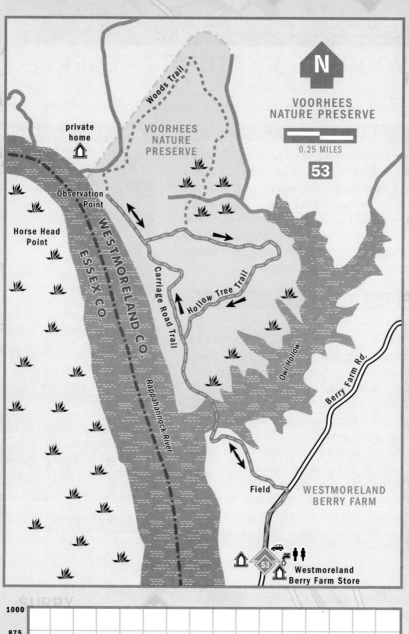

N

0.25 MILES

53

Woods Trail

private
home

VOORHEES
NATURE
PRESERVE

Observation
Point

Horse Head
Point

WESTMORELAND CO.
ESSEX CO.

Carriage Road Trail

Hollow Tree Trail

Rappahannock River

Owl Hollow

Berry Farm Rd.

Field

WESTMORELAND
BERRY FARM

53

Westmoreland
Berry Farm Store

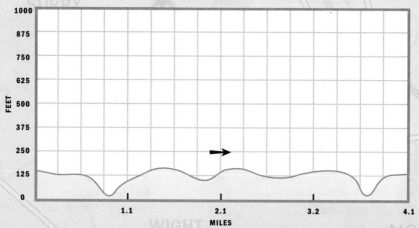

Voorhees and is now part of its Chesapeake Rivers Program, which aims to protect unspoiled parcels of Virginia's Northern Neck and Middle Peninsula. Voorhees, like the state-owned Caledon State Park and Natural Area upstream (see page 38), is a bald-eagle sanctuary. Visitation is banned during the winter nesting season.

Begin your hike by backtracking along Berry Farm Road, passing beside a barn and orchard on your left, then a field. Continue approximately a quarter mile from the farm store before turning left, off the road and onto a mowed double-track. The vestiges of an old vineyard extend to your right then give way to trees. A hexagonal picnic table sits in the shade as you approach the trailhead proper.

Follow the signed, yellow-blazed trail south beneath chestnut and northern red oaks. A beech-sycamore forest thickened by tall hollies grows in the ravine on your right. The valley widens to reveal the grassy marsh of Owl Hollow just before the path curves left to descend a slope braced with wooden beams. Switchback right to reach the Rappahannock shoreline. You promptly approach the preserve signboard.

The trail then turns slightly inland to cross Owl Hollow on a lengthy wooden bridge. Approach quietly and you may find beavers at work in the swamp or herons stalking prey. Across the bridge a steep cliff towers above the wide Rappahannock, its clay face almost white in the sunlight. Eagles and ospreys often perch in the pines that fringe the cliff, scanning the river below for fish.

To skirt the cliff, your path bends to the right and passes through a soggy flat where small logs in the trail bed serve as an improvised boardwalk. You'll then curve north and climb through a small valley shaded by yellow poplars. A small streamlet runs on trail left, and a log wall braces the path on the right. Reaching the top of the draw, a view of the Rappahannock opens before you, just below the steep bluff.

The trail veers right to run north along the riverfront side of a triangular plateau. Notice the level forest floor stretching inland on your right. Chestnut oaks and mountain laurel thrive in the well-drained soil near the cliff top, but the interior forest has an uncanny bottomland-like appearance, thick with grass, vines, and yellow poplars. Continue past the first trail junction, remaining on the Carriage Road Trail when the Hollow Tree Trail forks right.

A steep-sided runoff channel has eroded a wide bowl against the Rappahannock, pressing the trail inland. It dips slightly to make the curve then again runs along the bluff top. Members of the red-oak family abound in the forest here, including Southern and Northern red and bear oak. When the Hollow Tree and Carriage Road Trails rejoin, continue north on the latter.

Through a thin screen of trees, the quarter-mile-wide river is visible immediately below. West of Voorhees, Horse Head Point juts into the river, giving the appearance of a long island. Just slightly wider than the river itself, the marshy peninsula forces the river more than a mile north before it rounds an oxbow to head south. The trail begins to descend slightly as it approaches the turnaround overlook. Tread lightly, as bald eagles often use the overlook to scout for fish in the water below. Just before a sign noting the trail's end, a view of the Rappahannock opens on your left. Exercise caution when approaching the bluff. Though laurel and small trees cling to the steep slope, its eroding sand offers little traction.

Behind you, descending sharply to the northeast, is a sand-and-pebble trail. Some maps identify this as the Woods Trail. No signage on the ground acknowledges the path, but it has been cleared of recent deadfalls. By hiking it, you add 1.2 miles to your overall hike. The sub-loop begins with a quick descent to come within close view of a private home. Turn right to skirt the preserve boundary on roomy single-track. Follow the twisting trail upstream of the slender creek on your left. After heading north through an airy flat, the path veers right to ascend to upland oak forest.

There it joins an old roadbed and makes a long run northeast, keeping a narrow valley on trail left. Upon intersecting another double-track, make a sharp right turn for a level, southeastward stint. Beyond a small parcel of pines, another valley drops away on trail left. As the trail curves south, it enters a roomy beech forest and begins descending to the northern reaches of crescent-shaped Owl Hollow. A wide decrepit bridge crosses the rivulet, the vestige of an old forest road. A shipping pallet just downstream serves today's foot traffic. Crossing the stream, a wide marshy plain extends on left and right. Ahead, the trail climbs a steep, wooded hillside to meet the Hollow Tree Trail.

To stick with the main trails and follow the hike as mapped here, simply back-track from the overlook to its northernmost junction with the Hollow Tree Trail. Turn left onto the Hollow Tree Trail and follow it east through oak-dominated woods. A sweeping view of a valley on trail left opens just in advance of an unmarked but dis-cernable junction where the Woods Trail arrives from downhill on the left.

The Hollow Tree Trail continues due east along the northern side of this trian-gular plateau. It remains fairly level but dips slightly as it passes above the gullies that feed Owl Hollow. Rounding a small knoll, the path then heads southwest. Here, more gently sloping hills stretch away on your left. A sign denotes the trail's name-sake at the head of a wide drainage on trail left. The gnarled, ancient oak is indeed hollow, and younger visitors can squeeze inside for a photo.

Continue on beyond the tree, with vine-draped forest stretching away on your right. Just after veering left, your path rejoins the Carriage Road Trail. Turn left and retrace your steps through Owl Hollow and on to the berry farm. On a hot day you'll be ready for a strawberry sundae when you get there.

# WAHRANI NATURE PARK

### ▶ IN BRIEF

On rainy afternoons, mist enshrouds the fern-blanketed hills at Wahrani Nature Park, evoking the Smoky Mountains rather than Tidewater Virginia. Though modest by Appalachian standards, the distinct climbs along this route lead hikers to a sweeping overlook and a pair of colonial graves.

### ▶ DESCRIPTION

In 2001 New Kent County assumed jurisdiction over the 138-acre parcel encompassing this long-standing nature trail, making it the first holding of the county's fledgling parks department. Until recently, this route was alternately referred to as the Chesapeake Nature Trail, because Chesapeake Corporation owned the land, or the Warreneye Nature Trail, in honor of the eighteenth-century Warreneye Church that once stood here. In 2003 New Kent renamed the area Wahrani Nature Park to reflect the word's Native American origins. That same spelling is now applied to a swamp south of the park. In their efforts to anglicize the indigenous term, colonists also came up with Warrenigh, Warreny, and Warren I.

New Kent was settled more than a century before the American Revolution and inhabited by tribes of the Powhatan Confederacy prior to that. It was in New Kent that George Washington wed Martha Dandridge Custis. Located on the Pamunkey River a couple miles northwest of the park, Eltham Plantation was among the finest of its era and home to Washington's brother-in-law

### ▶ DIRECTIONS

From Richmond take I-64 east to Exit 220, VA 33. From Williamsburg or Newport News, head west on I-64. Exit onto VA 33 heading northeast. The entrance to the park is on your right after 3.8 miles on VA 33. The trailhead's small gravel lot is visible just before the turn.

### ⓘ KEY AT-A-GLANCE INFORMATION

**LENGTH:** 3.1 miles

**CONFIGURATION:** Loop with out-and-back spur

**DIFFICULTY:** Moderate

**SCENERY:** Steep hillsides in mature hardwood forest, numerous rivulets, ridgetop-pine woods, eighteenth-century gravestones

Exposure: Well-shaded

**TRAFFIC:** Low

**TRAIL SURFACE:** Dirt

**HIKING TIME:** 1.5 hours

**SEASON:** Open daily during daylight year-round

**ACCESS:** No fee; not recommended for wheelchairs

**MAPS:** None at present; take the map included here

**FACILITIES:** Parking area with signboard and trashcan

**SPECIAL COMMENTS:** Following acquisition of the park from Chesapeake Corporation, New Kent County grafted new triangular-plastic blazes atop a preexisting network designated by painted blazes. The old and new blazes often coincide but sometimes conflict. The numbered posts en route predate county management. While booklets identifying them are now absent from the trailhead, newer maps have yet to replace them. You can reach New Kent County Parks at (804) 966-8502.

UTM Trailhead Coordinates for Wahrani Nature Park

UTM Zone (NAD27)   18S

Easting   0335621

Northing   4152441

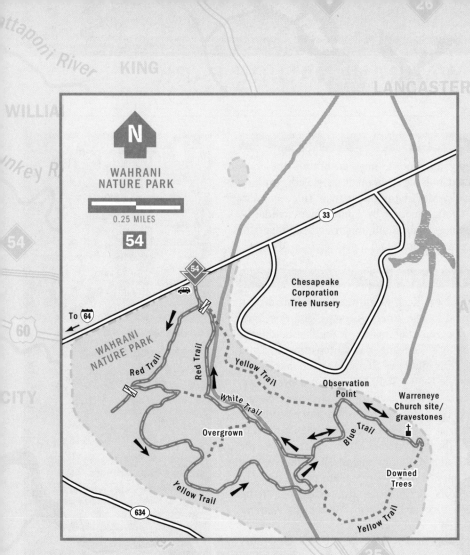

N

WAHRANI
NATURE PARK

0.25 MILES

54

To 64

WAHRANI
NATURE PARK

Red Trail

Red Trail

Red Trail

Yellow Trail

White Trail

Overgrown

Yellow Trail

Yellow Trail

634

33

Chesapeake
Corporation
Tree Nursery

Observation
Point

Warreneye
Church site/
gravestones

Blue Trail

Downed
Trees

Yellow Trail

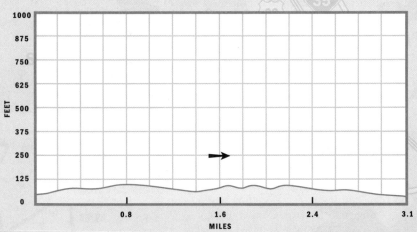

Burwell Bassett. The first president recalled visits to Eltham in his diary, and the Washingtons frequently joined the Bassetts for Sunday worship at Warreneye Church.

Also known as the Upper Church of Blisland Parish, Warreneye Church was built in 1703. It was already in disrepair when soldiers of the Richmond Militia camped there during the War of 1812. One, Samuel Mordecai, wrote: "The church was set on a high elevation overlooking the junction of the Pamunkey and Mattaponi Rivers at the formation of the York. It was by the old road, the Colonial highway, that ran from Eltham to Williamsburg. In 1814, only the walls and a part of the roof remained."

The route mapped here takes you to the site of Warreneye Church, though all that remains today are two flat gravestones, easily spotted thanks to a much newer white picket fence. Dated 1736 and 1745 the gravestones display varying degrees of erosion. The better-preserved stone includes an ornate circular crest. Families can make an educational adventure of this hike, teaching children about history and archaeology by making rubbings of the stones with crayon and butcher paper.

Setting out from the parking area, the trailhead is distinguishable by a tall sign with rules but no map. The path forks almost immediately. Head right, following a low-level sign for the Main Trail. This small marker, like the numbered posts along the trail, is a vestige of the privately built nature trail. The county added new diamond-shaped blazes to distinguish three trails by color: red, yellow, and white. These often (but not always) correspond to the painted blazes of the older color-coded network, which also included a blue-blazed path.

As you begin this trek, you'll notice diamond-shaped blazes of all three colors along the path. You'll also spy bright green club moss growing on the forest floor amid a mixture of pines and younger hardwoods. Water runoff often clears the sandy trail of leaves and sometimes puddles remain behind. You'll soon pass a triple-trunked tulip poplar—also known as yellow poplar—on trail left. Many more of these grow on the hillside ahead. First, however, the trail curves left to squeeze between two steep-sided knolls. Ferns grow on these wet banks, and exposed tree roots protrude from them. Short wooden boardwalks guide the trail over muddy seeps before it emerges onto a hillside, which slopes steeply away on the left.

Tulip poplars give way to pines, their needles blanketing the trail, before the trail makes a sharp left downhill. The old grade you've just followed continues along the hill, but a log blockade serves to deter anyone dismissive of the blazes. The trail descends past the sawed remains of several downed trees, the hulking remains of which will likely lie nearby for years. In the small valley the path veers right then left to meet a sandy-bottomed stream. A wooden footbridge spans the rivulet in a lush fern garden. Just ahead, the white-and-yellow-blazed trail heads to the right, crossing another footbridge over a seasonal stream before rising uphill. Follow this path, as you will rejoin the red-blazed path, which heads straight here, on your return trip.

As you ascend along a mossy trail studded with roots, a network of small streams is visible behind and below you. Beech trees prevail in this damp wood. The trail begins a wide curve to the left and continues climbing, passing a wooden bench on the right for anyone wishing to catch their breath. Though ferns still dot the ground, the forest makeup shifts slightly as you gain elevation, with an increased presence of white and chestnut oaks as well as broad-leafed shagbark hickories. The climb now behind you, the trail undulates and winds gracefully, maintaining its elevation as the hillside land drops steeply away on the left.

Logs placed along the trail outline a bend to the right, and soon a white-blazed connector trail enters on trail left. This path links to another downhill, on which you will return. However, trailside vegetation, thriving in the abundant sunlight left by downed trees, now crowds the path. If the trail is passable, interested hikers can take the spur to see an eroding cliff located about halfway down the path. The cliff, and the boulders that have broken away from it, is studded with seashells, testimony to an ancient sea that once covered this region.

The fauna presently inhabiting this mature hardwood forest and the parcels of younger woods that lie ahead include white-tailed deer and wild turkeys, both of which I spotted here. The turkey spotted me first, and the audible whoosh of air beneath her broad wings turned my head.

Beyond the spur, the path descends to a seasonal stream then rises again to another hillside. It soon crests, then descends just as quickly, passing through a pine wood before reaching a power-line clearing. Cross the clearing, looking for songbirds in the brush. Zigzag right then left upon entering the woods opposite. You've now left behind the newer diamond blazes and are following yellow-painted blazes. You will next turn left onto a path marked by blue-painted blazes. After crossing two streams on wooden footbridges, you'll spot a bench and a sign for the Loop Trail and then the turn. The old yellow-blazed path does continue beyond the turn and ultimately reaches the gravestones. However, numerous downed pines on its easternmost stretch render the trail impassable.

The blue-blazed path, by contrast, winds around the base of a small ridge then traverses a wet bottomland valley. Cross four modest rivulets, three on wooden spans, before passing a mossy embankment. The path alternately approaches then retreats from the power-line clearing, which it roughly parallels, until cresting on a pine ridge. About 500 feet in on the blue-blazed trail, watch for a trail on your left—your return route.

After climbing to the ridgeline, the trail curves right to an overlook on the left. A bench faces a vista of the Mattaponi and Pamunkey Valleys. The rivers join to form the York 3 miles northeast. Continue east along a trail carpeted with pine needles to reach the eighteenth-century gravestones. They are easily discernable on trail right. The blue-blazed path has rejoined the yellow loop on the ridge, and the latter continues downhill from the knoll on which Warreneye Church once stood. However, the gravestones make a suitable turnaround, as downed pines obstruct the way ahead.

Retrace your steps along the ridge and downhill. Do not follow the yellow blazes west from the lookout. This older loop recrosses the power-line clearing then passes through a meadow before re-entering woods near the trailhead. However, its junction with the diamond-blazed network is blocked. So, instead, descend from the ridge and look for a right turn before returning to the stream-laced bottomland. Recross the power-line clearing here, on a path with both blue- and white-painted blazes. It rejoins an unobstructed portion of the white diamond–blazed trail in the woods ahead, first passing through mixed forest and paralleling a creek on the right. Bear right at a junction where the white trail heads in both directions. You will soon return to the loop on which you set out, blazed with red, white, and yellow diamonds. Turn right to make a few more creek crossings, relishing the wild character of this park even as you return to the trailhead.

# WALLER MILL PARK

Waller Mill Park took a beating in 2003, and its premier hiking trail, the 2.9-mile Lookout Tower Trail reopened just prior to publication of this guide. The 5-mile mountain-bike trail remained closed, but Waller Mill still has enough amenities to rival a day-use state park—and a dog park is in the works.

## ▶ DESCRIPTION

The first Virginians never saw Waller Mill Reservoir; it was constructed in 1942. However, colonists and speculators representing the Virginia Company of London no doubt explored the area. They would have seen the present shore as hilltops overlooking the now-flooded valley of Queen's Creek, which still drains east from the reservoir to the York River. However, in light of one intriguing historic account, it's possible those English colonists were not the first Europeans to attempt settlement here. According to the story, it was along Queen's Creek that ill-fated Spanish Jesuits attempted to establish a mission in 1570 (though some suggest that New Kent County's Diascund Creek was the more likely locale).

Led by Friar Juan Baptista Segura, the expedition numbered fewer than a dozen, and only two survived: their teenaged assistant, Alonso de Olmos, and an Algonquian native christened Don

## ▶ DIRECTIONS

From Richmond take I-64 east to Exit 234, VA 646. From Newport News head west on I-64. Exit onto VA 646 heading southwest. After 1.5 miles turn left onto US 60. Drive 2.3 miles to Airport Road (VA 645), turning left again. The entrance to the park is on your right after 1.7 more miles, shortly after crossing the reservoir on a bridge. Ample parking is available north of the park office.

## ⓘ KEY AT-A-GLANCE INFORMATION

**LENGTH:** 3.9 miles, but either the 2.9-mile Lookout Tower Trail or 1-mile Bayberry Nature Trail can be walked separately; optional 2-mile paved trail and 0.75-mile dirt trail are east of the office.

**CONFIGURATION:** Figure-eight

**DIFFICULTY:** Easy on Bayberry Natur Trail, moderate on Lookout Tower Trail

**SCENERY:** Turtles, waterfowl, and paddlers on Waller Mill Reservoir; mixed forest, some fields along old railroad grade

**EXPOSURE:** Mostly shaded, more open at lake's edge and along railroad grade

**TRAFFIC:** Moderate; high near park office

**TRAIL SURFACE:** Paved along railroad grade, dirt on nature trail

**HIKING TIME:** 2.5 hours

**SEASON:** Open daily during daylight year-round (exact hours vary, available online)

**ACCESS:** No fee; hike route not recommended for wheelchairs but paved trail is accessible

**MAPS:** Available at park office; brochure without map available online at www.ci.williamsburg.va.us/rec/parks.html#waller

**FACILITIES:** Picnic tables, grills, restrooms, vending machines, volleyball nets, playing fields, fishing docks, boat launch ($2 fee), boat rentals (prices vary)

**SPECIAL COMMENTS:** Contact the park office at (757) 259-3778 or the Williamsburg City Parks office at (757) 259-3760.

**UTM Trailhead Coordinates for Waller Mill Park**

**UTM Zone (NAD27)  18S**

**Easting  0348961**

**Northing  4130972**

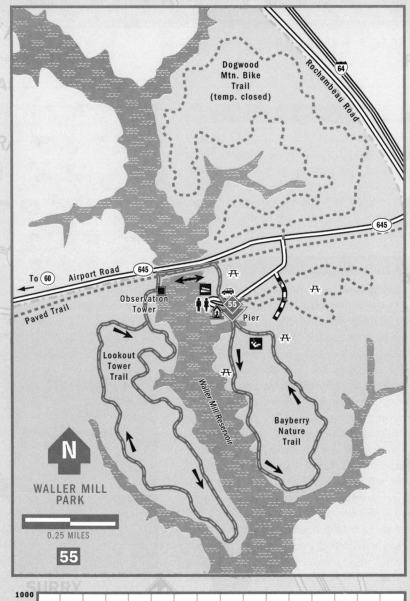

Dogwood
Mtn. Bike
Trail
(temp. closed)

Rochambeau Road

64

645

To 60   Airport Road

645

Observation
Tower

Paved Trail

Pier

55

Lookout
Tower
Trail

Waller Mill Reservoir

Bayberry
Nature
Trail

**N**

**WALLER MILL PARK**

0.25 MILES

55

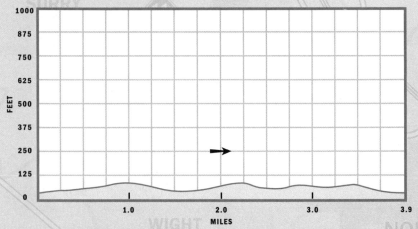

Luis. Don Luis had been taken from Ajacan, as the Spanish called Virginia, by an expedition sent to explore the Bahia de Madre de Dios, now the Chesapeake Bay, in 1560. Educated in Mexico, he was to serve as the Jesuits' interpreter and help lead his native tribe toward his adopted faith.

The apparent advantage of an Algonquian guide convinced Segura that Spanish troops need not accompany the expedition. As it happened, Don Luis was quickly reabsorbed into his native tribe. The Spaniards were thus left defenseless and unable to communicate with the native Indians. Celebrating mass in a crude hut, the mission persisted for some five months. However, in February 1571 Don Luis murdered three priests sent to beckon him to back to the mission. He then led a band of tribesmen to the mission, where they stealthily killed the remaining Jesuits.

That was the account of the teenage de Olmos, who was spared and later escaped to be rescued by a Spanish resupply ship in 1572. Sent to avenge the murders, Spanish troops hung eight native Indians accused of participating in the raid. However, Don Louis was never found. An improbable legend holds that he survived to instigate a 1622 raid on the Jamestown settlement in which 347 colonists perished.

That colony, of course, persisted, and plantations were established along Queen's Creek in the 1640s. Its waters also served to power gristmills for the first plantations and for centuries thereafter. Today, a millstone some four feet in diameter welcomes visitors outside the Waller Mill Park office. It was found in the lake during a 1963 dam upgrade and may have been part of the park's namesake mill, which was swallowed in 1942 by the rising waters. Also submerged beneath the 343-acre reservoir was the site of Oak Grove School, which is commemorated by a historical marker near the office. Established in 1911, during an era of entrenched racial segregation, the school provided education to area African Americans until 1940, when a lightning strike set the two-story schoolhouse ablaze.

Constructed by the federal government to provide water to World War II naval recruits training at Camp Peary to the north, Waller Mill Reservoir was sold to the City of Williamsburg in 1945 and still provides drinking water for much of the area. The 2,400-acre park along the shore was not established until 1972. Since then, however, it has become a favorite sunny-day destination for Williamsburg residents, with amenities to match. Picnic shelters and grills host family gatherings; fishing piers and rowboats afford anglers the opportunity to land striped and largemouth bass, carp, and foot-long black crappie; rental canoes and kayaks invite paddlers to explore the shoreline; and trails invite everyone—seniors, joggers, cyclists, and nature lovers—to stretch their legs.

Unfortunately, hurricane and storm damage effectively closed the park's trails in 2003. It was well over a year before the Lookout Tower Trail and the western half of the Bayberry Nature Trail were reopened. Now the two loops can be paired with a short section of the recently paved railroad grade paralleling Airport Road to create a 3.9-mile figure eight. Visitors have the option of hiking either loop on its own (the paved trail still serves as a necessary link to the Lookout Tower Trail). The park also offers twin exercise trails, one designed especially for seniors, and will reopen more than five miles of mountain-bike trail.

The Bayberry Nature Trail begins just south of the park office via a wooden footbridge that spans an inlet of the lake. Pause here to survey your rental-boat options at the dock or toss breadcrumbs to the panhandling geese and turtles below—a popular pastime with younger visitors. Bear right across the bridge, passing Shelter 1, and follow the sandy, root-laced path south. You'll spot numbered posts, which refer you to entries in guide booklets available from the park office. Formerly there were 72 stations along the loop, though several that identified trees have been felled by high winds. Even without the help, you'll recognize many of southeast Virginia's most common hardwoods—white oak, sweet gum, beech, and hickories—shading equally familiar thickets of holly.

After winding along the lakeshore, the path soon reaches a memorial meditation bench overlooking a small inlet. A second bench awaits farther down the path, backed by holly and shaded by a mammoth red oak. The trail then circles northward and uphill to pass through an open wood. The abundance of downed trees here has made room for opportunistic overgrowth beside the path.

Continue on, with small inlets of the lake visible on your right. After crossing the upper reaches of a drainage that feeds a finger of the lake below, the reservoir fades from view. The path bears left to pass first a shelter then the playground on the right as you reapproach the bridge that leads back to the office. Turn right to pass beside the office and then traverse the parking area.

Continue north past picnic tables through a beech glade. After passing volleyball nets on the left, you will reach the Asphalt Bike/Walk Trail on a former railroad grade. It leads right (east) approximately 0.5 miles, passing the park entrance, the seniors' walking trail, and the mountain-bike trail en route. To the left, the trail continues 1.5 miles before reaching a turnaround.

To reach the Lookout Tower Trail, turn left onto the asphalt and continue across the bridge over the lake with Airport Road running parallel on your right. Ahead, a sign directs you left, off the path, and uphill to the observation tower, which is braced against the steep hillside above the lake. After a few moments watching the boats below, head south along the bluff above the lake.

The Lookout Tower Trail traces the shore south through mixed forest. It tends to stay above the lake but dips through several creek drainages. Rounding the southern tip of a peninsula, the trail bears right (north). A narrow finger of the lake stretches along the path, and the trail soon dips to the water's edge. You'll then climb back onto the hillside above the lake and continue north as it recedes behind you. Enjoy this final woodland stretch as the trail begins to wind generally east.

Upon reintersecting the trail above the lake, turn left and head back downhill to the paved trail, which you can exlpore if you wish. Farther west along the paved trail, red maple and tulip-poplar trees shade relaxation benches, and some fields also border the path, offering promising butterfly- and bird-watching. Otherwise, simply retrace your steps to the parking area.

Waller Mill Park makes a fine addition to a tourist itinerary that includes nearby attractions at Jamestown, Williamsburg, and Yorktown. An afternoon at the lake can have restorative effects on young children whose appetite for historic sites doesn't match that of their parents or siblings. Consider pairing this hike with a picnic or paddle. The flat water at Waller Mill Reservoir is a good place to try out canoeing or kayaking for the first time.

# WALNUT CREEK PARK

## ▶ IN BRIEF

Choose from a short loop southeast of Walnut Creek Lake or its longer counterpart northwest of the reservoir. The former, popular with trail runners, leaves the main parking area near the beach; the latter departs from a trailhead lot closer to the entrance. The two can be linked using one of two short connectors.

## ▶ DESCRIPTION

Walnut Creek Park offers a wide range of outdoor recreation to residents of Albemarle County and nearby Charlottesville. Anglers cast from boats or the shore, with good odds for landing largemouth bass, catfish, and sunfish in the stocked 45-acre lake. Disc-golfers hone their skills on the park's newly built course. In the summer, families crowd the beach and nearby playground.

But Walnut Creek Park is best known for the 15 trail miles that lace its 480 acres. Area mountain bikers built most of the trails, and their preference

## ▶ DIRECTIONS

From Richmond follow I-64 northwest to Exit 121. Exit southbound on US 20. Continue southwest for 8 miles before turning right onto VA 708, which is signed for Walnut Creek Park. Drive almost 3 miles northwest, then turn left onto VA 631. The park-entrance road is located on the left, 0.6 miles ahead. Upon entering the park, wind downhill on the paved road to reach the main trailhead parking area, next to the lake, on the right. This is the trailhead for the longer loop. To reach the beach and most facilities, continue along the park road until it terminates. This is the trailhead for the shorter loop. It's also possible to arrive via US 29 south from Charlottesville. Drive just over 6 miles south of I-64, then turn left onto VA 708. Continue 3 miles before turning right onto VA 631.

## ℹ KEY AT-A-GLANCE INFORMATION

**LENGTH:** 5-mile loop, 2-mile loop, 0.3- or 0.75- mile connector, plus numerous spurs

**CONFIGURATION:** 2 loops that leave from separate trailheads but can be linked

**DIFFICULTY:** Difficult on long loop, moderate on short loop

**SCENERY:** Walnut Creek Lake, rocky Walnut Creek, young pine and cedar thickets, mature chestnut-oak forest on rocky hillside, stone chimney at old homesite

Exposure: Well-shaded except lakeside

**TRAFFIC:** Moderate

**TRAIL SURFACE:** Dirt single-track

**HIKING TIME:** 3 hours long loop, 1 hour short loop

**SEASON:** Trails open daily 7 a.m.–sunset year-round; beach and facilities open Memorial Day–Labor Day

**ACCESS:** Free to hike; swimming $3 for county residents, $2 ages 4–12, $4.50 and $3 for nonresidents; trails not recommended for wheelchairs

**MAPS:** Available at park in season and online at www.albemarle.org/parks; map depicted on trailhead signboard

**FACILITIES:** Restrooms, concessions, picnic tables, grills, disc-golf course, swimming beach (10 a.m.–8 p.m. in season), boat launch, canoe rentals ($5 per hour)

**SPECIAL COMMENTS:** The network is convoluted; don't expect to find blazes at every intersection. Contact Albemarle County Parks at (434) 296-5844.

**UTM Trailhead Coordinates for Walnut Creek Park**

**UTM Zone (NAD27)   17S**

**Easting   0711650**

**Northing   4200288**

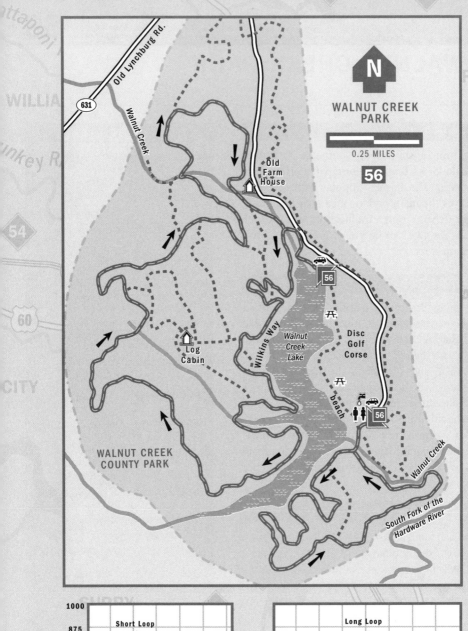

Old Lynchburg Rd.

631

Walnut Creek

WILLIA

54

60

CITY

**N**

**WALNUT CREEK PARK**

0.25 MILES

56

Old Farm House

56

Walnut Creek Lake

Disc Golf Corse

Wilkins Way

Log Cabin

beach

56

WALNUT CREEK COUNTY PARK

Walnut Creek

South Fork of the Hardware River

Che

ATTHEW

HAM

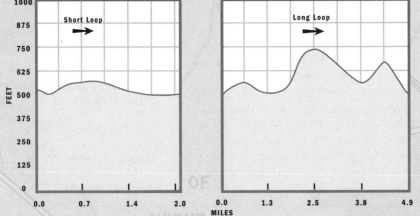

| FEET | | | | | |
|---|---|---|---|---|---|
| 1000 | **Short Loop** → | | | | |
| 875 | | | | | |
| 750 | | | | | |
| 625 | | | | | |
| 500 | | | | | |
| 375 | | | | | |
| 250 | | | | | |
| 125 | | | | | |
| 0 | | | | | |

0.0    0.7    1.4    2.0

**Long Loop** →

0.0    1.3    2.5    3.8    4.9

MILES

for frequent ups and downs and twists and turns is evident. However, the network sees roughly as many pedestrians as cyclists, notably trail runners. A tapestry of one dozen distinct paths, the trail system offers many permutations, but scant signage complicates matters. To keep things simple, you can choose one of the two loops outlined below. For more mileage, you can use a connector trail and hike them both.

## SHORT LOOP

This 2-mile outing begins at the main parking lot, which is just uphill of the swimming beach and concession building. A service road loops down to the beach from the southwest corner of the parking lot. The trail heads left from this asphalt surface as a gravel double-track descending toward the lake. The path narrows to dirt single-track as it runs along the lake to traverse the dam. Note the connector trail that heads left before crossing the dam, then veer right once across the dam.

Young mountain-laurel bushes climb the mossy slope on trail left, while the lake stretches away on your right. The trail rises slightly as it curves inland through pine-dominated woods to reach a trail junction. Turn right here. The trail now twists with the topography to remain generally level, twice leaving the lakeshore only to return.

The trail veers decidedly inland to traverse a parcel of pines, some felled by disease, then winds beside multiple piles of granite stones, perhaps amassed here by trail builders or farmers before them. Heading south, a barbwire fence runs on trail right. Bike traffic has exacerbated trail potholes in a few spots, but the single-track remains passable.

Ahead, a cluster of red cedar signifies an old homesite, where you will spy the remains of a stone chimney and foundation on trail right. Next, bear right again upon reaching a second junction with the cutoff trail. Another fence appears on trail right as you proceed along a bluffline to crest a small knoll. At the base of the steep hillside across the fence flows the South Fork Hardware River. Walnut Creek drains from the lake to its confluence with the river approximately 0.2 miles beyond the trail.

As it descends from the ridge, your path curves left to draw along the creek. Proceed upstream amid abundant hornbeams. A bend in the trail grazes the creek just as great sheets of rock thrust skyward from the opposite bank. Perpendicular to the streambed, these successive walls of lichen-spotted rock force the water into a narrow channel. Look for additional rock formations ahead as you proceed through a grassy floodplain studded with poplars. The trail ultimately veers left and rises away from the creek to rejoin the dam-top path on which you arrived.

## CONNECTOR

It's possible to simply walk half a mile past the picnic area, across a meadow, and through a small wood to link the two loops. A single-track connector runs east of the park road in the woods bordering. To follow it, take the trail leading southeast (downstream) on the northern side of the dam. The path runs beside Walnut Creek, then turns a sharp left uphill within sight of the vertical rock walls in the streambed. Crest the hill and bear left to an overlook. You'll notice disc-golf "holes" in this area. The trail then proceeds north, staying close to the road. It grazes the asphalt near the northern parking lot, and you can cross the street to pick up the longer loop.

## LONG LOOP

Before setting out from the designated trailhead parking lot (north of the beach lot), study the map on the central signboard. The trail departs from the northern shore of the lake below the park road. This stretch of single-track amid reeds tends to be muddy. Next you must ford Walnut Creek before it empties into the lake. Do so cautiously, then take your first left to head southward along the shore.

Successive lefts will keep you close to the shore, ensuring that you stay on the main loop, Wilkins Way (shown red on the map, but sporadically blazed). Your first inland stint entails several ups and downs intended to amuse cyclists, but, by following the trail clockwise, you retain the option of retreating after 3 miles and a major climb. Opting to press on, you'll have made the widest loop available.

Crossing numerous laurel-clad runoff gullies, the path generally follows the lakeshore then curves right to trace a small inlet of the lake. You'll double back and cross a feeder stream shortly beyond a trail junction. Bypass the trail that heads right to an old log-cabin site, a hub for many of the paths crisscrossing the interior of this loop.

Your trail reapproaches the lake on a narrow, club moss–carpeted peninsula opposite the beach. The path then bends westward, running between an arm of the lake and a pine wood. A slight rise precedes a definitive right, away from the tapering inlet. The trail soon begins a steady climb 250 feet up Ammonett Mountain. You won't top the peak, which crests at 974 feet, but you will switch back beside lichen-dotted boulders and beneath mature chestnut oaks.

The mountaintop is visible uphill on the left as the trail levels out. Numerous windblown trees lie scattered in the woods. The trail temporarily veers east as it dips to cross the upper reaches of a streamlet. Another appreciable climb follows. As you climb, look for an old stone chimney, the remains of a former farmstead, on trail right. A right at the chimney leads downhill to the log cabin. The larger loop, however, rises on, briefly heading west then doubling back. Catch your breath on the downhill stint that follows.

The trail soon forks, descending on either side of this tapering ridge. You may follow Wilkins Way left for a shorter, rougher descent; however, the route mapped here makes a right to maximize mileage and enjoyment of a leisurely downhill. Bypass the next junction and then take the following left. This path curves around a hillside as it drops toward Walnut Creek and an old farmhouse comes into view across the valley. Just beyond the reunion of the Red Trail with your own, the pathway fords the stream.

After rock-hopping across Walnut Creek, wider and shallower here, follow the trail downstream. The path tunnels through dense thickets of pines then cedars on its twisting ascent from the creek. Near the meadow-covered hilltop, approach a trail intersection and turn right to traverse an open glade where pines and post oaks find purchase in the drier upland soil. The path then curves right to descend a hillside clad in young hardwoods, including clammy locust. The forest is dotted with piles of iron-red stones as the trail runs parallel to the park road.

Near the base of the slope, pass the tin-roofed, weathered-wood farmhouse on your left between the trail and road. Beyond it, the trail nears Walnut Creek on the right. The rocky trail descends to bisect the remains of a stone wall ahead. Continue to return along a grassy, cedar-dotted power-line clearing. The creek meets the lake just ahead. The parking area is visible a short distance on.

# WESTMORELAND STATE PARK

Leaving from its trailhead along the park road, the Turkey Neck Trail heads southeast then forks to create a loop. Hiked clockwise, the loop descends a ridge to trace Big Meadow Run through a swampy valley. Follow a lengthy boardwalk to the sandy Potomac River shore for views of Horsehead Cliffs before turning around to complete the loop. Optional trailheads let you interchange the strings on this balloon hike.

▶ **DESCRIPTION**

One of the commonwealth's first state parks, Westmoreland was constructed by the New Deal–era Civilian Conservation Corps and opened in 1936. With shovels and wheelbarrows, young men left jobless by the Depression were put to work building roads and trails. The trees they felled served to build the historic conference center, with its rough-hewn log beams and flooring (for more on the young men who served in the

▶ **DIRECTIONS**

From Richmond head north on I-95 to Exit 104. Follow VA 207 almost 12 miles to the town of Bowling Green, where it merges with US 301. Continue northeast on US 301 through Fort A. P. Hill and across the Rappahannock River. After almost 18 miles, turn right onto VA 3 (from Fredericksburg, you can arrive eastbound on VA 3). Drive almost 18 miles west to VA 347, and turn left, following signs for the state park. Continue a mile and a half, paying your entrance fee along the way, and park at the Turkey Neck Trail trailhead on the right side of the road. You may also park at the visitor center, visible just ahead. To reach the swimming pool, picnic, and boat-launch areas, turn left at the visitor center and continue less than a mile downhill. (See description for alternate trailheads within the park.)

**KEY AT-A-GLANCE INFORMATION**

**LENGTH:** 3.6 miles, 3 or 5.5 miles using optional access trails

**CONFIGURATION:** Balloon

**DIFFICULTY:** Moderate

**SCENERY:** Upland hardwood forest, a wide marshy creek valley, a sandy Potomac Beach

Exposure: Well-shaded in forest, exposed on boardwalk and at the shore

**TRAFFIC:** Moderate

**TRAIL SURFACE:** Dirt with one extensive boardwalk, sandy along beach

**HIKING TIME:** 3 hours

**SEASON:** Open daily 8 a.m.–5 p.m. year-round, campground open March–December, pool open daily Memorial Day–Labor Day

**ACCESS:** Parking costs $2 on weekdays, $3 on weekends; swimming pool costs $3 for adults, $2 for children ages 3–12, $4 and $3 on weekends; campsites cost $18–$23 per night, cabins cost $44–$50. Visitor center, restrooms, campground, and pool are wheelchair accessible; most trails not recommended for wheelchairs.

**MAPS:** Available at visitor center, on trailhead signboards, and online

**FACILITIES:** Restrooms, visitor center, riverside picnic area, swimming pool, campground, cabins, convention center, Potomac River Retreat center, amphitheater, boat launch, boat rentals (prices vary)

**SPECIAL COMMENTS:** Call the park at (804) 493-8821 or visit www.dcr.virginia.gov/parks/westmore.

**UTM Trailhead Coordinates for Westmoreland State Park**

**UTM Zone (NAD27)   18S**

**Easting   0336340**

**Northing   4225845**

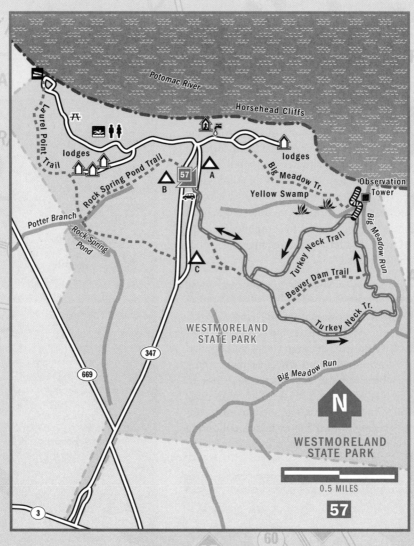

WESTMORELAND
STATE PARK

N

WESTMORELAND
STATE PARK

0.5 MILES

57

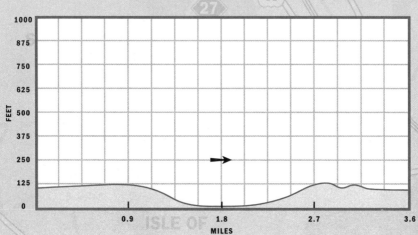

CCC, see Pocahontas State Park, page 162). Stationed atop the 150-foot Horsehead Cliffs, the center overlooks the wide Potomac River.

Shale-dolomite cliffs run the along much of the park's almost 2-mile shoreline. Gradually eroding, the whitish cliffs are crowned with wind-shaped pines. Visitors often take to rented kayaks or canoes in order to approach the striated rock face and scan it for fossils, reminders of the ancient sea that once covered the Chesapeake Bay basin. The visitor center displays a collection of shark's teeth recovered from the cliffs, one of several exhibits on Chesapeake ecology.

Anglers with modern marine life in mind can rent boats near the Potomac River Retreat (a newer facility than the original conference center). Nearby, at the western base of the cliffs, swimmers and sunbathers enjoy an Olympic-size pool, and picnickers fill the tables along the sandy shoreline.

This northwestern corner also offers an alternate trailhead for the hike outlined here. The Laurel Point Trail departs from the boat launch just west of the retreat center. It gets off to a steep start then climbs moderately on, skirting a cluster of cabins. The path then descends to cross a streamlet running beside Rock Spring Pond. Bound by Westmoreland's tall bluffs, the pond drains west as Potter's Branch. After feeding into Canal Swamp, itself a tributary of Pope's Creek, the water meets the Potomac near the site of George Washington's birth. The Laurel Point Trail, however, bends eastward to scale a hillside forested with towering beech trees. After crossing the park road, continue through Campground C to reach the loop portion of the Turkey Neck Trail via a short spur. Turn right and continue as described below. This longer option totals 5.5 miles.

To shorten your hike, consider using the other optional trailhead, found east of the visitor center near the park's amphitheater. The Big Meadow Trail heads east from a roadside sign and is convenient to the park's easternmost group of (two-bedroom) lodges. This path, like Turkey Neck, is a CCC original, and follows a long ridgeline before dipping to reach its namesake, Big Meadow Run, near the observation tower mentioned below. Hike the loop portion of the Turkey Neck Trail and this option amounts to almost 3 miles.

The proper start to the balloon-shaped Turkey Neck Trail is on the right-hand side of the park road just south of the visitor center. Facing the signboard map, a spur leads left to the visitor center, but take the trail leading right (northeast). The blue-blazed path briefly parallels the park road on your right as it rounds the top of a drainage. Ferns cling to the steep-sided ravine on your left, shaded by Northern red, bear, and chestnut oaks. Yellow poplar and red maple thrive in the valley below, where young beeches replace holly in the understory. Curving to the left shortly after the park road falls out of sight, the path veers steadily deeper into the forest.

Turn left to stay with the Turkey Neck Trail when the spur to Campground C heads right. Pass through a parcel of mixed forest where Virginia pines and mountain laurel green the woods in winter. Your wide, sandy path dips twice then curves right to undulate once more before reaching a trail junction. The Turkey Neck Trail heads in two directions here; follow it to the right, as signed for the Beaver Dam Trail. (You will return to this junction after making a loop.)

Ahead, bypass the Beaver Dam Trail when it heads left. (You can use the Beaver Dam Trail to make a figure eight if you wish, adding a mile to your total, or use it to cut off the northwestern segment of the Turkey Neck balloon, reducing your hike by about half a mile.) The wide Turkey Neck Trail continues along a broad, level hilltop that abounds with white and Southern red oaks. The path extends east onto a ridge, and inlets of Yellow Swamp on Big Meadow Run are visible below.

Descend from the ridge to the valley floor on wooden steps as a view of the creek-fed swamp opens before you. Approach quietly, and you well may find a heron stalking prey or a woodpecker hammering at the still-standing tree trunk of a downed tree. Work your way along the base of the hillside, green with patches of ferns and club moss. The trail here is narrow and laced with exposed roots. A boardwalk stretch aids your passage north beneath the bluffs, but watch for a muddy stretch that follows before the trail climbs just slightly onto the hillside.

To your right, water-tolerant red maples, also fittingly called swamp maples, dot the grassy marsh. Stands of poplar rise across the marshgrass expanse. An early autumn visit will find Yellow Swamp ablaze in color. The Beaver Dam Trail descends to enter on your left just before Turkey Neck ascends a small flight of wooden steps, opening to a vista of the Potomac ahead. Beech trees shade the final stretch of trail before you reach a lengthy boardwalk with an observation platform constructed at its center.

As you follow the L-shaped boardwalk out across the marsh, look for small crabs scuttling about in the muck below. Perched in the observation platform, patient visitors can see beavers and muskrats gliding through the marsh, ospreys and hawks circling overhead, and turtles coming out to sun themselves on fallen trees. At the boardwalk's terminus, the Big Meadow Trail heads left, but follow a spur to the right to visit the beach.

Strewn with driftwood, clamshells, and flotsam, the narrow, rustic beach runs west beneath rising cliffs. Fallen trees evidence the ongoing erosion. Natural-history buffs can scramble over them and walk a short distance along the beach to scan the cliff face for fossils. If you're staying in one of the lodges, consider taking the Big Meadow Trail to this spot early in the morning, when the rising sun illuminates the east-facing cliff wall.

To complete this hike, retrace your steps across the boardwalk and turn right. The Turkey Neck Trail traces the periphery of a black-water swamp on the right, then traverses a short boardwalk before rising out of the bottomland and onto a narrow ridge. Initially, mountain laurel crowds the path, with holly displacing it as the ridge widens. A few tall specimens of Virginia pine grow amid the oaks and beeches above. The winding path soon regains the hilltop junction noted above, where a right turn leads you back along a familiar trail to your starting point.

Virginia's Potomac shoreline is rich with history, and Westmoreland State Park makes a good base camp for anyone looking to couple outdoor recreation with excursions to nearby historic sites. Bordering the park on the west is Stratford Hall, birthplace of Robert E. Lee. The plantation manor and grounds are open for tours. For details call (804) 493-8038 or visit www.stratfordhall.org. Just west of Stratford Hall is George Washington's Birthplace National Monument, with a short hike of its own (see page 94).

# WILLIS RIVER TRAIL, CUMBERLAND STATE FOREST

## IN BRIEF

A joint project of the Virginia Department of Forestry and the Old Dominion Appalachian Trail Club, the Willis River Trail twice skirts its namesake river and makes extensive runs along equally scenic tributaries. The 16-mile trek (one-way) takes in swampland, open forest, and hilltop meadows to finish along placid Winston Lake.

## DESCRIPTION

The Willis River Trail's northern trailhead is scarcely a mile west of Royal Oaks, the colonial homestead of Jesse Thomas. A member of the Continental cavalry, Thomas was recuperating at home on June 2, 1781, when he learned that British commander Cornwallis had dispatched troops to take Baron

## DIRECTIONS

From Richmond travel west on US 60 (Midlothian Turnpike). Continue through Midlothian and Powhatan toward Cumberland. East of town, turn right onto VA 45. After 0.6 miles, turn left onto VA 624, and follow it 5.5 miles north. Turn right onto VA 608 at a T intersection. Drive 2.25 miles, then turn right onto gravel Warner Forest Road for the last half mile. The trail heads southbound from the road's cul-de-sac.

To reach the Willis River Trail's southern terminus from US 60, continue beyond Cumberland and turn right onto VA 629. Park at the Winston Lake picnic area on the right at 3.1 miles. Follow the stairs from the streamside picnic area to reach the trail. If you're leaving a shuttle vehicle here, continue north (right) on VA 629 for 3 miles, passing Bear Creek Lake on the right. Turn left at a T intersection with VA 622 and continue half a mile. Veer right with VA 623, which will become VA 624. After 4 miles bear left with VA 608. Turn right on Warner Forest Road 2.25 miles ahead.

## KEY AT-A-GLANCE INFORMATION

**LENGTH:** 16 miles

**CONFIGURATION:** End-to-end

**DIFFICULTY:** Hard

**SCENERY:** Wooded swamps, hardwood and pine forests, the Willis River and its rocky tributaries (Reynolds, Horn Quarter, and Little Bear Creeks), Winston Lake

**EXPOSURE:** Shaded except in brief meadow and road stints

**TRAFFIC:** Low

**TRAIL SURFACE:** Dirt, predominantly single-track; a few double-track sections

**HIKING TIME:** 8 hours

**SEASON:** Trails are open daily during daylight year-round but best avoided during hunting seasons (see below)

**ACCESS:** No fee; a pedestrian-only trail not recommended for wheelchairs

**MAPS:** Available at forest office and state park

**FACILITIES:** Parking areas at either trailhead, picnic area, and boat launch; adjacent Bear Creek Lake State Park offers restrooms, a campground, and concessions

**SPECIAL COMMENTS:** Portions of the state forest are open to hunting with the proper license. Call the forest office (434) 983-2175 for details; check with VDGIF to determine annual hunting seasons (call (804) 370-1000 or visit www.dgif. virginia.gov/hunting). Contact Cumberland State Forest at (804) 492-4121, or visit www.vdof.virginia.gov/stforest/index-csf.

---

UTM Trailhead Coordinates for
Willis River Trail,
Cumberland State Forest

UTM Zone (NAD27)   17S

Easting   0745899

Northing   4167030

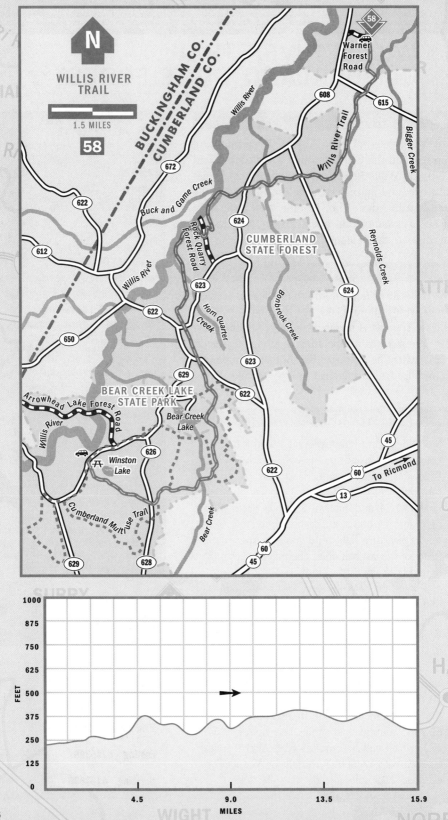

Friedrich von Steuben, the German nobleman-mercenary, who at Benjamin Franklin's request set to work training the American army. In the middle of a rainstorm, Thomas rode his horse Fearnaught as far north as the James and then swam the river to warn von Steuben near the town of Columbia.

The tale is a fitting introduction to Cumberland County, recalling as it does Paul Revere's famous ride. Established in 1749, Cumberland was the first Virginia county to make an official call for self-rule (despite being named for the Duke of Cumberland, uncle of King George III). On April 22, 1776, the county's Committee of Safety, convened to address mounting unrest, issued a proclamation. Read from the balcony of Effingham Tavern, it told delegates to the Virginia Convention: "We therefore, your constituents, instruct you positively to declare for Independency, that you solemnly abjure any allegiance to His Britanic Majestey and bid him good night forever."

Beyond the marker at the end of Warner Forest Road is a swinging bridge made of wooden poles and steel cables. The sagging span is noticeably weathered. Some hikers will be relieved to know that the Willis River Trail doesn't cross it. You, however, may wish to venture out above the river and gaze downstream. Birches arc above the greenish waters gliding east toward the James. The Willis River Trail heads south into the woods and out of sight of the river.

The path runs upstream along a swampy, unnamed tributary, crossing sandy feeder branches. Views open across a small bog on trail left. Red oaks dominate the hillside, and birches dot the bottomland. You'll find mossy boulders in the headwaters of this tributary, which you cross just before intersecting VA 615. Turn left onto the paved road to cross Reynolds Creek. White blazes then signal a right turn into the woods.

The trail climbs a bluff overlooking a swamp. Wood ducks and beavers hide in this small wetland. Ahead, the trail runs through an open hardwood forest then a dense mixed wood on the hillside east of Reynolds Creek. A short, steep descent brings you to a rock-hop ford of about ten feet. Moss colors the creek's sandy banks and water noisily flows over angular rocks. Once across you'll veer momentarily away through white oaks and young cedars, then return to the creek as you follow it upstream and south. After crossing a feeder branch, the red maples and hornbeams of the bottomland recede as you ascend a piney ridge.

The Willis River Trail follows a double-track cushioned with pine needles before turning right onto gravel Toll Gate Forest Road. Follow the road to its junction with VA 624, roughly 4 miles into the hike. Cross the road to follow a rivulet downhill through oak-dominated forest. Hikers must scramble around downed trees at numerous points along the trail, but the stretch ahead entails the most obstacles. Veering away from the rivulet, you intersect Bonbrook Creek, a sandy brook with pebble-strewn shoals. Once across, bear right and downstream before making a left uphill.

Head westbound through thick, younger hardwoods to again bisect VA 624. Turn left with the road then bear right, away from the road and an intersecting double-track. The trail descends steadily to reach the Willis River at mile 6. Turn left to head upstream beside the river, not quite as wide here but still smooth and draped with birches. After a brief riverside stretch, the trail bends left. You'll soon draw along a small, rocky tributary. Rounding the top of this drainage, the trail briefly runs beside a clear-cut field on the left and a stand of pines on the right. You'll intersect Rock Quarry Forest Road near a wooden gate then descend by single-track back to the Willis River.

Enjoy a blufftop stretch overlooking the river before descending briefly to traverse airy riparian bottomland. A meadow extends on the opposite bank as the river rounds a bend. Soon your path bears left and uphill, passing a ramshackle wooden privy. Next, climb upstream along Horn Quarter Creek in a scenic, steep-sided valley. Shelves of gray stone, spotted green by moss and lichen, line the watercourse. Turning right to ford the creek, you'll climb out of the valley on a wide path.

The trail soon joins an old dirt road. At an intersection follow the double-track that bears right, away from a loblolly-pine plantation. The wide path becomes a rutty, soggy stretch before the Willis River Trail turns beyond a streamlet. Follow single-track to reach the VA 622 and VA 623 intersection. Here, the Willis River Trail begins a half-mile roadside walk south on VA 622. Ahead, at the intersection of VA 622 and VA 629, look for it on the right.

Rounding the headwaters of two small streams, the trail continues through young hardwoods to reach a double-track connector to Bear Creek Lake State Park, at mile 11. A right takes you less than a quarter of a mile to the state park, where you'll find the only legal camping along the Willis River Trail. Continuing straight, the trail descends along a rivulet to meet another connector that leaves right to access the state park's own trail network. Bearing left, you'll soon reach Little Bear Creek, a scenic stream dotted with beaver dams and green pools. The trail follows this channel for almost a mile, fording it halfway then running against a steep bluff.

Bearing right to climb away from the creek, you'll soon cross Bear Creek Forest Road on a piney ridge. Then promptly dip to reach Bear Creek itself, fording near a tributary then making a long, steady climb. The hardwoods in this valley also give way to pines as you rise to a hilltop just before intersecting Booker Forest Road. The Willis River Trail turns left with the road and follows it more than a quarter of a mile to VA 628. Across the paved road, the trail makes a single-track run through mixed forest.

You'll soon pass a cleared hillside visible on trail right. Chestnut and Northern red oaks grow on the hilltop ahead, and young birch trees in the understory line the trail as you descend to an unnamed stream. Cross then follow the rocky channel. Heading west toward Winston Lake, the stream widens and its flow slackens. Before recrossing the creek, continue a short distance to find a small rocked-in spring at the edge of the lake. Then head north through the woods overlooking Winston Lake. The trail undulates beneath you slightly then traverses a glade of white pines before passing the spillway on your right. Just before reaching VA 629, turn left to descend a stone stairway and reach a rustic picnic shelter, the Willis River Trail's southern terminus.

For a three-day hiking excursion: set out from the swinging bridge southbound on the Willis River Trail for an 11-mile day. Spend the night at Bear Creek Lake State Park (see page 18), then continue on to the Willis River Trail terminus at Winston Lake. Enjoy a picnic, then pick up the Cumberland State Forest Multiuse Trail (see page 70) for the southern half of its loop. Turn right, eastbound, onto the Willis River Trail from Booker Forest Road, then turn right at Bear Creek Forest Road. Pick up the Cumberland Multiuse Trail access spur that heads left and return to the park for a second night. Your day-two total will be 14.5 miles, but you won't have to lug your tent. On day three, simply retrace the string of your balloon hike.

# YORK RIVER STATE PARK

## ▶ IN BRIEF

At 2,550 acres, York River State Park encompasses a great diversity of terrain and ecosystems. Visitors likewise enjoy numerous options for exploring the park's estuarine marshes, the sandy shoreline of the tidal York, and the wooded ridges overlooking both. This balloon hike can be extended to the east or west.

## ▶ DESCRIPTION

Prior to English colonization, Mattaponi and Pamunkey Indians inhabited the York River shoreline. As settlers converted former hunting grounds to crop fields, the tribes withdrew inland and upriver along their namesake tributaries, which converge to form the York ten miles northwest of the park. Tobacco grown for export was the Virginia farmer's lifeblood, and Taskinas Creek was a point of departure for tobacco headed downriver to Yorktown then on to Bristol or Birmingham.

Today all that remains of the Taskinas Plantation tobacco warehouse are the wooden, "corduroy," roads visible along the muddy creekbank at low tide. The park visitor center displays Native

## ▶ DIRECTIONS

From Richmond head east about 37 miles on I-64; from Williamsburg head west on I-64 8 miles. Take Exit 231, and drive north 1 mile on VA 607. Turn right onto VA 606 and continue 2 miles to the signed park entrance road (VA 696) on the left. Follow the road 2 more miles to the entrance station (awkwardly located on the right-hand, passenger, side of the road) and, after paying your parking fee, park on either side of the road. The visitor center, with the York beyond it, is straight ahead. Croaker Landing boat launch, a noncontiguous portion of the state park, lies further north along VA 607 and requires a signed right turn onto VA 605.

## ℹ KEY AT-A-GLANCE INFORMATION

**LENGTH:** 6.4 miles, plus 5.6 miles of spurs (most out-and-back)

**CONFIGURATION:** Balloon

**DIFFICULTY:** Moderate

**SCENERY:** Upland woods, creek-fed marshland, York River beach

**EXPOSURE:** Mostly shaded, open on Backbone Trail and along the river

**TRAFFIC:** Low; higher near visitor center

**TRAIL SURFACE:** Dirt and gravel

**HIKING TIME:** 3 hours

**SEASON:** Trails open daily 8 a.m.–dusk year-round; main season runs May–October

**ACCESS:** No camping allowed; parking costs $2, $3 on weekends in season; restrooms, picnic shelters, and visitor center are wheelchair accessible.

**MAPS:** Maps are available at the park; another is online at www.dcr.virginia.gov/parks/yorkriver.

**FACILITIES:** Visitor center, gift shop, restrooms, vending machines, playground, boat-rental pier, fishing pier, picnic tables and shelters. In-season bike, canoe, and kayak rentals available (prices vary).

**SPECIAL COMMENTS:** Consider the park's unlimited one-day bike-and-boa rental offer, a steal at $5 per adult and $3 per child. You can bike the necessary but bland Backbone Trail and explore Taskinas Creek by boat. Call the park office at (757) 566-3036

---

**UTM Trailhead Coordinates for York River State Park**

**UTM Zone (NAD27)  18S**

**Easting  0348266**

**Northing  4141896**

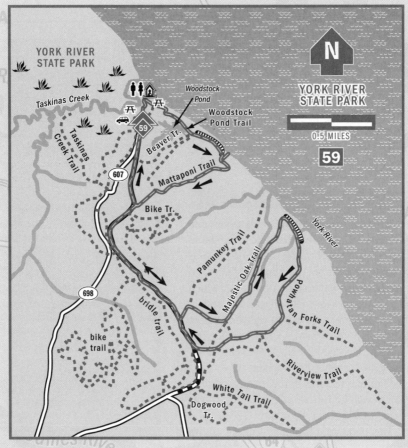

YORK RIVER
STATE PARK

Taskinas Creek

Taskinas
Creek Trail

Woodstock
Pond

Woodstock
Pond Trail

Beaver Tr.

Mattaponi Trail

Bike Tr.

Pamunkey Trail

Majestic Oak Trail

Powhatan Forks Trail

Riverview Trail

bridle trail

bike
trail

White Tail Trail

Dogwood
Tr.

York River

N

YORK RIVER
STATE PARK

0.5 MILES

59

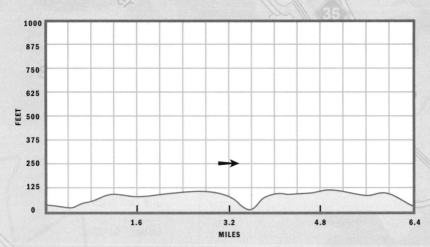

American artifacts unearthed on the property. Far-reaching, if not encyclopedic, the center examines the many lives of the York. Aquariums simulate Tidewater habitats, 20,000-year-old fossils tell of an ancient sea, and modern fishing gear testifies to the commercial importance of the Chesapeake Bay.

Descending the bluff west of the center a short, switchbacking, paved trail leads through a garden of native vegetation. The labeled flowers and shrubs make an excellent prehike primer on Virginia botany of the sort often overlooked. At the base of the hillside, the park's fleet of canoes and kayaks stands marshaled. Step out onto the small dock jutting into Taskinas Creek and scan the cattails opposite for great blue herons, great and snowy egrets, and long-billed Virginia rails. The Taskinas Creek Trail runs along the southern reaches of this marsh, leaving from the parking area. At press time the loop was still closed due to 2003's Hurricane Isabel, but odds are it will be reopened prior to your visit. If so, consider beginning or ending your hike with the 1.7-mile loop, which features several wooden boardwalks and puts you on eye-level with the dragonflies darting about this national estuarine-research reserve.

To follow the route as mapped, head east behind the visitor center. Take the Woodstock Pond Trail southeast, passing sand volleyball courts, a playground, then a shelter. Woodstock Pond comes into view as the trail descends a small hill. The freshwater pond was created as a water source when the surrounding territory was farmland. In the 1950s it was stocked with largemouth bass and bluegill; a small fishing pier juts out over the water on trail right. Pass between the cattail-lined pond and the York River before bearing inland and uphill. Presently, you will reach the hike's first junction. Turn left onto the Mattaponi Trail, a single-track path through pines and the occasional black walnut.

A short-but-steep descent brings you to a boardwalk through a marsh at least 50 feet wide that is fed by a meandering streamlet only a few feet across at low tide. Cattails and marsh grasses grow waist high along the boardwalk, but peer through their stalks to the mud below, and you will see one- to two-inch fiddler crabs scuttling about. As many as 200,000 fiddler crabs can inhabit a single acre of marsh. Nevertheless, males, distinguished by a single large claw, are aggressively territorial, often battling other males who invade the vicinity of their burrows.

Across the boardwalk, the trail continues beneath diminutive Virginia pines and water oaks, discernable by their scarcely lobed leaves. Ascend a hillside braced by wooden beams to reach the bluff's top. The York is slowly eroding this band of ancient sedimentation even as mud and silt deposits accumulate on the river bottom. Be cautious when approaching the edge; the trees now lying along the shore 30 feet below toppled when this bluff gave way. A bench affords you the chance to rest and look out across the York.

The path then veers right, passing beeches and white oaks with ferns beneath. A beach-access trail soon heads left. Follow this short spur through a culvert to the water's edge. Swimming is prohibited and downed trees complicate a lengthy beach walk, but look among the flotsam for seashells and scan the crumbling bank for fossils. You'll almost certainly spot clamshells, but whale teeth are a real coup.

Return to the Mattaponi Trail and turn left. The path enters a more open glade, then seemingly evaporates. Look to your right for a roadbed heading southwest. After a level one-third mile through lofty hardwoods, this dirt road climbs to meet the park's gravel Backbone Trail. Turn left and soon the other fork of the Backbone enters on the right. Note the junction, as you'll take a left here to return to the parking area.

Now, however, proceed southwest along the wide gravel path, passing an entrance to the Laurel Glen mountain-bike trail on your left. The Backbone then makes a distinct curve eastward, with the park's entrance road visible on trail right. The two soon part ways. Accompanied by a power line, the Backbone now progresses southeast, with mountain biker's Black Bear Run and Marl Ravine Trails visible on the left and the equestrian Meh-Te-Kos Trail running parallel on the right.

After passing through a wooden gate, which blocks horses from the northern reaches of the park, continue south with forest on your left and fields veiled by a thin barrier of pines to the right. Just as I was questioning this wide, exposed path, a pair of quail darted across the trail before me and into the field. At the first left beyond the wooden gate, the Pamunkey Trail departs. Follow it into the woods, a blend of yellow poplar, Virginia pine, white oak, and holly. Just a short walk ahead, the aptly named Spur Trail heads right. Follow the Spur to hike the route mapped here, but consider hiking the entire 0.77-mile Pamunkey as an out-and-back if you wish. It follows a finger of land bordered by marshy creeks to an overlook of the York.

Follow the spur past an area carpeted with ferns and another opened to the sky by downed pines, then turn left onto the Majestic Oak Trail. Make a gradual but steady descent from 100 feet in elevation to almost sea level. The land falls away steeply on either side of this pebble-studded trail, so that the crowns of tall trees are visible at eye level. You'll find the Majestic Oak Trail's namesake hard to miss as you approach the York. Just before the path curves right and downhill to a boardwalk, it passes a white oak, unquestionably one of the oldest in the park, with a trunk five feet in diameter.

Pause at the bench overlooking the river ahead or dangle your feet from the boardwalk and take in the view of the York River. Across the boardwalk, wind up a set of wooden-beam stairs to pass through a stand of Virginia pines on a sandy path. Now on the north fork of the Powhatan Forks Trail, you must regain the elevation lost en route to the water's edge. Unlike the proceeding ridge path, this trail climbs a wider hill through mixed woods. Having made the hilltop, the east fork of Powhatan Forks tempts you back to the river. This 0.46-mile spur option departs left at an intersection marked by a 7-trunked yellow poplar.

Continuing west, back toward the Backbone, you will traverse an area scarred by storm damage. The 1.4-mile Riverview Trail meets your path twice on the left. The Riverview Trail also intersects the Backbone to the west. As its name suggests, the out-and-back optional spur follows a ridge to another marshy creek junction with the York.

Still more options await just a bit farther east (left when you regain the Backbone Trail). The White-Tail and Dogwood Lane Trails, each 0.75 miles, leave left just before the Backbone's terminus. The former is an upland loop, while the latter follows a short ridge to the bottomland confluence of two small streams. These spurs access some of the more remote and scenic reaches of the park and offer good wildlife watching and photography prospects. Bring plenty of water and some snacks, and you can easily spend the day exploring York River State Park.

To stick with the more modest, 6.4-mile loop, simply return along the Backbone Trail. Bear left when it forks, passing the short Beaver Trail from Woodstock Pond on the right. Pass behind the entrance station to reenter the parking area.

# ZOAR STATE FOREST

▶ **IN BRIEF**

Divided into two noncontiguous parcels, Zoar State Forest has two separate hikes, each with its own character. The Main Trail passes the Pollard family farmstead and highlights forestry practices en route. The Nature Trail traces the scenic Mattaponi River and its tributary, Herring Creek.

▶ **DESCRIPTION**

The town of Ayletts was named for William Aylett, whose colonial estate was located here. In 1782 Robert Pollard purchased the land north of town that would become his family's farmstead. According to forest literature Ayletts was, at the time, a crossroads of such ill repute that Pollard named his home Mount Zoar in reference to the Biblical city where Lot took refuge after fleeing Gommorah. Flames engulfed the manse in 1885. The present structure was erected in 1890. It remained in the family until 1987, when it was donated to the state by Pollard's great-great-grandson. The white hilltop house now serves as the forest office.

Like all of Virginia's state forests, 378-acre Zoar is self sustaining. Unlike most it includes

▶ **DIRECTIONS**

From Richmond follow US 360 northeast to the hamlet of Ayletts (approximately 20 miles beyond I-295). In Ayletts turn left onto VA 600. To reach the Pollard homestead—now the forest office—make an immediate left onto VA 606. There is a sign indicating this turn. The trailhead for the Main Trail is located 0.2 miles ahead on the right. The forest office/farmhouse is up the hill, a trailhead signboard advises visitors to park in a small lot outside the often-locked gate. To reach the Nature Trail, continue straight on VA 600 for 1.7 miles, then turn right at a forest sign. The trailhead is located in the northern corner of the first parking lot, to the right of the gravel road. A second lot down the road accesses the canoe put-in.

## ℹ KEY AT-A-GLANCE INFORMATION

**LENGTH:** Main Trail, 1.8 miles; Nature Trail, 1.4 miles

**CONFIGURATION:** Loops on noncontiguous parcels of land

**DIFFICULTY:** Easy

**SCENERY:** Hardwood-forested bluffs, boggy bottomland, and the Mattaponi River along the Nature Trail; a pine plantation, wetland pond, and old farmhouse

**EXPOSURE:** Limited shade on Main Trail, well-shaded on Nature Trail

**TRAFFIC:** Low

**TRAIL SURFACE:** Dirt, with some gravel double-track on Main Trail

**HIKING TIME:** 2 hours

**SEASON:** Open daily during daylight year-round

**ACCESS:** No fee; mountain biking allowed only on Main Trail; trails not recommended for wheelchairs

**MAPS:** On pamphlets and signboards at trailheads and online at www.dof. virginia.gov/stforest/index-zsf.shtml

**FACILITIES:** Parking, boat launch in northern section, office located in house in the southern section

**SPECIAL COMMENTS:** The Nature Trail is divided into the Mattaponi Bluffs and Herring Creek Loop sections. Guides detailing the stops along each are available online. A similar guide for the Main Trail is available at the trailhead but not on the Web. Contact the forest office at (804) 769-2962.

---

**UTM Trailhead Coordinates for Zoar State Forest (Main Trail)**

**UTM Zone (NAD27)   18S**

**Easting   0314234**

**Northing   4184086**

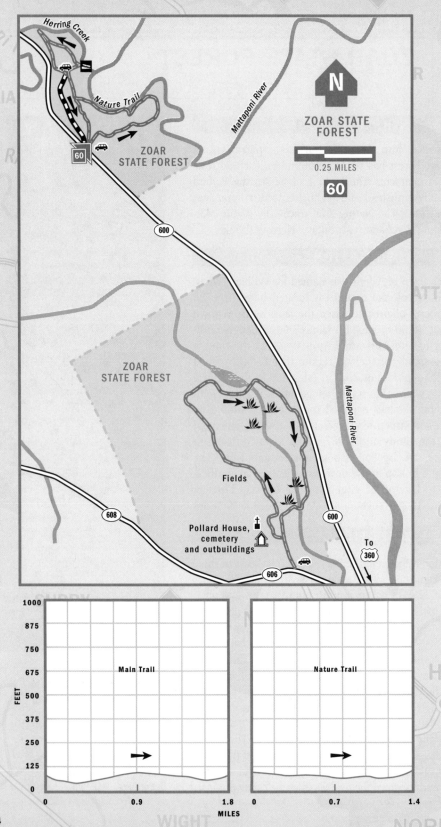

crop fields still under cultivation, in addition to forestry demonstration areas, and hunting by permit. Fishing is also allowed. The forest maintains a canoe put-in on the Mattaponi, allowing paddlers to make a 4-mile oxbow trip to the Virginia Department of Game and Inland Fisheries boat landing at US 360.

Though they can't be combined—unless you want to take a 2-mile road walk—the forest's two trails total 3.2 miles, and both can be hiked in a single visit.

## MAIN TRAIL

A booklet detailing the Main Trail at Zoar is available from a signboard in the parking area. With a focus on forestry education, it details the sights and environments along the route. Begin by heading up the gravel double-track that leads to the old Pollard home, which is shaded by a broad beech and numerous cedars. The road passes below the home on the east, then curves up between it and the family cemetery. In addition to the brick-walled graveyard, several outbuildings surround the house. When the gravel ends, follow a mowed path behind (west of) the graveyard. The path borders a cultivated field on the left and a barn on the right before it turns to the right. Downhill, turn left upon intersecting another mowed path that is a continuation of the entrance road. An open-sided metal maintenance shelter stands on trail left.

The Main Trail now proceeds between two fields, one recovering from an intentional burn, the other routinely tilled. In each you will find native shrubs and grasses that serve as both cover and food source for rabbits, quail, and songbirds. Another mowed path enters on the right. This out-and-back spur leads to a field planted with warm-season grasses designed to attract young quail. Along the loop, the cultivated field reappears on your left as the shrubbery on your right rises to a hardwood forest.

The trail then veers right to enter the woods on a wide path. The Main Trail continues beneath tall willow oaks and alongside sassafras and cedar saplings before the tree population shifts to include more Virginia pines. After crossing a small creek on a rudimentary bridge, turn right upon reaching a T intersection. A left here takes you on an out-and-back spur to four demonstration plots also planted with pines but in different densities.

The creek you just crossed feeds a swampy wood ahead on trail right, shaded by river birch and red maple. The creek then drains into a wetland pond visible on both sides of the raised trail. A small wooden dock on the left provides views across the marsh. Rotting tree trunks protrude from the shallow impoundment, and grasses fringe the pond.

Beyond the water, 20-year-old pines shade the needle-covered trail until it approaches VA 600. A wood-beam blockade prevents auto access ahead; and the Main Trail turns right, passing a recently logged area on the left. A power line overhead further detracts from the loop's easternmost stretch, but sweetgums thriving in the now-abundant sunlight will soon provide an added buffer from the road.

The Main Trail ultimately bears right, away from the road, to traverse a demonstration wetland road. Water pooled about the tree trunks on your right is covered, at least in the summer, with a bright green layer of tiny aquatic plants. The effect is at first eerie, then intriguingly surreal. Orange jewelweed and cardinal flower lend their brilliant colors to the scene. The Pollard house is visible uphill as you emerge from the trees. Simply follow the path and turn left at a T intersection to return to your car.

## NATURE TRAIL

Subdivided into the Mattaponi Bluffs and Herring Creek Loops, Zoar's Nature Trail is a single-track journey through mature forest and riparian bottomland. Download trail guides from the Web to ensure that you will have a key to the route's 22 numbered stops. The first appears just beyond the trailhead, at a T intersection. Stop 1 indicates this is an upland bluff. Turn right and trace the bluff a short distance to the second stop, where a bench invites you to gaze 50 feet down to the Mattaponi River floodplain.

Turn sharply left to descend a path braced by wooden beams and bordered by wild rhododendron. Leaving behind the upland mix of holly, red cedar, white oak, and mockernut hickory trees, enter a fern-carpeted forest of beech, river birch, red maple, and swamp chestnut oak. A boardwalk guides you over a streamlet, scarcely flowing on dry days. Continue along an earthen path crisscrossed by roots and blanketed by moss. The easy-to-follow trail crosses a larger creek on a wooden bridge, then a smaller seasonal stream. The numbered stops proceed with the route, highlighting various forest features and species.

The trail first approaches the Mattaponi at a scenic bend in the river. Birch trees shade the smooth-flowing water. From the river's edge, the trail cuts left, bisecting a small peninsula before rejoining the river headed upstream. Occasional overgrowth crowds the trail but invariably recedes. Views of the river on trail right reward your persistence. Look for turtles sunning on rocks and beavers that have gnawed trees along the trail. The path traverses additional culverts on wooden bridges, periodically venturing inland to more open glades, including a mature stand of holly.

Approaching its halfway point, the trail turns left, inland, to cross an old river channel on a boardwalk. Sedimentation and erosion have rerouted the river, but this low-lying area still holds water and is routinely drenched by the surging river. Across the boardwalk, ascend a tall flight of wooden steps to regain the bluff. Turn right and continue, first descending gradually then steeply to emerge in a gravel parking area.

At the base of the bluff, you'll see two paths heading north and uphill on stairs from the lot. Take the path on the right. Approaching it, you'll see a third, eastbound spur that departs right to the canoe put-in and views of Herring Creek's confluence with the Mattaponi. Herring Creek was named for the fish that spawn here in the spring. The term "river herring" refers to either of two difficult-to-distinguish species: Alewife and blueback herring. River herring have drawn fishers since colonial times, but modern anglers are more likely after striped bass that forage for herring hatchlings.

The Nature Trail rises from the lot to the bluff above Herring Creek. After curving westward through open forest above the creek, the trail reaches a T intersection. Turn right for an out-and-back visit to the 20-foot-wide creek. Relax for a moment on the sandy shore before returning uphill and continuing straight through the intersection. The trail briefly comes within sight of VA 600 before curving away to the left, with traffic audible through the trees. The trail guide highlights a beech tree perforated by small cavities—one almost expects a pair of owl eyes glaring back—and an oak with a goiter-like growth on its trunk.

The Nature Trail's northernmost loop is soon completed, as you descend back to the canoe put-in parking lot. Continue forward, ascending back to the blufftop trail on which you arrived. You'll pass the wooden stairs on your left, then wind slightly through an abundance of rhododendron and laurel before reaching an intersection. A right takes you back to the trailhead lot.

# 60 Hikes within 60 MILES

## RICHMOND
### INCLUDING WILLIAMSBURG, FREDERICKSBURG, AND CHARLOTTESVILLE

## APPENDIXES AND INDEX

# APPENDIX A:
## LOCAL SHOPPING FOR HIKERS

You can find anything you want on the Internet, but you can't try on boots.

**Blue Ridge Mountain Sports**
10164 West Broad Street
Glen Allen, VA 23060
(804) 965-0494

**Blue Ridge Mountain Sports**
Barack's Road Shopping Center
1125 Emmet Street
Charlottesville, VA 22903
(434) 977-4400

**Blue Ridge Mountain Sports**
Chesterfield Towne Center
11500 Midlothian Turnpike
Richmond, VA 23235
(804) 794-2004

**Blue Ridge Mountain Sports**
Marketplace Shoppes
4655-303 Monticello Avenue
Williamsburg, VA 23188
(757) 229-4584

**Chesterfield Plaza**
1520 West Koger Center Boulevard
Richmond, VA 23235
(804) 897-5299

**Creeks at Virginia Center**
9940 Brook Road
Glen Allen, VA 23059
(804) 261-1853

**Dick's Sporting Goods**
Rio Hill Shopping Center
1940 Rio Hill Center
Charlottesville, VA 22901
(434) 974-5640

**L. L. Bean Factory Store**
5715-66B Richmond Road
Williamsburg, VA 23188
(757) 259-9403

**Orvis Outlet**
3040 Richmond Road
Williamsburg, VA 23188
(757) 258-0767

**Short Pump Mall**
11800 West Broad Street,
Suite 1096
Richmond, VA 23233
(804) 360-8165

**Spotsylvania Mall**
290 Spotsylvania Mall
Fredericksburg, VA 22407
(540) 548-1200

**Stony Pointe**
9204 Stony Pointe Parkway
Richmond, VA 23235
(804) 253-0800

# APPENDIX B:
## CLUBS AND ORGANIZATIONS

In addition to hiking clubs, this list includes some running clubs that support trail runs and conservation groups that sometimes lead educational outings. There are also numerous local "Friends of" groups that support the parks and public lands described in this guide; inquire with management at your favorite park.

**BikeWalk Virginia**
P.O. Box 203
Williamsburg, VA 23187-0203
(757) 229-0507
www.bikewalkvirginia.org

**Charlottesville Track Club**
P.O. Box 495
Charlottesville, VA 22902
(434) 293-6115
www.avenue.org/ctc

**The Chesapeake Bay Foundation**
1108 East Main Street, Suite 1600
Richmond, VA 23219
www.cbf.org

**Colonial Road Runners**
P.O. Box 657
Williamsburg, VA 23187
www.colonialroadrunners.org

**Fredericksburg Area Running Club**
P.O. Box 3653
Fredericksburg, VA 22402
www.farc.org

**Ivy Creek Foundation**
P.O. Box 956
Charlottesville, VA 22902
(434) 973-7772
www.avenue.org/icf

**The Nature Conservancy in Virginia**
490 Westfield Road
Charlottesville, VA 22901
(434) 295-6106
www.nature.org/virginia

**Northern Neck Audubon Society**
P.O. Box 991
Kilmarnock, VA 22482
www.northernneckaudubon.org

**Old Dominion Appalachian Trail Club**
P.O. Box 25283
Richmond, VA 23260-5283
joinodatc@mindspring.com

**Outdoor Adventure Social Club of Greater Charlottesville**
420 East Main Street, Suite 3
Charlottesville, VA 22902
(434) 760-HIKE

**Peninsula Track Club**
P.O. Box 11116
Newport News, VA 23601
www.peninsulatrackclub.com

**Potomac Appalachian Trail Club**
118 Park Street, Southeast
Vienna, VA 22180
(703) 242-0315
www.patc.net

**Richmond Area Road Runners**
P.O. Box 8724
Richmond, VA 23226
www.rrrc.org

**Richmond Sports Backers**
100 Avenue of Champions, Suite 300
Richmond, VA 23230
(804) 285-9495
www.sportsbackers.org

**Richmond Audubon Society**
P.O. Box 26648
Richmond, VA 23261
www.richmondaudubon.org

**Rivanna Trails Foundation**
P.O. Box 1786
Charlottesville, VA 22902
(434) 923-9022
www.avenue.org/rivanna

**Tidewater Appalachian Trail Club**
P.O. Box 8246
Norfolk, VA 23503
www.tidewateratc.com

**Virginia Chapter of the Sierra Club**
6 North 6th Street, no. 102
Richmond, VA 23219
(804) 225-9113
www.virginia.sierraclub.org

**Virginia Conservation Network**
1001 East Broad Street, Suite 410
Richmond, VA 23219
www.vcnva.org

# INDEX

# INDEX

# INDEX

# INDEX

# INDEX